Governance and Regionalism in Asia

In the decade since the Asian financial crisis the ten states of Southeast Asia that form ASEAN, together with China, Japan and South Korea have formed the basis of a community intended to support the well-being of its member states, markets and peoples. This highly successful regionalisation was not anticipated by the region's leaders, however, and as a result, policy makers are increasingly talking about 'meeting fatigue' and the need to find a better way to govern regional affairs. Among the reforms being considered is a shift towards a more rules-based culture as well as the more explicit incorporation of both private sector and civil society organisations into the policy processes. In short, ASEAN+3 is seeking to develop new norms and processes for its networks and institutions.

This book explores the pressures currently influencing East Asian policy debates, analysing the trend towards deeper integration and the emergence of a governance model for managing regional processes. Combining state and subnational perspectives in conjunction with an examination of the role of the business community and civil society organisations, this book highlights the policy challenges confronting regionalism and governance in East Asia, including key issues such as the rule of law, financial cooperation and a case study on disaster management.

Nicholas Thomas is an Associate Professor in the Department of Asian and International Studies at the City University of Hong Kong.

Politics in Asia series

Formerly edited by Michael Leifer
London School of Economics

**ASEAN and the Security of
South-East Asia**
Michael Leifer

**China's Policy towards
Territorial Disputes**
The case of the South China
Sea Islands
Chi-kin Lo

India and Southeast Asia
Indian perceptions and
policies
Mohammed Ayoob

Gorbachev and Southeast Asia
Leszek Buszynski

**Indonesian Politics under
Suharto**
Order, development and pressure
for change
Michael R.J. Vatikiotis

**The State and Ethnic Politics in
Southeast Asia**
David Brown

**The Politics of Nation Building
and Citizenship in Singapore**
*Michael Hill and
Lian Kwen Fee*

Politics in Indonesia
Democracy, Islam and the
ideology of tolerance
Douglas E. Ramage

**Communitarian Ideology and
Democracy in Singapore**
Beng-Huat Chua

**The Challenge of Democracy
in Nepal**
Louise Brown

Japan's Asia Policy
Wolf Mendl

**The International Politics
of the Asia-Pacific, 1945–1995**
Michael Yahuda

**Political Change in
Southeast Asia**
Trimming the banyan tree
Michael R.J. Vatikiotis

Hong Kong
China's challenge
Michael Yahuda

Korea versus Korea
A case of contested legitimacy
B.K. Gills

Media and Politics in Pacific Asia
Duncan McCargo

Japanese Governance
Beyond Japan Inc
Edited by Jennifer Amyx and Peter Drysdale

China and the Internet
Politics of the digital
leap forward
Edited by Christopher R. Hughes and Gudrun Wacker

Challenging Authoritarianism in Southeast Asia
Comparing Indonesia and
Malaysia
Edited by Ariel Heryanto and Sumit K. Mandal

Cooperative Security and the Balance of Power in ASEAN and the ARF
Ralf Emmers

Islam in Indonesian Foreign Policy
Rizal Sukma

Media, War and Terrorism
Responses from the Middle East
and Asia
Edited by Peter Van der Veer and Shoma Munshi

China, Arms Control and Nonproliferation
Wendy Frieman

Communitarian Politics in Asia
Edited by Chua Beng Huat

East Timor, Australia and Regional Order
Intervention and its aftermath in
Southeast Asia
James Cotton

Domestic Politics, International Bargaining and China's Territorial Disputes
Chien-peng Chung

Democratic Development in East Asia
Becky Shelley

International Politics of the Asia-Pacific since 1945
Michael Yahuda

Asian States
Beyond the developmental
perspective
Edited by Richard Boyd and Tak-Wing Ngo

Civil Life, Globalization, and Political Change in Asia
Organizing between family
and state
Edited by Robert P. Weller

Realism and Interdependence in Singapore's Foreign Policy
Narayanan Ganesan

Party Politics in Taiwan
Party change and the democratic
evolution of Taiwan, 1991–2004
Dafydd Fell

State Terrorism and Political Identity in Indonesia
Fatally belonging
Ariel Heryanto

Governance and Regionalism in Asia

Edited by Nicholas Thomas

Routledge
Taylor & Francis Group

LONDON AND NEW YORK

First published 2009
by Routledge
2 Park Square, Milton Park, Abingdon, Oxon, OX14 4RN

Simultaneously published in the USA and Canada
by Routledge
711 Third Avenue, New York, NY 10017

Routledge is an imprint of the Taylor & Francis Group, an informa business

First issued in paperback 2011

Typeset in Times New Roman by
Taylor & Francis Books

British Library Cataloguing in Publication Data
A catalogue record for this book is available from the British Library

Library of Congress Cataloging in Publication Data
Governance and regionalism in Asia / edited by Nicholas Thomas.
      p. cm. – (Politics in Asia series)
    1. Regionalism–Asia. 2. Asia–Politics and government–1945– 3. Asia–
Economic conditions. I. Thomas, Nicholas, 1970–
    JQ24.G68 2009
    341.24′7–dc22

                                                        2008030159

ISBN10 0-415-45699-9 (hbk)
ISBN10: 0-415-66715-1 (pbk)
ISBN10 0-203-88385-3 (ebk)

ISBN13 978-0-415-45699-9 (hbk)
ISBN13: 978-0-415-66715-9 (pbk)
ISBN13 978-0-203-88385-3 (ebk)

Contents

Illustrations

Contributors

Douglas Arner is Director of the Asian Institute of International Financial Law and an Associate Professor at the Faculty of Law, University of Hong Kong. He is author, co-author or editor of nine books, including *Financial Stability, Economic Growth and the Role of Law* (Cambridge University Press, 2007) and *Financial Markets in Hong Kong: Law and Practice* (Oxford University Press, 2006). He has been a consultant with, among others, the Asian Development Bank, APEC, the World Bank, and the European Bank for Reconstruction and Development.

Mely Caballero-Anthony is an Associate Professor and Head of the Centre of Non-Traditional Security Studies at the Rajaratnam School of International Studies (RSIS), Nanyang Technological University, Singapore. Her research interests include regionalism and regional security in Asia-Pacific, human and non-traditional security issues, and comparative politics. Her latest publications include *Regional Security in Southeast Asia: Beyond the ASEAN Way* (ISEAS, 2005), *Understanding Non-Traditional Security in Asia: Dilemmas in Securitisation* (Ashgate, 2006) and *UN Peace Operations and Asian Security* (Routledge, 2006).

Jaewoo Choo is an Associate Professor of Chinese Foreign Policy in the Department of Chinese Studies at Kyung Hee University, Korea. His research interests include Chinese foreign policy, China's relations with developing countries, Sino-Korea/North Korean relations and China's energy security policy. His recent publications include: 'Mirroring North Korea's growing economic dependency on China: political ramifications', *Asian Survey* (Vol. 48, No. 2, 2008), pp. 343–372; and book chapters in *Korea and New Asia* (2007), *China in the International Order* (2007), and *China Rising: Reaction, Assessments, and Strategic Consequences* (2007).

James Cotton is a Professor of Politics, University of New South Wales at The Australian Defence Force Academy. His most recent book is (edited with John Ravenhill), *Trading on Alliance Security: Australia in World Affairs 2001–2005* (Melbourne: Oxford University Press, 2006).

Paul Davidson is a Professor in the Department of Law, Carleton University, where he teaches international economic law, and is the Chair of the Carleton Committee on Asian Studies (CAS). He is also a barrister and a solicitor. His current research interests and publications focus on the legal frameworks for economic cooperation in the Asia-Pacific Rim.

Alain Guilloux is the former CEO of Médecins Sans Frontières in Hong Kong. He has over 25 years of experience working with development and aid projects in Asia, Europe, Africa and Latin America. His research focuses on governance, particularly with relation to humanitarian actions and public health issues. His next book – *Taiwan, Humanitarianism and Global Governance* – is forthcoming with RoutledgeCurzon.

Kanishka Jayasuriya is the Acting Director and Principal Senior Research Fellow at the Asia Research Centre, Murdoch University. His most recent books are: *Reconstituting the Global Liberal Order* (Routledge, 2005) and *Statecraft, Welfare and the Politics of Inclusion* (Palgrave/ Macmillan, 2006).

Stephanie Lawson is a Professor of Asia-Pacific Studies at the University of Birmingham. Her research interests encompass the study of culture, ethnicity, nationalism, and democracy, and combine comparative and normative approaches to the study of world politics with a special focus on the Asia-Pacific. Recent books include *Culture and Context in World Politics* (2006), *Europe and the Asia-Pacific: Culture, Identity and Representations of Region* (2003), *International Relations* (2003) and *The New Agenda for International Relations: From Polarization to Globalization in World Politics?* (2002).

Paul Lejot is a Visiting Fellow at the Asian Institute of International Financial Law, The University of Hong Kong and a Visiting Research Fellow of the ICMA Centre, University of Reading. His interests focus on law and finance, notably legal influences on financial development, instruments, institutions and markets in Asia and elsewhere. He is a former investment banker.

Thomas G. Moore is an Associate Professor in the Department of Political Science, University of Cincinnati, USA, where he teaches courses on US foreign policy, international political economy and East Asian politics. His current research focuses on international relations in East Asia, with particular emphasis on Chinese foreign policy.

Isabelle Saint-Mézard was a Post-Doctoral Fellow in the Centre of Asian Studies, The University of Hong Kong, where she coordinated the China-India Project from 2003 to 2006. She currently teaches at the Institut d'Etudes Politiques in Paris and at the Institut National des Langues et Civilisations Orientales. Her research interests and publications focus on India's foreign policy and Asian regionalism.

Nicholas Thomas is an Associate Professor in the Department of Asian and International Studies at the City University of Hong Kong. His current research interests and publications focus on East Asian regionalism, Chinese foreign policy and non-traditional security. His most recent publication is *Advancing East Asian Regionalism* (co-edited with Melissa Curley, RoutledgeCurzon, 2007).

Wei Wang is an Associate Professor of Law at Fudan University Law School, Shanghai, China. He is a former Chinese lawyer. His study interests include international financial law, international economic law and public international law.

Hidetaka Yoshimatsu is a Professor of Politics and International Relations in the Graduate School of Asia Pacific Studies, Ritsumeikan Asia Pacific University, Japan. His current research interests include Japan's foreign economic diplomacy and regional cooperation in East Asia.

Preface

In December 2005, to mark the realisation of the East Asian Summit, the Centre of Asian Studies at the University of Hong Kong convened a meeting on Governance and Regionalism in Asia. With a keynote address by former ASEAN Secretary-General Rodolfo C. Severino Jnr., the participants of that meeting sought to understand the implications for regional institutions and norms of this new Summit and its related processes. In the period since that initial meeting, the participants have been further developing their analyses of the emerging regional order, taking into account the many political, economic and social changes that have occurred at the regional and domestic levels.

The East Asian Summit was landmark meeting for the region, although not necessarily in the ways envisaged by its sponsors. In introducing the East Asian Summit ahead of schedule, its proponents failed to address the biggest challenge now facing Asia: namely, how to govern the region? What institution best meets the needs of its constituent members? What are the values and identities that these members should express or affirm? Who is 'in' the region and who is 'out'? What is the future of the region – a mere collection of states with common interests or an East Asian Community? This volume is a first step towards addressing that challenge and answering its related questions.

This volume has adopted a similar structure to that of the East Asian Summit, with chapters on ASEAN, its three Northeast Asian partners, as well as analyses of Australia and India's role in regional affairs. It then moves on to exploring some of the key issues arising from these intended (and unintended) patterns of integration before considering what happens when the Asian region engages with other regions. In doing so, this volume intends to meet the needs of three important audiences: those academics and students who are interested in this topic and its many remarkable aspects; the policy makers whose job it is to make sense of regional dynamics and the theoreticians who are seeking to better understand the functions and scope of governance at the regional level – a relatively little-explored field outside of the European experience. It is hoped that this volume will shed some light on this very rich and complex topic, generating interest and encouraging future research endeavours.

Nicholas Thomas
June 2008, Hong Kong

Foreword

Governance and regionalism in Asia

Rodolfo C. Severino Jnr

The relationship between regionalism and governance is a subject whose time has come. There have been many conferences, seminars, speeches and books on either regionalism or governance, but rarely have the two been blended together. And yet, they are closely linked. Indeed, a group of countries cannot effectively or successfully pursue regionalism without attending to issues of governance, both at the national and at the regional levels. This I have found in my years of involvement with the Association of Southeast Asian Nations and in my studies of regionalism around the world.

I will give some examples from the ASEAN experience. ASEAN has been considered to be one of the most successful regional associations among developing countries. Through its very existence, the personal networking that it has promoted, the mutual confidence that it has developed, and the delicate dynamics that its member states have conducted in relating to one another – through all this, ASEAN has helped to keep the peace among its members and advance the stability of the region.

Beyond keeping the peace and fostering stability, ASEAN has set for itself the objectives of regional economic integration and regional cooperation in dealing with transnational problems. These, for ASEAN, are part of the essence of regionalism. As we shall see, for integration and cooperation, the notion of governance is indispensable – at the national and regional levels – although the linkage between regionalism and governance is not often made.

ASEAN member states have made clear their recognition that they must integrate the regional economy if they are to maintain the momentum of the region's economic growth and if they are to be capable of facing up to the competitive challenges from continent-sized economies like China and India and from economic groups elsewhere in the world. However, ASEAN's leaders and other officials are very rarely explicit in acknowledging that domestic reforms and improvements in regional, as well as national, governance are necessary for regional economic integration.

Governance and regional integration

In 1992, the ASEAN countries agreed that they would no longer engage in just economic cooperation; they would take a giant step forward and seek to integrate their economies into one regional market. They would do this, first, by removing tariffs on and non-tariff barriers to trade among them. Thus, they agreed to set up the ASEAN Free Trade Area (AFTA). Under that agreement, the ASEAN countries were to cut their tariffs each year until tariff levels reached 0–5 per cent by a certain date; that date was later advanced twice. They also committed themselves to removing non-tariff barriers to intra-ASEAN trade within a certain timeframe.

At that time, the Treaty of Asunción, creating MERCOSUR, had just been concluded. The Final Act of the Uruguay Round of Multilateral Trade Negotiations had just been signed. The Maastricht Treaty creating a single market in Western Europe was in the final stages of negotiation. The North American Free Trade Agreement would be concluded towards the end of the year. Regional arrangements were being put together, in parallel with global efforts to remove barriers to trade. At the same time, Deng Xiaoping's reforms were beginning to show results in China, and economic reforms were starting to take hold in India, both countries, especially China, becoming magnets for foreign direct investment.

These developments created many opportunities for the ASEAN countries; they also posed enormous competitive challenges. ASEAN knew that the economies of its members could not maintain their remarkable growth rates if they remained economically fragmented as a region, if they stayed as a collection of small national economies, instead of being the one vast, integrated regional market that they could become.

ASEAN also knew that there was more to regional economic integration than the removal of tariffs on trade among its members. Non-tariff barriers had to be dismantled, too. The application of the preferential tariffs enjoyed by intra-ASEAN trade had to be properly and effectively administered, principally by the customs authorities. Product standards had to be harmonised. Transportation, by land, sea or air, had to be made freer, easier and less expensive. Trade in services, which had been accounting for a greater and greater share of the member countries' economies and trade, had to be freed up.

ASEAN thus agreed to adopt cooperative measures for advancing these other elements of regional economic integration. As we have seen, the AFTA agreement provides for the elimination of non-tariff barriers. ASEAN has agreed to apply the World Trade Organisation (WTO) system of customs valuation and the post-clearance audit method of undertaking customs inspections. It has harmonised the nomenclatures used by member states in administering customs tariffs. The ASEAN countries have meshed their standards for twenty products that they agreed in 1997 to designate as priorities for standardisation, safety standards for seventy-one electrical and electronic products, and electro-magnetic conformance for ten such goods.

Aware of the importance of transportation to the integration of the regional economy, the ASEAN countries agreed in 1998 to facilitate the passage of goods in transit and to mutually recognise their commercial vehicle inspection certificates. In November 2005, they signed the long-pending agreement on multi-modal transport. In 1995, the ASEAN countries agreed to liberalise trade in services beyond what they had committed under the WTO. They have made specific mutual commitments in air transport, business services, construction, financial services, maritime transport, telecommunications and tourism.

These are the agreements, the frameworks and the foundations for regional economic integration. However, by themselves they do not tell us anything about their impact on the national economies and societies of the member states and on the lives of their peoples, or even about whether the agreements are being carried out. To answer these questions, we have to look for answers in the area of governance.

Governance and transnational problems

The linkage between regionalism and governance is not limited to regional economic integration or other forms of economic regionalism. It is evident, too, in the regional response to transnational problems, such as environmental pollution and international terrorism, although, again, only rarely is the relationship explicitly made.

In response to the disastrous haze that enveloped large parts of the region in 1997 and 1998, ASEAN concluded in 2002 an agreement committing the parties to ensure that 'activities within their jurisdiction or control do not cause damage to the environment and harm to human health of other States or of areas beyond the limits of national jurisdiction.' It also obligates them to cooperate in preventing and monitoring trans-boundary haze pollution, including providing information if requested. The agreement lays down rather specific obligations for preventing land and forest fires, fighting them, and mitigating the damage caused by them, individually and in cooperation. The agreement is now in force, although not all ASEAN countries have ratified it.

Needless to say, the agreement will only be as effective as the ability and willingness of each party, particularly the country or countries in which the fires take place, to carry out its provisions. In some critical cases, this would mean overcoming the strong resistance put up by powerful interests that profit from the deliberate burning of forests – again, a question of governance.

Southeast Asian countries have achieved some notable successes in arresting terrorists and breaking up terrorist cells. A key factor in these successes has been the sharing of intelligence on the ground. Clearly, much depends not only on the quality of the intelligence but also on the effectiveness of law enforcement and the efficacy of the judicial system. The broad framework of governance has much to do with all this.

Regional governance

The effectiveness of a regional enterprise requires a certain quality of governance not just at the national level. Regional governance, too, has a critical role to play. The more advanced the degree of regionalism, the higher the ambition of the region in terms of regional integration, the more important the role of regional governance.

This is why, when ASEAN agreed in 1992 to create the ASEAN Free Trade Area, it decided at the same time to strengthen the ASEAN Secretariat, so that a regional institution could at least manage the process of regional economic integration. However, the Secretariat still lacks the power and authority to ensure compliance with ASEAN agreements or even to invite attention to instances of non-compliance. ASEAN still does not have a credible mechanism to settle disputes over the implementation of its agreements. Now that ASEAN has declared its intention to move toward an ASEAN Economic Community, it needs effective institutions for regional governance even more. It needs regional institutions – in this case, largely the Secretariat – to research and analyse issues and make policy recommendations on them, to take initiatives on its own, to establish benchmarks to measure progress toward ASEAN objectives, and to speak with authority on behalf of the Association. It needs an objective and credible dispute-settlement mechanism whose decisions are legally binding, not just for economic agreements but for all. The ASEAN Charter that ASEAN's leaders signed in November 2007 aims to strengthen the Association's institutions and regional governance. It is now up to the member states to make full use of its provisions.

In sum, the experience of ASEAN shows that any endeavour toward regionalism requires good and effective governance – at the level of the nation and at the level of the region itself. Without it, the region will not fully achieve its objectives. Without it, regional governance will fall short of its potential.

Acknowledgements

This volume is the final result of a decade-long project that has explored various aspects of East Asian regionalism and led to over a dozen books and many more articles. It arises from a regional and international network of scholars and officials devoted to better understanding the regional dynamics now emerging in Asia. The editor would particularly like to thank those who contributed to this particular volume. Their patience and dedication to this project has been incredible.

Without the necessary funding the project that underpinned this volume would not have been possible. The editor would like to extend a special note of thanks to the Japan Foundation Asia Center for its support of this volume as well as a number of other projects that have been undertaken by the Centre of Asian Studies over the years.

Many thanks to Teresa Tsai and Cathy Wong from the Centre of Asian Studies' administration staff for their invaluable assistance in preparing the manuscript for publication. A sincere debt of gratitude is also due to Stephanie Rodgers, Sonja van Leeuwen, Chris Hook and Leanne Hinves at RoutledgeCurzon for their wonderful guidance and editorial support.

Abbreviations

AAECP	ASEAN Australia Economic Cooperation Programme
AANEA	Atmosphere Action Network East Asia
ABAC	ASEAN Business Advisory Council
ABF1	Asian Bond Fund
ABF2	Asian Bond Fund II
ABMI	Asian Bond Market Initiative
ACD	Asia Cooperation Dialogue
ACPMECS	Ayeyawady-Chao Phraya-Mekong Economic Cooperation Strategy
ACSC	ASEAN Civil Society Conference
ADB	Asia Development Bank
ADMER	Agreement on Disaster Management and Emergency Response
ADMM	ASEAN Defence Ministers Meeting
ADRRN	Asian Disaster Reduction & Response Network
AEC	ASEAN Economic Community
AEM	ASEAN Economic Ministers
AEPF	Asia–Europe People's Forum
AERR	ASEAN Emergency Rice Reserve
AFAS	ASEAN Framework Agreement on Services
AFTA-CER	ASEAN Free Trade Area with Australia and New Zealand
AFP	Australian Federal Police
AFSIS	ASEAN Food Security Information System
AFSIT	ASEAN Food Security Information and Training
AFTA	ASEAN Free Trade Area
AIPMC	ASEAN Inter-Parliamentary Caucus for Democracy in Myanmar
AMAF	ASEAN Ministers on Agriculture and Forestry
AMEICC	AEM-METI Economic and Industrial Cooperation Committee
AMF	Asian Monetary Facilities
AMM	ASEAN Ministerial Meeting
ANZUS	Australia–New Zealand–United States
APA	ASEAN People's Assembly
APEC	Asia-Pacific Economic Cooperation group

APT	ASEAN+3
ARF	ASEAN Regional Forum
ARPDM	ASEAN Regional Programme on Disaster Management
ARSP	ASEAN Regional Surveillance Process
ASA	ASEAN Swap Arrangement
ASC	ASEAN Security Community
ASCC	ASEAN Socio-Cultural Community
ASEAN	Association of Southeast Asian Nations
ASEAN+3	ASEAN plus China, Korea and Japan
ASEAN-CER	ASEAN plus Australia and New Zealand
ASEAN-ISIS	ASEAN Institutes of Strategic and International Studies
ASEF	Asia–Europe Foundation
ASEM	Asia Europe Meeting
ASEMUS	Asia–Europe Museum Network
AU	African Union
BCIM	Bangladesh, China, India and Myanmar
BIMP-EAGA	Brunei Darussalam-Indonesia-Malaysia-Philippines East ASEAN Growth Area
BIMSTEC	Bangladesh, India, Sri Lanka, Thailand Economic Cooperation
BIS	Bank for International Settlements
BIT	bilateral investment treaty
BSA	bilateral swap arrangement
CACO	Central Asian Cooperation Organisation
CARE	Cooperative for Assistance and Relief Everywhere
CASS	Chinese Academy of Social Sciences
CBM	Confidence-Building Measure
CECA	Comprehensive Economic Cooperation Agreement
CEPEA	Comprehensive Economic Partnership in East Asia
CEPT	Common Effective Preferential Tariff
CFSP	Common Foreign and Security Policy
CLMV	Cambodia, Laos, Myanmar and Vietnam
CMI	Chiang Mai Initiative
CSCAP	Council for Security Cooperation in the Asia-Pacific
CSCE	Conference on Security and Co-operation in Europe
CSO	civil society organisation
CSTO	Collective Security Treaty Organisation
DG	Directors-General
DMR	daily mortality rate
DPRK	Democratic People's Republic of Korea (North Korea)
DSB	Dispute Settlement Body
DSM	dispute settlement mechanisms
EABC	East Asian Business Council
EAC	East Asian Community
EAEC	East Asian Economic Caucus

EAEG	East Asian Economic Group
EAERR	East Asia Emergency Rice Reserve
EANET	Acid Deposition Monitoring Network in East Asia
EAS	East Asian Summit
EASG	East Asian Study Group
EAVG	East Asia Vision Group
ECJ	European Court of Justice
EEC	Eurasian Economic Community
EMEAP	Executives' Meeting of East Asia-Pacific Central Banks
EPG	Eminent Persons Group
ERIA	Economic Research Institute of ASEAN and East Asia
ETWG	Group of Experts and a Technical Working Group on Economic and Financial Monitoring
EU	European Union
FAO	Food and Agriculture Organisation
FDI	foreign direct investment
FDL-AP	Forum of Democratic Leaders of the Asia-Pacific
FOCP	ASEAN-ROK Future Oriented Cooperation Projects Fund
FPDA	Five Power Defence Arrangements
FTA	free trade area
FTAAP	Free Trade Area of the Asia-Pacific
G-7	Group of Seven
GATS	General Agreement on Trade in Services
GATT	General Agreement on Tariffs and Trade
GMS	Greater Mekong Sub-region
GNI	gross national income
HLTF	High Level Task Force
HRD	human resource development
IAI	Initiative for ASEAN Integration
IAIS	International Association of Insurance Supervisors
IAP	Individual Action Plans
ICRC	International Committee of the Red Cross
ICT	information and communications technology
IDEA	Initiative for Development in East Asia
IDRI	Indonesian Danareksa Research Institute
IFRC	International Federation of Red Cross and Red Crescent Societies
IGO	intergovernmental organisation
IIMA	Institute for International Monetary Affairs
ILO	International Labour Organisation
IMF	International Monetary Fund
IMT-GT	Indonesia-Malaysia-Thailand Growth Triangle
INTERFET	International Force for East Timor
IOSCO	International Organisation of Securities Commissions
IPE	international political economy

IPR	intellectual property rights
IRC	International Rescue Committee
ISEAS	Institute of Southeast Asian Studies
JFPR	Japan Fund for Poverty Reduction
JICA	Japan International Cooperation Agency
JICAK	Japan, India, China, ASEAN, South Korea
JPF	Japan Platform
JSCOT	Joint Standing Committee on Treaties
KIEP	Korea Institute for International Economic Policy
LDP	Liberal Democratic Party
METI	Ministry of Economic, Trade and Industry (Japan)
MICS-Asia	Model Inter-Comparisons of Long Range Transport and Sulphur Deposition in East Asia
MILF	Moro Islamic Liberation Front
MNC	multinational corporation
MNLF	Moro National Liberation Front
MOF	Ministry of Finance
MOFA	Ministry of Foreign Affairs
MoU	memorandum of understanding
MPAT	Military Planning Augmentation Team
MSF	Médecins Sans Frontières
NAFTA	North American Free Trade Agreement
NBIP	Non-Binding Investment Principles
NEAC	Northeast Asian Conference on Environmental Cooperation
NEACD	Northeast Asian Cooperation Dialogue
NEACEC	Northeast Asian Conference on Environmental Cooperation
NEARGA	Northeast Asia Regional Government Association
NEASD	Northeast Asian Security Dialogue
NEAT	Network of East Asian Thinktanks
NGO	non-governmental organisation
NPC	National Party Congress
NSC	New Security Concept
NSS	National Security Strategy (United States)
NTS	non-traditional security
ODA	official development assistance/overseas development aid
OECD	Organisation for Economic Cooperation and Development
OREI	Office of Regional Economic Integration
OSCE	Organisation for Security and Cooperation in Europe
PAFTAD	Pacific Trade and Development Council
PBEC	Pacific Basin Economic Council
PD	preventive diplomacy
PECC	Pacific Economic Cooperation Council
PKO	peace-keeping operation
PMC	Post-Ministerial Conference
PNG	Papua New Guinea

POSCO	Pohang Iron and Steel Company
PRC	People's Republic of China
PSI	Proliferation Security Initiative
PTA	preferential trading agreements
QDR	Quadrennial Defense Review
RAD	ROK-ASEAN Dialogue
RATs	Regional Anti-Terrorist Structure
RHAP	Regional Haze Action Plan
RMSI	Regional Maritime Security Initiative
ROK	Republic of Korea
RTA	Regional Trade Agreement
SAARC	South Asian Association for Regional Cooperation
SAF	Singapore Armed Forces
SAPA	Solidarity for Asian Peoples Advocacy
SCF	Special Cooperation Fund (ASEAN-ROK)
SCO	Shanghai Cooperation Organisation
SKRL	Singapore–Kunming Railway Link
SMART	Special Malaysian Rescue Team
SOM	Senior Officials Meeting
SPDC	State Peace and Development Council
TAC	Treaty of Amity and Cooperation
TC	tropical cyclone
TDRI	Thailand Development Research Institute
TEU	Treaty on European Union
TI	Transparency International
TIFA	Trade and Investment Framework Agreement
TMRR	Technical Meeting on Rice Reserve
TRIMS	Agreement on Trade-Related Investment Measures
TRIPS	Agreement on Trade-Related Aspects of Intellectual Property Rights
UNDP	United Nations Development Programme
UNEP	United Nations Environment Programme
UNESCAP	United Nations Economic and Social Committee for the Asia and the Pacific
UNHCR	UN High Commissioner for Refugees
UNICEF	United Nations Children's Fund
UNMISET	United Nations Mission of Support in East Timor
UNOCHA	United Nations Office for the Coordination of Humanitarian Assistance
UNTAET	United Nations Transitional Administration in East Timor
VAP	Vientiane Action Programme
WFP	World Food Programme
WHO	World Health Organisation
WMD	weapons of mass destruction
WTO	World Trade Organisation

1 Understanding regional governance in Asia

Nicholas Thomas

Introduction

The birth of the Association of South East Asian Nations (ASEAN) in 1967 was a modest event for an organisation that is rapidly becoming the hub for East Asian integration. Such modesty is, however, not surprising when the history of the region immediately prior to the creation of ASEAN is considered. In the aftermath of the Second World War, three other regional groupings had been created as Southeast Asian states sought to foster security and economic development in the region and at home.[1] Each one had failed, brought down by either intraregional tensions or geopolitical shifts. Given that the objectives of the earlier organisations were also incorporated into ASEAN, its modest beginning was perhaps a reflection of the difficulties these other groups had faced in maintaining their momentum and cohesion.

But the region was changing. ASEAN's arrival coincided with the rapid development in all four dragon economies – Taiwan, South Korea, Hong Kong and Singapore – and the start of Japanese investment into Southeast Asia. Over the next decade the development of the ASEAN economies – supported by inflows of regional and international foreign direct investment – helped to promote social and economic capital. At the same time, conflicts between member states began to lessen – creating a space for cooperative activities at the regional level. During this same period China emerged from the shadow of the Cultural Revolution and began to increase its involvement in world affairs. The opening up of China provided a further economic stimulus to Southeast Asia, with most ASEAN members sending trade and political delegations to China during this time.[2] Reflecting their increased socio-economic and political capacities as well as a desire to deepen regional ties, the ASEAN leaders met at the end of this decade to sign the Treaty of Amity and Cooperation (TAC) and the Declaration of ASEAN Concord. With these agreements in place ASEAN gained a framework for an institutional and normative identity, which continues to develop today.

Over the next two decades ASEAN expanded the scope of its intraregional cooperation. Three key events can be seen as having a significant impact on shaping this cooperation. First, Vietnam's intervention in Cambodia (1978–1990) forced ASEAN members to work together in developing a common negotiating position and achieving a mutually desired outcome. Although the influence of ASEAN in developing the Paris Accords is debatable, it is clear that this experience highlighted for ASEAN the opportunities to be gained from deeper collaboration on regional and international issues.[3] Second, the end of the Cold War removed many of the geopolitical obstacles that had impeded regional cooperation – not only in Southeast Asia but also between Southeast and Northeast Asian states. These two events not only encouraged ASEAN members to work collectively but also provided the organisation with the necessary political and economic space in which to do so.

The third key event was the 1997 Asian financial crisis. This had a number of significant outcomes for the region. The most important outcome was the understanding that Southeast Asian and Northeast Asian states were not only intraregionally connected: they were also pan-regionally linked. In other words, problems in one state could not only spill over to neighbouring states – detrimentally affecting their ability to provide economic stability and socio-political security for their peoples – but they were not confined to a single subregion and could spread, to impact on other states across East Asia. The 1997 Asian crisis also fostered the belief that this was a problem for the region to deal with. The International Monetary Fund (IMF)'s interventions were not viewed favourably by most affected governments, who perceived the organisation to also be furthering a US-centred policy rather than solely focusing on alleviating the crisis.[4] Finally, it again reinforced the idea that deeper cooperation could yield synergistic results for the benefit of all states, economies and peoples in the region. The task was how to achieve such cooperative outcomes, given that the regional response to the 1997 crisis was driven by states and external actors rather than by ASEAN.

During this period ASEAN expanded its membership to include all ten Southeast Asian countries. It has also enlarged its cooperation to include the three main states of Northeast Asia. This success has presented the region with a singular challenge, namely how to integrate these disparate countries, with their different needs, capacity levels and worldviews. This was already a pressing issue when ASEAN moved to incorporate Cambodia, Laos, Myanmar and Vietnam in the 1990s. The inclusion of China, Japan and South Korea – with their own sets of interests, norms and worldviews – in the ASEAN+1 and ASEAN+3 (APT) dialogues further complicated the situation.

An unexpected challenge to the relevance and focus of ASEAN's work emerged in the late 1980s and 1990s with the creation of numerous other organisations and networks with an interest in East Asia. The Asia-Pacific Economic Cooperation (APEC) group was established in 1989; with a focus on economies rather than states, this is the only regional organisation with Taiwan and Hong Kong as members. The ASEAN Regional Forum (ARF) has – since its inception in 1994 – involved members with very different political and security norms from those in the core Southeast Asian countries. The Asia Europe Meeting (ASEM) dialogue began in 1996 and was the first regional organisation to have China, Japan and South Korea grouped with the then seven-member ASEAN, as representatives of Asia. The region also witnessed an expansion of subregional initiatives throughout the 1990s – such as the Greater Mekong Sub-region (GMS), the Brunei Darussalam-Indonesia-Malaysia-Philippines East ASEAN Growth Area (BIMP-EAGA) and the Indonesia-Malaysia-Thailand Growth Triangle (IMT-GT). Most ASEAN states were members of one or more of these regional and subregional groupings, all of which required resources (both human and capital) in order to achieve their respective agendas. The redirection of these resources meant that member states had less capacity to commit to regional projects, requiring a hierarchical prioritisation of regional initiatives based on members' self-interest.

In order to avoid the fate of the pre-ASEAN groups – all of whose utility was diminished by other events – and to clarify its position in this emerging constellation of regional bodies, the organisation sought to refine its *raison d'être* by developing a blueprint for institutional evolution. To this end, at the 1999 Informal ASEAN Summit, regional leaders agreed to establish an eminent persons group – the East Asia Vision Group (EAVG) – to find a way forward for the region. In their final report, towards an East Asian Community (EAC), the 13 members of the EAVG noted that they aimed to 'offer a common vision for East Asia that reflects the rapidly changing regional and global environment, as well as provide direction for future cooperation among East Asian nations'.[5] This vision encompassed private sector actors and civil society organisations operating in conjunction with states to further regional integration. It also placed ASEAN at the centre of regional integration efforts, even as it acknowledged the work being undertaken by other institutions – such as APEC. In other words, the report not only offered a final destination, an EAC, but a roadmap as to how to get there.

In the period since this report was handed down there have been a number of other studies and initiatives undertaken whose effect has been to speed up the process of regionalisation and governance in Asia. While some of these have been significant in articulating a grand vision for what the region should look like – the East Asian Community as described in the Bali Concord II, for example – there has been relatively little work published on the fine details as to how this end point will be achieved, with competing visions held by different members, leading to the region's collective leadership preferring to see this aspect of regionalisation as more of a work in progress.

These various initiatives have created new opportunies for dialogue and cooperation all of which need to be integrated with each other. Indeed, there are presently in excess of 700 ASEAN meetings held each year. ASEAN's success in its expansion has, therefore, become an impediment to the smooth functioning of the organisation and limits its ability to realise its many objectives. This tension – between deeper and wider regionalisation, on the one hand, and better institutional functionality, on the other – has led policy makers in Asia to seek new partners, for both policy formulation and execution. Even as states remain the key actors in regional institutions, the broadening out of the policy processes has involved actors from the private sector as well as civil society.

In order to understand the implications of this tension for East Asia, this chapter draws on the governance literature to model the articulation of regional institutions and norms by regional actors. In particular, this chapter seeks to go beyond traditional state-centric analysis by incorporating examples of sub-state and non-state actors in a multilevel governance framework. Three examples highlighting the evolution of regional governance – the APT process, the East Asian Summit (EAS) and the drafting of the ASEAN Charter – are then presented. These cases highlight many of the ambitions and struggles implicit in the governance formation process. As observers of Asian regional affairs have noted, the process of regional integration and governance has faced numerous problems. Some of these have been resolved over time, while others remain as impediments to regional affairs. This chapter focuses several of the more serious obstacles to the further development of Asian regional governance before concluding and presenting a summary of the chapters that follow.

Modelling regional governance

Governance 'remains an elusive theory, defined and conceptualized in various ways'.[6] Originally located within the nation-state, it has since expanded to the global and – most recently – regional levels. Roseneau describes governance as encompassing 'the activities of government, but it also includes any actors who resort to command mechanisms to make demands, frame goals, issue directives and pursue policies'.[7] According to Marks and Hooghe, these activities and the authority that underpins the decision-making mechanisms can take place either within 'general purpose' jurisdictions – at the 'international, national, regional, meso, local' levels – or within 'specialized jurisdictions' that operate across these five levels, according to a given problem.[8]

At the domestic level there are numerous ways in which the term governance is used. Krahmann states that at the 'national and sub-national levels, the term governance is used primarily in four ways. The first treats governance as a generic category synonymous with the concepts of political system or state structure ... The second usage concerns the reform of public administration since the 1980s. It refers mainly to the devolution of political authority from national administrative agencies to sub-national bodies ... The third use regards the governance of particular policy sectors ... And the final usage concerns the analysis of corporate governance.'[9] Weiss suggests a further eight ways in which the term is used, of which the following is arguably the most relevant: 'The concept of governance refers to the complex set of values, norms, processes and institutions by which society manages its development and resolves conflict, formally and informally.'[10]

Global governance has similar characteristics to that of governance at the domestic level. As with many other theories of international relations, it emerged from the post-Cold War debate on the new international order. Held and McGrew describe it as a 'thickening web of multi-lateral agreements, global and regional institutions and regimes, transgovernmental policy networks and summits'.[11] Halabi adds to this understanding of global governance by further suggesting that it 'marks the acceptance of regulations at the global level out of a conviction that such regulations will enable actors to seek wealth in an orderly fashion and in accordance with the norms of the international system'.[12] The willingness by different actors to engage in globalised processes of governance arises due to recognition (principally by governments) of the 'limitations to their resources and capabilities in dealing with global issues' and a desire to overcome these limitations so as to gain greater benefits.[13] Embedded in this understanding of global governance is an implied universalist philosophy or policy agenda to which states, their respective subnational bodies, market institutions and social organisations are requested, to varying degrees depending on the relationship of the referent actor to the global processes, to conform if they wish to draw from the globalisation process.

Regional governance is a relatively new addition to the discourse and remains heavily influenced by Eurocentric models. As Phillips notes, governance at this level is concerned 'with supranationalism and the attractive notion of "multi-level governance"',[14] albeit in a more intensive mode than that witnessed on the global plane. Governance at this level also implies a more concentrated sharing of norms and histories, usually within a geographically defined area. With respect to the European Union (EU), Hooghe and Marks describe this phenomenon as 'a polity-creating process in which authority and policy-making influence are shared across multiple levels of government – sub-national, national and supranational. While national governments [remain] formidable participants in EU policy making, control has slipped away from them.'[15] In the case of Africa, Söderbaum suggests that this loss of authority has been exacerbated through the regionalisation of 'shadow networks' where transnational patronage and criminal networks serve to unevenly redistribute resources and authority to the 'rich and powerful and those with jobs'.[16] However, rather than only conceive this diminution of control in a zero-sum and negative sense (through slippage or a loss of authority), it can also be considered in a more positive light, where states choose to pool their sovereignty in order to achieve synergistic outcomes that could otherwise not be realised. In East Asia, this pooling of sovereignty can be seen within the APT area, where there is 'clear trend to enacting common policies that are binding on member states'.[17]

At the regional level another variant of governance can also be identified, that of pan-regional governance. Thus, in addition to the vertical articulations of governance Hooghe and Marks put forward, there is also a horizontal expression of regional governance. This is expressed when regions begin to work together at a meta-level which remains below the global plane, constructing interlocking transnational epistemic communities. An example of this can be seen in the growing array of dialogues within – and related to – the ASEM process.

Payne compares the development of a regional governance as 'multi-level governance in the EU', 'hubs and spoke governance in North America' and 'pre-governance in Asia-Pacific'. Despite Payne's observation regarding the operational differences in governance it can still be suggested that, at the global and regional levels, states foster the development of regional governance primarily through a series of multilateral arrangements that coordinate the relations between the member states 'on the basis of generalized principles of conduct'.[18] This approach by Ruggie serves to link both institutions and norms together in the expression of transnational forms of governance. Nel et al. build on Ruggie's observation by suggesting that while an institution may have a set of 'meta-norms', 'certain substantive norms conceptually and ethically fit the institution of multi-lateralism better than others'.[19] In terms of what constitute such meta-norms within an institutional-type arrangement, Krasner proposes a:

> set of implicit or explicit principles, norms, rules and decision-making procedures around which actors' expectations converge in a given area … Principles are beliefs of fact, causation and rectitude. Norms are standards of behaviour defined in terms of rights and obligations. Rules are specific prescriptions or proscriptions for action. Decision-making procedures are prevailing practices for making and implementing collective choice.[20]

If Ruggie, Nel et al. and Krasner are brought together, then it could be expected that within regional institutions there would be a set of meta-norms which would reflect general international norms but that these would exist with and be influenced by a specific set of substantive norms generated through the actors' shared identities or objectives. The extent to which such substantive norms would be subordinated to or given primacy over the meta-norms would reflect the degree to which the actors operating within the regional institution found a commonality between the two sets of norms – concerning either general purpose or specialised jurisdictional issues. Acharya, in discussing this issue with respect to Asian regionalism, found that some meta-norms are more readily 'localised' than others, because of the congruence between the external norms and the pre-existing regional norms. The degree to which norm localisation can take place depends on a set of variables, including 'the positive impact of the norm on the legitimacy and authority of key norm-takers, the strength of prior norms, the credibility and prestige of local agents, indigenous cultural traits and traditions and the scope for grafting and pruning presented by foreign norms'.[21]

These substantive norms can be further subdivided into two categories: constitutive norms and regulative norms. Constitutive norms serve to 'define the organisational or institutional mechanisms related to the operation of the object or scenario under analysis'.[22] Such norms, for example, serve to define the scope of public–private interactions or the extent of civil society engagement with states or institutions operating at the regional and transnational levels. In extending this concept, Jayasuriya suggests that:

> the emerging fabric of governance is best understood in the sense that there is a simultaneous recognition that region-wide regulatory frameworks ... can be implemented and policed at the local level so that what is formed is a system of multilevel governance that connects international organisations ... with regional entities ... and various national agencies or even sub-national or local entities.[23]

Regulative norms 'define the rules of conduct which state what is appropriate' behaviour for member states.[24] These may be further considered as either formal or informal. Formal norms serve to bind members to specified actions or codes of conduct. At the regional level, the European Union is the best example of an institution with a formal set of regulative norms. Informal norms are uncodified and flexible. They draw on the shared histories and cultural values which the participants perceive as creating a basis for undertaking common actions for mutually desirable outcomes.

Whereas formal norms require the support of an enabling institution able to enforce the regulative process, informal norms can be developed in a less institutionalised setting. While ASEAN is a good example of a regional organisation that draws upon such informal regulative norms, it is by no means the only such case. The African Union (AU), the Shanghai Cooperation Organisation (SCO) or the South Asian Association for Regional Cooperation (SAARC) all utilise similar informal norms in seeking regional objectives. It should also be noted that formal and informal norms frequently coexist in all regional institutions. Moreover, without the types of shared values that first create informal norms, formal regulative norms could not be developed.

Given the above observations, it can be postulated that – at the regional level – the shared cultural and historical basis of such substantive norms would mean that these would form the default position for the regional organisation and its members, except when external norms (either as meta-norms or when transmitted from other regions) gained primacy. Further, in more heterogeneous organisations these norms would be correspondingly more contested as different members vied to become 'norm setters' in order to advance their own agendas.[25] Under such conditions, the objectives of the organisation would be a continuous process of renegotiation with a 'lowest common denominator' approach defining the outcomes. As an organisation expanded its membership base or extended the range of actors involved in the formulation and realisation of its objectives, this process would become concomitantly more congested. Such a case can be seen where regional organisations move from a core number of elite-state policy makers to incorporate a set of new actors without a streamlining or codification of its substantive or meta-norms. The case of East Asia, which has over the last decade developed a multilevel approach to regional governance with a new set of state, substate and non-state actors, is considered next.

Multilevel Asian governance

Multilevel governance refers to an extension of the policy-making processes to include actors outside the state. This concept is most readily used in the global governance literature but it is being increasingly used in analyses of European regional governance.[26] Although this volume is neither contending that Asia is as advanced in this aspect as Europe nor suggesting that Asia is necessarily following a European model in its regional endeavours, a similar process of including non-governmental and substate actors in regional policy formulations can be identified.

Since the 1999 ASEAN Summit, the region has been moving towards a more integrated system of Asian governance. Institutionally, this is typified by a number of new processes, such as the ASEAN Economic, Security and Socio-Cultural Communities. However, what is important is that as East Asia integrates, its policy processes are expanding beyond the realm of state-based actors to involve private sector organisations and civil society actors as envisaged by the EAVG report.

In terms of state-based organisations, the region has developed a set of institutions at the pan-regional (ASEM), regional (ASEAN), subregional (GMS or BIMP-EAGA) and sectoral levels (APEC) whose cumulative impact is to foster a set of networks centred on the East Asian region. While some of these are linked in various ways – for example, ASEAN, ASEAN+1, APT and the East Asian Summit – others operate in parallel (such as APEC) and only overlap in terms of actors and (sometimes) agendas.

With ASEAN as the core institution, the countries of Southeast Asia are actively engaging in the broadest set of dialogues and programmes with surrounding states. Although these dialogues were initially bilateral (such as ASEAN+1), they soon became multilateral (APT). Since the creation of the East Asian Summit, these dialogues are expanding into multilateral endeavours – with the inclusion of Australian, Indian and New Zealand representatives. Below the level of the state, substate actors are also forming networks across the region based on shared norms and policy agendas. Provincial and municipal authorities are developing bi- and multilateral sister-state and sister-city arrangements. One example of the latter case can be seen with the East Asia (pan-Yellow Sea) City Conference, which involves '10 cities in East Asia to promote sustainable urban development'.[27]

Subregional organisations such as the GMS, BIMP-EAGA, the Kunming Initiative and the Mekong–Ganges Cooperation Group also serve as catalysing forces for closer regional cooperation between smaller sets of regional states with higher areas of common interests. The role of regional states in other Asian organisations and networks with wider or different geographical foci (such as the SCO or the SAARC) serves to provide additional opportunities for the sharing and development of norms and identities.

Sectorally based organisations or networks such as APEC, the ARF or Shangri-La Dialogue – whose activities focus on specific policy areas (for instance, economics or security) – again serve regional processes but under a more open-regionalism model, where non-regional states with interests in Asia work with regional actors to achieve mutually desirable outcomes. These are, in turn, supported by Track-Two groups, for example, the Council for Security Cooperation in the Asia-Pacific (CSCAP). These groups not only supply a wider policy space for participating states to engage with their counterparts, they also provide an additional channel for the engagement of non-state actors in policy processes. In doing so, they create 'a positive atmosphere that is conducive to the formation of [a] regional identity'.[28]

Outside of state-centric organisations, regional governance processes are also developing within private sector and civil society networks. Indeed, in considering the private sector, it is possible to identify the creation of open-regional governance processes well in advance of those in the political realm. Both the Pacific Basin Economic Council (PBEC) and the more academically inclined Pacific Trade and Development Council (PAFTAD) were established in 1968. Although the 'principal participants in [these fora] have been private players ... they have developed and exercised influence in the evolution of government policy through the establishment of regional cooperation arrangements'.[29] These two organisations, in conjunction with the Pacific Economic Cooperation Council (PECC – created in 1980) and APEC group, helped to foster regional economic and financial governance across the Asia-Pacific.

However, all four organisations are based on an open-regional governance model. In 2004, a more narrowly defined financial and economic governance process was initiated when the East Asian Business Council (EABC) was launched in the lead-up to the ASEAN Leaders' Summit. Unlike the Pacific-focused organisations, the EABC's membership was limited to representatives from the APT states.[30] Moreover, the EABC was created in response to a request by regional leaders who wanted to 'establish an East Asian Business Council to promote private sector participation'[31] in regional policy processes.[32] The coexistence of the PBEC and the EABC (and other related organisations) reflects an ongoing tension between an open model of participation in regional affairs and a more geographically narrow model where members are only drawn from the thirteen states within the APT group.

Civil society organisations (CSOs) are also beginning to become more involved in regional governance. At the Track-Three level, the ASEAN People's Assembly (APA) serves as a consultative mechanism between 'governments, think tanks and civil society groups'.[33] While it should be noted that this consultation process is quite uneven, with some regional governments opposed to the idea of the inclusion of CSOs in regional governance processes, the linking of the APA participants with regional policy processes 'will inevitably [have an] impact on the norms and modalities of ASEAN'.[34] Such an impact allows for the 'horizontal and vertical co-ordination of public policies in ways that "are more sensitive to the societal environment than the traditional mode of governing"'.[35]

Beyond the development of Track-Three levels of governance are other formalised linkages between regional institutions and civil society organisations. As of mid 2008, for example, there were fifty-seven CSOs affiliated with ASEAN.[36] Other institutions, such as ASEM, not only hold pan-regional civil society meetings but also create interfaces between civil society and governments. While such interfaces may lead to tensions between 'Eastern' and 'Western' proponents of civil society behaviour, within the two sides these meetings help to promote the development of the respective identities and norms on the two sides. In addition, outside of the Track-Three processes there are many more civil society organisations either working at the regional level or simply collaborating with their counterparts in other Asian countries, whose collective impact helps support the social and cultural development of an East Asian Community.

Hence, over the last decade it is possible to see a multilevel expansion of governance at the regional level in East Asia. Although the current processes remain heavily state based, there is an identifiable shift towards including non-state actors in institutional processes. Despite the fact that private sector representatives generate the least resistance to their inclusion in policy processes, there is also a clear willingness to engage with civil society organisations – at least on the part of some member states and regional institutions. These new actors are also accompanied by a different set of identities and norms from those which the regional institutions had earlier encompassed. Despite the fact that the impact of these new actors is limited because their involvement is restricted by the existing members, they represent an additional source of pressure on the further development of regional governance in East Asia.

Evolving institutions and norms

Even as the region seeks to develop closer ties, the actors and their shared norms which underpin the process of regionalisation and institution formation are changing. ASEAN has moved from being a five-member group focused on economic development and national security to encompass all ten Southeast Asian states. At the same time as the last few states joined,

ASEAN expanded its regional processes to incorporate the three major Northeast Asian states of China, Japan and South Korea. The creation of the East Asian Summit has further widened participation in regional affairs from thirteen to sixteen member states; with Australia, India and New Zealand now taking part in regional heads of government meetings as well as an expanding array of functional cooperation dialogues. The ASEAN-centred principles of consensus-based informal decision making and non-interference in each other's affairs are also gradually changing as the group evolves; an example can be seen in the call for an ASEAN Charter. However, these developments are not without tensions – internally within ASEAN, and in the relationships with their partners as well as between the partners themselves. In seeking to understand regional governance in Asia, these three cases are worth exploring, so as to better appreciate how the governance of the region may develop in future.

ASEAN+3

In 1997 – amid the fallout of the Asian crisis – the first APT meeting was held. Although it would be another two years before the heads of all thirteen states were present, the meeting demonstrated East Asian perceptions that the futures of Southeast Asia and Northeast Asia were inextricably linked.[37] If the regional states were to avoid a reoccurrence of the financial crisis, as well as manage the negative externalities resulting from the twinned processes of modernisation and globalisation, then they had to develop synergistic mechanisms that built state capacities while limiting negative spillovers into their neighbours' affairs.

At the successive APT Summits the process of integrating the region has developed rapidly. Outside the leadership level, the APT process has steadily expanded to include Agriculture and Forestry Ministers, Economic Ministers, Energy Ministers, Finance Ministers, Foreign Ministers, Labour Ministers and Tourism Ministers. In addition, combined meetings have begun to be held just between the +3 Ministers, spurring the creation of complementary linkages in Northeast Asia.[38] Below the Ministerial level, there are now also Senior Officials Meetings (SOMs) of the APT group. The SOMs act as policy coordinators for the respective state-based bureaux.[39] Implementing the Ministerial and SOM decisions are the APT Directors-General (DG).

Outside the explicit +3 framework there have, since 1997, been a growing number of other meetings that have brought the Northeast Asian states into a closer cooperative arrangement with their Southeast Asian counterparts. These meetings usually involve a subset of the thirteen members and focus on a specific issue. An example of this type of meeting was the anti-drugs meeting that took place in Denpasar in November 2001. Although it was organised by Southeast Asian states and focused on the use of and trade in illegal narcotics in Southeast Asia, the meeting also included Chinese and

Japanese (but not South Korean) delegations.[40] As a result, an agreement was signed to combat drugs in Southeast Asia, which incorporated the resources of both Chinese and Japanese governments. In addition, a number of bilateral and multilateral cooperative arrangements between various regional governments were signed.[41] There has also been a deepening of regional integration via the ASEAN+1 dialogues, which serve as a parallel initiator of region projects between ASEAN and its three Northeast Asian partners on a bilateral basis.

At the 2003 APT Summit in Bali the process of developing a regional community advanced with the release of the Bali Concord II proposal. This proposal called for the establishment of an ASEAN Community comprised of three pillars – an ASEAN Economic Community (AEC), an ASEAN Security Community (ASC) and an ASEAN Socio-Cultural Community (ASCC). It was envisaged that within each of these pillars community-building activities would be undertaken that would promote the deeper integration between the ten member states. Although this was an ASEAN-focused initiative, it had significant ramifications for APT community building, given the centrality of ASEAN to the wider EAC concept.

Since the release of Bali Concord II, efforts to promote APT integration have increased. At the 2004 Summit ASEAN released the Vientiane Action Plan to accelerate community building, particularly through faster integration of eleven priority sectors as well as mapping a series of areas within the three pillars for further development. It was also at this meeting that the East Asian Summit was first discussed in a formal manner, with ASEAN and its +3 partners agreeing to hold the first summit the following year. Although the following two summits were – to a certain extent – overshadowed by the initiation of the East Asian Summit process, the community-building process (under APT auspices) continued. Importantly, the 2005 APT Summit affirmed that 'the ASEAN Plus Three process will continue to be the main vehicle in achieving [East Asian cooperation and community building], with ASEAN as the driving force and with the active participation of the ASEAN Plus Three countries, in order to promote shared ownership'.[42]

Over the following two summits, the APT continued to develop, although the position of APT as the key enabling mechanism for wider East Asian integration between ASEAN and the three main Northeast Asian states began to shift. The Chairman's statement from the tenth APT Summit only declared APT to be 'an essential part of the evolving regional architecture, complementary to the East Asian Summit and other regional fora'.[43] At the Singapore Summit in November 2007 the centrality of APT to community-building efforts was seen with the release of a ten-year work plan for the group. This work plan closely mirrors regional governance efforts being called for in ASEAN but seeks to extend the integrative capacity of the region by drawing in the three Northeast Asian partners in a systematic and coherent manner.[44]

Hence, what began ten years ago as an informal meeting confined to the leadership level has now become a formal process, incorporating a wide range of activities. In ASEAN+1 and APT, these linkages are developing as the basis for an East Asian Community, as envisaged in the EAVG and East Asian Study Group (EASG) reports. This community-building process has expanded beyond the leaders to include an ever-increasing range of ministers, senior and other officials. Beyond the realm of the policy elites there is also a broad range of commercial and social bodies that are developing contacts with similar entities in either the ASEAN or APT areas.[45] These bodies are forging epistemic communities that reach across state boundaries to integrate sets of policy, market and social actors into a regional framework. However, since 2005, the role of APT in community-building efforts has been somewhat uncertain, with the early introduction of the East Asian Summit. As the EAS represents an alternate evolutionary path for regional integration and community-building, it is worthwhile exploring its impact on the development of regional governance.

The East Asian Summit

At the APT meeting in 2001 the East Asian Vision Group submitted its report to the regional leadership. Under the heading of institutional development, the EAVG called for the evolution of the APT meetings into an East Asian Summit (EAS).[46] This call was advanced by the subsequent EASG report in 2002, which saw the EAS as 'a desirable long-term objective ... that [built] on the substantive comfort levels of the existing APT framework'.[47] However, whilst the region's senior officials and eminent persons saw the EAS as a long-term goal, intraregional politics and ambitions saw the EAS brought forward to 2005.

One of the pressures behind for the early realisation of the EAS was the decision in 2003 for ASEAN to seek to create an East Asian Community, based on the APT group. Although not explicitly linked in any of the preceding documents, the EAS was generally seen by regional policy makers as the logical pinnacle of the EAC meeting series. Such a goal would not only allow for a clear evolution from the APT to the EAC but would also allow for a greater role to be taken by China, Japan and South Korea in regional affairs – as called for the EASG report.[48]

A second pressure for the EAS to be held sooner rather than later was the proposal by Malaysia for it to host an APT Secretariat. During 2002, Malaysia had been very active in pushing for a new Secretariat for APT. Such an organisation, Malaysia argued, would not only lighten the administrative load of the ASEAN Secretariat but would also allow Asia to speak with one voice in global affairs.[49] However, the idea of a separate secretariat was opposed by other ASEAN members. Even though Malaysia subsequently modified its proposal – initially by suggesting that the new body could still remain administratively under the ASEAN Secretariat and later by retitling the body as the APT bureau[50] – it continued to be opposed by the other ASEAN states. One of the key concerns was the view that the proposition was another attempt by Malaysia to start the East Asian Economic Grouping (EAEG), an earlier Malaysian proposal for an Asian economic bloc that had been sidelined by the other ASEAN members.

A third, split pressure came from Northeast Asia. On the one hand, China was seeking a venue to increase its presence in regional affairs. As Yamakage has noted, it 'is clear that China is trying to exert influence over the formation of an East Asian order by drawing closer to ASEAN and preparing to march in step with it and that China is positioning itself to play a leadership role'.[51] Indeed, the timing of the successful China-ASEAN free trade agreements and other bilateral accords has meant that the China-ASEAN relationship has become the institutional and normative yardstick by which ASEAN's other regional relationships are measured. China's actions generated a responsive pressure from Japan as it sought to limit the expansion of Chinese influence in the region. In addition to expressing its reservations to the early introduction of the EAS, Japanese Prime Minister Koizumi in 2002 also called for the inclusion of Australia and New Zealand in any future EAC 'thereby hinting at a strategy of increasing the number of democratic nations in such a community'.[52]

These contending pressures combined to push the EAS onto the agenda of the 2004 Summit in Vientiane, but it was far from clear how the new meeting would function. The EASG report had seen the Summit as a natural evolution of the APT Summit; however, the forced introduction of the EAS meant that this evolution was not possible. Instead the EAS was placed alongside the existing ASEAN and ASEAN+ summits, limiting its capacity to drive community-building processes. Tensions also arose within the group as to who should participate in the EAS, with 'Singaporean, Thai and Indonesian support for enlargement from the ASEAN+3 formula to include India (as well as Australia and New Zealand) being at odds with the more limited role proposed by Malaysia, Cambodia and Vietnam'.[53] However, it should be noted that Indonesia was only ever marginal in its support for the EAS process, possibly because it foresaw a diminution of its own regional influence in any such body where China and Japan were equal members.[54] China also opposed the expansion of the inclusion of the three new participants, even as Japan supported it. By the time of the first East Asian Summit it had been agreed that Australia, India and New Zealand would participate in the meeting. Russia had also wanted to join the group – with the support of Indonesia, Malaysia and Singapore – but was blocked by other members on the basis that it had not shown sufficient interest in the region.[55]

With all the divisions and disagreements in the lead-up to the inaugural EAS in Kuala Lumpur in December 2005, it was always unlikely that the meeting would produce a significant result – beyond the fact that all sixteen participating states met as equals for the first time in an Asian dialogue. This was reflected in the Summit declaration, which simply noted that it was a 'forum for dialogue on broad strategic, political and economic issues of common interest and concern with the aim of promoting peace, stability and economic prosperity in East Asia'.[56] One area where the EAS was distinctly different from other ASEAN-related fora was the stated intent of the group 'to strengthen global norms and universally recognised values'.[57] Although such an aim could be interpreted as stemming from the inclusion of the three new, democratic members, this aim actually served to highlight a core normative difference between the EAS and the other ASEAN-related fora, which may restrict its impact in future EAC affairs.

The second EAS was held in Cebu in January 2007. Unlike the inaugural meeting, the second Summit produced a statement outlining a number of areas for future cooperation (including education, energy, finance, public health and disaster management).[58] While some initiatives stemming from the second meeting (such as the EAS meeting on disaster management hosted by India in November 2007) are new, many duplicate or repeat existing programmes.[59] One of the more concrete results of the second EAS was an agreement to form a Track-Two study group for the 'Comprehensive Economic Partnership in East Asia (CEPEA)', an EAS-zone FTA. The idea for the CEPEA is based on the fact that all sixteen members have either signed or are in the process of negotiating FTAs with each other.[60] If realised, the CEPEA would be a significant achievement for the EAS. However, the initiative would appear to duplicate existing efforts to form regional FTAs. In addition, given that the China-ASEAN FTA has become the template for the Japan-ASEAN, ROK-ASEAN and India-ASEAN FTA discussions – and that these FTAs, in turn, inform the negotiating position for other FTAs which these states consider – it is difficult to envisage what a CEPEA could significantly offer beyond that which is already emerging in substance.

The third East Asian Summit, in Singapore in November 2007, served to consolidate the projects and processes between the sixteen members. With the primary focus on economic integration as the foundation of regional integration, the EAS approved the creation of a new 'Economic Research Institute of ASEAN and East Asia (ERIA) to be accommodated temporarily at the ASEAN Secretariat' as well as the initiation on an informal Senior EAS Finance Officials dialogue.[61] Other projects that advanced regional integration were in the areas of energy cooperation and disaster relief management. However, the final statement from the EAS also indicated that the Summit was no longer being considered as the lead process in regional integration. As the Chairman's statement noted:

> [The] East Asian Summit is an important component of the emerging regional architecture and would help build an East Asian community. It should play a complementary and mutually reinforcing role with other regional mechanisms, including the ASEAN dialogue process, the

ASEAN Plus Three process, the ARF and APEC in community building efforts.[62]

Hence, between the first three summits, cooperation between the sixteen members has begun to expand. However, while cooperation has expanded, the EAS has lost its central place in the construction of an East Asian Community and become simply one of many such mechanisms that support this goal. It is noteworthy that the language used to describe many of the EAS activities (for example, ministerial 'retreats' or 'luncheons' rather than meetings and 'ad hoc' rather than formal) serves to play down both the level of the participants as well as the importance of any outcomes.[63] Indeed, it is already clear that the EAS may not live up to its potential as the driving body for community-building endeavours in East Asia. As former ASEAN Secretary-General Rodolfo Severino stated:

> The East Asian Summit does not yet, at least for now, provide sufficient basis for a community. What it could provide are the political environment, the high-level network of contacts and the regional processes for accelerating economic integration among the participants, integration that is already happening under pressure from market forces.[64]

When this statement is contrasted with the 2005 and 2007 statements on APT it is clear that there is a competitive tension developing between the two processes, rather than the two developing in a mutually reinforcing framework. As a result, in the near term, regional policy makers are refocusing on the APT – rather than the EAS – as the key body in building an East Asian Community.[65] This would imply that, even as the APT has reached out to the three countries with high-level and long-standing ties to East Asia, the regional preference is for an EAC created on a narrower basis than was proposed in the EASG report. This conclusion is, in part, supported by the declaration issued at the end of the first EAS, which stated only 'that the efforts of the East Asian Summit to promote community building in this region will be consistent with and reinforce the realisation of the ASEAN Community'.[66] This is a far lesser objective when compared to that called for by the EASG. Hence, what is being formed is an East Asian region based on a series of concentric circles, with ASEAN at its core; a set of overlapping relations with China, Japan and South Korea (via the ASEAN+1 and APT dialogues) in an immediate periphery (which may merge with the core in a future EAC); a zone of important but non-regional relations (composed of the non-APT EAS states); and then a more distant grouping of other states with whom the region has a relationship.

The 'return' to an East Asian-only based model of regionalisation may also imply a reaffirmation of a regional set of norms distinct from those that are perceived to be held by non-East Asian actors. An example of where such norms have been articulated can be seen in the debate over the ASEAN Charter.

The ASEAN Charter

Although the idea of a clearer expression of ASEAN's norms, objectives and scope of operations had been around for decades, formal consideration of a Charter for the organisation only began in April 2005 at a working group meeting of Southeast Asian foreign affairs directors.[67] By the time of the Kuala Lumpur ASEAN Summit later that year the need for such a document had been agreed upon. In particular, the formulation of an ASEAN Charter was seen as a necessary stage in the codification and development of ASEAN's institutional practices and norms.[68]

The submission of the Eminent Persons Group (EPG) Report on the ASEAN Charter at the January 2007 ASEAN Summit stimulated further debate on the ways forward for the organisation. The most far-reaching recommendation from the EPG Report was to provide ASEAN with a legal identity and enforcement measures. This shift will move the institution away from its informal origins. Given that such informality has been frequently highlighted as part of the 'ASEAN Way', the creation of a legal foundation for the organisation – if adopted – will not only change it institutionally but will also affect its operating norms. Further, the enforcement measures proposed not only covered the creation of dispute settlement mechanisms (DSMs) in 'all fields of ASEAN cooperation'.[69] While DSMs have gradually been introduced in ASEAN free trade agreements, the expansion of their presence to all areas of activity will further serve to formalise the institution. Moreover, even though the EPG recommendations continue to uphold the principles of non-interference and respect for sovereignty, the effective inclusion of DSMs in all areas of ASEAN activity means that such enshrined norms will gradually be reduced in scope and impact. If ASEAN does adopt these new measures it is also difficult to envisage the +3 partners being exempt from eventual compliance.

At the conclusion of that Summit, the EPG Report was handed to a High Level Task Force (HLTF) to develop the EPG recommendations into a Charter. Very quickly the more ambitious proposals from the EPG were dropped. At a retreat in March 2007 'the idea of an ASEAN Union as the highest Community-building goal in ASEAN was rejected, as were the provisions for suspensions, expulsions and withdrawals. Voting as a decision-making tool was not mentioned, as consultation and consensus are still sacrosanct.'[70] The EPG recommendation for a regional human rights commission also divided the HLTF, with Indonesia and the Philippines supporting the proposal but other countries – notably Myanmar and Singapore – opposing the move.[71] At the July ASEAN Ministerial Meeting (AMM), the region's foreign ministers agreed to include broad reference to a human rights commission but were unable to go into specifics, deferring more detailed discussions until later in the year.[72]

At the third EAS in November 2007, the ASEAN Charter was formally adopted. While it did not realise the ambitious vision – as first proposed by former ASEAN Secretary-General Severino – it did advance the process of institutionalising ASEAN. However, as noted by regional observers, the final draft reflected a point of least resistance across two fault lines, the first, between the older and newer members of the group, the second, between those states more supportive of democracy, human rights and civil society engagement and those who favour a more conservative approach. The result of these divisions meant that while the less-contentious issues (such as a second leadership meeting just for the ASEAN states, upgrading the status of the ASEAN Secretary-General and creating an ASEAN Ambassadorial corps) were approved, others such as the proposed ASEAN Human Rights body were only agreed to in principle, and on even more problematic concerns (such as adjusting the level of members' financial contributions) no agreement was reached.[73]

What has been interesting in terms of the development of regional institutions and the espousal of accompanying norms is the post-EAS debate, where a number of countries (principally Indonesia and the Philippines) have been resisting ratifying the ASEAN Charter precisely because it does not go far enough. While it is likely that the Charter will be ratified by all countries before the end of 2008, the deep public divisions that the watered-down Charter exposed show that the region is far from unified when it comes to articulating a common mission and vision.

What emerges from the APT and East Asian Summit processes as well as the ASEAN Charter debates is that a profound evolutionary tension exists within the organisation. From the preceding analysis it is clear that there are multiple divisions in terms of the further development of institutional structures and norms. When these discussions are expanded to include China, Japan and South Korea they become even more complex, in terms of the bilateral issues not only between ASEAN and its +3 partners but also between the three Northeast Asian states as well. The decision in 2004 to hold an East Asian Summit involving three new states only further stretches organisational aims and capacities. At its heart, this problematic situation stems from a lack of directional clarity within ASEAN. If ASEAN is to remain the institutional and normative hub of regional activities in East Asia, then its internal capacity must be strengthened and its goals be more comprehensively achieved. Of course, institutional incoherence is not the only challenge facing the region. There is a range of other obstacles to regional governance, some of which are discussed in the following section.

Obstacles to regional governance

Three issues, in particular, stand out as potential obstacles for the further development of Asian regional governance, namely, sovereignty, leadership and trust. These issues cut across the earlier-mentioned issues of institutional development and norm creation. Successfully addressing them will provide a positive impetus to deeper regionalisation and governance in Asia; although a far deeper willingness to integrate for regional – and not just state – benefits will have to be evidenced for such success to be realised. To a certain extent these three challenges are interrelated, but for analytical reasons they will be treated separately.

Sovereignty

What institutional form the East Asian region ultimately takes will depend on the attitude of its members towards their own sovereignty. The example of the EU offers the possibility that states can relinquish a measure of sovereignty to a regional organisation without failing or losing popular legitimacy. The EU example also demonstrates that greater benefits can be derived from cooperating regionally instead of pursuing growth-oriented agendas individually. That greater benefits can be accrued when states cooperate with each other can also be evinced from the outcomes of multilateral organisations such as the United Nations or the World Trade Organisation. At the regional level, the benefits should be more easily derived because the concept of shared norms and identity implies a policy environment more conducive to cooperation and agreements.

However, within East Asia, the shared norms and identity are blocked by the underdeveloped identity of many regional states. It can be posited that an uncertain state identity can lead to an unnecessarily strong affirmation of those aspects that are considered fixed. In the case of post-colonial regimes or of new states, what could be termed the 'over-promotion' of sovereignty is part of the normative behaviour of the state. It has also been argued that greater economic development requires greater involvement in global processes that correspondingly entails a more flexible understanding of sovereignty. In reviewing the political history and economic development of the region, most states are either post-colonial or new and most are not yet fully integrated into global economic processes.[74]

The question that then arises is whether or not sovereignty matters. The EU is the only example of a regional organisation that has successfully pooled its member states' sovereignty to achieve synergistic outcomes. Other organisations, such as CARICOM (the Caribbean Community), the Andean Community, or MERCOSUR (the Southern Common Market), have their own internal challenges that have left them comparatively under-regionalised.[75] In East Asia, while benefits have been and are being delivered to the ASEAN member states, it is arguable as to whether these represent the best outcome that could have been supplied. None of these benefits is predicated on the development of an EU form of regionalisation. This then leads to the dilemma, as to what extent the benefits resulting from EU integration is a result of the processes involved or a result of the unique nature of the collective of European states that comprise the union. Without another successful model(s) of the regional integration that clearly followed the EU model this 'process vs culture' problem cannot be resolved. It can, however, be concluded that within East Asia there is a trend towards more integrated forms of regional engagement. These deeper, 'third wave' forms may lead to a tipping point where sovereignty is exchanged for additional benefits. However, this point has not yet been reached, with the norms that would be required for such an exchange to take place still absent from most regional dialogues. Instead the region remains characterised by a collection of states attempting to guard their respective sovereign positions while still attempting to derive benefits from their regional association. Hence, the creation of an ASEAN Community and its eventual expansion to include China, Japan and South Korea in an East Asian Community arrangement remains a long-term proposition, even with the ASEAN Concord II and the ASEAN Charter as guiding documents.

Leadership

The process of creating a region requires a state to assume a leadership role. Normally such a state is already in a dominant position regionally and has the resources to influence other states. According to Mattli, the existence of 'leader states' usually assumes a single state able to develop the regionalist cause;[76] however, it has also been postulated that 'a coalition of leading states may provide the requisite leadership for successful integration'.[77] The problem with the 'leader state' concept in the APT process is twofold. First, within the core ASEAN group, there is no such leader state. Indonesia is the largest state in terms of population and geographical spread. However, Indonesia lacks the resources to drive the regional processes forward. Singapore has the resources but lacks the size and has a troubled relationship with other neighbouring countries. Of all the ASEAN states, only Thailand has the potential to assume such a leadership role but its capacity is currently only that of a middle-sized ASEAN country.

Second, all the ASEAN states are under-qualified for a leadership role when compared with the +3 Northeast Asian countries. As ASEAN expands its cooperation and integration with these three countries, their scope to exert a leadership function will increase. The problem then becomes one of which of these countries should lead. Even though it is still going through a prolonged economic downturn, Japan still has the largest economy in the region and is well placed to contribute to regional growth. However, any overt leadership bid would trigger a response born of lingering resentment over Japanese actions during the Second World War; something that still detracts from Japan's regional relations. China is the biggest regional state in terms of geographical spread and population. In time it may also supplant Japan's pre-eminent economic status. However, the lack of transparency within Chinese decision-making processes, its continued threat of force over Taiwan and in the South China Sea, make it an uncertain regional partner at best. Compared to its two neighbours, South Korea has neither the size nor the resources to drive regional processes. Instead, it is contributing to regional developments in certain niche areas, for example the East Asian Vision Group.

Complicating the potential contribution each of these three countries could make is the fact that they also experience periods of diplomatic tension arising from their ongoing competition for regional leadership as well as from other cultural and historical triggers. Indeed, the ongoing policy division between APT and the EAS can be alternatively viewed as part of the leadership struggle between China and Japan. The successful inclusion of Australia, India and New Zealand into the EAS was a victory for Japan over China's more narrowly focused vision of which states should be included in an East Asian Community. However, the reassertion of the APT process as the framework for such a community represents a success for China in reshaping the policy debate. Until there is a consensus between these two powers and ASEAN as to the future arrangements of a regional community, it will be extremely difficult for a regional leader to emerge.

Given these issues, it is not currently feasible that Mattli's leadership model can be applied in East Asia. Webber takes a broader approach, suggesting that 'a coalition of leading states may provide the requisite leadership for successful integration'.[78] As the region still lacks a single state able to drive regional integration forward it is more likely that Webber's concept of a group of states will be the most likely scenario for East Asia. But even if this is the case, such a group has not yet emerged from the ASEAN or wider APT groupings. What seems to be the case is that interest-driven politics is determining which state or states take the lead on particular issues. It may be that the work of APT may, over time, highlight the operations of a particular group of states, but until the regional norms develop to a sufficient extent as to ensure a common approach to all the issues, this interest-driven approach to regional leadership is likely to continue.

Trust

The formation of common norms and a shared identity is predicated on mutual trust and understanding. Although it has been said that the absence of armed conflict in the region since ASEAN's inception is – at least in part – due to an adherence to the pacific nature of the 'ASEAN Way', such a conclusion is marred by frequent differences of opinion within the ASEAN group that have occasionally spilled over into hostile actions. Even when such actions are not undertaken, the high level of distrust between member states can be considered detrimental to the development of the aforementioned norms and identity, as is frequently evidenced between Malaysia and Singapore, for example. Indeed, in reviewing intraregional relations, it is not possible to find a single country that does not have a fractious relationship with at least one of its neighbours. Sometimes these issues are a result of economic problems, at other times because of territorial disputes. Still others are due to negative externalities from internal political issues, while clashes of culture also generate problems between member states.

Most of these problems are resolved over time between the parties involved. Some, such as the various Malaysia–Singapore disputes, appear to be intractable. This lack of trust has held up regionalisation in East Asia. A good example of this is the High Council proposed in the Treaty of Amity and Cooperation for resolving internal disputes. While the utility of such a dispute-resolution mechanism is beyond doubt, the membership of such a body is a major hurdle. Given that it is based on ASEAN's consensus approach, it is hard to envisage that Myanmar would agree to have Thailand adjudicate in any of its disputes with other states. Similarly, Thailand would be loath to allow Cambodia or Laos to play a similar role. Where disputes are sufficiently serious and intractable – such as those involving territory – ASEAN states have preferred to take the problems to international tribunals for resolution, rather than allow other members to decide. The call by the ASEAN Charter EPG for an enforceable dispute resolution mechanism to be used in all areas of ASEAN's activities may signal a new willingness of member states to allow for internal adjudication. However, ASEAN has never operated a dispute resolution mechanism and it is questionable whether states with clearly different views as to how the region should behave and develop would be willing to acquiesce to such a supranational body.

Conclusion

The future of East Asia must be based on what has gone before. Since the formation of ASEAN in 1967, the region has undergone tremendous change. What began as simply one organisation in a succession of such groups has developed into the hub of East Asian regionalisation. Whether it is in ASEAN+1, APT or the EAS dialogues, ASEAN – institutionally and normatively – lies at the core of the integration process. However, ASEAN's success in positioning itself at the heart of regional affairs has generated its own problems. With over 700 meetings per year as well as responsibilities in other fora, ASEAN members face a severe bottleneck in the institution's capacity. With three partner states in Northeast Asia and three new states from South Asia and Oceania, ASEAN now also has to engage with a far more complex set of norms than was previously the case.

To address this, ASEAN has commissioned a number of reports charting the way forward for the organisation. It has also sought to increase its own capacity through the incorporation of private sectors and civil society organisations in policy processes. At the same time, substate and non-state actors in Asia have been developing ties with their counterparts across the region. Subregional organisations have also become active in advancing micro-regionalism between subsets of Asian states. The conduct of these new regional actors acts as catalysts for the advancement of regional integration across multiple levels. In addition, the creation of APT and the EAS indicates that a core/periphery model is forming across these levels – with ASEAN at the core, the +3 states in a close semi-periphery and the EAS states in a more distant space.

However, even as this model of regional governance is being created, it is clear that the region remains divided by different visions for the future trajectory of its institutions and norms. As the formation of the EAS and the drafting of the ASEAN Charter clearly show, the region is far from united in its aspirations. Institutionally there is a clear division between states that continue to favour ASEAN as the regional core and those that prefer APT to assume that role. Although the second aim may become the regional reality, it is not clear what would happen to ASEAN and the meetings peculiar to Southeast Asian interests. In terms of norm articulation and development, the debate over the drafting of the ASEAN Charter demonstrates that some regional states are more willing to embrace ideals that could externally impinge on members' domestic affairs, while others prefer their unitary non-interference comfort zone be maintained without challenge. These divisions are overshadowed by other obstacles that cut across all actors and agendas and which, if not addressed, hold the potential to block further regionalisation and governance in Asia. These obstacles limit ASEAN or APT members' ability to fully engage with their regional institutions. As a result, members revert to a default position whereby they simply operate within an association of states rather than within a collective body, bound by shared norms and able to make binding decisions.

If the region is to develop an East Asian Community, then these issues and obstacles need to be addressed and overcome. As the subsequent chapters in this volume show there is a clear willingness on the part of some regional actors to resolve these problems and to advance regional governance. However, there are also conservative coalitions who prefer a more limited and cautious approach to regional cooperation. In the absence of a clearly defined goal based on well-defined steps that set out what must be done (and in what order) for the region to be considered successfully integrated, it is not possible to conclude which of these sets of actors is adopting the correct approach. In the absence of such a conclusion, the focus of any analysis must shift towards identifying contemporary issues of importance to the region. As the preceding material has suggested, understanding the ways in which regional actors are choosing to work with each other in shaping the East Asian region and the impact this has on the accompanying institutions and norms is critical. Without such knowledge not only will the present state of regional affairs be misinterpreted, but future opportunities for advancing East Asian regional governance may be missed.

Structure of the book

In order to better understand regional governance in Asia the volume is divided into three parts. The first part of the book (Chapters 1 and 2) covers the overarching themes and issues. The second part explores the role of state and other actors and their contribution to the evolution of regional institutions and norms (Chapters 3–8). The third part reviews policy developments and systematic topics before concluding (Chapters 9–13).

Chapter 2, by Mely Caballero-Anthony, explores regional governance in ASEAN and its related dialogues, paying particular attention to the implications of an East Asian Community. Anthony extends the Asian regional governance model presented in this chapter before reviewing the development of the ASEAN Security and Economic Communities. Going beyond traditional elite-centric studies, Anthony considers the role of non-state and substate actors in regional policy processes. Anthony is able to establish how the developments in the region are being influenced by actors outside the state structures, who are engaging in the transformation of the regional order. In concluding, Anthony suggests that, while the utilisation of regional governance structures has benefited ASEAN, more needs to be done to ensure that the community-building project remains an ongoing concern.

Chapters 3–5 review the impact of the three Northeast Asian states – Japan, South Korea and China – on regional governance in Asia. Chapter 3, by Hidataka Yoshimatsu, analyses Japan's contribution to regionalism and governance. Yoshimatsu concentrates his analysis on Japan's contribution to rules-based governance through its involvement in the creation of regional economic and financial architectures. Extending his analysis to cover the state's engagement with substate and non-state actors, Yoshimatsu is able to clearly show how Japanese participation in regional affairs is helping to forge a multilevel governance structure, even though domestically the relationship between these actors remains largely hierarchical rather than horizontal. This participation is based on a normative adherence to equity and social justice, which, Yoshimatsu demonstrates, underlies Japan's commitment to its Asian governance.

South Korea has held an ambiguous role in East Asian affairs. Despite the facts that South Korea has been an integral part of APT since its inception and that it was a South Korean proposal that led to the East Asian Vision Group being formed, the country has not been as enmeshed with the wider region as its two Northeast Asian neighbours. In Chapter 4, Jaewoo Choo assesses South Korea's involvement in East Asian regionalism and its contribution to governance processes. Choo suggests that South Korea's primary focus on Northeast Asian affairs, its relationship with North Korea and its ties to the United States meant that its institutional ties to the wider East Asia are relatively recent. Although South Korea began sectoral talks with ASEAN in 1989 and became a full dialogue partner in 1994, it was only after the 1997 crisis that a new phase of engagement began, despite resistance from some domestic political and economic interests. Nonetheless, Choo argues that, as a middle power, South Korea is well placed to contribute to the further development of regional institutions and norms, even as it seeks to balance its more immediate geopolitical environment.

In the period since the 1997 Asian crisis the China–ASEAN relationship has emerged as the key axis in regional affairs. However, even as China is emerging as a dominant state with countries in Southeast Asia, it is also expanding its ties and influence in the three other regions on its borders. In Chapter 5 Nicholas Thomas explores the implications of these relations on the development of regional governance in Asia. Thomas shows how China's utilisation of institutionalised and non-institutionalised forms of regional engagement is serving to create a second normative hub in the region. However, a diverse set of restrictions currently prevents China from realising any leadership ambitions. These restrictions leave ASEAN and its related dialogues as the main institutional and normative hub in Asia.

The creation of the East Asian Summit in 2005 brought three new actors into a closer regional dialogue with the members of APT. Chapters 6 and 7 review the impact that two of these actors – Australia and India – are having on the development of regional governance. 'Is Australia an Asian country?' was a long-running political debate though the 1980s and mid 1990s in that country. The federal election of the conservative coalition of Liberal and National parties in 1996 seemed to end that debate with a policy redirection to ties with the United Kingdom and the United States. However, contrary to some expectations, relations between Australia and the countries of East Asia have grown rapidly. In Chapter 6, James Cotton analyses the growth of bilateral and regional ties and considers Australia's impact on regional governance. Cotton's paper shows that even though Australia is now a member of the East Asian Summit, it still allocates a significant preference to bilateral ties. Despite this preference, Cotton's chapter illustrates how multilevel governance networks are emerging between Australia and the region – tying the two sides ever more strongly together.

It is indeed an ironic twist of history that – as Isabelle Saint-Mézard notes in Chapter 7 – a country such as India, which had championed early forms of regional integration and contributed so significantly to the initial creation of regional norms, should find itself on the periphery of contemporary Asian regional governance. Yet the enactment of India's 'Look East' policy has – since the early 1990s – allowed it to develop a new generation of ties with the countries of East Asia. The formation of these ties has not been without a number of challenges. The underlying economic liberalisation theme of the 'Look East' policy has met with domestic resistance from various sectors of local industry. The need to engage with Myanmar, as a cost of being involved in regional dialogues, has resulted in normative shifts in Indian foreign policy; while the need to work with China – a country towards which India still has significant foreign and defence concerns – has divided policy makers. Despite these problems, India is actively seeking deeper ties with East Asia. Through its involvement in the EAS, India may well achieve its goals, although the refocus on APT as the basis of an East Asian Community may require India's policies to be rethought.

One country that is not of the region but is nevertheless deeply enmeshed in regional affairs is the United States. Policy choices made by the United States – even when in other parts of the world – can have direct or secondary effects on regional power balances and strategic directions. In Chapter 8, Thomas Moore presents a detailed study of US–Asian relations and the influence the United States has on the formation of Asian regional governance. With case studies on security and economic governance, Moore demonstrates how regional engagement is being supported by a plethora of non-state actors from both the private sector and civil society. What emerges from these case studies is a picture of growing – although asymmetric – interdependence between the United States and the region, where the United States remains a key state, even as dynamics within APT and in terms of the rise of China alter the way the relationship is expressed.

Part 3 of this volume commences with an exploration of the role of law in governing Asian regionalism. In Chapter 9, Paul Davidson compares relationship-based governance to rules-based governance with respect to regional economic activity. Drawing on a range of institutional case studies – from ASEAN, the WTO and APEC – Davidson is able to show how the use of rules-based governance is essential for the development of economic interdependence and development. While the 'ASEAN Way', emphasising relations-based regimes, may have limited the region's ability to successfully integrate, Davidson demonstrates how the outcomes from the East Asian Summit process may be signalling a shift towards a greater utilisation of rules and regulations as a vehicle for the further advancement of regional governance. Davidson suggests that the APEC model, which combines both approaches, may be a way forward for the region, especially when it comes to the types of regional trade agreements that underpin much of East Asia's integration.

Chapter 10, by Douglas Arner, Paul Lejot and Wei Wang, analyses the extent to which economic and financial forms of regional governance have developed in East Asia. Exploring both the financial imperatives and development initiatives that the region has undertaken in the post-1997 period, Arner et al. argue that the outcomes in financial integration have not matched the concurrent political rhetoric. In seeking to understand why this is the case for a sector that is so critical to regional integration processes, the authors suggest that not only are ASEAN socio-cultural norms conservative when it comes to reforms, but the 'ASEAN Way' and similar norms are not conducive to the development of transparent, market-based solutions. The main point of this chapter is that Asian financial integration is modest as compared to trade and economic integration largely because states have been as yet unwilling to surrender national sovereignty to the extent that would allow it to develop further. Furthermore, in harmony with Davidson's findings, the authors conclude that if the region is to maximise its efforts in financial integration it needs to develop an open institutional and legal framework within which such activities can take place. Without such a framework, the region will remain ill-equipped to advance regional financial governance or to prevent the reoccurrence of a future financial crisis.

Alain Guilloux, in Chapter 11, explores a different area of regional governance – that of disaster management. Using the 2004 tsunami as a case study (and with reference to the 2008 tropical cyclone Nargis), Guilloux examines the role of state, private sector and non-state actors in responding to manmade or natural disasters. Although Guilloux is able to show that a broad structure for these actors to respond to such crises is in place, he demonstrates that it is not likely that the region will utilise a governance approach because of a range of institutional and normative obstacles. As many of these obstacles are seen in other areas of regional integration, Guilloux's findings broadly echoe the conclusions of Arner et al. – namely, that there is a significant gap between rhetoric and reality in regional discourse. Unless that gap is bridged, the region will remain exposed to future calamities and crises.

The penultimate chapter, by Stephanie Lawson, is concerned with regional identity formation and its implications for the development of regional governance. Drawing on ASEM as a case study, Lawson is able to contrast the formation of Asian cultural values with their European counterparts. Even though such values are fluid, responding to the environment in which they are placed, they implicitly shape the collective norms that are the foundation of regional integration. The author's analysis highlights the heterogeneous set of cultural values that are held by different state and non-state actors within the region. When this observation is considered against the findings of the previous chapters, it could be suggested that, while such diversity provides a rich cultural environment for regional engagement, it may also be one reason why East Asian regionalisation proceeds at its current pace.

The book concludes with a chapter by Kanishka Jayasuriya, who synthesises the key issues raised across all the chapters. Drawing on the governance literature and the case studies presented in the volume, Jayasuriya shows just how far regional governance has developed since the 1990s. Consequently, the regional space in which governance activities take place has both expanded and become more complex. There are new sets of actors and issues that occupy a regulatory landscape much changed since the 1990s. Not only are more states now engaged in regional integration processes but there is a multitude of subnational, private sector and civil society actors who have been drawn into policy processes. At the same time, the scope of the policy debates that engage these actors has expanded. Although economic and financial matters remain at the core of the East Asian Community-building endeavours, almost all areas of domestic policy concerns are now represented at the regional level. This policy formulation brings both benefits and costs to the participants. Benefits, in terms of expanded capacities to better meet domestic needs, but also costs, insofar as involvement in regional processes restricts the ability of the participants to act in a completely unilateral manner, one that is divorced from regional consequences. Hence, East Asia is at a crossroads. How the collective regional leadership chooses to manage its affairs will have enormous implications for the successful integration of its states, economies and peoples. This volume is intended to contribute to this emerging debate.

Notes

1 For more on the precursors to ASEAN see: Curley, Melissa and Nicholas Thomas. 'Advancing East Asian Regionalism: An Introduction', in Melissa Curley and Nicholas Thomas (eds). *Advancing East Asian Regionalism.* (London: RoutledgeCurzon, 2007), pp. 1–25.
2 Indonesia suspended diplomatic relations with China in 1967, after suspecting the PRC of involvement in an attempted coup d'état in 1965. Full relations were only restored in 1990. Singapore officially recognised the PRC in 1992.
3 For the most recent volume to explore this debate see: Jones, David Martin and M.L.R. Smith. *ASEAN and East Asian International Relations: Regional Delusion.* (Cheltenham: Edward Elgar, 2006).
4 There is a large body of literature that has been written on the regional impact of the 1997 Asian crisis. One of the clearest pieces of analysis can be found in: Narine, Shaun. *Explaining ASEAN: Regionalism in Southeast Asia.* (Boulder, CO: Lynne Rienner, 2002), pp. 139–166.
5 East Asian Vision Group. 'Letter of Transmittal', *Towards an East Asian Community.* 31 October 2001.
6 Kjær, Anne Mette. *Governance.* (Cambridge: Polity Press, 2004), quote on back cover.
7 Roseneau, James. *Along the Domestic-foreign Frontier: Exploring Governance in a Turbulent World.* (Cambridge: Cambridge University Press, 1997), p. 145.
8 Marks, Gary and Liesbet Hooghe. 'Contrasting Visions of Multi-level Governance', in Ian Bache and Matthew Flinders (eds). *Multi-level Governance.* (Oxford: Oxford University Press, 2004), pp. 15–30.
9 Krahmann, Elke. 'National, Regional and Global Governance: One Phenomenon or Many?', *Global Governance.* (Vol. 9, No. 3, 2003), pp. 324–325.
10 Weiss, Thomas. 'Governance, Good Governance and Global Governance: Conceptual and Actual Challenges', in Rorden Wilkinson, (ed.). *The Global Governance Reader.* (London: Routledge, 2005), p. 70.
11 Held, David and Anthony McGrew (eds). *Governing Globalization: Power, Authority and Global Governance.* (Cambridge: Polity Press, 2002), p. xi
12 Halabi, Yakub. 'The Expansion of Global Governance into the Third World: Altruism, Realism, or Constructivism?', *International Studies Review.* (Vol. 6, No. 1, 2004), pp. 21–48.
13 Krahmann, Elke. 'National, Regional and Global Governance: One Phenomenon or Many?', p. 330.
14 Phillips, Nicola. 'Governance after Financial Crisis: South American Perspectives on the Reformulation of Regionalism', *New Political Economy.* (Vol. 5, No. 3, 2000), p. 385.
15 Marks, Gary and Liesbet Hooghe. *Multi-level Governance and European Integration.* (Lanham, MD: Rowman and Littlefield Publishers, 2001), p. 2
16 Söderbaum, Frederik. 'Modes of Regional Governance in Africa: Neoliberalism, Sovereignty Boosting and Shadow Networks', *Global Governance.* (Vol. 10, No. 4, 2004), pp. 419–436.
17 Thomas, Nick. 'Building an East Asian Community: Origins, Structure and Limits', *Asian Perspective.* (Vol. 26, No. 4, 2002), p. 88.

18 Ruggie, John. 'Multilateralism: The Anatomy of an Institution', in John Ruggie (ed.). *Multilateralism Matters: The Theory and Praxis of an Institutional Form.* (New York: Columbia University Press, 1993), p. 11.

19 Nel, Philip, Ian Taylor and Janis van der Westhuizen. 'Multilateralism in South Africa's Foreign Policy: The Search for a Critical Rationale', *Global Governance.* (Vol. 6, No. 1, 2000), p. 44.

20 Krasner, Stephen. 'Structural Causes and Regime Consequences: Regimes as Intervening Variables', *International Organization.* (Vol. 36, No. 2, 1982), p. 186.

21 Acharya, Amitav. 'How Ideas Spread: Whose Norms Matter? Norm Localization and Institutional Change in Asian Regionalism', *International Organization.* (Vol. 58, No. 2, 2004), p. 269.

22 Hufty, Marc. 'The Governance Analytical Framework', a concept paper prepared for the International Symposium on *Governance: Towards a Conceptual Framework.* (Geneva: Graduate Institute of Development Studies, 22–24 November 2007), p. 16.

23 Jayasuriya, Kanishka. 'Introduction: The Vicissitudes of Asian Regional Governance', in Kanishka Jayasuriya (ed.). *Asian Regional Governance: Crisis and Change.* (London: RoutledgeCurzon, 2004), pp. 7–8.

24 Op. cit.

25 This term is drawn from: Wiener, Antje. 'Contested Compliance: Interventions on the Normative Structure of World Politics', *European Journal of International Relations.* (Vol. 10, No. 2, June 2004), pp. 189–234.

26 For a good discussion of this see: Kjær, Anne Mette. *Governance.* pp. 59–122.

27 Schreurs, Miranda. 'Problems and Prospects for Regional Environmental Cooperation in East Asia', in Melissa Curley and Nicholas Thomas (eds). *Advancing East Asian Regionalism.* pp. 212–213.

28 Kim, Beng Phar. 'Asia's Informal Diplomacy', *Harvard International Review.* (Vol. 23, No. 1, Spring 2001), pp. 38–41. For more on the role of Track-Two groups see: Simon, Sheldon. 'Evaluating Track II Approaches to Security Diplomacy in the Asia-Pacific: The CSCAP experience', *The Pacific Review.* (Vol. 15, No. 2, 2002), pp. 167–200 and Kraft, Herman. 'The Autonomy Dilemma of Track Two Diplomacy in Southeast Asia', *Security Dialogue.* (Vol. 31, No. 3, 2000), pp. 343–356.

29 Terada, Takashi. 'Nagano Shigeo: Business Leadership in the Asia Pacific Region and the Formation of the Pacific Basin Economic Council', *Australian Journal of Politics & History.* (Vol. 47, No. 4, 2001), pp. 475–489.

30 See comments in: 'Malay Businessmen Must Exploit East Asian Business Council', *Pertubuhan Berita Nasional Malaysia.* 17 April 2004.

31 See: US-ASEAN Business Council. 'ASEAN+3 (China, Japan and South Korea)'. http://www.us-asean.org/ASEANOverview/asean+3.asp. Accessed 6 August 2007.

32 For more on this topic see: Thomas, Nicholas. 'Developing a Regional Economic Community', in Melissa Curley and Nicholas Thomas (eds). *Advancing East Asian Regionalism.* pp. 137–157.

33 See: http://asean-isis-aseanpeoplesassembly.net/index_new.htm. Accessed 6 August 2007.

34 Caballero-Anthony, Mely. 'ASEAN and Civil Society: Enhancing Regional Mechanisms for Managing Security', in Hadi Soesastro and Carolina Hernandez (eds). *Twenty-Two Years of ASEAN-ISIS: Origin, Evolution and Challenges of Track-Two Diplomacy.* (Yogyakarta: Centre for Strategic and International Studies). http://asean-isis-aseanpeoples assembly.net/pdf/asean_and_civil_society.pdf, p. 25. Accessed 6 August 2007.

35 Kazancigil, Ali as quoted in ibid. p. 26.

36 See: *Register of ASEAN-affiliated CSOs.* http://www.aseansec.org/6070.pdf. Accessed 29 May 2008.

37 Alwi Shihab, *Speech at the Opening of the 33rd ASEAN Ministerial Meeting*, (Bangkok: 24 July 2000).
38 Although these meetings remain hostage to negative sentiments between Japan and China and, to a lesser extent, between Japan and South Korea.
39 SOMs can also act as policy initiators for the ASEAN+3 grouping. In May 2001, the ASEAN Committee on Science and Technology convened its first +3 meeting in Phnom Penh before it was initiated at the +3 ministerial level.
40 'ASEAN drugs conference in Bali', *The Jakarta Post*, 7 November 2001.
41 In the case of China this was particularly important, as the flow of drugs through the Mekong region is known to cross over into Chinese territory. Coordination of anti-drug campaigns with the PRC government was therefore essential. Japan is a long-standing supporter of anti-drug efforts in the region, providing both financial and human resources to lesser-developed countries, which is why Japan was an important player at the Denpasar meeting. Source: Press Release, *First Meeting of the Accord Plan of Action Task Forces*. (Bali, Indonesia: 12–14 November 2001).
42 See *Chairman's Statement of the Ninth ASEAN Plus Three Summit*. (Kuala Lumpur: 12 December 2005). http://www.aseansec.org/18042.htm. Accessed 14 November 2007. Comments in [ ] added for clarity.
43 *Chairman's Statement of the Tenth ASEAN Plus Three Summit*. Cebu, Philippines, 14 January 2007. http://www.aseansec.org/19315.htm. Accessed 14 November 2007.
44 See *ASEAN Plus Three Cooperation Plan, 2007–2017*. http://www.aseansec.org/21104.pdf. Accessed 10 December 2007.
45 See Thomas, Nick. 'ASEAN+3: C/community Building in East Asia', *Journal of Internatioal and Area Studies*. (Vol. 8, No. 2, December 2001), pp. 1–19.
46 *Towards an East Asian Community: Region of Peace, Prosperity and Progress*. The East Asian Vision Group Report, 2001. p. 17.
47 *Final Report of the East Asia Study Group*. East Asian Study Group. Phnom Penh, 4 November 2002. p. 59.
48 Ibid. p. 59.
49 'Malaysia Pushes for ASEAN+3 Secretariat', *Channel NewsAsia*. 6 October 2002 and 'ASEAN+3: Prelude to EAEG's Formation', *Malaysia Economic News*. 10 August 2002.
50 Hamsawi, Roziana. 'KL Seeks to Set up Asean+3 Bureau', *New Straits Times*. 4 November 2002.
51 Yamakage, Susumu. 'The Construction of an East Asian Order and the Limitations of the ASEAN Model', *Asia-Pacific Review*. (Vol. 12, No. 2, 2005), p. 7
52 Ibid. p. 8
53 Camroux, David. 'Towards an Asian Community: The East Asian Summit, Kuala Lumpur'. http://www.ceri-sciencespo.com/archive/jan06/artdc.pdf. Accessed 7 August 2007.
54 'ASEAN Fails to Agree on East Asian Summit Plan', *Japan Economic Newswire*. 27 November 2004.
55 'ASEAN Split over Russian Membership of East Asian Summit: Malaysia', *Agence France Presse*. 7 December 2005.
56 *Kuala Lumpur Declaration on the East Asian Summit*. (Kuala Lumpur: 14 December 2005). http://www.aseansec.org/18098.htm. Accessed 7 August 2007.
57 Ibid.
58 See: *Chairman's Statement of the Second East Asian Summit*. (Cebu: 15 January 2007). http://www.aseansec.org/19302.htm and 'Asia Second East Asian Summit Prioritizes Cooperation in Energy, Finance, Education, Bird Flu Control and Natural Calamity Alleviation', *Financial Times Information*. 17 January 2007.
59 See: *Opening Statement by External Affairs Minister Shri Pranab Mukherjee at Press Briefing in Manila*. (New Delhi: Ministry of External Affairs, 31 July

2007). http://mea.gov.in/cgi-bin/db2www/meaxpsite/coverpage.d2w/coverpg?sec = pr&filename = pressrelease/2007/07/31pr02.htm. Accessed 8 August 2007.

60 See: *Chairman's Statement of the Second East Asian Summit.* (Cebu: 15 January 2007). http://www.aseansec.org/19302.htm; Tamura Akihiko. 'Extrovert Regionalism', *Journal of Japanese Trade.* 1 July 2007 and Goh Sui Noi. 'Green Light for Study on 16-nation Trading Bloc', *The Straits Times.* 16 January 2007.

61 *Chairman's Statement of the 3rd East Asian Summit.* (Singapore: 21 November 2007). http://www.aseansec.org/21127.htm. Accessed 10 December 2007.

62 Ibid.

63 'East Asian Summit Ministers in Malaysia Discuss Enhanced Cooperation', *British Broadcasting Corporation.* 26 July 2006.

64 Severino, Rodolfo. 'Presentation on East Asian Economic Integration', *ISEAS Regional Forum Outlook 2006.* (Singapore: 5 January 2006), p. 5.

65 'East Asian Summit Ministers in Malaysia Discuss Enhanced Cooperation', *British Broadcasting Corporation.* 26 July 2006.

66 *Kuala Lumpur Declaration on the East Asian Summit.* (Kuala Lumpur: 14 December 2005). http://www.aseansec.org/18098.htm. Accessed 7 August 2007.

67 Villamor, Marites. 'Work on ASEAN Charter Begins with Cebu Meet', *Business-World.* 11 April 2005.

68 Severino, Rodolfo. 'Why Asean should Have a Charter', *The Straits Times.* 5 December 2005.

69 *Report of the Eminent Persons Group on the ASEAN Charter.* December 2006. p. 21.

70 'Limited Time to Salvage the ASEAN Charter', *The Nation.* 11 June 2007.

71 'Indonesia Holds Ground on ASEAN Charter', *The Jakarta Post.* 15 June 2007 and 'Drafting of ASEAN Charter Turns Lively', *Malaysia General News.* 27 July 2007.

72 'ASEAN Charter to Include Human Rights Commission', *The Financial Times.* 31 July 2007.

73 See, for example, Rekhi, Shefali. 'Asean Charter to Turn Region into Community', *The Straits Times.* 28 October 2007 and Chongkittavorn, Kavi. 'ASEAN Charter Ready, but Clear Divisions Show Through', *The Nation.* 15 October 2007.

74 As measured, for example, by both OECD and WTO membership.

75 Although this is not to imply that the EU's quest for deeper regionalisation is not without its own operational challenges and uncertainties.

76 Mattli, Walter. *The Logic of Regional Integration: Europe and Beyond.* (Cambridge: Cambridge University Press, 1999), pp. 73–77.

77 Webber, Douglas. 'Two Funerals and a Wedding? The Ups and Downs of Regionalism in East Asia and Asia-Pacific after the Asian Crisis', *The Pacific Review.* (Vol. 14, No. 3, August 2001), p. 345.

78 Ibid. p. 345.

2 Evolving regional governance in East Asia

From ASEAN to an East Asian Community

Mely Caballero-Anthony

Introduction

One of the most interesting developments in East Asia has been the launching of the East Asian Summit (EAS) in December 2005. Spearheaded by the Association of Southeast Asian Nations (ASEAN), this decision to create yet another layer of multilateral arrangement in the region came just two years after ASEAN announced its vision of an ASEAN Community by the year 2020, at its 9th ASEAN Summit in 2003. The first EAS was held on 14 December 2005 in Kuala Lumpur, Malaysia and in conjunction with the holding of the 11th ASEAN Summit. It brought together the ten member states of ASEAN, the three Northeast Asian states – China, Japan and Korea – plus Australia, New Zealand and India.

The 'premature' launching of the EAS (it was only supposed to be realised in 2010) has come at the time when ASEAN is embarking on a number of initiatives to realise its vision of an ASEAN Community. Set within the framework of Bali Concord II, the ASEAN Community was to be established through the setting up of three pillars, namely: the ASEAN Security Community (ASC), the ASEAN Economic Community (AEC) and the ASEAN Socio-Cultural Community (ASCC).[1] The implications of the EAS for ASEAN's goal of an ASEAN Community and relationship of the EAS with the other main East Asian organisation – ASEAN+3 (APT) – have drawn considerable attention.

While the member states of the EAS comprise the core members of APT, its configuration (ASEAN+3+3) and strategic thrusts are supposed to be different from the latter. To be sure, these three regional groupings – ASEAN, APT and the EAS – are separate entities, despite having ASEAN as the core foundation. Moreover, even as APT can be seen as a logical extension of the Southeast Asian grouping to a larger East Asian entity, the EAS as it is presently constituted is not necessarily so path dependent. In fact, the inclusion of India and the longer-term plans to bring the United States (US), the European Union (EU) and Russia into the EAS not only defy geographical logic but also raise a number of questions as to the objectives behind the conceptualisation of the EAS.

These interesting developments in Southeast Asia and the wider region therefore prompt a number of issues to be raised, such as: what does the new EAS mean for regionalisation in East Asia and how will the inclusion of the three non-East Asian countries into the regional processes change the dynamics of regionalism in this part of the world? What is the significance of ASEAN's three-pillared community to regional governance, and how inclusive and participatory are the visions of an ASEAN and/or an East Asian Community?

Dealing with such a large topic may well be considered as a potential recipe for an incoherent study on evolving regionalism in the region. That said, a more manageable approach to understanding these shifting patterns of regionalism in Southeast Asia and beyond is to tease out commonalities in approaches and objectives and to examine them within the framework of 'new regionalism' and its linkage to global governance. It is not, therefore, the intention of this chapter to address all the issues raised above. Instead, the main objectives of this study are twofold. First, to identify the mechanisms which have emerged from ASEAN and APT in providing a framework for managing intra- and interregional relations. Second, to examine the implications of these regional mechanisms on regional governance, particularly in providing for spaces for regional actors – both state and non-state – to mitigate the attendant instabilities and security challenges brought on by the rapid, structural changes in the global environment.

The insights offered in this study speak to the wider literature on new regionalism and global governance. In particular, the study seeks to examine the broader issue of whether the developments in East Asia reflect efforts by different actors in the regional arena to reform global governance through the development of norms and institutions and the strengthening of regional identities. In this regard, one would note the significant articulation by certain groups, be it in an ASEAN, APT and or EAS context, of certain resonant themes, including: building a (regional) community; creating caring communities; fostering partnerships for prosperity; and attaining human security. It could therefore be suggested that the extent to which these themes/goals are being achieved forms an integral part of regional governance through new regionalism in Asia.

Against this background, this study argues that regionalism in East Asia, particularly as seen through the emerging trends in ASEAN and the ASEAN-plus configurations, is becoming more robust and goes beyond the usual characterisation of informal processes and weak institutions. While many of the new, emerging mechanisms may be deemed to be largely reactive rather than pro-active, they nevertheless reflect the growing desire of regional players – including, but not exclusively, state actors – to be actively engaged in transforming the regional order: from one that had been largely state-centric and more pre-occupied with state security and development to one that is more responsive to issues of human security and development. These varying configurations of regional grouping therefore compel an examination as to whether the 'new regionalism' that is occurring in Asia has become more participatory and inclusive, and perhaps more democratic.

New regionalism and governance

Before proceeding to analyse the significance of these emerging multilateral arrangements in the region, the term 'new' regionalism needs to be first understood and its relationship to governance – particularly regional governance – examined. To start with, much of the work on 'new' regionalism has focused on the expanded and multidimensional forms of interstate cooperation and integration that cover a wide range of areas from economic, political, security to the social and cultural aspects. The expansion of these functional areas beyond the conventional goals of region-based free trade regimes or security alliances depicts salient trends found in the emerging patterns of interstate relations, particularly the participation of new actors in the regional arena. Hettne describes the 'new' or 'second-generation' regionalism as having the following characteristics: (1) deep economic integration with political elements; (2) multilevel governance; (3) devolution within states; (4) a strong international legal framework; and (5) cooperation among many dimensions. Hettne also argues that these new patterns of interstate actions reflect a compelling need by regional players to integrate non-economic issues of justice, security and culture with trade and economics and this [appears to be] driven by the 'political ambition of establishing regional coherence and identity'.[2]

In a recent study on regionalism, Grugel also describes 'new regionalism' as a route that states could take to be able to 'mediate the range of economic and social pressures generated by globalisation'.[3] Given the weakening of state responses, mediation in this sense refers to the ability of states and other actors to organise themselves and craft appropriate responses to mitigate the destabilising impact of global forces. Similar ideas are also found in the literature on international political economy (IPE) on global governance, such as the work of Robert Cox, who had also suggested that regionalism provided the means for regional actors to pursue alternative approaches to reform the world order that had been dominated by market-led, neo-liberal approaches to globalisation, almost devoid of the 'human face'.[4] What many of these ideas on new regionalism point to is the emerging trend for more spaces to be opened for states and collectivities to react to the complex impact of globalisation, by 'strengthening regional control when traditional centralised sovereignty no longer functioned and bargaining collectively with extra-regional powers'.[5] Hence, when set against the context of global governance, new regionalism provides another layer of governance within the global polity,[6] which allows for shifts in patterns of regulations through market discipline, elite consensus, and dissemination of norms.[7]

Among the latest works on 'new regionalism', perhaps Jayasuriya best captured all these dynamic ideas when he described new regionalism as projects of 'regional governance'.[8] Jayasuriya added that these 'regional governance' projects could be vastly diverse, providing different models that are dependent on the political, economic and security context within which these projects take place. Indeed, as also noted by Grugel, new regionalism 'is not of one piece' and 'the institutional linkages, the coalitional structures and the policy context that sustain it vary ... and are not identical.'[9]

Jayasuriya and Grugel's observations are very pertinent when one starts to peel off the layers of the multi-forms of regional groupings that have emerged in East Asia. Grugel, in particular, draws attention to issues of participation and inclusion by non-state actors in the myriad regional processes that are taking place. Although Grugel notes that the activism of a broad range of society-based actors and their relationships with state actors can often be conflictual,[10] nevertheless, his attention to the participation of other actors prompts us to probe further and examine whether the engagement of these society-based actors or civil society organisations has a significant bearing on how regional norms – be it contested or agreed upon – are translated into regional institutions or lost in the field of ideas on regional governance that abound in the region. In sum, the framework provided by new regionalism and governance better locates the kind of regionalism that is taking place in East Asia and helps us to better understand the evolving processes that are found in ASEAN and APT and possibly to link them with the establishment of the EAS.

Given the wide range of issues and processes that are found in the region, we can narrow our study of regional governance by looking at the four central elements that Jayasuriya had identified in examining regional governance project(s). These are: a stable set of international economic strategies; a distinctive set of governance structures which enables regional economic governance; a set of normative or ideational constructs that not only makes possible a given set of regional governance structures but also makes possible the very definition of regions; and a convergence of domestic coalitions and political economy structures across the region, which would facilitate the coherent construction of regional political projects.[11]

The main foci of this chapter are the set of the governance structures and the set of normative and ideational constructs outlined by Jayasuriya. These are adapted to an analysis of the type of regional mechanisms that can be found in ASEAN, APT and, as far as possible, the EAS. By concentrating on governance structures and normative/ideational constructs the evolution of regional norms, how such norms are contested and the extent to which these norms are being challenged and modified can be examined. In utilising this approach, it should be possible to draw linkages between these norms and the kinds of regional governance mechanisms which have emerged in East Asia that are specifically aimed at attaining human security and human development in the region. In doing so, this chapter seeks to extend the analytical model presented in Chapter 1.

Against this framework, the paper proceeds in five sections. Following this introduction, section two provides a broad overview of the evolving regionalism in the region, starting with a brief discussion on ASEAN's history as a regional organisation and highlighting some of the significant mechanisms that have emerged as ASEAN member states continue with their projects on regional governance through their twinned goals of attaining a secure and economically developed region. In this regard, the discussion is primarily focused on the evolving security mechanisms (writ large) that are geared toward maintaining regional peace and security, leading to ASEAN's latest project on building an ASEAN Security Community.[12] Section three links the evolving mechanisms in ASEAN with emerging mechanisms found in the APT, mainly focusing on the regional financial cooperation projects that are geared to addressing the issues of economic security and development in the region. Section four then proceeds to examine how these varying efforts at the ASEAN and APT levels speak to the goal of establishing an ASEAN or an East Asian community. In particular, the issues of participation and inclusion of non-state actors in the regional processes that are taking place are examined, before drawing out their implications for regional governance, human security and development. The chapter concludes with some observations on the future direction of regionalism and governance in East Asia.

The ASEAN story: an ongoing regional governance project on security and development

ASEAN's notion of a secure region has always been the twin pursuit of economic security and political stability. Hence, a concise way of analysing ASEAN processes on security and development is to focus on the relevant developments leading to the adoption of two of the pillars of the ASEAN community – the ASC and the AEC – and, in doing so, to highlight some of the mechanisms that have emerged. Before this can be undertaken, however, it is first necessary to briefly outline the historical developments that led to the establishment of the ASC and the AEC.

Developing ASEAN

The formation of ASEAN in 1967 was to provide the member states with a stable structure of relations for managing and containing interstate tensions that had defined the regional environment during that period, particularly between neighbouring states like Malaysia and Indonesia that had earlier been embroiled in *konfrontasi* in 1963. As reflected in ASEAN's more recent history, this process of 'regional reconciliation' was eventually extended beyond the boundaries of the original, non-communist member states[13] to include the other five states in Southeast Asia, regardless of their political orientation.[14] Thus, the creation of ASEAN provided the core structure for regional collaboration that underpinned the promotion of regional peace and security in Southeast Asia. In doing so, it established a set of mechanisms that allowed for the governing of regional affairs. Although initially targeted on constructing a security community whose goal it was to ensure that no member states would ever go to war with each other, in the last two decades these mechanisms and their underlying norms have begun to evolve, encompassing new actors and new ideas.

Up until the 1997 Asian financial crisis, most of the regional mechanisms found in ASEAN were aimed essentially at building a de facto security community. Why de facto? ASEAN's notion of security community can be regarded as a more informal adaptation of Deutsch's security community, which is defined as:

> a group that has become integrated, where integration is defined as the attainment of a sense of community, accompanied by formal or informal institutions or practices, sufficiently strong and widespread to assure peaceful change among members of a group with 'reasonable' certainty over a 'long' period of time.[15]

Acharya has located ASEAN's experience in security community building by presenting the Association and its adherence to norms built around the 'ASEAN Way' as a nascent security community, underpinned largely by its relative success in developing a collective identity – the kind of 'we-feeling' identified by Deutsch – which is a key feature of the management of regional conflict.[16] Acharya's important work provided a revisionist approach to the notion of security community, which had been largely informed by the European experience of integration, to capture the experience of regional organisations in the developing world that had followed a different trajectory in managing regional security beyond the conventional security approaches of deterrence, power balancing and collective security.

Norm building for a regional security community has therefore been based on approaches determined by the ASEAN Way, but has also expanded to define all areas of ASEAN's governance project. As ASEAN expanded to first include the other five Southeast Asian states and, more recently, the three Northeast Asian states, it has strongly promoted the careful cultivation, socialisation and adherence of these regional norms. These norms, first codified in the ASEAN Treaty of Amity and Cooperation (TAC), include: non-interference in internal affairs of states; respect for national sovereignty, non-use of force in the settlement of intraregional disputes; and effective cooperation.[17] The TAC is arguably the only indigenous regional diplomatic instrument that allows for the peaceful settlement of disputes.

However, the development of ASEAN's security community project goes beyond the construction of norms for security purposes to spill over into other areas of cooperation.[18] This can be witnessed in the cautious building of structures to facilitate the implementation of the various functional cooperation projects that ASEAN initiated in tandem with the process of norm creation. These structures can be seen in the numerous institutionalised meetings that take place under the ASEAN umbrella, including: the ASEAN summits, the annual and ad hoc meetings of ASEAN foreign ministers (AMM), meetings of ASEAN economic ministers, and meetings of other ministers as well as meetings of ASEAN senior officials (SOMs), directors-general and expert groups; all of which foster regional political and security cooperation. These meetings provide the important venues and opportunities for bilateral and regional issues to be addressed. As a result, over time ASEAN has generated a number of formal instruments that are indicative of the multifaceted nature of this organisation and the many areas of functional cooperation that define ASEAN. Among these are the ASEAN Bali Declaration I (1976) and Bali Declaration II (2003), Zone of Peace, Freedom, and Neutrality (1971), ASEAN Declaration on the South China Sea (1992), ASEAN Free Trade Area (1992) and the ASEAN Regional Forum (ARF) Concept paper (1995).[19]

All the numerous declarations, agreements and treaties have provided a comprehensive framework for managing interstate relations and promoting closer political and economic cooperation in ASEAN.[20] In brief, these mechanisms have, in their own ways, been important and useful in promoting regional security. When viewed within the context of building a security community, these types of regional structures – described as Acharya as 'soft institutions'[21] – can also be categorised as low-key security approaches that promote trust and confidence building through established habits of dialogue, observance of regional norms and building loose/informal institutions to support these process-oriented approaches to preventing regional conflicts and promoting regional cooperation.[22]

It should also be noted that these are the same approaches ASEAN drew upon when it helped to establish the ARF in 1994. The creation of the ARF was, in fact, seen as ASEAN's attempt to extend to the Asia-Pacific region its processes of conflict avoidance *writ large* through fostering constructive dialogue, and consultation of political and security issues.[23] Hence, the process of regional reconciliation that was earlier confined to ASEAN was expanded to become an 'inclusive' form of regionalism with the establishment of a security forum covering the vast expanse of the Asia-Pacific. Thus, in bringing together the like-minded and the non like-minded states, the ARF was also supposed to be counted as one among the many building blocks that make up several 'islands of peace'.

Perceptible shifts in regional mechanisms and norms

Until the onset of the 1997 Asian financial crisis, the loosely structured 'security community' of ASEAN had served its members well. In fact, ASEAN was once hailed as one of the most successful regional organisations in the developing world. The events of 1997, however, cast significant doubt over the future of this group.

Much has already been written about the impact of the 1997 Asian financial crisis on ASEAN.[24] To be sure, the 1997 crisis (and those that followed) became a watershed in ASEAN's history.[25] For one thing, it exposed the inadequacy of ASEAN member states to deal internally and collectively with crises that challenged regional stability and security. One of the more difficult challenges was the crisis in East Timor in 1999. ASEAN and the ARF came under severe criticism for their inability to stem the violence and gross violations of human rights that followed. As noted in many accounts, ASEAN could not initiate any form of concerted action to prevent the conflict, and among the many reasons cited for this inability was member states' strict observation of the norm of non-interference in the domestic affairs of member states (in this case, Indonesia). It was not until the United Nations organised a peace-keeping mission under the framework of the International Force for East Timor (INTERFET) that violence was controlled and large-scale humanitarian relief operations were eventually carried out.[26]

Following the financial crisis and East Timor, East Asia has been beset by a number of other region-wide crises. Among these are the recurring regional environmental (haze) problem, rising incidents of terrorism after the 9/11 terrorist attacks in the United States, as well as the emergence of non-traditional security threats such as infectious diseases (SARS and avian influenza), illegal migration, and various forms of transnational crimes. Indeed, at one point, it appeared to be that the ASEAN de facto security community could be unravelling. Against the lack of institutional capacity, ASEAN responded by instituting a number of agreements that resulted in the establishment of new regional initiatives to address problems and to encourage closer cooperation among member states. Among the more significant initiatives, were:

- The establishment of the ASEAN Troika to address the crisis in Cambodia in 1997, leading to its formalisation in 2000 to respond to future situations, which could likely affect ASEAN in political and security terms and would require collective action;
- Adoption of the ASEAN Vision 2020, in December 1997, and the Hanoi Plan of Action of 1998 that outlined the modalities of implementing the Vision 2020. The document basically outlined ASEAN's new direction in economic, political and socio-cultural areas, which later on became the bases for the establishment of the three-pillar ASEAN Community document in 2003;
- The adoption of the Regional Haze Action Plan (RHAP) in 1997 to provide a regional mechanism to fight regular forest fires and manage future haze/environmental problems;
- Institution of the Rules and Procedures of the High Council on the Treaty of Amity and Cooperation in Southeast Asia in 2001 to provide a mechanism for the settlement of disputes;

- The signing of the Agreement on Information Exchange and Establishment of Communication Procedures in 2002 to promote cooperation in combating transnational crimes, including terrorism;
- Declaration on the Conduct of Parties in the South China Sea (2002);
- The adoption of several measures to jointly contain infectious diseases, including the development of an ASEAN Centre for Disease Control (2003);
- Joint Declaration of the ASEAN Defence Ministers on Enhancing Regional Peace and Stability (2007); and
- Cebu Declaration on Energy Security (2007).

Hence, instead of unravelling, the structure that emerged was rather one of a visibly bruised and weakened organisation, but more focused on developing deeper institutional mechanisms for managing regional crisis. This change grew out of the awareness that the new challenges – from capital flows to emerging infectious diseases to terrorism – were transnational in nature and could no longer be solved unilaterally and would thus require even closer regional cooperation. It was recognised, however, that in the absence of strong institutions and the lack of enforcement mechanisms, the effectiveness of the types of ad hoc responses ASEAN had undertaken remained in doubt. Moreover, without a more formalised Secretariat, the effectiveness of future initiatives taken by ASEAN, which require – at the very least – close coordination and constant monitoring of responses among member states, would be severely handicapped. It was against this backdrop that the blueprints for the ASEAN Security Community and the ASEAN Economic Community were introduced.

The ASEAN Security Community

As noted earlier, the ASC is an integral part of the 3-pillar approach for building an ASEAN Community. This has been inspired by the ideals of ASEAN Vision 2020 that envisage a community of caring societies by the year 2020, one that is 'bonded together in partnership in dynamic development; living in peace, stability and prosperity'.[27]

The ASC owned much of its early conceptualisation to Indonesia, which was the then serving ASEAN chair. Based on the Indonesian concept paper, the ASC was to provide a regional framework for ASEAN members to handle security matters and disputes, instead of relying on the current mode of bilateral arrangements or international forums. Realising that most security issues in the region are now transnational, the ASC therefore puts emphasis on building regional capacity to address regional problems and, in the process, enhance regional cooperation. In essence, the concept of a security community 'was meant to provide a sense of purpose, a practical goal, and a future condition that all [ASEAN] members should strive for'.[28]

The idea of a security community, as conceptualised, was also meant to bring the security cooperation among ASEAN members to a higher plane. Since its launching in 2003, a number of ideas and modalities of the ASC had been deliberated upon both at the official and, more recently, at the non-official level.

The Vientiane Action Programme (VAP) (2004) had clearly laid out the areas – or strategic thrusts – to realise the idea of a security community. These are: political development, shaping and sharing of norms, conflict prevention, conflict resolution and post- conflict peace building (Box 2.1).[29] A closer look at the ASC blueprint reveals three significant points. Firstly, the elements found in the ASC reflect the 'new' security concept that is being promoted within ASEAN. These can be observed in the number of strategies and measures adopted in the VAP, which embody a new security framework that goes beyond ASEAN's traditional notion of comprehensive security and into the realm of human.

Secondly, while the security issues outlined in the ASC and the regional mechanisms suggested to respond to them may cover both traditional and non-traditional security issues, the emphasis on the latter is quite visible. These are reflected in the specific activities that urge for more cooperation in tackling non-traditional security issues such as transnational crimes and other trans-boundary problems, maritime security cooperation, law enforcement cooperation, and cooperation on environmental problems and infectious diseases.

Thirdly, one can also observe the greater emphasis placed on building regional capacity to address the number of non-traditional security (NTS) challenges facing the region. These include proposals for enhancing maritime security cooperation, including coordinated maritime patrols (especially in the Straits of Malacca), boosting cooperation on counter-terrorism, and others.[30] The other proposals on convening an annual ASEAN Defence Ministers Meeting (ADMM) and establishing a regional peace-keeping force are equally significant. So far, it appears that ASEAN has been moving speedily in carrying out these strategies, especially with the convening of the first ADMM in May 2006 and the subsequent announcement of its three-year work programme the following year.[31] As noted by Rodolfo Severino, former ASEAN Secretary-General, the ADMM can be 'considered mainly the formalisation of a process that has been unfolding for a number of years … [but] could strengthen the institutional framework of defence and security cooperation in ASEAN'.[32] These important initiatives are therefore indicative of the desire of ASEAN members to raise the level of security cooperation in the region to a higher plane.

While one could argue that many of these initiatives are declaratory in nature and would need to be assessed pending successful implementation, it is nevertheless important to point out that the kinds of measures outlined in the proposals are significantly different from previous types of regional modalities prevalent in ASEAN's cooperative arrangements. However, this

Box 2.1 Programme areas and measures

1   Political development (includes):

- Promote understanding of political systems, culture, etc. through person-to-person contact and Track-Two activities
- Promote human rights and obligations
- Establish institutional framework to facilitate free flow of information among ASEAN members
- Establish programmes for support and assistance to develop and strengthen the rule of law, judiciary systems, legal infrastructure, effective and efficient civil services, good governance in public and private sectors
- Increase participation of NGOs, including the ASEAN People's Assembly
- Prevent and combat corruption

2   Conflict prevention – includes the following strategies:

- Strengthen confidence-building measures
- Promote greater transparency
- Develop an ASEAN Early Warning System (EWS)
- Strengthen ARF Process
- Combat transnational crimes and other trans-boundary problems
- Promote ASEAN maritime security cooperation

3   Approaches to conflict resolution:

- Institute an ASEAN Dispute Settlement Mechanism on political and security areas (including suggestions to make the High Council a judicial body)
- Establish an Eminent Persons Group and an expert advisory committee to provide advice and extend assistance to conflict parties (only being discussed)
- Establish an ASEAN Peace-keeping Force

4   Post-conflict peace building:

- Establish a mechanism for delivery of humanitarian assistance, which may include providing safe havens in conflict areas, repatriation of refugees, etc.
- Establish a mechanism to mobilise necessary resources to facilitate post-conflict peace building (e.g. ASEAN Stability Fund)

Source: Derived from the *Vientiane Plan of Action* (ASEAN Security Community),   http://www.aseansec.org/VAP-10th%20ASEAN%20Summit.pdf.

point is often lost in the sweeping generalisations about the inability of ASEAN to address regional security challenges. These are significant in that they encourage a wider and deeper type of regional cooperation that is potentially intrusive into the domestic affairs of states. The current arrangements to combat terrorism in the region, for example, are illustrative of the type of intrusiveness that is at stake as members are encouraged to exchange intelligence information. Closely related to this are the current deliberations on the possibility of a transnational judicial system for cooperation in 'collecting evidence, investigating suspects and witnesses ... and extraditing criminals'.[33]

There is also the novel proposal of establishing an ASEAN peace-keeping force. In explaining the rationale for this proposal, a spokesperson for the Indonesian government had earlier remarked that 'ASEAN countries should know one another better than anyone else and therefore [we] should have the option ... to take advantage of an ASEAN peace-keeping force to be deployed if they so wish'.[34] Against ASEAN's experience and the participation of some countries in the peace-keeping and peace-building efforts in East Timor, the proposal for a regional peace-keeping force indicates a perceptible adjustment or even shift in the thinking about regional norms (as constituted in the ASEAN way). The implications for this initiative are therefore tremendous, yet bring to light an emerging new thinking on how some ASEAN member states regard the issues of sovereignty and non-intervention.

Although some ASEAN states had objected to the peace-keeping force proposal, on the grounds that it was 'too early' to consider setting up a force, and highly problematic because 'each country has its own policy about politics and the military',[35] it should also be noted that this proposal has not been completely rejected. Instead, in lieu of a regional peace-keeping force, the possibility of establishing a regional peace-keeping centre is currently being deliberated among ASEAN officials. One of the alternatives being mooted in lieu of a regional peace-keeping force is the idea of setting up a regional peace-keeping training centre. Moreover, military officials attached to the peace-keeping units in some ASEAN states, like Thailand, have already openly endorsed a similar idea of having a regional coordinating centre for regional peace-keeping units, including other measures like joint training exercises, and joint PKO courses. Thus, given the experience of ASEAN states (Thailand, Malaysia, Philippines, Singapore) in peace-keeping operations in the region – Cambodia and East Timor – one can be cautiously optimistic about its prospects, in the medium term.

That having been said, the cautious outlook adopted in this chapter does not, in any way, dismiss the potential problems and obstacles that many of these initiatives may encounter, given, among others, the lack of regional capacity in implementing many of the cooperative measures outlined in addressing transnational challenges, as well as the often-cited concern about protecting state sovereignty and upholding the principle of non-interference.

But the argument being made here is for balanced assessments of the ability of ASEAN to realistically push through with its strategies and plans, while at the same time being able to note the subtle changes that are being introduced in attempts at calibrating regional approaches to effectively address security issues, albeit in an incremental way. In this regard, it is necessary to be able to recognise and differentiate among the kinds of measures being adopted and to identify those that indicate fledgling attempts at going beyond the usual process-oriented, confidence-building measures which had been the preferred regional practice in ASEAN. That said, many of the regional measures recently adopted are in fact geared toward problem solving, involving: sharing of information (be it in intelligence gathering for combating terrorism and transnational crimes; or in expertise to address environmental pollution, etc.); developing certain types of regional surveillance systems for early warning on infectious diseases and natural disasters; providing relief in disaster management, rehabilitation and reconstruction, as well as providing humanitarian assistance; and more significantly, working toward coordinated procedures and even attempts at harmonising legal frameworks in addressing transnational crimes. In other words, from ad hoc mechanisms it is now possible to observe a type of creeping institutionalism in ASEAN, while working around the sensitive issues of sovereignty and non-interference – and toward promoting the concept of 'pooled sovereignty'. The ASC in its formulation has therefore integrated many of these modalities.

This optimism, however, has to be measured against the kinds of domestic challenges faced by countries in the region. These would include the lack of institutions and/or institutional capacity to carry out some of the regional initiatives agreed upon as well as the kind of political transitions that are taking place in the region that define the political and security environment of the respective states. One only has to look at the debates surrounding the Proliferation Security Initiative (PSI) and the Regional Maritime Security Initiative (RMSI) proposals to get a glimpse of the kinds of political and security dynamics taking place in the region that reflect the extent to which certain types of more intrusive initiative are regarded by states in Southeast Asia.

Against these considerations, it could nevertheless be concluded that the ASEAN Security Community concept comes at a time when the region is in the throes of significant changes. That a security community has been declared as a goal of ASEAN cooperation is certainly ambitious and beset with a number of challenges. What is clear is that ASEAN's security agenda reflects the wide spectrum of challenges facing the region – including the issue of economic security.

The ASEAN Economic Community

The idea of an ASEAN Economic Community was first proposed by Singaporean Prime Minister Goh Chok Tong at the 8th ASEAN Summit in Phnom Penh in 2002. The idea of the AEC was seen as a logical extension of the ASEAN Free Trade Area (AFTA) project that began in 1992. AFTA obligates ASEAN members to bring down or remove tariffs and non-tariff barriers to trade, under the Common Effective Preferential Tariff (CEPT). AFTA has been considered as a showcase project of ASEAN's regional economic cooperation, which demonstrated the resolve by member states to deepen economic integration in the region and, in the process, to enhance its competitiveness to investors. The eventual objective of the AEC therefore is to build on the success of AFTA and ensure the economic security of the region by creating opportunities for more markets and more trade.

Specifically, the AEC has envisioned ASEAN to be a single market by the year 2020 and a production base with free flow of goods, services, investments, capital and skilled labour.[36] In realising this vision, the ASEAN High Level Task Force (HLTF) on Economic Integration had unveiled a set of economic initiatives with clear deadlines to expedite the process of economic integration that has already been started. These initiatives include, among others, removing the remaining non-tariff barriers, the harmonisation of product standards, as well as the aim of allowing a limited movement of skilled and professional workers within the region.[37]

One of the most important recommendations by the HLTF was the creation of a more effective dispute settlement mechanism (DSM) with powers to make legally binding decisions in resolving trade disputes among member states. Since it is expected that the number of trade disputes will likely rise as the region moves towards a higher level of economic integration, a credible DSM would be extremely critical for the AEC to succeed. In this regard, plans are being discussed to (finally) strengthen the ASEAN Secretariat so as to improve its capacity to undertake some of the necessary functions in this area, including the possibility of setting up a legal unit within the Secretariat to provide legal advice on trade disputes. More significantly, in a stark departure from the ASEAN modality of decision making by consensus, ASEAN may also use the '2+X' formula besides the 'ASEAN-X' formula that had already been adopted in economic matters. The '2+X' approach allows two member countries that are ready to integrate certain sectors to go ahead while the others could follow later. This arrangement would also make it easier for countries such as Thailand and Singapore who want to realise the AEC before 2020.

The pressure on integrating the ten economies is revealing the different capacities within the grouping to realise the 2020 goal. At the 38th ASEAN Economic Ministers (AEM) meeting in August 2006, ministers from the more advanced economies called for the AEC to be realised by 2015.[38] This was supported by a Japanese proposal for the creation of a regional economic forum, the East Asia ASEAN Economic Research Center, to coordinate regional economic policies so as to ensure the acceleration of integration measures.[39] This goal was realised the following year at the annual ASEAN Summit when the ministers adopted the AEC Blueprint to realise the Economic Community by 2015 for all ASEAN members.[40]

Although these activities collectively represent a clear signal that the region is committed to deeper economic integration – with the potential for greater transnational policy coordination – the capability of the four less-developed economies of Cambodia, Laos, Myanmar and Vietnam to keep up with policy reforms remains questionable. What this proposal may well lead to is a two-track ASEAN Economic Community, one where the ASEAN-6 economies push to create a smaller-scale economic community.[41]

However, the push to create an ASEAN Economic Community is not the sole province of the regional states; the private sector also plays a formal role in advancing the AEC, with the ASEAN Business Advisory Council (ABAC) providing 'private sector feedback and guidance to boost ASEAN's efforts towards economic integration [and identifying] priority areas for considera- tion by the ASEAN Leaders'.[42] The ABAC was first mooted at the 2001 ASEAN Summit as a way of bringing business into the 'mainstream of [ASEAN's] economic activities' at a time when the region was still seeking to consolidate its economic recovery, advance regional integration and cope with the onset of another crisis – terrorism.[43] Since 2003, the ABAC has held a regular ASEAN Business and Investment Summit just before the annual ASEAN Summit. This timing allows for private sector issues to be fed into the summit discussions. It is worth noting that summits of the ABAC are not limited to only Southeast Asian companies but include representatives of foreign multinationals with a presence in the region as well as various business councils.

Hence, regional economic governance not only relies upon institutions and norms but also encompasses a set of actors beyond the state. What is inter- esting about both the ASEAN Security Community and the ASEAN Eco- nomic Community is that, although they are based on a discrete regional organisation focused on Southeast Asia, they implicitly stretch to encompass the three Northeast Asian states and identify a role for extra-regional actors, notably the United States in the case of the ASC and multi-national com- panies in the case of the AEC. The implications of these developments on regional mechanisms and governance in East Asia will be further elaborated upon in section four. Before this, it is necessary to understand the types of mechanisms and norms of APT.

APT: expanding the project on regional governance

Crises and APT

To start with, this section will briefly discuss the events that were relevant to the establishment of the APT and, in the process, provide a more coherent link between ASEAN and the APT. Most observations about the nature of economic cooperation in ASEAN had lamented the lack of cooperation in this area, especially at the height of the crisis in 1997.[44] However, it should be observed that, months before the currency crisis, there had been efforts by the ASEAN finance ministers and the ASEAN central banks to find modalities to protect the region from the increasing volatility of regional currencies. It is also important to note that the ASEAN banks had in fact provided large-scale support for the Thai baht in May 1997, when it was being attacked aggressively by currency speculators. However, against the massive capacity of currency speculators, the ASEAN central banks found themselves defenceless.[45]

During the crisis period, ASEAN convened several meetings at three levels (Heads of State/Government, Economic and Finance Ministers and Representatives from the private sectors) to develop an ASEAN response. The meetings came up with several measures to address the crisis, and among them was the establishment of a regional surveillance mechanism which was essentially aimed at promoting a more effective surveillance over the economic policies and practices of ASEAN members, facilitated by fuller disclosure of relevant economic data.[46]

The financial crisis therefore was the catalyst for the formation of the APT. As noted by Stubbs, 'for many ASEAN members, the crisis underscored the benefits of establishing formal economic links to the more developed economies of Japan and South Korea and the dynamic market of China as a means of averting any possible future crisis'.[47] Obviously, despite the fact that there was APEC, the inability of the latter to provide a coherent response to the affected economies of its member countries created disillusionment with this bigger grouping, which had more powerful and more economically endowed members like the United States. Hence, absent global economic governance, the initial impetus for the APT can be viewed as the region's attempt to hedge member states against future economic shocks and search for alternative mechanisms when current mechanisms proved inadequate in responding to economic, political and security challenges. As stated by Gyohten, 'the [Asian] crisis raised an issue of great importance that needs to be tackled by East Asia as a whole ... that is whether is it necessary for East Asia, like America and Europe to strengthen its regional cooperative ties ... East Asia has no mechanism for coping with its own problem'.[48] Clearly, the emergence of APT – a multilateral institution, albeit at the regional level – highlights and reinforces the issue of subsidiarity, when global institutions such as the International Monetary Fund (IMF) and the World Bank were perceived to be unable to provide the assistance and solutions required for specific regional problems.

It was within the framework of the ASEAN Summit that the APT began. It was at the 5th ASEAN Summit, held in Kuala Lumpur, Malaysia in December 1997 that ASEAN leaders met informally with the leaders of China, Japan and South Korea for the first time. Two years later, at the 7th ASEAN Summit, held in Manila in November 1999, the first APT Summit was formally convened, with the heads of all thirteen regional states present. The first joint statement produced in 1999 outlined the areas of cooperation in economic, social, political and security fields. Since then, the APT has emerged as a comprehensive framework with a wide range of agendas and conducts regular meetings not only during the summits but also with a wide variety of ministerial, official and expert meetings. The lens through which the APT has developed remains ASEAN, with many APT meetings held immediately following an ASEAN meeting on the same topic and adhering to the ASEAN modalities of consultation, consensus building and a rotating ASEAN-led chairmanship.

Like ASEAN, the APT has been characterised as a loose, informal institution. Nevertheless, despite the lack of any formal structure, treaty or formally binding agreement between the participating states 'the web of relations between the members has grown quickly since the first meeting of the heads of government'.[49] This web has led to a build-up of confidence between the thirteen states that has, in turn, allowed for a variety of projects to realise concrete products. Examples of these concrete products can be seen in two economic and financial cooperation projects that have taken place under the rubric of the Chiang Mai Initiative. The initiative has two main components: (1) an expanded ASEAN Swap Arrangement (ASA), and (2) a network of bilateral swap arrangements (BSAs) among the APT countries.

The ASA was originally established among the ASEAN-5 countries (Indonesia, Malaysia, Philippines, Singapore and Thailand) in 1997 and had a total facility of US$100 million. This was increased to US$200 million a year later and to US$1 billion under the Chiang Mai Initiative (CMI) (and with the inclusion of all ASEAN members). The BSAs, on the other hand, are a swap arrangement in which each party can request the other to enter into a swap transaction to provide liquidity support to overcome balance of payment difficulties in the specified currency up to a specified amount. By the end of November 2004, the accumulated value of the BSAs was US$36.5 billion.[50] Within two years the 'self-help and support mechanism of the Chiang Mai Initiative [had] made substantial progress [with] the Bilateral Swap Arrangements … [amounting] to over US$75 billion'.[51]

In mid 2005, the APT finance ministers agreed to further strengthen the CMI by making it a more effective and disciplined framework through a number of measures, including the integration and enhancement of the APT economic surveillance mechanism to enable early detection of irregularities and swift remedial policy actions, increasing the size of the available swaps by up to 100 per cent, and improving the drawdown mechanism, whereby the size of the swaps that could be withdrawn without the IMF-supported programme can be increased from the current 10 per cent to 20 per cent.[52] This was followed up in May 2006 when the APT finance ministers set up a new task force 'to further study various possible options towards an advanced framework of the regional liquidity support arrangement' and to enhance regional surveillance mechanisms.[53] The inputs for this framework were extended in 2007 when the Trioka of central bank governors met with the APT finance ministers to provide additional policy options.[54]

The measures outlined to enhance the CMI are important steps towards multilateralising the CMI so as to enable all countries to pool their financial resources. What this means is that an enhanced CMI could eventually create a regional mechanism such as the Asian Monetary Fund (AMF) that can then be used in the event of a financial crisis. (It is worth noting that an earlier attempt at establishing an AMF following the outbreak of the 1997 financial crisis failed, due to opposition from extraregional actors, principally the US and the International Monetary Fund.[55]) The significant inroads made by the APT in the area of financial cooperation reinforce a point made by Dieter and Higgott about an evolving 'monetary regionalism', where they argued that the 'East Asian region will become an increasingly potential domain within which to explore protection against financial crises [given that] "monetary regionalism" is now firmly in the agenda'.[56] Given that the levels of economic integration, particularly in trade, are already quite high in the East Asian region, deepening cooperation in trade and finance through the strengthening of CMI mechanism becomes even more important. As argued by Hamilton-Hart, the benefits of a strong regional mechanism for preventing and managing financial crises probably outweigh the costs involved.[57]

The APT, however, is envisioned to be more than just a mechanism of monetary regionalism. If one follows the proposals of the East Asian Vision Group (EAVG) released in 2001, the vision was to move East Asia from a region of nations to a bona fide regional community representing all levels of interest. In terms of security cooperation, it was envisaged that this would entail the further development of mechanisms and norms to ensure a stable region, the creation of a regionally representative voice in international fora, and 'the broadening of political cooperation with respect to national governance issues'.[58]

Moving beyond the realm of the state, security cooperation is also enhanced through the Track-Two work of the Council for Security Cooperation in the Asia-Pacific (CSCAP) and the Network of East Asian Thinktanks (NEAT). Although CSCAP, as an organisation under the ARF, involves extraregional partners, the focus of the CSCAP working and study groups remains East Asian. NEAT emerged from the EAVG report, which called for a network 'to be established to explore long term policy issues of strategic importance to the region'.[59] With its foci on regional political and security cooperation as well as economic and financial architecture, but a membership based on the APT states, NEAT draws upon experts, academics and policy makers in advancing community building.

On the economic front, the EAVG envisaged the integration of East Asian economies to serve as a catalyst for community building, eventually leading to the formation of an East Asian Economic Community (EAEC). In addition to the role of the states, the private sector was also identified as a key sector in this community-building process. The EAVG Report called for the establishment of an East Asian Business Council (EABC) – comprised of small and medium-sized enterprises from regional states as well as multi-national corporations based in East Asia – to contribute to the economic integration process.[60] The first meeting of the EABC was held in April 2004. Its mandate is to 'provide private sector perspective and feedback to the APT governments with the aim of deepening economic cooperation and linkages, and to strengthen cooperation among the private sectors of ASEAN, China, Japan and Korea'. As a measure of the EABC's policy influence, it presents its recommendations direct to the AEM and their senior officials.[61]

From the preceding discussions, it is possible to draw linkages from ASEAN to the APT in developing a larger community in East Asia. As it stands, economic integration has primarily driven the community-building process in the region since the 1997 financial crisis. In doing so, even as new mechanisms have been developed, the economic process has drawn upon many of the structures and norms that were first used for security coopera-tion. These two sectors now stand entwined at the heart of the East Asian Community-building process. As they seek to develop into the Security and Economic Communities, the two sectors have expanded to include new state actors as well as an array of non-state actors in the decision-making process. In order to properly understand the ways in which the APT has changed, the dynamics of interstate relations in the region need to also be examined, particularly if the nature of the multilevel interactions that take place within the grouping is to be comprehended and the implications for the formation of an East Asian Community are to be appreciated.

ASEAN – a binding regional hub?

One of the goals of the APT has been the institutionalisation of regional dialogues on issues beyond economics, to include political- and security-related topics as a means to strengthen cooperation. Similarly to the mod-alities adopted in the formation of the ARF, ASEAN's approach of con-fidence and trust building through dialogue was deemed to be the best way to bring the three Northeast Asian countries together, despite a history of rivalry and animosity. In this regard, the centrality of ASEAN in providing a space for fostering better relations among the three Northeast Asian coun-tries must be emphasised. One would note, for instance, that before the APT was formed, relations were established first at the ASEAN+1 level (ASEAN–Japan, ASEAN–China and ASEAN–South Korea), signalling the desire by all three countries to improve their relations with ASEAN. (This is one of the subjects discussed in the following three chapters.) In turn, this led to the upgrading of their relationships with ASEAN to full dialogue partnerships. In effect, the ASEAN+1 Summit became the foundation of the APT. Moreover, it was only at the 1999 Manila Summit that the heads of the three Northeast Asian states held their first trilateral meeting.

As already argued by many, it is in the interest of both ASEAN states and the three Northeast Asian states to commit to the APT process to minimise tensions in the region.[62] For ASEAN, its role in the APT has been viewed as a buffer between the uneven political and security relations between China and Japan. But how, exactly, is this buffer role played out? For one, the continued chairmanship of the APT process remains within the domain of ASEAN, and its practice of rotated chairmanship is rooted in the ASEAN practice of chairman by annual rotation and in alphabetical order (other than the recent exception of Myanmar stepping aside for the Philippines). Thus, while Japan and China are in competition for a leadership role in East Asia, having an ASEAN state as the chair diffuses competition, at least, within the APT process. Japan and China as well as Korea are therefore compelled to work with ASEAN and continue to promote their own individual relations with the grouping so as to maintain its influence in the region.

Similarly, the APT is important in providing a framework for Northeast Asian countries to meet in the sidelines of the APT summits and provide additional channels for them to discuss their bilateral relations; although, as the events of 2005/06 showed, when relations between any two of these countries deteriorate significantly so too does the utility of this additional framework. Nonetheless, an obvious benefit from these series of meetings that take place at the APT process is the positive climate of enhanced cooperation, fostered by institutionalised dialogue. Thus, while the ARF was seen as an extension of the ASEAN way of confidence and trust building, the APT can also be regarded as ASEAN's way of deepening the regional processes within a more focused geographical arena.

Apart from this tacit *mission civilatrice* of ASEAN, APT also provides the platform for ASEAN to maintain its political leverage and to tap the economic benefits from its linkages with China, Japan and Korea in order to reduce economic gaps in the region. This can be seen in the way the ASEAN +1 channel is maintained, thereby forming a separate yet integral part of the APT process. The +1 channel is already showing more results, as reflected in the nature of collaboration taking place between ASEAN and the three countries. China and ASEAN, for example, have entered into a free trade agreement in 2002. Negotiations have also been recently completed for an ASEAN and Japan Comprehensive Economic Partnership,[63] with a similar agreement also being gradually developed with South Korea. In addition to the economic ties, each of the three ASEAN+1 relationships has yielded a number of political, security and cultural agreements that have served to further deepen regional cooperation and integration. Moving beyond ASEAN's relations with the +3 states, a range of similar political, security and economic agreements have either been agreed upon or are in the process of being negotiated between ASEAN and India. This is further discussed by Isabelle Saint-Mézard in Chapter 7.

Most importantly, the APT framework has also been conducive to building of norms for a more stable and integrated East Asia. ASEAN's Treaty of Amity and Cooperation (TAC) has now been formally adopted as reference for the Code of Conduct of interstate relations in East Asia with the formal accession of all +3 countries to the TAC. The norms contained in the TAC – which were referred to earlier – are, thus, now the norms by which the thirteen regional states manage their relations. Former Malaysian Prime Minister Mahathir Mohamed has, in fact, claimed that the TAC is now the de facto East Asian charter for peace and good neighbourliness.[64]

Hence, despite the perceived lack of formal institutional capacity on the part of ASEAN and the APT, the current shape of cooperative developments among countries in East Asia supports the idea that a more structured and integrated community is emerging. Beyond security and economic linkages, one can see a gradually expanding pattern of multilateral cooperation in a variety of other areas. A key aspect of these cooperative fora is the way they involve state and non-state actors in policy dialogues. However, the argument can be made that, despite the broadening of these dialogues that are shaping the region, those participating in the process still only represent elite opinions. What is lacking in terms of regional governance, therefore, is an understanding of the role of the regional peoples and their societies in the community-building process. This is the subject of the following section.

Entrenching regional governance: the role of the people

From the foregoing discussions, the developments at the ASEAN and APT levels approximate some of the characteristics of the second-generation regionalism described in the literature, manifesting deeper economic integration, cooperation among many dimensions, and development of international legal frameworks. As to whether ASEAN and the APT have met the elements of Jayasuriya's framework of regional governance projects, the discussion so far supports the argument set at the start of the chapter that suggest that, in both the ASEAN and the APT processes, a more robust regionalism is emerging and that to manage these processes has required the development of governance structures (in terms of norms and institutions).

But robust regionalism also begs the question as to whether, in the quest for multilevel governance, the regionalism project has indeed become more inclusive and participatory. As has been seen, apart from regional state and market elites, there are comparatively few opportunities for social voices to be heard. This section argues that, unless this is addressed, the regional governance project that is supposed to be able to mediate the forces of globalisation and aim for a more balanced and socially responsible regional community is incomplete. New regionalism has been conceptualised as part of the global structural transformation in which non-state actors of many different types and levels of institutions, organisations and movements are included.[65] Where there needs to be further exploration in East Asia, therefore, is in the extent to which multilevel governance is beginning to take place within these regions.

Until the adoption of the ASEAN Community project, ASEAN has often been seen as a state-centric organisation and disconnected from the peoples in the region. Moreover, even in the ASEAN plus arrangements that emerged – the APT and the EAS – these had clearly been engagements and participation primarily at the government level. Hence, it was not until the announcement of the ASEAN Community that the grouping's new thrust of wanting to become a more inclusive regional governance project became evident. The clearest indication of this was at the 11th ASEAN Summit in 2005, when Malaysian Prime Minister Abdullah Badawi, speaking in his capacity as the ASEAN Chair, emphasised the need for ASEAN to be 'transformed' to become a more people-centred community.[66]

Prior to this announcement, however, were similar significant processes already taking place that were reflective of the ongoing evolution of ASEAN's institutional framework towards a more inclusive modality. These processes could be found at both the governmental and the non-govern-mental level. Insofar as the latter is concerned, the creation of the ASEAN People's Assembly (APA) and its attempts to engage with ASEAN officials are a perceptible trend in this direction. The APA, which was formed in 2000, is the first attempt to bring together a wide range of civil society organisations (CSOs) to discuss issues of concern to the peoples of Southeast Asia and to provide inputs to the ASEAN agenda-setting and decision-making process. Organised under the auspices of the ASEAN Institutes of Strategic and International Studies (ASEAN-ISIS), a Track-Two body in ASEAN, the APA had to experience a long gestation period, overcoming several obstacles before it could finally be established.[67] The decision by ASEAN officials to provide political space for CSOs came only after more than thirty years. Prior to APA's formal establishment in 2000, ASEAN has always been seen a 'club of elites'. As argued by Hernandez, if there had been earlier attempts by ASEAN to consult with civil society, it was mostly top-down in approach, 'where implementation rather than planning or stra-tegizing was open only to select circles seen as cooperative rather than con-structively critical or destructively confrontational'.[68] For Hernandez and the members of the ASEAN-ISIS, the APA was to become this regional mechanism 'meant to create a regular people's gathering where they would meet on a regular basis, discuss issues they consider timely, important and relevant; seek solutions for them and make recommendations to government on these matter'.[69]

Over the period since its formation, the APA has focused its engagement with ASEAN by outlining and pursuing an ambitious people's agenda that highlights the human security issues of the people in this region. This can be found in the APA's Action Plan, which had been in development since the organisation's inception. The Action Plan identifies seven areas that various groups within the APA are working on, which are aimed at bringing atten-tion to urgent security and development challenges and providing alter-native modalities for ASEAN governments to consider. These areas are: developing a human rights scorecard; identifying threats to democracy by developing 'democracy promoting indicators and/or democracy eroding indicators; developing a framework to evaluate the progress of gender mainstreaming; developing a Code of Ethics for (governance in) NGOs; promoting cooperation in tackling HIV/AIDS; promoting Cooperation Among Media groups; and developing the Southeast Asian Human Development Report'.[70]

From these seven areas, the APA's work on human rights and democracy are instructive in this discussion of the nature and prospects of the institutional engagement of regional civil society. In the area of human rights, for instance, the APA since 2001 has developed a human rights scorecard in the region with the aim of documenting the international human rights instruments to which each of the ASEAN members had acceded. The scorecard was further modified at the 3rd APA in 2003 to include monitoring national legislations, orders, decrees, rules and regulations that have been adopted by each of the ASEAN member states which would reflect their commitment to the international human rights instruments which they have ratified. This scorecard covers the wide spectrum of human rights protection, to include civil and political rights, social, economic and cultural rights, and the right to development. It is envisioned that data and other relevant information for this scorecard will be collected with the help of NGOs, local academics, donor agencies and other relevant actors.

As an ongoing project, the scorecard is primarily meant to be a useful tool to determine how far human rights promotion and protection have gone in the region. Human rights advocates could also use it as a neutral instrument in their work on the promotion of human rights.[71] This particular project dovetails with the work of a specific civil society group in the region – the Regional Working Group on Human Rights – that has been working for the establishment of an ASEAN Regional Human Rights Commission since 1993.

The engagement of the APA in the ASEAN process is a fascinating development, as are the implications of ASEAN's plans for starting a framework for political development in the region through the ASC. Even though the idea of democracy is now more openly articulated in the region, not only by the people but also by some governments in ASEAN, much remains to be seen with regard to the ability of the grouping to eventually set the standard and norms for intrastate conduct. Depending on the extent to which one puts value on the current ASEAN engagement with Myanmar, the jury is still out on how far the ASC can actually be a significant driver for more democracy and good governance in the region. The same can be said with regard to the question of whether regionalism, at least in Southeast Asia, is becoming also more inclusive. However, while dramatic change is never one of ASEAN's defining characteristics, the decision by Myanmar to give up its scheduled chairmanship of ASEAN in 2006 does provide a flicker of hope that 'peer pressure' may eventually have some effect. Similarly, the ongoing efforts by ASEAN parliamentarians to push for the 'suspension' of Myanmar from ASEAN are certainly indicative of shifting patterns of regional approaches towards good governance and non-intervention – albeit coming mostly from non-state actors.

Even with these tiny flickers, however, there remain major issues concerning the ability of ASEAN to adopt a set of regional standards on democracy and human rights. If, indeed, the notion of a security community that pursues human rights protection and promotion is part of building the 'we feeling' in the region, a pertinent question to examine is whether member states in the region have reached the point where these values are commonly shared. In this regard, the ASEAN Charter, which was adopted in November 2007, has presented both opportunities and challenges in embedding the goals of establishing a 'democratic, tolerant and participatory and open community'.[72]

The ASEAN Charter: opportunities and challenges for more participatory regionalism

The concept of an ASEAN Charter was proposed by Malaysia in 2004,[73] although the decision to draw up a Charter was formally announced at the 11th ASEAN Summit in 2005. The Malaysian concept paper, entitled *Review of ASEAN Institutional Framework: Proposals for Change*, had argued that in order to successfully transform ASEAN into an ASEAN Community, it would have to be prepared for profound changes, including in terms of its institutional framework. In response to this, the Charter can be seen as a way to review and revise ASEAN's current institutional framework, its working methods and rules, while creating a space where discussions on regional norms can be held.

The Summit's announcement of a Charter led to the appointment of a ten-person Eminent Persons Group (EPG) – one from each of the ASEAN states – with the mission of providing the ASEAN leaders with 'bold and visionary' recommendations and/or inputs for the Charter.[74] Apart from their official mandate, the EPG was also encouraged by the ASEAN leaders to conduct a series of consultations with civil society groups and business networks in keeping with the new thrust of the grouping to become a more inclusive organisation. The initiative for a bottom-up consultative process was announced by Malaysia's Prime Minister Abdullah Badawi, speaking in his capacity as the 2005 ASEAN Chair. According to Badawi, ASEAN had to be 'transformed' to become a more people-centred community.[75]

The announcement of the ASEAN Charter attracted a lot of attention, especially among the CSOs and NGO communities in the light of the invitation issued for them to get involved in the consultation process for the drafting of the Charter. To kick off the bottom-up consultative process, the EPG invited representatives from the different CSOs in the region to the first ASEAN-CSO meeting. This led to the convening of the first ASEAN Civil Society Conference (ACSC) in Malaysia on 7–9 December 2005, which brought together around 120 participants from CSOs in the region.[76] The first ACSC resulted in the preparation of a 'Statement of the ASEAN Civil

Society Conference to the 11th ASEAN Summit', which was subsequently submitted to the ASEAN heads of state at their first-ever interface with civil society group on 12 December 2005. Although the meeting only lasted for about 15 minutes, the representative of ACSC was able to submit and read out their statement on 'Building a Common Future Together'.[77]

The convening of the ACSC therefore started a new momentum among CSOs in the region to work closely by establishing a more coherent CSO mechanism to formally engage ASEAN.[78] This led to the formation of the Solidarity for Asian Peoples Advocacy (SAPA) in February 2006, which brought together twelve umbrella CSO organisations including Forum Asia and Third World Network.[79] After the first ASEAN-CSO meeting in Malaysia in December 2005, four other consultative processes took place during 2006 (Bangkok in February, Manila in March, Bali in April and Singapore in June).

Meanwhile, other informal parallel consultations took place. Having already worked quite closely with ASEAN-SOM, the ASEAN-ISIS was also invited to present their ideas about the Charter. The Track-Two group subsequently issued its own ASEAN-ISIS Memorandum No. 1 2006 on the ASEAN Charter which it submitted to the ASEAN Foreign Ministers meeting in Bali, Indonesia in April 2006, around the same time that the EPGs were conducting their second consultative meeting. The ASEAN-ISIS Memorandum approximated a full version of what it wanted to see included in the ASEAN Charter, such as ASEAN principles, organs and institutional arrangements, consultation and decision-making process, external relations, rights and obligations, financial matters and even sanctions.[80] There were also similar proposals that were submitted by other Track-Two institutions, like the Institute of Southeast Asian Studies (ISEAS), which prepared its own document on framing the Charter. ISEAS sent its report to the EPG and the ASEAN SOM in time for the 11th Summit in Kuala Lumpur.[81] Moreover, there were also other initiatives that emerged, albeit outside the official consultative process. For example, the ASEAN Trade Union Council had drawn up its own ASEAN Social Charter which it presented to the ASEAN officials in December 2005. The Social Charter was aimed at promoting common labour standards in ASEAN which would include employment stability, promotion of health and safety and just wages.[82]

After conducting five meetings, dubbed as 'Consultations with the People', the EPG finally submitted its recommendations to the ASEAN leaders at the 12th ASEAN Summit in Cebu, Philippines in January 2007. The EPG Report attracted a lot of attention for the boldness of vision and ideas that it presented. Furthermore, the fact that it was widely circulated and made easily available through the ASEAN Secretary website – a significant departure from the past practice of non-transparency – reinforced the perception, at least at that point in time, that Southeast Asia was indeed at the cusp of a new era of 'regionalism'. Two elements of this new regionalism are highlighted below:

First, on ASEAN's principles and norms, the EPG Report called for 'the active strengthening of democratic values, good governances, rejection of unconstitutional and undemocratic changes of government', as well as inclusion of 'the rule of law, including humanitarian law'. Clearly articulated also was the respect for human rights and fundamental freedoms.[83]

Second, on the rights and obligations of members, the Report included a provision for possible sanctions, specifically proposing that 'ASEAN should have the power to take measures to redress cases of serious breach of ASEAN's objectives, major principles ... such measures may include suspension of any of the rights and privileges of membership'.[84] Although the 'ASEAN Way' was not going to be completely discarded, it was going to be supplemented by a culture of adherence to rules which were, by the merits of the Charter, going to be legally binding.

In brief, the EPG Report indicated a potential sea change in the thinking among ASEAN elites. The recommendations on democracy and human rights and on obligations of member states, including the idea of adopting sanctions, reflected the emerging attitude that sticking to the lowest common denominator in standards of behaviour was no longer acceptable in a maturing ASEAN.

However, the turn of events that followed the submission of the EPG Report to the ASEAN Summit in January 2007 was foreboding. Although the Report was endorsed by the ASEAN, rifts among the ASEAN on a number of controversial issues began to emerge. Hence, between the summits in January and November 2007, a High Level Task Force was assigned to prepare the draft of the Charter which was to be approved by the leaders in time for the 40th anniversary celebrations of ASEAN in Singapore. But while the reported differences among ASEAN leaders indicated the possibility of a watered-down version of the Charter, the unexpected demonstrations in Myanmar in September 2007 had dramatically changed the mood in the region. The incidents and the violence that followed drew a swift and sharp response from ASEAN. Not only did ASEAN issue a joint statement expressing its 'revulsion' at the atrocities that had occurred, but it joined the rest of the international community in 'urging Myanmar to exercise utmost restraint ... seek political solution ... and release all political detainees including Aung San Suu Kyi'.[85]

Thus, the run-up to the November 2007 Summit in Singapore became highly eventful. Not only had Myanmar's attendance at the summit cast a shadow on ASEAN's 40th anniversary celebrations, but the mood was further dampened by the 'leaking' of copies of the draft Charter prior to the Summit which turned to be a 'watered-down' version of what the EPG Report had recommended. Making matters worse was the unexpected volte-face of Myanmar in not allowing UN envoy Ibrahim Gambari to brief the regional leaders on developments in that country after the host, Singapore, had already announced that such a briefing was slated to take place.

Despite the series of events that marred the ASEAN Summit and its 40th year celebrations, the Summit was nevertheless significant for the emerging and salient tensions that became visible not only within the community in

Southeast Asia but beyond. At the official level, it became clear that ASEAN elites were divided on how far to push ahead with the plans to establish a normative framework for ASEAN. Despite the declarations of the democratic norms in the Charter and the plans to establish a regional human rights body, it did not go far enough to operationalise how this regional body was going to function. Absent too was any provision for sanctions or punitive mechanism on violations of norms of democracy. However, it is interesting to note that Philippine President Gloria Arroyo broke protocol during the Summit when she announced that her country would be hard pressed to ratify the Charter unless the situation in Myanmar improved.

Tensions are also growing between ASEAN officials/leaders and civil society groups and Track-Two networks – with the latter expressing their disgust over the final outcome of the Charter and ASEAN's inaction on Myanmar in spite of tragic events that transpired prior to the Summit. For example, a prominent member of the ASEAN-ISIS network had urged the Indonesian parliament not to ratify the Charter and called for ASEAN to 'go back to the drawing board to come up with a more modest document commensurate with the state of affairs in ASEAN'.[86] Similarly, civil society groups who participated in the EPG consultative processes had openly criticised ASEAN's 'weak' Charter and declared that they were going to come up with their own people-oriented charter.

In brief, the 40th anniversary of ASEAN was marked by a number of defining moments which in turn have tremendous implications on the path toward the emerging regionalism in ASEAN. To be sure, transnational security challenges, and issues on human rights and democracy have reached a threshold where ASEAN elites and civil society groups are now pressing for these issues to be addressed and no longer swept under the carpet.

Thus, despite what appeared to be a lost opportunity in pushing for a more credible Charter, one still could argue that the momentum in pressing ahead with change is already gaining ground in the region, which in effect captures the new regionalism taking place in Southeast Asia.

Beyond ASEAN

The story in the wider region, however, is slightly different. So far, there is yet to emerge a dedicated trans- or interregional civil society group, similar to APA or the ASEAN Civil Society Conference, which could play a significant role in pushing for a more participatory and inclusive form of regional governance across East Asia. While much of the discourse at the official and Track-Two levels speaks about building an East Asian Community, what can only be discerned so far is a sense of promoting and sharing an idea, but without much thought on how exactly this notion of a community is going to be realised. What is also missing is a voice from civil society organisations that represent the wider region and are able to reflect shared notions of building an East Asian Community. Thus, while deepening security and economic integration could pave the way for community-building projects, the kind of community that could evolve may not be the same as the Deutschian notion of a community – the big C – especially in the light of the intractable and periodic tensions that define interstate relations in Northeast Asia.[87]

Nevertheless, despite these reservations, the fact remains that the notion of community-building continues to be a shared regional idea beyond ASEAN and APT – as witnessed at the 2005 East Asian Summit. In the Chairman's Statement of the EAS, the meeting acknowledged that the progress of community in East Asia had already advanced through the ASEAN and the ASEAN+3 processes. The holding of the EAS is therefore pitched to complement the ongoing processes under the APT and the ASEAN+1 processes.[88] As succinctly described by a former Japanese foreign ministry official, the APT and the EAS is a two-tiered approach to community building where norms are being developed and habits of cooperation are being fostered.[89] These are best seen in the criteria set by ASEAN for participation in the East Asia Summit, namely, the signing of the ASEAN TAC, being a formal dialogue partner of ASEAN, and having substantive cooperative relations with ASEAN. Thus, the establishment of the EAS is another example of an ASEAN-led approach toward an open and inclusive regionalism that is aimed at strengthening a set of norms and values which are geared to improvinh governance at the regional level.

Conclusion

The foregoing discussion has attempted to show how regional governance in East Asia – seen through the lens of developments in ASEAN, APT and, to a certain extent, the EAS – has evolved over time. In highlighting the various mechanisms that had emerged across the wide expanse of the political–security and economic areas of cooperation found in both ASEAN and APT, the conclusion is that regionalism in this region has indeed been robust. However, the expansion of regional norms and institutions to include governance remains limited, primarily mired at the level of policy elites – although more recent developments may indicate that this is changing.

There are at least two salient points that can be drawn from the above. First, as a regional governance project, ASEAN has shown throughout its history that it is able to have the capacity to effect positive changes within the organisation. Although weakened as a result of the series of crises, ASEAN was able to work from within to forge cooperation in responding to critical security and development issues and, in the process, also forged linkages with the other three Northeast Asia countries to form APT. In the process, not one but two interrelated regional organisations have evolved that are focused on strengthening cooperation among members as they confront the emerging and complex economic and security challenges facing the region. Second, ASEAN as a central actor in the region has not only provided the ties that bind the +3 states together but – through its norms and institutions – has also helped to develop the modalities for dialogue and cooperation among the +3 states and between ASEAN and the +3. In effect, ASEAN and the APT have provided and will hopefully continue to provide the regional framework to embed norms and rules to manage both intra- and interregional relations. However, how these two regional grouping will mesh with the EAS process remains to be seen.

A major challenge facing ASEAN, however, is to ensure that its efforts at building the ASEAN Community – through the ASC and AEC – can be sustained. While it may be premature to raise problems that the EAS could pose for the process of regionalism in East Asia, ASEAN must ensure that the community-building process that has begun be consolidated, otherwise the region may lose the important ties that bind states and people together. More importantly, given that the processes of engaging societal groups in ASEAN regional framework have already begun, the momentum needs also to be sustained for the ASEAN Community to become meaningful to the larger community of East Asian peoples.

So much has happened in the four years since the adoption of the Vientiane Action Plan in 2004. These developments, as discussed above, highlight the huge challenges ahead in shaping the normative framework of ASEAN beyond the goal of raising cooperation in ASEAN to a higher plane in all aspects – economic, political and security. Nevertheless, the stage has been set for a more inclusive region. This also means that elite politics in the region are now subject to contestation. The regional projects on the ASEAN Community and the ASEAN Charter therefore signal a significant new beginning for ASEAN. If ASEAN indeed wants to drive the community-building process in East Asia, it cannot afford to lose this opportunity to commence a new phase in the development of regional governance.

Notes

1 See *Declaration of the ASEAN Bali Concord II*. http://www.aseansec.org.15159.htm. For a recent analysis on this topic see: Curley, Melissa and Nicholas Thomas. 'Introduction: Advancing East Asian Regionalism', in Melissa Curley and Nicholas Thomas (eds). *Advancing East Asian Regionalism*. (London: RoutledgeCurzon, 2007), pp. 1–25.
2 Hettne, Bjorn. 'Globalisation and the New Regionalism: The Second Great Transformation', in Bjorn Hettne, Andras Inotai and Osvaldo Sunkel (eds). *Globalism and the New Regionalism*. (London: Macmillan, 1999), p. xvi
3 Grugel, Jean. 'New Regionalism and Modes of Governance – Comparing US and EU Strategies in Latin America', *European Journal of International Relations*. (Vol. 10, No. 4, 2004), p. 604.
4 See: Cox, Robert with Timothy Sinclair. *Approaches to World Order*. (Cambridge: Cambridge University Press, 1996).
5 Telo, Mario. 'Introduction: Globalisation, New Regionalism and the Role of the European Union', in M. Telo (ed.). *European Union and the New Regionalism*. (Aldershot: Ashgate, 2001), p. 7.

6 See: Payne, Anthony. 'Globalisation and Modes of Regionalist Governance', in Jon Pierre (ed.). *Debating Governance: Authority, Steering and Democracy.* (Oxford: Oxford University Press, 2000), pp. 201–218.
7 These points are derived from Murphy, Craig. 'Global Governance: Poorly Done and Poorly Understood', *International Affairs.* (Vol. 74, No. 4, 2000), pp. 789–803.
8 Jayasuriya, Kanishka. 'Introduction: The Vicissitudes of Asian Regional Governance', in Kanishka Jayasuriya (ed.). *Asian Regional Governance: Crisis and Change.* (London: RoutledgeCurzon, 2004), pp. 1–18.
9 Grugel, Jean. 'New Regionalism and Modes of Governance – Comparing US and EU Strategies in Latin America', p. 606.
10 Ibid. p. 618.
11 See: Jayasuriya, Kanishka. 'Introduction: The Vicissitudes of Asian Regional Governance'.
12 The argument here is that security in the ASEAN context is closely intertwined with economic development, as reflected in the regional concept of comprehensive security. See for example: Alagappa, Muthiah. 'Comprehensive Security: Interpretations in ASEAN Countries', in Robert Scalapino, Seizaburo Sato, Jusuf Wanadi and Han Sung-joo (eds). *Asian Security Issues: Regional and Global.* (Institute of East Asian Studies, University of California, Berkeley, 1988), pp. 50–78.
13 The five original ASEAN members were Indonesia, Malaysia, Philippines, Singapore and Thailand. Brunei Darussalam joined in 1984, immediately after its independence from the United Kingdom.
14 Vietnam joined ASEAN in 1995, followed by Laos and Myanmar in 1997 and finally Cambodia in 1999.
15 Deutsch, Karl (1961), 'Security Communities', as cited in James Rosenau (ed.). *International Politics and Foreign Policy: A Reader in Research and Theory.* (New York: Free Press, 1968), p. 98.
16 See: Acharya, Amitav. *Constructing a Security Community in Southeast Asia: ASEAN and the Problem of Regional Order.* (London: Routledge, 2001).
17 See: Article 2 of the *Treaty of Amity and Cooperation in Southeast Asia.* Indonesia, 24 February 1976.
18 For a longer treatment of this see: Caballero-Anthony, Mely. *Regional Security in Southeast Asia: Beyond the Asian Way.* (Singapore: Institute of Southeast Asian Studies, 2005).
19 For more this see, ASEAN Documents, ASEAN Secretariat.
20 It must be noted, however, that bilateral disputes (political and others) between ASEAN members are handled bilaterally through joint commissions and/or committees. For more on this, Caballero-Anthony, Mely. 'Mechanisms of Dispute Settlement: The Case of ASEAN', *Contemporary Southeast Asia.* (Vol. 2, No.1, 1999), pp. 38–67.
21 See: Acharya, Amitav. *Constructing a Security Community in Southeast Asia: ASEAN and the Problem of Regional Order.*
22 These issues are discussed in greater detail throughout: Caballero-Anthony, Mely. *Regional Security in Southeast Asia: Beyond the ASEAN Way.*
23 See: *The ASEAN Regional Forum: A Concept Paper.* 1995. http://www.aseansec.org/3635.htm. Accessed 20 August 2007.
24 See for example, Ruland, Jurgen. 'ASEAN and the Asian Crisis: Theoretical Implications and Practical Consequences for Southeast Asian Regionalism', *The Pacific Review.* (Vol. 13, No. 3), pp. 421–451; Henderson, Jeannie. *Reassessing ASEAN,* Adelphi Paper 323 (London: Oxford University Press for IISS, 1999); Garofano, John. 'Flexibility or Irrelevance: Ways Forward for the ARF', *Contemporary Southeast Asia.* (Vol. 21, No. 1, April 1999), pp. 74–94.

25 See: Caballero-Anthony, Mely. *Regional Security in Southeast Asia: Beyond the ASEAN Way*, especially pp. 194–231.

26 For more of this topic see: Martin, Ian. *Self-Determination in East Timor*. International Peace Academy Occasional Paper Series. (Boulder, CO: Lynne Rienner Publishers, 2001), and Sebastian, Leonard and Anthony Smith. 'The East Timor Crisis: A Test Case for Humanitarian Intervention', in Daljit Singh (ed.). *Southeast Asian Affairs 2000*. (Singapore: Institute for Southeast Asian Studies, 2000), pp. 64–83.

27 See *ASEAN Vision 2020*. http://www.aseansec.org. Accessed 5 November 2007.

28 'Indonesia Proposing ASEAN Security Community Concept', *Jakarta Post*, 16 June 2003. http://www.thejakartapost.com. Accessed 6 November 2007.

29 See *Vientiane Action Programme*. http://www.aseansec.org./VAP-10thASEAN Summit.pdf. Accessed 20 November 2007.

30 For more discussion on the security dimensions of the ASC, see among others, Caballero-Anthony, Mely. 'Regional Structures and Responses to Security Challenges in Southeast Asia', *Indonesian Quarterly*. (Vol. 33, No. 1, May 2005), and Ho, Joshua. 'Recent Developments and Regional Initiatives in the Straits of Malacca', *IDSS Commentary*, 26 May 2006.

31 See: *Joint Declaration of the ASEAN Defence Ministers on Enhancing Regional Peace and Stability*. Singapore, 14 November 2007. http://www.aseansec.org/ 21135.pdf. Accessed 24 April 2008.

32 Severino, Rodolfo. *Southeast Asia in Search of an ASEAN Community*. (Singapore: Institute of Southeast Asian Studies, 2006), p. 206.

33 'Reports from the China-ASEAN Prosecutors-General Conference', Kunming, 8 July 2004 from *Xinhua News Agency*, accessed from http://web.lexis-nexis.com.

34 'Indonesia Proposes Southeast Asian Peacekeeping Force', 21 February 2004. http://www.aseansec.org/afp/20p.htm. Accessed 14 November 2007.

35 See 'Asean's Peace', *The Straits Times* (Singapore), 8 March 2004.

36 The ASEAN Vision 2020 envisaged 'a stable, prosperous and highly competitive ASEAN Economic Region in which there is a free flow of goods, services and investments, a freer flow of capital, equitable economic development and reduced poverty and socio-economic disparities.' (p. 12).

37 See: *Recommendations of the High-Level Task Force on ASEAN Economic Integration*. http://www.aseansec.org. Accessed 16 November 2007.

38 See, for example: 'Malaysia urges ASEAN to aim for 2015', *The Associated Press*, 14 August 2006; Othman, Azlan. 'Brunei Singapore PM Seeks Quicker ASEAN Economic Integration', *Borneo Bulletin*. 12 August 2006; and Ng, Pauline. 'ASEAN to speed up integration', *The Business Times Singapore*, 26 July 2006.

39 'Japan to pledge US$86 mln to finance East Asian economic forum', *Asia Pulse*, 18 August 2006.

40 See: *Declaration on ASEAN Economic Blueprint*. 20 November 2007. http:// www.aseansec.org/21081.htm. Accessed 24 April 2008.

41 This is discussed in: 'Philippines to call for economic integration at Asean meeting', *Asia Pulse*. 21 August 2006.

42 See: 'Objectives of the ASEAN BAC'. http://www.asean-bac.org/index.php? option = com_content&task = view&id = 13&Itemid = 27. Accessed 10 November 2007.

43 Press Statement by the Chairman of the 7th ASEAN Summit and the *5th ASEAN+3 Summit*. (Bandar Seri Begawan: 5 November 2001). http://www. aseansec.org/5317.htm. Accessed 10 November 2007.

44 For a good treatment of this issue see: Narine, Shaun. *Explaining Regionalism in Southeast Asia*. (Boulder: Lynne Reinner, 2001).

45 There have been numerous accounts of ASEAN's concerted response to the currency crisis. See for example, Soesastro, Hadi. 'ASEAN during the Crisis',

ASEAN Economic Bulletin. (Vol. 15, No. 3, December 1998), and Funston, John. 'ASEAN: Out of its Depths', *Contemporary Southeast Asia.* (Vol. 20, No. 3, April 1998), pp. 22–37.
46 This idea was later on expanded within the ASEAN plus Three (APT) framework in the establishment of the APT early warning systems. See the Asian Development Bank *Asian Economic Monitor,* July 2002, p. 24.
47 Stubbs, Richard. 'ASEAN Plus Three: Emerging East Asian Regionalism?', *Asian Survey.* (Vol. 42, No. 3, 2002), p. 449.
48 Gyohten, Toyoo. 'East Asian Initiative Needed in Crises', *Institute for International Monetary Affairs Newsletters.* (No. 6, 1999), p. 7 (English translation).
49 Webber, Douglas. 'Two Funerals and a Wedding? The Ups and Down of Regionalism in East Asia and Asia-Pacific after the Asian Crisis', *The Pacific Review.* (Vol. 14, No. 3, 2001), p. 340.
50 For more on this see: Thomas, Nicholas. 'Developing a Regional Economic Community in East Asia', in Curley, Melissa and Nicholas Thomas (eds). *Advancing East Asian Regionalism.* (London: RoutledgeCurzon, 2007), pp. 137–157
51 See: *Chairman's Press Statement of the Seventh ASEAN+3 Foreign Ministers Meeting.* (Kuala Lumpur: 26 July 2006). http://www.aseansec.org/18579.htm. Accessed 10 December 2007. The text was slightly altered for grammatical purposes.
52 *The Joint Ministerial Meeting of the 8th ASEAN+3 Finance Ministers' Meeting.* (Istanbul: 4 May 2005). http://www.aseansec.org/17448.htm. Accessed 10 December 2007.
53 See: *The Joint Ministerial Statement of the 9th ASEAN+3 Finance Ministers' Meeting.* (Hyderabad: 4 May 2006). http://www.aseansec.org/18390.htm. Accessed 10 December 2007.
54 See: *Joint Ministerial Statement of the 11th ASEAN Finance Ministers' Meeting.* (Thailand: Chiang Mai, 5 April 2007). http://www.aseansec.org/20471.htm. Accessed 20 April 2008.
55 Hew, Denis and Mely C. Anthony. 'ASEAN and ASEAN+3 in Post Crisis Asia', *NIRA Review.* (Vol. 7, No. 4, Autumn 2000), pp. 21–26.
56 Dieter, Heribert and Richard Higgott. 'Exploring Alternative Theories of Economic Regionalism: From Trade to Finance in Asian Cooperation', *Working Paper No. 89/02.* (University of Warwick: Centre for the Study of Globalisation and Regionalism, 2002), p. 2.
57 Hamilton-Hart, Natasha. 'Cooperation on Money and Finance: How Important? How Likely?', in Kanishka Jayasuriya (ed.). *Governing the Asia Pacific: Beyond the 'New Regionalism.* (London: Palgrave Macmillan, 2004), p. 96.
58 See: *Towards and East Asian Community: Region of Peace, Prosperity and Progress.* East Asian Vision Group Report 2001. p. 3.
59 Ibid. p. 18.
60 Ibid. pp. 10–11. See also: East Asia Study Group. *Final Report of the East Asia Study Group.* (Phnom Penh: 4 November 2002), pp. 20–21.
61 'Rafidah to Open Inaugural East Asian Business Council Meeting', *Bernama,* 12 April 2004.
62 For example: Terada, Takashi. 'Constructing an 'East Asian' Concept and Growing Regional Identity: From EAEC to ASEAN+3', *The Pacific Review.* (Vol. 16, No. 2, 2003), pp. 251–277, and Stubbs, Richard. 'ASEAN Plus Three: Emerging East Asian Regionalism?', *Asian Survey.* (Vol. 42, No. 3, 2002), pp. 440–455.
63 See: *ASEAN SG Hails Completion of the Signing of the ASEAN-Japan Comprehensive Economic Partnership Agreement.* 15 April 2008. http://www.aseansec.org/21471.htm. Accessed 21 April 2008.
64 Mahathir, Mohamed. 'Towards an Integrated East Asia Community', *Keynote Address at the Second East Asia Forum.* (Kuala Lumpur: 6 December 2004). http://www.aseansec.org/16952.htm. Accessed 11 December 2007.

65 See: Hettne, Björn 'Globalisation and the New Regionalism: The Second Great Transformation', in Björn Hettne, András Inotia and Osvaldo Sunkel (eds). *Globalism and the New Regionalism*. (London: Macmillan, 1999), pp. 1–24.
66 See *Chairman's Statement of the 11th ASEAN Summit on 'One Vision, One Identity, One Community'*. http://www.aseansec.org/18040.htm. Accessed 11 December 2007.
67 For a summary on the conceptualisation and establishment of APA, see: Caballero-Anthony, Mely. 'Non-State Regional Governance Mechanism for Economic Security: The Case of the ASEAN People's Assembly', *The Pacific Review*. (Vol. 17, No. 4, 2004), pp. 567–585.
68 Hernandez, Carolina. *A People's Assembly: A Novel Mechanism for Bridging the North-South Divide in ASEAN*. (Unpublished manuscript, 2002), pp. 10–11.
69 Ibid. p. 8.
70 See *Second APA Report: Challenges Facing the ASEAN People*. (Jakarta: Center for Strategic and International Studies, 2003), pp. 5–7.
71 Carolina G. Hernandez, 'Towards an ASEAN Human Rights Scorecard: A Concept Paper and Proposal', March 2003, cited in Kraft, Herman. 'Assessing Human Rights in Southeast Asia: The Need for an Instrument', presented at the 11th ASEAN-ISIS Colloquium on Human Rights, 12–13 February 2004. I am grateful to Herman Kraft for sharing this information with me.
72 *Vientiane Plan of Action*, 2004, p. 7.
73 The idea of having an ASEAN Charter, however, is not new. According to a Malaysian senior official at the Foreign Ministry, the idea was first articulated at the 7th ASEAN Ministerial Meeting in 1974; however, at that time, it was considered to run counter to the ASEAN practice of informal, flexible processes as well as its principles of consensus. See Karuppanna, Ilango. *The ASEAN Community and ASEAN Charter: Toward a New ASEAN*. (Manuscript, 2005).
74 The EPG is composed of 10 representatives from each of the ASEAN member countries and chaired by Musa Hitam, who is the former Deputy Prime of Malaysia and Chairman of Malaysia's Human Rights Commission (*Suaram*).
75 See *Chairman's Statement of the 11th ASEAN Summit on 'One Vision, One Identity, One Community'*. http://www.aseansec.org/18040.htm. Accessed 10 December 2007.
76 See, 'ASEAN Civil Society Speaks Out', *JustWord E-com*. http://www.just-internaional.org/commentary/E%20News%20Jan%2006.htm. Accessed 10 April 2006. The Asian Civil Society Conference brings together a number of civil society groups in the region and is coordinated by the Universiti Institut Teknologi Mara (UiTM), Malaysia.
77 See *Statement of the ASEAN Civil Society Conference to the 11th ASEAN Summit*, reproduced in http://www.focusweb.org/content/view/774/27/. Accessed 27 July 2006.
78 Prior to this was the regular convening of the ASEAN Peoples' Assembly (APA), which was established in 2000 (see note 49).
79 'SAPA core group spearheads coming strategies in engaging ASEAN'. http://www.forum-asia.org/news/in_the_news/10Apr06_sapa.shtml. Accessed 25 July 2006.
80 *ASEAN-ISIS Memorandum No. 1, The ASEAN Charter*, 18 April 2006.
81 See *Framing the ASEAN Charter: An ISEAS Perspective*. (Singapore: Institute of Southeast Asian Studies, 2005).
82 See 'Charter to protect workers in ASEAN', *The Star*, 5 December 2005.
83 See *Report of the Eminent Persons Group on the ASEAN Charter*, 30 December 2006, p. 2. http://www.aseansec.org. Accessed 25 July 2006.
84 Ibid. p. 4.

85 *Statement by ASEAN Chair, Singapore's Minister for Foreign Affairs George Yeo.* (New York: 27 September 2007). http://www.aseansec.org/20976.htm. Accessed 29 November 2007.
86 Wanandi, Jusuf. 'ASEAN's Charter: Does a mediocre document really matter?', *The Jakarta Post*, 26 November 2007.
87 For more on the Big 'C' versus little 'c' variants of regional communities see: Thomas, Nicholas. 'ASEAN+3: C/community building in East Asia?', *Journal of International and Area Studies.* (Vol. 8, No. 2, December 2001), pp. 1–19.
88 See: *Chairman's Statement of the First East Asia Summit.* (Kuala Lumpur: 14 December 2005).
89 See: Tanaka, Hitoshi. 'The ASEAN+3 and East Asia Summit: A Two-Tiered Approach to Community Building', *East Asia Insights.* (No. 1, Tokyo: Japan Center for International Exchange, January 2006).

3 Japan and regional governance in East Asia

Expanding involvement, stagnated influence?

Hidetaka Yoshimatsu

Introduction

Globalisation is one of the most conspicuous phenomena in the current international world. Growing linkages through enhanced flows of trade, capital and foreign direct investment have linked economies and societies in various parts of the world. Globalisation has also produced socio-political problems that a single state is usually unable to resolve unilaterally. Given this situation, the state frequently needs to resolve such problems in collaboration with other states and non-state actors, including intergovernmental organisations (IGOs) and non-governmental organisations (NGOs). Further, the types of networks, institutions and norms required to yield a positive outcome necessitate a different way of governing problems, one that draws in a range of different actors and different levels of domestic and international society. This is a reason why the governance paradigm has emerged as a critical policy tool in international society as well as in various regions, including Europe, North America and East Asia.

While Europe and North America developed certain forms of regional governance, Asia-Pacific, including East Asia was regarded as 'pre-governance'.[1] This characterisation of East Asia derives partly from attitudes of leading states in the region. For a long time, Japan, the major economic power in the region, did not show meaningful leadership in developing regional cohesion and regional governance in East Asia. Since the late 1990s, however, the Japanese government has proposed various schemes and programmes designed to consolidate a regional grouping and promote cooperation within the group. Policy areas where Japan has been involved have expanded from financial and economic cooperation to environmental, agricultural and energy fields.

There are three key questions that must be considered in any study of Japan's recent attempts to develop collective mechanisms and programmes to manage political, economic and social affairs in East Asia. In what areas has Japan made substantial commitments to the development of regionalism and regional cooperation? How are the major aspects of governance reflected in such commitments? What problems are found in Japan's undertaking in regional affairs in terms of governance formation? This chapter seeks to suggest possible answers to each of these questions.

In seeking answers to these questions, this chapter advances two core propositions. First, that Japan has intensified its involvements in the development of regionalism in policy fields represented by financial/monetary management, food security and environmental protection, and that such involvements have contributed to the sprouting of regional governance in East Asia. Second, that Japan's engagements are still weak in terms of governance formation, largely because of weak coordination among government agencies, underdeveloped perception of governance ideals, and the growing geopolitical nature of its regional policies. Before examining Japan's concrete activities for regionalism and regional governance, the chapter first reviews the literature on regionalism and governance and identifies the major elements of regional governance.

Regionalism, regional governance and East Asia

The objective of this chapter is to link Japan's roles and commitments in East Asia to the development of regionalism and regional governance in the region. To realise this objective, it is necessary to understand what is meant by the terms regionalism and governance. Regionalism can be defined as 'cooperation among governments or non-government organisations in three or more geographically proximate and inter-dependent countries for the pursuit of mutual gain in one or more issue-areas'.[2] The essence of regionalism becomes clear in comparison with regionalisation. Regionalisation is the undirected and autonomous economic processes that lead to higher levels of economic interdependence within a given geographical area.[3] In the case of regionalism, emphasis is given to 'political' aspects, where government policies and formal institutions lead the development of interdependence and cohesion within a given geographical area.

In East Asia, the development of regionalism has lagged far behind Europe and North America. However, moves towards regionalism have gathered momentum since the late 1990s. The first summit of the Association of Southeast Asian Nations (ASEAN) with China, Japan and South Korea (ASEAN+3) took place in December 1997, to celebrate ASEAN's thirtieth anniversary and to discuss collective responses to the Asian financial crisis. At the Second ASEAN+3 (APT) Summit in 1998, the East Asia Vision Group (EAVG) was established, accepting a proposal by South Korean President Kim Dae-jung to develop a coherent blueprint for advancing East Asian regionalism.[4] The APT summits have since developed as a comprehensive forum to discuss political, economic, social and security issues in the region. In the Joint Statement on East Asia Cooperation, issued at the conclusion of the third summit in 1999, member states advocated cooperation bringing together Northeast and Southeast Asia in political–security areas as well as in economic and social fields.

Cooperation under the APT framework has expanded to encompass an ever-widening range, from major policy areas to functional issue areas. The finance ministers of the region held the first APT finance ministers' meeting in April 1999. The first meeting of APT economic ministers was held in May 2000, while that of foreign ministers was organised two months later. The APT countries organised the first ministerial meeting in functional issue areas in succession: for agriculture in October 2001; for tourism in January 2002; for environment in November 2002; for energy in June 2004; and for telecommunications and information technology in August 2004. By the end of 2007, cooperation under the APT framework showed steady progress to cover sixteen sectors and have forty-eight mechanisms to facilitate and implement cooperative initiatives, with a new set of four sectors ('rural development and poverty eradication, disaster management, minerals and women issues') being advanced from 2008 onwards.[5]

While regionalism has gradually gained momentum in East Asia, this fact does not necessarily mean that regional governance has developed concurrently. Governance is a vague concept, with various definitions. A notable definition is provided by the Commission on Global Governance: 'the sum of the many ways individuals and institutions, public and private, manage their common affairs. It is a continuing process through which conflicting or diverse interests may be accommodated and cooperative action may be taken.'[6] Some scholars put emphasis on authority, referring governance to 'spheres of authority at all levels of human activity that amount to systems of rule in which goals are pursued through the exercise of control'.[7] Others stress the collective nature of governance, as exemplified by a definition: 'the processes and institutions, both formal and informal, that guide and restrain the collective activities of a group'.[8]

Regional governance is the regionalised dimension of governance. Deriving the essences from the above definitions, it is possible to consider regional governance as the processes that manage common regional affairs and draw cooperative action through formal institutions and informal mechanisms created at the regional level. Since regions are socially constructed entities, a particular region has a multitude of ideas, regionalisation strategies and modes of governance.[9] In this respect, Payne characterises Asia-Pacific as a mode of 'pre-governance', a market-driven form of regionalism which lacks the multilevel regional policy networks associated with Europe and the 'hub and spoke' characteristics of North American governance.[10]

As touched upon in the two previous chapters, an understanding of major elements of regional governance is a prerequisite in evaluating a state's commitments to the development of regional governance. Although the articulation of regional governance is different from that of either national governance or global governance, nonetheless there are significant similarities between the three levels.[11] Accordingly, it is possible to draw the elements of regional governance from the overall character of governance. This chapter will highlight three elements of regional governance: norms, actors and mechanisms.

In realising governance at the regional level, it is particularly important to encompass a set of socio-political norms with universal character. These norms include equity and equality, social justice and sustainability. The maintenance of equity and social justice has become a critical issue in the current international setting that is characterised by neo-liberal globalisation. Neo-liberal globalisation has advanced market liberalisation for efficient functions and level playing-field competition, leaving the maintenance of equity and justice in society and sustainable development out of the main agenda. Accordingly, regional governance supports not only norms where there is adherence across the region but also those socio-political norms whose attainment is desirable but which have otherwise become difficult to achieve through efforts at the individual national level.

The realisation of socio-political norms has much to do with the issue of which actors are involved in governance formation. A distinctive feature of governance is the sustaining coordination and coherence among a wide variety of actors with different purposes and objectives. What previously were indisputably roles of government have been increasingly seen as issues of the 'commons' that involve commitments by both state and non-state actors.[12] Thus, governance goes beyond traditional notions of government or formal public authority by relaxing the boundaries between the state and society or between the public and private sectors. Indeed, states remain vital and active participants in regional public affairs, but they are no longer the only actors who initiate policies, nor do they necessarily dominate the resulting processes of public affairs. Various non-state actors such as IGOs, NGOs, and subnational governments have an important role to play in creating governance structures at the regional level.[13]

Equally important is that the relationships between the state and non-state actors in the process of governance formation are not confined to vertical, hierarchical structures in which non-state actors comply with the directives of states. Their relationships are embedded into horizontal networks in which mutually interdependent state and non-state actors collaborate in pursuing common desired ends. Moreover, at the regional level such networks may cross state boundaries, creating transnational coalitions of interest.

The third element is the mechanisms by which the development of regional governance is realised. A key aspect of these mechanisms is the way in which they seek to regulate social, economic and political risk rather than simply through a redistribution of resources. Previously, governments developed mechanisms for allocating resources through direct intervention. However, the globalised economy requires increasing regulations and harmonisation of domestic affairs in a wide range of issue areas, from economics and finance through to social or environmental issues.[14] A rules-based form of governance is necessary for making regulation and harmonisation effective and transparent. In the process of achieving such rules-based governance, the depoliticisation of economic and social management needs to be advanced by reducing the discretionary nature and raising transparency and accountability in policy formation. Furthermore, regional projects need to compensate for the institutional weaknesses at the domestic level that disturb the development of states' regulatory capacities.[15]

In brief, socio-political norms and mechanisms of equity and social justice are key ingredients in the formation of regional governance, and the participation of actors other than states plays a meaningful role in this pursuit. Furthermore, rule-based regulatory systems support and maintain the process of governance formation. An important point in governance formation within a region is that a particular state often leads this process. In North America, the United States is a typical example. In Latin America, Brazil, the regional hub state, has propelled and defined the system of governance.[16] In East Asia, Japan's relative influence vis-à-vis China declined, due to a protracted economic slump in the 1990s and its awkward attitudes towards regional leadership. However, Japan, which still accounts for two-thirds of the entire gross domestic product (GDP) in East Asia, retains significant capabilities to promote institution building in the region and mobilise resources for this objective. In the following section, the ways in which Japan has committed to the development of regionalism and regional governance are examined, with a focus on three elements of governance: rules-based regulatory systems, the participation of non-state actors, and the pursuit of socio-political norms.

Japan and rules-based regional governance

As discussed in the previous chapter, the 1997 Asian financial crisis was a key incident that urged leaders in East Asia to develop collective initiatives for closer regional cohesion. The East Asian countries have subsequently advanced regional monetary and financial cooperation as a way of preventing a recurrence of the financial crisis, with a set of formal institutions and rules gradually developed in support of this objective.

At the second APT finance ministers' meeting in May 2000, the ministers announced the Chiang Mai Initiative (CMI). The initiative aimed to provide liquidity support to member countries that faced short-run balance of payment deficits, through an extension of the existing ASEAN swap arrangements and the development of a network of bilateral swap agreements (BSAs) that included Japan, China and South Korea. The BSA networks under the CMI have developed rapidly. The number of the BSAs increased from eight in July 2002 to sixteen by April 2005, while the cumulative value grew from US$17 billion to US$75 billion between July 2002 and May 2006.[17] In order to supplement the BSAs, the East Asian financial authorities began to deliberate on the fostering of the Asian bond market. Its objective was to enable the private and public sectors to raise and invest long-term capital without currency and maturity risks. In October 2002, then

Thai Prime Minister Thaksin Shinawatra formally proposed an idea of fostering the Asian bond market, and other governments supported it. In June 2003, the central banks and monetary authorities of eleven Asian and Oceanian countries set up the Asian Bond Fund (ABF1), which invested in dollar-denominated bonds. In May 2005, they agreed to launch Asian Bond Fund II (ABF2), which would invest in local currency-denominated bonds. This is discussed in greater detail in Chapter 10.

A critical cause of the Asian financial crisis lay in the fact that East Asia had not developed effective surveillance mechanisms for monetary and financial affairs. Learning from this bitter experience, the East Asian countries began to develop feasible economic and financial review systems collectively. At the fourth APT finance ministers' meeting in May 2001, the ministers agreed to exchange data on capital flows bilaterally on a voluntary basis to facilitate effective policy dialogues. Moreover, the APT members have institutionalised economic reviews and policy dialogues at the ministers' level annually and at the deputies' level twice a year to discuss economic and financial developments in the region. These systems are designed to ensure the early detection of irregularities in the region's economies, coupled with the implementation of remedial policies and actions.

At the eighth APT finance ministers' meeting, in May 2005, several important agreements were reached. First, the ministers agreed to integrate APT economic surveillance into the CMI framework. This change was intended to allow for the quick detection of problems through the development of effective regional surveillance capabilities. Second, the ministers agreed to establish a collective decision-making mechanism of BSAs. This was a first step towards multilateralisation, so that the relevant BSAs would be activated collectively and promptly in case of emergency. They also agreed to study further routes towards multilateralising the CMI. This meant that the CMI would be a more rules-based, institutionalised system, including the establishment of a secretariat to conduct regional economic surveillance and to set up criteria for activating the CMI. Third, the ministers agreed to revise the drawdown mechanism. They paid due attention to the CMI's character to supplement the existing international financial arrangements. At the same time, the size of swaps that could be withdrawn without the IMF-sponsored programme would be increased from the previous 10 per cent to 20 per cent. Given that the previously held high link to the IMF-supported programme was regarded as a retreat from an Asian attempt to increase its autonomy in financial affairs, this change had vital implications for the distinction of the regional from the global.

Since the May 2005 meeting, the region's finance ministers have been seeking to consolidate the gains that have been made since the 1997 crisis, as well as exploring new forms of financial cooperation. The 2006 meeting was notable for its decision to launch a Group of Experts and a Technical Working Group on Economic and Financial Monitoring (ETWG) to act 'as an independent economic assessment vehicle for this region' as well as a new deputy finance ministers' taskforce to consider ways to create a post-CMI 'advanced framework of the regional liquidity support arrangement'.[18] The 2007 meeting of the APT finance ministers sought to increase regional financial resilience by fast-tracking various financial sectors that were considered more open to reform as well as advance cooperation in taxation matters.[19] With the financial shocks presented by the sub-prime crisis and the rising costs of staple foods in 2008, the finance ministers acted to accelerate the liberalisation of financial services in a bid to continue to make ASEAN an attractive region for foreign direct investment.[20]

In addition to the CMI, Japan has been deeply involved in the development of other forms of financial architecture in East Asia. The CMI was the first achievement of APT cooperation with substantial institutional frameworks. Interestingly, it was unclear who took the political lead in creating the CMI. However, behind the scenes there is no doubt that the initiative was Japan's. Japan had already concluded BSAs with South Korea and Malaysia as a part of the New Miyazawa Initiative, and proposed to expand and combine agreements among East Asian countries.[21] The Japanese Ministry of Finance (MOF) undertook informal negotiations to gain explicit support from the United States. While the US government adamantly opposed the Asian Monetary Fund in autumn 1997, it did not object to the CMI. This was partly because Washington recognised the need for regional facilities as measures to prevent the recurrence of the disruptive 1997 financial crisis. At the same time, the MOF successfully lobbied Washington about its merits. A senior MOF official recalled that at the time it was tough to convince Washington that the initiative would be completely different from the AMF.[22]

The MOF has made efforts to create viable surveillance mechanisms in East Asia. When the APT finance ministers agreed to exchange data on capital flows bilaterally in May 2001, Japan concluded an agreement for this objective with five countries (Indonesia, South Korea, the Philippines, Thailand and Vietnam). In order to facilitate this process, the MOF established the Japan–ASEAN Financial Technical Assistance Fund under the ASEAN Secretariat in September 2001. The fund was intended to assist ASEAN members to improve their monitoring, collection and reporting systems on capital flows. Furthermore, the MOF sent its bureaucrats and other specialists in finance to several Southeast Asian countries under the auspices of the New Miyazawa Initiative. These specialists, dispatched to the central bank or finance ministry in the recipient countries, offered assistance and guidance to develop human resources regarding financial and fiscal policies as well as government bond management and other areas.[23]

The second area where Japan has contributed to the creation of a regional, rules-based governance structure is in agriculture. In this area, East Asian countries have gradually developed institutions and rules designed to promote food security in the region. The formal initiative for this objective was launched at the first meeting of the ASEAN Ministers on Agriculture and

Forestry (AMAF) +3 in October 2001. At that meeting, the ministers agreed to begin studying specific cooperation under the APT framework to alleviate poverty and strengthen food security in East Asia. They agreed to task Thailand to coordinate a study on the East Asian rice reserve system and to coordinate the improvement of the ASEAN Food Security Information System (AFSIS).[24]

In December 2001, a study team on the rice reserve system began to conduct the review on rice reserves in the APT countries. The results of the study were discussed at the Technical Meeting on Rice Reserve (TMRR), gatherings of directors-general of relevant government agencies, which were held three times between April and October 2002. One of the recommendations put forward by the TMRR was to undertake a three-year pilot project of the potential of an East Asia rice reserve system, prior to the establishment of the East Asia Emergency Rice Reserve (EAERR).[25] The proposal to conduct the pilot project was approved at the third AMAF+3 meeting in October 2003, and the pilot project began in early 2004. The project showed significant progress in developing a rules-based system by formulating the protocols for the release of EAERR stocks as well as the criteria for the utilisation of national rice stocks earmarked for the ASEAN Emergency Rice Reserve (AERR) under the EAERR scheme.[26] Moreover, a secretariat of the EAERR was set up at Bangkok in 2004 in order to manage the pilot project and coordinate various social development activities.[27] Although the secretariat was a small body, its establishment had critical meaning as a development to implement ministers' agreement through the institutional system.

As for AFSIS, the agricultural ministers approved ASEAN's proposal for the establishment of the AFSIS project at the second AMAF+3 meeting in October 2002.[28] The AFSIS project will facilitate food security planning, implementation, monitoring and evaluation for the APT countries through the systematic collection, analysis and dissemination of food security data and information. The project, started in January 2003, consisted of two main components: human resource development and information network system development. The ASEAN Food Security Information and Training (AFSIT) Centre was established under the Thai Ministry of Agriculture and Cooperatives as the secretariat of the AFSIS project.[29]

The Japanese government has sustained the region's efforts to establish a feasible food security system from its initial conceptualisation. Although a formal agreement to consider the rice reserve system in East Asia was reached at the AMAF+3 meeting in October 2001, prior consultation was conducted under Japan's strategic initiative. In Japan, a study group of the international food stockholding framework was established in April 2001 as an advisory body to the head of the Food Agency. The group aimed to develop a new international food stockholding framework from that which the Japanese government had proposed during the WTO agricultural negotiations in December 2000. The Japanese government regarded regional cooperation to strengthen the AERR as the first step towards the creation of an international food stockholding scheme. In April 2001, cooperation on rice reserves was discussed at a senior officials' meeting of the AMAF+3, and the Thai government reported the current state of rice reserves in East Asia. Three months later, the ASEAN Workshop on Food Security Cooperation was held in Thailand. The participants recommended that a feasibility study should be undertaken on the creation of a new rice reserve system in East Asia so as to improve and reinforce the AERR framework. During this process, Japan and Thailand took the lead in assisting other countries' recognition of food security as a common regional issue.[30]

After the AMAF+3 meeting decided on a study on the East Asia rice reserve system, the Japanese government extended cooperation with Thailand through the Japan International Cooperation Agency (JICA). JICA commenced a survey on project research in January 2002, and conducted the Development Study on an East Asia/ASEAN Rice Reserve System from May to November 2002. The discussions at the TMRR had been undertaken in accordance with the progress of the study.[31] JICA also provided Thailand with personnel and with technical assistance in organising the TMRR. The mechanisms for the EAERR reflected recommendations in the final report of the survey. Importantly, due consideration was paid to the harmonisation with the existing international rules and systems in establishing the EAERR mechanisms. For instance, the harmonisation with the 'Principles of Surplus Disposal' of the Food and Agriculture Organisation (FAO) was emphasised as a basic tenet for the EAERR.[32]

At the Seventh AMAF+3 meeting in late 2007, Japan was again active in supporting the further development of the EAERR as well as the second phase of the AFSIS project.[33] However, the global and (particularly) regional shortfall in rice and other staple goods in early 2008 suggested that, even though East Asian states were committed to developing new mechanisms, they were not yet ready to implement them in full.

The Japanese government has also engaged in the development of the AFSIS project. Although Thailand coordinated the project, it was funded by the Japanese Ministry of Agriculture, Forestry and Fisheries. The AFSIS project has been conducted in close collaboration with other Japan-funded projects such as an FAO regional project 'Strengthening Regional Data Exchange System on Food and Agricultural Statistics in Asia and Pacific Countries' and a JICA project 'Agricultural Statistics and Economic Analysis Development', which ran for six years (2001–2007).[34] JICA has also assisted human resources development by organising, for example, a Seminar for the Directors-General of Agricultural Statistics and Information in ASEAN in January 2003.

These examples serve to briefly highlight the ways in which Japan works to foster regional governance at the state level. Despite the fact that it does not necessarily assume an obvious leadership position, Japan nonetheless plays a key role in developing regional mechanisms and norms. In the first case, Japan was the core actor but opted for a low-key approach. In the second case, Japan again played a significant role in terms of providing essential resources to realise programme objectives, but again opted for another partner to be seen as the leader. This is a frequently observed aspect of Japan's regional relations, with the development role often in conjunction with another regional state (such as Thailand) or organisation (such as ASEAN), although in certain cases it also partners with international organisations operating in a regional context. However, as noted earlier, the construction of regional governance involves actors beyond the state sector. Japan's collaboration with these non-state actors is the subject of the next section.

Governance and the role of non-state actors

Some of Japan's commitments to regionalism and governance formation in East Asia have been sustained by close collaboration with non-state actors. While this collaboration includes a wide range of issues, two areas where this work is most noticeable are the regional economic and environmental governance sectors, encompassing Track-Two networks, subnational agencies and non-governmental organisations.

In the process of advancing monetary and financial architectures, for example, the Japanese Ministry of Finance has sought to develop institutional mechanisms and rules in close collaboration with research institutes. In partnership with the Institute for International Monetary Affairs (IIMA) and the Asia Development Bank (ADB) Institute, the MOF has organised various research projects concerning the Asian economies and the development of regional financial cooperation.[35] This trilateral cooperation has been expanded into a regional network as these institutes developed relationships with their counterparts in other Asian countries, deepening ideas about desirable economic development and management for the region. An example of this was seen when the ADB Institute took the lead in establishing the Asian Policy Forum in December 1999. The forum, comprising seventeen Asian research institutes, aimed to provide intellectual and analytical leadership in Asian economic policy communities. The MOF also proposed the establishment of the ASEAN+3 Research Group at an informal APT Finance and Central Bank Deputies' meeting in November 2002, and its establishment was agreed upon during the sixth APT finance ministers' meeting in August 2003. This group aimed to explore tangible measures to strengthen financial cooperation and promote financial stability in the region by soliciting academic inputs from researchers and research institutes in the APT countries.

The outcomes of the discussions at these academic forums have influenced the development of monetary and financial cooperation in East Asia. As already explained, an idea of fostering the Asian bond market was formally proposed by Thai Prime Minister Thaksin in October 2002. However, the importance of fostering the Asia-based bond market was also discussed at the Asian Policy Forum. In October 2001, the Asian Policy Forum issued a policy report entitled *Policy Recommendations for Designing New and Balanced Financial Market Structures in Post-Crisis Asia*. One of recommendations in the report was the fostering of corporate bond markets. Kanit Sangsubhan, a senior official of the Thai Ministry of Finance and an advocate of the Asian bond market, was involved in activities of the Asian Policy Forum,[36] an example of where networks and actors overlap to support the creation of new institutions designed to foster regional economic governance.

Some of the agreements reached at the eighth APT finance ministers' meeting in May 2005 were based on recommendations by the APT Research Group. In 2004, the group released two reports: *Towards a Regional Financial Architecture for East Asia* and *An Exchange Rate Arrangement for East Asia*. The former report was based on research conducted by IIMA, the Korea Institute for International Economic Policy (KIEP), the Chinese Academy of Social Sciences (CASS), the Thailand Development Research Institute (TDRI), and the Indonesian Danareksa Research Institute (IDRI).[37] The report recommended that arrangements under the CMI should be revised so as to strengthen their effectiveness and that surveillance and financial assistance should be coordinated under an APT institution.[38]

Another field where Japan has promoted the formation of regional governance in collaboration with non-state actors is that of environmental protection. A first major initiative to conserve regional environments in Northeast Asia was the creation of the Northeast Asian Conference on Environmental Cooperation (NEAC). The NEAC's first meeting was held in Niigata, Japan in 1992, and an annual meeting has been organised for information exchange and policy dialogue between China, Japan, South Korea, Mongolia and Russia. The NEAC has been attended by environmental experts from relevant national government agencies, local governments, research institutes and NGOs of the participant countries. The NEAC has also been joined by observers from United Nations-related agencies including the United Nations Environment Programme (UNEP), the United Nations Development Programme (UNDP), and the United Nations Economic and Social Committee for the Asia and the Pacific (UNESCAP).

Japan's undertakings in environmental protection were seen in broader East Asian initiatives. Between 1993 and 1997, the Japanese Environment Agency hosted a series of meetings on trans-boundary air pollution, inviting experts from nine countries (China, South Korea, Mongolia, Russia, Indonesia, Malaysia, the Philippines, Singapore and Thailand). In 1998, on the basis of these meetings, the agency successfully persuaded participants to form the Acid Deposition Monitoring Network in East Asia (EANET), comprising thirteen countries in Northeast and Southeast Asia.[39] The aim of the EANET is to stimulate regional efforts for environmental sustainability and the protection of human health by monitoring acid deposition in participating countries in line with standardised monitoring guidelines and technical manuals.

The EANET has undertaken its activities in close collaboration with non-state actors. Its secretariat was transferred to the UNEP's regional office in Bangkok in 2002. The participating research institutes have used shared guidelines and technical manuals to compile and evaluate data on acid deposition collected at national monitoring sites. Moreover, the EANET's operations have been supplemented by the Model Inter-Comparisons of Long Range Transport and Sulphur Deposition in East Asia (MICS-Asia), which was co-funded by the International Institute for Applied System Analysis located in Austria and the Central Research Institute of the Electric Power Industry of Japan.[40] Interestingly, the EANET is also proving to be a window into Japan's views on the norms for regional governance. At the EANET's Ninth Session of the Intergovernmental Meeting in November 2007, Japan argued for targets to remain non-binding, while Russia led an argument for legally binding instruments so as to assure the organisation's financial basis. This argument divided the group, although in the end the matter was referred back to the Secretariat without immediate resolution.[41]

A critical feature of Japan's involvement in environmental conservation is the role subnational governments have played in establishing a basis for regional cooperation. A typical example can be found in environmental cooperation between China and Japan. When then Japanese Prime Minister Ryutaro Hashimoto made a formal visit to China in September 1997, Hashimoto and Premier Li Peng reached an agreement on Japan–China Environmental Cooperation for the Twenty-First Century. One of two projects in this cooperation was to establish model cities in China to promote environmental protection, with the cities of Dalian, Chongqing and Guiyang being selected.[42] Japanese municipalities then took the cooperation further through sister-city programmes.

One of these programmes was undertaken by Kitakyushu city, which has promoted cooperation with Dalian. When Chinese state councillor Song Jian visited Kitakyushu in December 1993, the city proposed the Dalian Environmental Demonstration Zone Project as a pilot project to disseminate successful outcomes throughout China. The following year, this project was selected as a priority project by the Chinese State Environmental Protection Administration. Kitakyushu city drafted an Environmental Master Plan for Dalian, and successfully encouraged the Japanese government to make the plan a part of an official development assistance (ODA) project. The ODA project, jointly implemented by JICA and Kitakyushu city from December 1996 to March 2000, evaluated Dalian's environmental conditions from various aspects, such as technologies, administrative operations and city planning. The utilisation of ODA funds for a project initiated by a subnational government implied a new direction for Japan's development assistance.[43]

Another example of subnational cooperation can be seen between Hiroshima and Chongqing. The two cities signed a friendship agreement in 1986 and began environmental cooperation in 1990. Hiroshima city implemented various activities, including the dispatch of technical advisors, hosting of trainees and the implementation of joint research projects. In an expansion of these ties Hiroshima prefecture and Sichuan province (where Chongqing is located) have also begun the Sichuan Province Joint Environmental Protection Project. Hiroshima, Hiroshima prefecture, Sichuan province and Chongqing jointly established the Research and Communication Centre for Acid Rain Research in 1993. The centre has implemented research and monitoring of acid rain and searched for prevention mechanisms.

Japan's cooperative activities in the development of economic and environmental architecture have the potential to lead to the formation of multi-level regional governance, in which the national government becomes one in a broad set of actors operating at different levels, from the local to the regional or international. Multilevel governance in Europe has contributed to the steady development of regional integration and improvement of livelihood of local communities.[44] However, unlike Europe, East Asia lacks a formal supranational organisation that constitutes a coordinating hub for multilevel governance processes. Nevertheless, this has not impeded the formation of governance structures in East Asia. Subnational government actors and other non-state actors have implemented cooperative projects designed to create a feedback loop of knowledge and processes to enhance economic stability and environmental conservation, drawing in support from national government agencies and IGOs. Many of these projects occur within a geographical location conterminous with the APT group, further fostering a sense of regional identity but allowing for the development of extraregional ties. If these activities are systematically coordinated, there is a high possibility for the emergence of feasible governance in economic and environmental affairs.

Japan's regional norms – equity and social justice

In the new millennium, the Japanese government has shown a greater interest in promoting equity and social justice, paying consideration to poverty alleviation, social development and economic disparity among East Asian countries. A notable initiative in this respect was the establishment of the Japan Fund for Poverty Reduction (JFPR) under the ADB in May 2000, with an initial contribution of US$90 million.[45] The JFPR aimed to support well-targeted activities for poverty reduction and social development and to stimulate the self-help capacity of the poor and broad stakeholder participation at the community level. As of December 2007, approved JFPR grants amounted to US$274.5 million, with a total of 107 projects.[46] The JFPR has been used for various projects for improvement in social development and poverty eradication. For example, projects in Indonesia have piloted creative schemes for community-based school management as well as improvements in the quality of education. Another project – this time in the Philippines –

promoted strategic private sector partnerships for urban poverty reduction that helped to provide poor communities with basic urban services and risk-prevention programmes against fires, floods and typhoons.[47]

The Japanese Ministry of Foreign Affairs (MOFA) embarked on a distinctive programme for poverty issues: the Initiative for Development in East Asia (IDEA). Japanese Prime Minister Junichiro Koizumi announced this initiative during his visit to Southeast Asia in January 2002. The IDEA aimed to review development experiences utilising ODA in East Asia and to share expertise and lessons for the further development of the region. In August 2002, MOFA held a ministerial-level meeting for the IDEA in Tokyo. At that meeting, the participants stressed the need to pay more attention to low-income regions with problems of poverty and income disparity in East Asia, and confirmed that the realisation and enhancement of good governance would be a major challenge to the stability and sound economic development of the region.

The Japanese government's emphasis on poverty and social development can also be seen in its partnership with ASEAN to narrow development gaps between member states. When ASEAN finally achieved its goal of representing all ten Southeast Asian states in the late 1990s, the region faced the challenge of addressing socio-economic disparities between the four newer members (Cambodia, Laos, Myanmar and Vietnam – CLMV) and the older and wealthier states.[48] Accordingly, Singaporean Prime Minister Goh Chok Tong proposed the Initiative for ASEAN Integration (IAI) at the fourth informal ASEAN Summit in November 2000. The IAI is designed to narrow the developmental divide between ASEAN members by promoting equitable economic development and alleviating poverty in the CLMV states. In order to attain these objectives, the old members set up various projects for human resource development and technical assistance. In addition to the old members, ASEAN's dialogue partners and various IGOs have supported a number of IAI projects.[49] Japan has also begun to work with China in this region, with the first Japan–China Policy Dialogue on the Mekong Region being held in late April 2008. The intent of this new dialogue is to identify areas of cooperation for trade, development and investment opportunities.[50]

Following the announcement of the IAI, the Japanese government began to contribute to the IAI through the ASEAN–Japan Solidarity Fund, the Japan–ASEAN General Exchange Fund and JICA. Japanese-initiated projects have included the provision of information technology equipment, an irrigation system management programme and an attachment programme at the ASEAN Secretariat for junior diplomats. Cooperation for the IAI was given further emphasis in the Tokyo Declaration issued at the Japan–ASEAN Summit in December 2003. The declaration stated that a key goal of the bilateral relationship would be to 'strengthen cooperation and support for the realisation of ASEAN integration goals by implementing projects, particularly those under the Initiative for ASEAN Integration (IAI)'.[51] An interesting statement in the Japan–ASEAN Action Plan attached to the declaration was to '[s]upport ASEAN's initiative to hold ASEAN Governors Conferences to provide platforms for poor provinces and cities of ASEAN to share their best practices on poverty alleviation and mobilise resources for the implementation of poverty alleviation programmes'.[52] This phrase implies consideration of the solution of poverty and social development problems by creating an organised feedback loop to accumulate expertise and practices at the subnational level.

Outside of the institutional mechanisms, Japan has provided substantial levels of aid to Southeast Asian countries. For instance, in 1999 and 2000 Indonesia was the primary recipient of Japan's bilateral ODA, and Vietnam, Thailand and the Philippines were among the top six recipients. In the new millennium, Japan began to give more emphasis to a region-based approach focused on poverty reduction and social development. In line with this change in direction, Japan began expanding coverage of its regional ODA. This change is most clearly seen in the fact that by 2004 the primary recipient of ODA was India, although Southeast Asia still remains an area of key concern for Japanese assistance.[53] Another interesting change has been the reduction in Japanese ODA to China in terms of both monies and the scope of funded projects.[54] Hence, although the IDEA and support for the IAI provide a clear indication of Japan's attempts to resolve development problems in Asia, promoting a set of norms for equal access to resources and opportunities within the region, it is a nuanced approach with a clear alignment towards South and Southeast Asia.

Domestic and regional constraints

Domestic constraints

While Japan has been pro-actively involved in the advancement of regionalism and regional governance in East Asia, its expanding involvement has not necessarily led to its growing influence in the region. There are at least two domestic constraints in promoting regional governance. First, Japan's regional projects are hampered by weak coordination between different ministries. This has led to various programmes launched by national agencies for regional cooperation not being coordinated in a consistent and strategic manner. Indeed, ministries have often embarked on programmes and initiatives with similar objectives as a way to increase ministerial influences in a given policy area. Ministerial rivalry of this nature was frequently observed between MOFA and METI (the Ministry of Economic, Trade and Industry) in funding development projects in Indochina.

MOFA supported the development of Indochina countries through the Forum for the Comprehensive Development of Indochina. The Forum, established in 1995, was intended to be a gathering for debates and exchanges of views on the development of Cambodia, Laos and Vietnam. METI, however, wanted to have its own networks and channels for the development of Indochina. Accordingly, METI established the AEM-METI Economic and Industrial Cooperation Committee (AMEICC) in 1998. The AMEICC aimed to promote industrial development through the creation of infrastructure and improvements in business environments and industrial and trade financing. While the Forum and AMEICC had different objectives (development in the former and industrial development and cooperation in the latter), concrete activities – such as human resource development aid – were similar.

The lack of coordination between the different ministries was again shown in a new concept paper for the development of the Greater Mekong Sub-region (GMS), which was presented at the Japan–ASEAN Summit in December 2003. The concept paper reflected the diverse interests of a number of government agencies with programmes operating in the area. MOFA hoped to demonstrate Japan's involvement in Indochinese development programmes through the allocation of a considerable amount of resources (US \$15 billion over a three-year period). MOF's interests were reflected in proposals for further collaboration with the ADB and the development of bond markets in the countries. METI's input was revealed in the promotion of Japanese firms' trade investment activities in the region. Thus, the concept was a mosaic of various ministries' policies and preferences, not an integrated national strategy. The strong inter-ministerial rivalry prevented Japan from taking optimal advantage of its financial resources and experiences of institution building for the development of desirable regional governance structures.

Strong political leadership is necessary for overcoming the problem of ministerial sectionalism. However, Japan's political conditions in the mid 2000s show limitations in political leadership. Japan's decade-long recession in the 1990s was partly due to political instability caused by frequent changes in prime ministers, who had been chosen through the LDP's (Liberal Democratic Party) faction politics. Prime Minister Koizumi established a leadership style independent of faction politics, and his successor Shinzo Abe pursued political management, not relying on the LDP's factions. Abe also tried to push forwards bureaucratic reforms through strengthened regulations on the *amakudari* practice of government bureaucrats landing lucrative jobs in the private sector. However, the Abe cabinet lasted just one year and was succeeded by that of new Prime Minister Yasuo Fukuda in September 2007. Whereas the Fukuda administration adopts flexible and soft postures towards Asian diplomacy, its dependence on the LDP's factions and bureaucrats makes it difficult to enhance political leadership so as to coordinate interests among ministries.

The second problem is relevant to the perception of governance ideals. As discussed, the Japanese government has been placing increased emphasis on the formation of governance ideals, which is reflected in its expanding commitment to poverty reduction and social development. However, the projects that Japan launched in other East Asian countries often failed to incorporate related aspects of its governance strategy, such as social justice. This was the case with Japan's concept paper on development in the GMS. The three pillars of the concept paper were the enhancement of economic cooperation, the promotion of trade and investment, and the strength of linkages with IGOs. The main target of economic cooperation was the development of infrastructure – as represented by the East-West Economic Corridor – and the construction of a second East-West Corridor. Scant regard was paid in the concept paper to sustaining social justice and poverty alleviation.

The weak promotion of governance ideals is also apparent in Japan's collaboration with non-state actors. Even though the Japanese government has gradually developed linkages with non-state actors, the majority of such actors – those who have influenced Japan's commitments to East Asia – have largely come from academia and business circles. The involvement of non-elite, civil society organisations in policy processes has remained comparatively weak. As previously discussed, environmental conservation is one sector where the Japanese government has attempted to foster collaboration with non-state actors. However, even in this area, collaboration with civil society organisations remains primitive. The example of the Japanese government-sponsored EANET that has been undertaking monitoring of acid deposition in thirteen East Asian countries is one such case. There is also an NGO network called the Atmosphere Action Network East Asia (AANEA), which is 'the only standing environmental NGO network in Northeast Asia'.[55] The AANEA's main objective is to enhance common understanding of the state of air pollution and climate change in East Asia. To achieve this objective the group has established a network for monitoring acid deposition throughout the region. Although the EANET and the AANEA conducted similar activities for the same purpose, meaningful collaboration has not developed between the two bodies.[56] The NEAC has served as a forum where administrative officials and experts involved in this conference have exchanged information about the changing state of regional environments, for the deepening of common understandings of the problems facing East Asia. At successive NEAC meetings, the participants shared a view that NEAC should search for the wider involvement of other stakeholders, such as local governments, NGOs and research institutes. The repeated inability of the official group to expand its membership, given the existence of a well-known and active civil society network, implies that the drive behind such statements (and hence the involvement of NGOs) remains weak.

Even in cases where non-state actors are involved in the development of regional projects, the relations between state and non-state actors have been basically hierarchical, not horizontal. The state agencies utilise non-state actors represented by the epistemic circles in order to give authority to ideas and projects on which the former have already decided. The non-state actors' independent inputs into initiatives for governance formation have been limited.

What are the main causes of these two problems? Jayasuriya, in reviewing the domestic foundations of foreign policy making, holds that a state's capacity to pursue certain kinds of regional political projects is embedded in the configuration of power and interest in its domestic political economy.[57] Since the early 1990s, Japan has undergone a considerable transformation in the core aspects of its political and economic systems. The *keiretsu*-based economic and industrial systems have been changed so much that the long-lasting six financial *keiretsu* dissolved, while the 'sub-governmental' iron triangle, which comprises key industrial sectors, bureaucrats and politicians, has been gradually eroded, due to Prime Minister Koizumi's reform initiatives. Furthermore, the reorganisation of government ministries in January 2001 enhanced the power of the prime minister and cabinet at the expense of that of central bureaucrats. While the prime minister has since been able to enhance his coordinating role and leadership, the cabinet secretariat deepened its authority by assuming the planning and drafting of important national policies.[58] Prime Minister Koizumi also tried to promote smoother coordination among ministerial agencies through personnel exchanges.[59] However, these reforms have not led to significant alterations in the operation of the bureaucracy and strong inter-ministerial rivalries remain as a problem.

The problem of the weak promotion of governance ideals in Japan's regional relations is mirrored in its domestic reforms. This is most typified in the government's relationship with the private sector and NGOs. In 2000, the Japanese government established the Japan Platform (JPF). The JPF was intended to forge closer working ties with NGOs and business associations, so as to provide emergency relief in natural disasters and refugee situations through an equal partnership of the public, private and civil sectors. Despite this intent, ODA for disaster relief and refugee crises remains less than transparent, with a low public disclosure of information. This public sector mentality has prevented the development of a partnership between the three sectors, but particularly with the NGOs. Some government officials retain a mentality that NGOs and businesses are merely subcontracting bodies to implement individual aid programmes, not equal partners in promoting international cooperation. Thus, the failure of Japan to adequately implement domestic reforms has hampered its ability to generate policies and meet its governance commitments. The inadequate reform process has prevented Japan from making leading contributions in the development of Asian regional governance.

Regional constraints

Japan's commitment to regional governance is also affected by regional politics in general, and in rivalry against China in particular. This was typically shown in the evolution of the East Asian Summit (EAS), a venue to promote governance formation in East Asia. In response to deepening debates on the East Asian Community (EAC) and EAS, the Japanese government formulated the *Issue Papers*, which were presented to the APT foreign ministers' meeting in July 2004. The papers, whose objectives were to consider the implications of East Asian cooperation and to create a political momentum for the EAC, elucidated Japan's concrete ideas on the EAC, the EAS and functional cooperation.[60] In seeking to promote the EAC the Japanese government identified several criteria that were presented in the 2005 Diplomatic Bluebook under three pillars. These criteria included: the need to first accrete functional cooperation efforts rather than attempt immediately to create institutional frameworks; to secure openness, inclusiveness and transparency as 'open regionalism'; and to promote regional cooperation along the lines of universal rules and values such as democracy, human rights, market economy and WTO rules.[61] These criteria were largely incorporated in the Kuala Lumpur Declaration, which was issued at the first East Asian Summit in December 2005.[62]

In 2007 the Diplomatic Bluebook added a further pillar to Japan's regional goals, namely the creation of an 'Arc of Freedom and Prosperity'. Although the Arc begins in the Baltic States and Central Europe, its main geographic focus is on Asia, especially Central, South, Southeast and Northeast Asia. The Arc concept takes the three pillars idea forward. With an 'emphasis on universal values such as freedom, democracy, fundamental human rights, the rule of law, and the market economy', MOFA argues that 'it is only when citizens are free that political stability and economic prosperity will come to last'.[63] Interestingly, the graphical representation of this concept draws the Arc as an almost complete circle around China, possibly indicating a clear demarcation in Japanese policy making between its values and those of its closest rival.

A problem in Japan's approach to the EAC and EAS was slight attention to regional 'governance'. While the Japanese government put emphasis on the values and norms in the creation of an EAC, these were not used with the intent of fostering the formation of regional governance. This is apparent in the *Issue Papers*, which articulated Japan's ideas about the EAC. In the papers, 'governance' was used only once in reference to community building and even this was simply a quote from the 2001 EAVG report rather than a new policy initiative. Instead, what the Japanese government stressed in terms of community building was the necessity of a functional approach to support institutional developments, coupled with the creation of a sense of community. It can therefore be concluded that an improvement in regional governance was not a major concern. Moreover, the strong emphasis on democracy, human rights and market economy could have a detrimental influence on governance discussions by diverting resources in such norms as equity and social justice away from less contentious areas of functional cooperation. Even though the guarantee of democracy and human rights contributes to improved political and social institutions and thus to a more equitable region, it is unrealistic to expect that the more authoritarian states (such as China or Myanmar) will show notable progress in guaranteeing democracy and human rights in anything but the long term. Indeed, the apparent stress on these values could, in fact, lead to a less cohesive region by serving as wedges between the more democratic and libertarian APT members and their authoritarian counterparts.

The universal values were convenient vehicles for Japan's regional diplomacy. On the one hand, the advocacy of these values enabled Japan to show clearer leadership in looking ahead to the future of East Asia. On the other hand, Japan could use them as a tool to reduce the influence of China, which has difficulty in realising these values. However, the outright stress on these values risked repercussions from China. In fact, Chinese Premier Wen Jiabao stated at the second EAS meeting in January 2007 that 'China will respect, as always, the diverse nature of cultures, religions and values in East Asia and promote both dialogue on an equal footing among civilizations and cultures and exchanges among them'.[64] The stress on the diverse nature of regional cultures and values was apparently China's answer to Japan's advocacy of universal values.

Japan's political calculations were also seen in its relations with ASEAN. The day before the 2005 EAS commenced, Prime Minister Koizumi and the ASEAN leadership held the Ninth ASEAN–Japan Summit. The leaders released a joint statement entitled *Deepening and Broadening of ASEAN–Japan Strategic Partnership*.[65] This was the first time Japan had used the term 'strategic' in its documents with ASEAN and represented an upgrading of the bilateral relationship. The statement identified areas and directions of cooperative programmes such as the negotiations on the ASEAN–Japan Comprehensive Economic Partnership, combating transnational crime and terrorism, and support for the formation of the ASEAN Community. The statement contained concrete programmes for promoting social development and reducing the development gap among ASEAN members. Japan promised to provide new financial assistance to support ASEAN integration through an additional US$70 million tranche for the ASEAN Development Fund and the ASEAN–Japan Cooperation Fund. It also promised to support efforts to prevent avian influenza, including the provision of Tamiflu for 500,000 people in Southeast Asia. Although not directly expressed in terms of assisting regional governance, these commitments are designed to promote social development, which underpins any articulation of governance in Asia.

However, beyond concerns for regional social development, the statement and accompanying programmes were also launched in order to maintain Japan's influence with ASEAN against a rising China. The statement itself was intended as a contrast to the 2003 *Joint Declaration on the ASEAN–China Strategic Partnership for Peace and Prosperity*, while the use of the declaration's phrase 'deepening and broadening' to describe the bilateral relationship implied that both parties had engaged in a strategic partnership for a long time (predating ASEAN's ties with China). Moreover, the statement stressed that the relationship should be premised on the principles in the Treaty of Amity and Cooperation and other principles of international law, global norms and universally recognised values. Japan sought to differentiate its relations with ASEAN from China's ASEAN relations by stressing 'universally recognised values' over functional cooperation.

This is not to suggest that Japan's functional cooperation efforts have been lagging behind its promotion of universal norms and practices. Following the 2005 joint statement, Japan has been very active in seeking to ground its relationship with ASEAN in a variety of functional areas, the most important of which is the economic relationship, which ASEAN members frequently cite as a sector where Japan could have been more effective. In April 2008, Japan and ASEAN finally concluded their negotiations for the Economic Partnership Agreement. This agreement is ASEAN's first comprehensive economic agreement, in that it covers trade in goods and services as well as investment and other forms of cooperation.[66] Not only will this agreement allow for closer economic ties between Japan and ASEAN, but it will complement similar agreements already signed between ASEAN–China and ASEAN–Korea, possibly paving the way for a region-wide economic agreement to be negotiated. Japan has also been active in supporting new youth-exchange programmes and in developing regional approaches to energy security.[67] However, while ASEAN has long argued that Japan should be more engaged in the region and also seek a strong bilateral relationship to offset the growing strength of ASEAN's China ties, it is not apparent that, in the period since the 2005 joint statement, either it or Japan's related programmes have been able to mitigate the growing influence of China in the region.

Conclusion

The main objective of this chapter has been to examine how Japan has engaged in the development of regionalism and regional governance in East Asia. In doing so, it has highlighted the three elements of governance within an analytical framework: a rules-based approach, the involvement of non-state actors and commitments to socio-political norms. What has emerged suggests that while Payne's conceptualisation of Asia as being in a state of pre-governance has a degree of validity, it can also be proposed that what is developing is otherwise characteristic of a 'hubs and spokes' model of regional governance, with the hub of ASEAN and – for the purpose of this chapter – the spoke of Japan.

Some of Japan's engagements in regional cooperation have contributed to the development of rules-based institutional systems. East Asian countries have gradually developed rules-based systems in order to create a stable regional order, with accompanying institutions and norms. The Japanese MOF took the lead in launching the CMI, surveillance mechanisms and the Asian bond market. In the agricultural sector, Japan's efforts have seen two major regimes established: the East Asian Emergency Rice Reserve and the ASEAN Food Security Information System. While both are still under construction, they incorporate a regionally agreed-upon set of rules for the creation of stable systems for food security. The Japanese agricultural ministry and JICA have provided substantial financial and technical support for the evolution of these systems.

Importantly, the development of a regional financial architecture has been sustained through the activities of epistemic groups sponsored by the Japanese government. The MOF and its affiliated research institutes have fostered research networks that have provided intellectual input for managing financial and monetary affairs in East Asia. Environmental conservation is another area where Japan has created opportunities for non-state actors to make a contribution to regional governance. The Japanese government took the lead in launching regional forums for environmental protection, such as the NEAC and EANET. In these forums, non-state actors were involved in formulating and implementing policies. Equally important was that several subnational governments in Japan have also engaged in bilateral cooperation and regional environmental governance.

As for commitments to socio-political norms, Japan's regional commitments began to incorporate equity and social justice norms into its Asia policy, particularly after the new millennium. This feature was revealed in the establishment of the JFPR within the ADB, the launching of the IDEA and Japan's support for the IAI. For a long time, Japan tackled poverty alleviation and social development through its bilateral ODA programmes but, more recently, Tokyo has placed greater emphasis on a region-based approach to addressing these problems.

In contributing to these various initiatives, Japan has supported the development of regional integration and better governance in East Asia. However, these contributions have been hampered by two key domestic problems: (1) the lack of coordination and sustainability in its regional strategies, as different government agencies were more interested in the impact that programmes had on domestic power structures than in regional cooperation, and (2) the weak promotion of governance structures, actors or ideals, with the roles offered to non-elite, non-state actors being more limited than could have otherwise been the case. The root cause of these problems lay in inadequate domestic reforms to the political economy that would have produced strategic initiatives for governance improvement in East Asia. A third problem lay in Japan's perceptions of the regional balance of power. Even though Japan has launched a number of programmes that will improve regional governance, these have been implemented less from an interest in governance and more from a desire to check the growing influence of China.

Despite these problems, Japan continues to play an important role in the development of governance and regionalism in Asia. It is a role that will expand so long as Japan's development of its regional relations continues to proceed in a positive manner. Either with its partners in the APT process or with the extraregional states in the EAS, Japan has shown a capacity to play a major role in the formation of multilevel processes that cross national boundaries and further regional integration.

Notes

1 Payne, Anthony. 'Globalization and Modes of Regionalist Governance', in Pierre Jon (ed.). *Debating Governance.* (Oxford, New York: Oxford University Press, 2000), pp. 214–215.
2 Alagappa, Muthiah. 'Regionalism and Conflict Management: A Framework for Analysis', *Review of International Studies.* (Vol. 21, No. 4, 1995), p. 362.
3 Hurrell, Andrew. 'Regionalism in Theoretical Perspective', in Louise Fawcett and Andrew Hurrell (eds). *Regionalism in World Politics: Regional Organization and International Order.* (New York: Oxford University Press, 1995), p. 39.
4 Three years later, the group submitted a report on 'An East Asian Community' to APT leaders, which referred to the evolution of the APT Summit to an East Asian Summit and the establishment of an East Asian Free Trade Area.
5 On the former point see: *ASEAN Plus Three Cooperation.* http://www.aseansec. org/16580.htm. Accessed 20 October 2007. On the new sectors for cooperation see: *Chairman's Statement of the Eleventh ASEAN+3 Foreign Ministers' Meeting.* Singapore, 20 November 2007, http://www.aseansec.org/21096.htm. Accessed 24 April 2008.
6 Commission on Global Governance. *Our Global Neighborhood.* (New York: Oxford University Press, 1995), p. 2.
7 Rosenau, James. *Along the Domestic-Foreign Frontier: Exploring Governance in a Turbulent World.* (Cambridge: Cambridge University Press, 1997), p. 145.
8 Keohane, Robert O. and Joseph S. Nye. 'Introduction', in Joseph S. Nye and John D. Donahue (eds). *Governance in a Globalizing World.* (Washington, DC: Brookings Institution Press, 2000), p. 12.
9 Söderbaum, Fredrik. 'Modes of Regional Governance in Africa: Neoliberalism, Sovereignty Boosting, and Shadow Networks', *Global Governance.* (Vol. 10, No. 4, 2004), pp. 420–421.
10 Payne. 'Globalization and Modes of Regionalist Governance', pp. 211–215.
11 Krahmann, Elke. 'National, Regional, and Global Governance: One Phenomenon or Many?', *Global Governance.* (Vol. 9, No. 3, 2003), pp. 323–346.
12 Pierre, Jon and B. Guy Peters. *Governance, Politics, and the State.* (New York: St. Martin's Press, 2000), pp. 4–5.
13 For more on this point see: Keohane, Robert and Joseph Nye. 'Introduction', pp. 1–41.
14 Jayasuriya, Kanishka, 'Introduction: The Vicissitudes of Asian Regional Governance', in Kanishka Jayasuriya (ed.). *Asian Regional Governance: Crisis and Change.* (New York: Routledge, 2004), pp. 5–6.
15 Phillips, Nicola. 'The Rise and Fall of Open Regionalism: Comparative Reflections on Regional Governance in the Southern Cone of Latin America', *Third World Quarterly.* (Vol. 24, No. 2, 2003), p. 229.
16 Phillips, Nicola. 'Regionalist Governance in the New Political Economy of Development: "Relaunching" the Mercosur', *Third World Quarterly.* (Vol. 22, No. 4, 2001), pp. 579–580.
17 See: *The Joint Ministerial Statement of the 9th ASEAN+3 Finance Ministers' Meeting.* Hyderabad, 4 May 2006. http://www.aseansec.org/18390.htm. Accessed 24 April 2008.
18 Ibid.
19 See: *Joint Ministerial Statement of the 11th ASEAN Finance Ministers' Meeting.* Chiang Mai, 5 April 2007. http://www.aseansec.org/20471.htm. Accessed 24 April 2008.
20 For more on this meeting see: 'ASEAN Meet in Vietnam Sees Service Liberalization Pact Initialled', *Xinhua*, 4 April 2008.
21 Kishimoto, Shuhei. 'Ajia kinyu senryaku no tenkai' [The evolution of financial strategies for Asia], in Akira Suehiro and Susumu Yamakage (eds). *Ajia Seiji*

Keizai Ron: Ajia no Nakano Nihon wo Mezashite [The Theory of Asian Political Economy: Searching for Japan in Asia]. (Tokyo: NTT Shuppan, 2001), p. 305.

22 *Nikkei Kinyu Shimbun*, 12 May 2000, *Asahi Shimbun*, 24 May 2000.

23 Kishimoto, Shuhei. 'Ajia keizai saisei misshion hokoku no igi to jinzai shien' [The implication of the mission for revitalization of the Asian economy and assistance to human resources], *Fainansu.* (June, 2000), pp. 75–77.

24 *The Joint Press Statement of the First Meeting of the ASEAN Agriculture and Forestry Ministers and the Ministers of the Peoples Republic of China, Japan and Republic of Korea (AMAF+3)*. Medan, 5 October 2001. http://www.aseansec. org/547.htm. Accessed 24 November 2007.

25 The EAERR aimed to establish a cross-supply arrangement for rice from food-surplus to food-deficit countries during normal conditions and in time of emergency. For details of the EAERR: http://www.eaerr.org/index.php.

26 The AERR was established in 1979 by the ASEAN Food Security Reserve Agreement. Despite its rather long history, the AERR has never been used operationally and its stock did not reflect the practical minimum stock required for anticipating emergency situations.

27 The EAERR has conducted activities to support people who experience food shortage due to national disaster or man-made calamity. For instance, during 2006, the EAERR provided rice aid with the people affected by flood, volcano eruptions, typhoon, or oil spillage in Indonesia and the Philippines. The EAERR has also committed to poverty alleviation in the member countries. In December 2004, EAERR began the Cooperation Project on Poverty Alleviation and Malnourishment Eradication in Laos. This project aimed to improve rice production areas by the refurbishment of irrigation canals as well as household food security by the provision of nutritious food and clean water.

28 For the details of the AFSIS see http://afsis.oae.go.th/.

29 The centre has coordinated various programmes such as a training course on statistical survey techniques (December 2003), a workshop on the construction of the information network system (February 2004), and a workshop on improvement of the quality of agricultural statistics (April 2005).

30 Oba, Mie. 'Higashi Ajia ni Okeru Shokuryo Anzen Hosho Kyoryoku no Sinten' [The development of food security cooperation in East Asia], *Kokusai Seiji.* (No. 135, 2004), p. 33.

31 Pacific Consultant International. *Taikoku Higasi Ajia Shokuryo Anzen Hosho Oyobi Kome Bichiku Shisutemu Keikaku Chosa: Saishu Hokokusho* [Thailand: Survey on East Asian food security and rice reserve system: the final report]. (Tokyo, Pacific Consultants International, 2002), pp. 1–4.

32 The Principles of Surplus of Disposal stipulates that food aid is to be additional to those commercial sales which can be reasonably assumed to have taken place in the absence of concessional terms.

33 See: *The Seventh Meeting of the ASEAN Agriculture and Forestry Ministers and the Ministers of Agriculture of the People's Republic of China, Japan and Republic of Korea (7th AMAF Plus Three)*. Bangkok, 2 November 2007. http:// www.aseansec.org/21028.htm. Accessed 24 April 2008.

34 For more information see: *Report on the Fifth Focal Points Meeting and Technical Session*. Siam Reap, 7–9 March 2007. http://www.faorap-apcas.org/docs/ RDES%20Meetings/Fifth_Focal_Points.pdf, pp. 24- 36. Accessed 24 April 2008.

35 The ADB Institute was established in Tokyo in December 1997. The Institute aimed to provide intellectual bases for pursuing the appropriate development paradigms for Asia, which were composed of the balanced combination of the role of market, institutions and the government.

36 Oba, Mie. 'Tsuka kinyu kyoryoku to FTA ni miru nihon no higashi ajia chiiki keisei senryaku' [Japan's regional strategy towards East Asia in terms of

monetary and financial cooperation and FTA], in Susumu Yamakage (ed.). *Higashi Ajia Chiiki Shugi to Nihon* [Japan and regionalism in East Asia]. (Tokyo: Nihon Kokusai Mondai Kenkyujo, 2003), p. 165.

37 For the summary of the report see: http://www.mof.go.jp/jouhou/kokkin/frame_2. html. Accessed 13 February 2005.

38 Shimura, Noriko. 'Higashi ajia ni okeru chiiki kinyu kyoryoku no shinten' [The development of regional financial cooperation in East Asia], *International Economic and Financial Review.* (No. 6, 2004), p. 4. http://www.iima.or.jp/pdf/ IER_2004/ir04_no6.pdf.

39 Including Mongolia and Russia but not Singapore or Brunei. For more details about the EANET: http://www.eanet.cc/.

40 Tsunekawa, Keiichi. 'Why so Many Maps There? Japan and Regional Cooperation', in T.J. Pempel (ed.). *Remapping East Asia: The Construction of a Region.* (Ithaca, NY: Cornell University Press, 2005), p. 139.

41 See: *The Ninth Session of the Inter-governmental Meeting on Acid Deposition Monitoring Network in East Asia.* Vientiane, 19–20 November 2007. http://www. eanet.cc/event/ig/ig09.pdf. Accessed 24 April 2008.

42 Ministry of the Environment. *Kankyo Hakusho 2001* [White Paper on the Environment 2001]. (Tokyo: Gyosei, 2001), p. 343.

43 Kitakyushu city has sought to expand the network of environmental cooperation from bilateral to regional. In December 1997, the city organised the Conference on Environmental Cooperation among Asian Cities. This conference was attended by representatives from six cities – Surabaya, Semarang (Indonesia), Batangas, Cebu (Philippines), Ho Chi Minh (Vietnam) and Penang (Malaysia). At the conference, participants agreed to conduct continuous and concrete cooperation for environmental protection under city linkages. In 2000 and 2001, Kitakyushu city dispatched experts and conducted training for Batangas city staff members on the optimal disposal of domestic waste.

44 Hooghe, Liesbet and Gary Marks. *Multi-Level Governance and European Integration.* (Lanham, MD: Rowman and Littlefield, 2001).

45 The total amount of the fund increased to US$325.8 million as of March 2004. For the details of the JFPR: http://www.adb.org/ Documents/Brochures/JFPR/ default.asp. Accessed 24 April 2008.

46 Asian Development Bank. Semi-Annual Progress Report to the Government of Japan on the Japan Fund for Poverty Reduction (JFPR) for the Period Ending 31 December 2007. (Manila: February 2008), p. 5. http://www.adb.org/Documents/ Reports/JFPR/2007/semi-ann ual-jul-dec2007.pdf. Accessed 25 April 2008.

47 The Japanese government also set up a similar fund, the Japan Social Development Fund (JSDF) in June 2000, which is administered by the World Bank. The JSDF aimed to support innovative programmes which directly respond to the needs of the poorest and most vulnerable groups in society. As of March 2005, the Japanese government had provided over US$250 million to the JSDF and over 160 grants, amounting to more than US$180 million, had been approved.

48 Despite decrease in per capita GDP in the old ASEAN members since 1996, the gap between the two groups remained stark. The four Indochina countries contributed only 8 per cent of total GDP in 2003, compared with their 28 per cent contribution in terms of population.

49 As of February 2006, 129 projects were at various stages of implementation. Funding was secured for 108 projects, of which 66 projects were completed, 24 projects were under implementation, and 18 projects secured firm funding and were in the planning stage. Source: ASEAN Secretariat. 'Progress of IAI Work Plan: Status Update, as of 10 February 2006', p. 1. http://www.aseansec.org/ 17947.doc. Accessed 14 December 2007.

50 See: Ministry of Foreign Affairs. 'The First Japan-China Policy Dialogue on the Mekong Region'. http://www.mofa.go.jp/announce/event/2008/4/1179410_932. html. Accessed 25 April 2008.

51 *Tokyo Declaration for the Dynamic and Enduring Japan-ASEAN Partnership in the New Millennium*, p. 4. http://www.mofa.go.jp/region/asia-paci/asean/year2003/summit/tokyo_dec.pdf. Accessed 14 December 2007.

52 'Japan-ASEAN Action Plan', p. 8. http://www.mofa.go.jp/region/asia-paci/asean/year2003/summit/action.pdf.

53 Shuji, Uchikawa. 'The Position of India in Asian Economy from a Japanese Perspective', paper presented at the IDE-JETRO *International Symposium on Economic Integration in Asia and India: What is the Best Way of Regional Cooperation?* Tokyo, 8 December 2005. http://www.ide.go.jp/Japanese/Lecture/Sympo/pdf/uchikawa_summary.pdf#search = %22japan%20ODA%202004–05% 22. Accessed 10 May 2007.

54 Mochizuki, Mike. 'Between Alliance and Autonomy', *Strategic Asia*. (Washington: The National Bureau of Asian Research, 2005). http://www.nbr.org/pub-lications/strategic_asia/pdf/sa04_4japan.pdf#search = %22japan%20ODA% 202004–05%20southeast%20asia%22. Accessed 10 May 2007.

55 Nam, Sangmin. 'Ecological Inter-dependence and Environmental Governance in Northeast Asia: Politics versus Cooperation', in Paul G. Harris (ed.). *International Environmental Cooperation: Politics and Diplomacy in Pacific Asia*. (Boulder: University Press of Colorado, 2002), p. 182. The AANEA was established in 1995 with financial support from the Japanese Fund for Global Environment. It consists of seventeen NGOs in seven countries and economies (China, Japan, South Korea, Mongolia, Hong Kong, Taiwan and Russia).

56 Takahashi, Wakana. 'Problems of Environmental Cooperation in Northeast Asia: The Case of Acid Rain', in Paul G. Harris (ed.). *International Environmental Cooperation: Politics and Diplomacy in Pacific Asia*. (Boulder, CO: University Press of Colorado, 2002), p. 240.

57 Jayasuriya, Kanishka. 'Embedded Mercantilism and Open Regionalism: The Crisis of a Regional Political Project', in Kanishka Jayasuriya (ed.). *Asian Regional Governance: Crisis and Change*. (New York: Routledge, 2004).

58 Shinoda, Tomohito. *Kantei Gaiko: Seiji Ridashippu no Yukue* [Diplomacy by Prime Minister: Tracing Political Leadership]. (Tokyo: Asahi Shimbunsha, 2004), pp. 34–36.

59 In February 2002, Prime Minister Koizumi ordered the promotion of personnel exchanges among the ministries, aiming to increase the ratio of exchange in some 1,400 senior posts from 3 per cent in 2004 to 10 per cent in 2007. In summer 2004, 14 ministries and agencies exchanged officials for 40 posts in addition to the existing 47 posts.

60 For the *Issue Papers* see: http://www.mofa.go.jp/mofaj/area/asia/e_asia/index.html.

61 Ministry of Foreign Affairs. *Gaiko Seisho 2005* [Diplomatic Bluebook 2005]. (Tokyo: Gyosei, 2005).

62 For instance, the declaration contained a phrase that 'the East Asia Summit will be an open, inclusive, transparent and outward-looking forum in which we strive to strengthen global norms and universally recognised values.'

63 See: Ministry of Foreign Affairs. *Diplomatic Bluebook 2007*. http://www.mofa.go. jp/policy/other/bluebook/2007/html/index.html. Accessed 28 April 2008.

64 Wen, Jiabao. 'Be Open and Inclusive and Achieve Mutual Benefit and Common Progress', *The First East Asia Summit*. Kuala Lumpur, 14 December 2005. http://www.fmprc.gov.cn/eng/topics/zgcydyhz/ ninthasean/t230642.htm. Accessed 10 May 2007.

65 *Joint Statement of the Ninth ASEAN-Japan Summit Deepening and Broadening of ASEAN-Japan Strategic Partnership*. http://www. aseansec.org/18076.htm. Accessed 10 May 2007.

66 'ASEAN SG Hails Completion of the Signing of the ASEAN-Japan Comprehensive Economic Partnership Agreement'. 15 April 2008. http://www.aseansec.
   org/21471.htm. Accessed 25 April 2008.
67 See respectively: 'Japan Contributes USD 247 Million to ASEAN for Youth
   Exchanges and to Boost Economic Partnership', 23 March 2007. http://www.
   aseansec.org/20459.htm; and *Chairman's Statement of the Third ASEAN+3
   (China, Japan, and Korea) Ministers on Energy Meeting*. Vientiane, 27 July
   2006. http://www.eppo.go.th/inter/asean/AMEM24/amem3-E.html. Both accessed
   25 April 2008.

4 South Korea and East Asian regionalism

Policies, norms and challenges

Jaewoo Choo

Introduction

South Korea has systematically engaged with East Asian regionalism only since the post-Cold War era. During this period, South Korea (hereafter Korea) has undergone two significant policy shifts in its regional activities – first towards Northeast Asia, and later towards the wider East Asian region. Korea developed its modern regional foreign policy with the commencement of the Sixth Republic under former president Roh Tae-woo in 1988. However, at that time the primary focus of Korea's regional policy was on the integration process in Northeast Asia. Even though Korea launched an official dialogue with ASEAN in 1989, its main diplomatic concerns focused on relations with the surrounding powers, namely the United States, China, Japan, and the former Soviet Union, and the impact of those relations on its ties with North Korea (DPRK).

Korea's regional horizon was forcibly broadened as it came to terms with the fallout of the 1997 Asian financial crisis. For Korean policy makers, it was not until this event that the underlying enmeshment of ties between Northeast and Southeast Asia was substantially recognised. Korea's attention to and interest in East Asian regionalism were further stimulated when the heads of all regional states gathered later that year to discuss ways of healing the economic wounds of the crisis-ridden countries and of preventing the recurrence of a similar crisis in the future. The resulting formulation of ASEAN Plus Three (APT), comprising all thirteen regional states, further advanced Korea's engagement in East Asian regional affairs.

The 1997 crisis was significant for Korea's regionalism policy because of the profound effect it had on the structure and distribution of power in the region. It did not take long before Korea realised its comparatively reduced status in regional processes, especially as compared to the rise of China. Until the mid 1990s, for instance, Korea was regarded as the most likely state capable of mediating between China and Japan, because of its economic advantage over China and good political ties with Japan.[1] However, the rise of China, coupled with Korea's economic setback, undermined its ability to influence regional events – either in Northeast or in Southeast Asia. The more recent incorporation of India, Australia and New Zealand into regional dialogues via the East Asian Summit (EAS) has had similar implications for Korea's future policy impact in East Asian regional affairs.

Korea is now clearly a middle power in a region where a number of greater and lesser regional powers coexist. As such, it could be expected that Korea's foreign policy would undergo the adjustments and reforms necessary to enhance its regional position and status. However, this does not seem to be the case, as the Roh Moo-hyun administration promoted a policy platform designed to transform the country into a hub nation of Northeast Asia. It has yet to develop a policy with an inherently larger regional orientation towards East Asia. It has also yet to present an overall and comprehensive official foreign policy for developing relations with Southeast Asia. Although Korea has been an active participant in a number of ASEAN-related multilateral dialogues and has successfully developed a framework for free trade with Southeast Asia, it has not come up with a policy framework that will allow observers to understand its underlying fundamental interests, goals and strategies.

This chapter argues that Korea needs to have a policy commensurate with its changing status and profile in order to contribute in any meaningful way to the fruition of East Asian regionalism. Korea's desire to make constructive contributions to the cause of East Asian regionalism was well manifested in its initiatives to found the East Asia Vision Group (EAVG) and the subsequent policy body known as East Asian Study Group (EASG). These groups were both initiated by former president Kim Dae-jung. Furthermore, in 2003 his successor Roh Moo-hyun claimed to turn the country into an economic hub of Northeast Asia. What is paradoxical about these initiatives is the lack of consistent policy support by the government, successor administrations often refusing to follow their predecessor's policies in this regard. Roh's government, for instance, halted backing for various ongoing activities, including financial support to the EAVG and EASG, leaving them to continue in name only. Roh's government remained passive and inactive over the idea of a hub, mainly because of its obsession with domestic political reform issues. Nevertheless, it is expected that president Lee Myong-bak will try to do better in regionalism diplomacy, following his inauguration in February 2008.

The purpose of this chapter is not to focus on the reasons underlying Korea's failure to develop an appropriate regional policy, but to examine what policies have been enacted and what it would take to develop a sustained regional foreign policy in future. This chapter comprises five sections. The next section reviews the evolution of Korea's regionalism policy in order to better understand the driving forces behind it. Following this, the third section briefly deals with the Roh administration's position on the issue of East Asian regionalism. The fourth section takes a realistic look at Korea's current position in the larger framework of regionalism (within East Asia) and examines the potential role for middle powers in order to provide a theoretical framework for Korea's case, which is dealt with extensively in the following section.

Regionalism in Korean foreign policy

Regionalism began to emerge as one of the guiding principles of Korea's foreign policy in the early 1990s. This can be attributed to Korea's recognition of the impact that the end of the Cold War, deepening economic interdependence and globalisation would have on its regional environment. Also, Korea sought to embrace regionalism as part of its foreign policy for a number of other domestic and external reasons. From the domestic perspective, Korea's economic achievements and subsequent success with democratisation were instrumental in developing a more outward-looking foreign policy. Not only did its political and economic advancement provide a strong basis for the development of supporting domestic political structures for international affairs, but they were also seen as part of a maturing process whereby Korea was ready to take the next step and realise its capacity to be a player in regional affairs.[2]

Korea's growing international profile, coupled with an apparent decline in the US and Japanese presence in East Asian affairs, propelled it to pursue a more independent and autonomous set of interests at regional level. This is clearly manifested in the articulation of the 'Northern Diplomacy' policy during Roh Tae-woo's administration (1988–1993). Since then, Korea has undergone a number of political and economic phases during which regionalism has gradually become one of the guiding principles in the conduct of its diplomacy.

Northern Diplomacy was the first indigenous Korean foreign policy in terms of its autonomous development as a result of external pressures. The policy was conceived as being a means to normalise relationships with former socialist states, mainly the People's Republic of China (PRC) and the former Soviet Union. It was also intended to be conducive to the promotion of peace and stability on the Korean Peninsula as a first step towards the eventual peaceful unification of the two Koreas. However, the scope of the policy was much wider than just being concerned with North–South relations and the issue of reunification.

First, it represented an expansion in the scope of Korea's foreign policy geographically, as well as in terms of its acceptance of other political ideologies. Under the Northern Diplomacy framework, ideology was no longer a restricting factor in Korea's diplomatic engagement, so long as it was not detrimental to national interests. This fundamental shift provided the basis for Korea's recognition of China in 1992. Second, the focus on the international environment of the Korean Peninsula made Korean policy makers pay more attention to the importance of the surrounding regions (not only Northeast Asia and Southeast Asia but also the broader Asia-Pacific) at a time when broader efforts at regional cooperation were also beginning.

Moreover, growing socio-economic and political interdependence with sur-rounding countries created the option for other states to contribute to a resolution of the intra-Korean dispute. Third, as the first Korean foreign policy with a truly outward-looking vision and autonomous orientation, it created a solid basis for the advancement of Korea's regional diplomacy.

The Kim Young-sam administration (1993–98) capitalised on the legacy of the Northern Diplomacy by promulgating the policy of 'New Diplomacy'. While Northern Diplomacy was grand in both its geographical scale and its ideological openness, New Diplomacy was designed to focus on practical challenges arising from then recent developments in international affairs. It was driven by five core strategic concerns: (1) a response to globalisation; (2) a need to diversify diplomatic relationships; (3) a pluralist approach to national interests; (4) support for regional cooperation; and (5) an orienta-tion to the future.[3] As noted in this list, engagement with regional actors and institutions was officially supported and pursued. Special emphasis was also given to the scope of Korea's diplomatic efforts across the Asia-Pacific and to the various strategic measures, in particular, support for multilateral regional initiatives which could be adopted in support of its goals. In other words, the New Diplomacy was a result of Korea's adjustment to changing international and regional structures and their accompanying institutions.

In the course of this adjustment, Korea became more attentive to the international and regional expression of such values as: democracy, liberty, freedom, welfare and human rights. This was a reflection both of the grow-ing liberalisation of its domestic political landscape and of the impact of the end of the Cold War system in allowing the rise of a host of international actors, including individuals, international institutions, transnational civil society networks and governmental organisations. The growing importance of these groups was seen in their contribution to peace and stability on the Korean Peninsula, which further encouraged President Kim's government to proactively improve relations with them. During his administration, Korea was highly visible in a wide variety of regional forums, such as: the Asia-Pacific Economic Cooperation (APEC) group, the ASEAN Regional Forum (ARF), the Northeast Asian Cooperation Dialogue (NEACD), the North-east Asian Security Dialogue (NEASD), the Council for Security Coopera-tion in the Asia-Pacific (CSCAP) and the Asia-Europe Meeting (ASEM) dialogues.

During this period, the New Diplomacy model was extensively expanded in both scope and range, as Korea sought cooperation not only in the security and political arenas but also in the economic, socio-political and environmental realms. All these efforts, however, later proved not to come without a price. As Korea reached outwards, it progressively pursued a policy of its own global engagement. For example, Korea successfully joined the ranks of Organisation for Economic Cooperation and Development (OECD) members, although without sufficient policy countermeasures against the progress of globalisation and the international flow of capital.

However, simply from an economic perspective, Korea's economic development was regarded as being at the required level for OECD membership and thus capable of managing globalisation.

However, the reality of Korea's economic structure and practice was otherwise. Some early signals and warnings came simultaneously from the different sectors of the Korean economy. 'The current account deficit widened from 2 per cent of GNP in 1995 to 5 per cent in 1996' with a slowdown in the growth rate of exports from 31 per cent to 15 per cent. This was coupled with a decline in the rate of growth of GNP from 14.6 per cent to 7.1 per cent and a rise of foreign debt from US$78 billion to US$100 billion, as well as a series of bankruptcies filed by the top-ranking conglomerates (such as Hanbo Iron & Steel Co., Jinro and the car manufacturer KIA).[4] In 1997, Korea's foreign debt stood at US$170 billion and it was hedged, which meant that the subsequent fall in the value of the Korean won by 50 per cent during the 1997 Asian crisis doubled the foreign debt load. Korea's debt problem was not perceived to be large enough to have caused the economic crisis by 'traditional criteria such as the debt–export ratio and the debt–GDP ratio'.[5] Instead, its debt problem was attributed in part to weak financial systems and poor corporate governance practices. As events unfolded they were interpreted by market analysts as signs of the inherent structural weakness in the Korean economy.

Apart from these economic factors, a failure of corporate social responsibility further exacerbated the impact of the 1997 Asian crisis. This was the result of long-standing practices of corruption and cronyism in Korea's public and private sectors, effectively facilitated by the government-led economic drive, by which the government became the mighty patriarch of Korean businesses and banks. The Korean government basically treated the financial institutions as means to 'mobilize financial resources and allocated funds to specific industries'.[6] Companies and banks were able to satisfy financial needs under government guarantee. Creditworthiness or company portfolio was often neglected. The prudential regulations of the banking system were simply not followed and the regulatory environment was very weak. Under these circumstances, the opening of the economy to movement of capital – primarily as a consequence of Korea's accession to the World Trade Organisation (WTO) (1995) and the OECD (1996) – made Korea much more vulnerable to all the problems generated by structural economic weakness, corruption and lack of transparency in business–government relations.[7]

In addition, Korea's memberships to the WTO and the OECD naturally led to a decrease in the level of government guarantees and thus 'made it difficult for the Korea government to ease the financial difficulty of firms and banks, as it had done before by providing policy loans and subsidies, and other less obvious measures'.[8] One of the most salient results was the bankruptcies filed by over 10,000 firms in 1997.[9] Inherent fragility in Korean corporate governance and financial institutions, coupled with the government's failure to make timely adjustment in these areas with the passage of several important reform measure,[10] all contributed in one way or another to the nation's bankruptcy. By the time the 1997 Asian crisis reached Korea in December 1997, Korea's foreign debt was at US$170 billion. Its trade deficit recorded US$20 billion, doubling from the previous year. Its foreign reserves were down to US$7.5 billion after the exodus of US$25 billion in the month of November 1997 alone. It all left in the form either of short-term loan payment or retreat by the hedge funds. With the debt–equity ratio of the Korean government-backed private sector reaching 3:4,[11] and the ratio of non-interest paying loans to total loans by commercial banks reaching 6.1 per cent, Korea's solvency was imperilled. Korea had to turn to the International Monetary Fund (IMF) for help, which came in the form of a rescue package of US$58 billion that included a series of political and economic reforms.

As was the case in other regional states and institutions reviewed in this volume, the crisis made Korea realise the vulnerability of its economy to exogenous shock and the depth of its integration with the region. Hence, the negative lesson from the crisis was a positive catalyst for Korea's commitment to East Asian regionalism. Prior to the 1997 Asian crisis there was a strong consensus among policy makers and academics as to the region's high degree of interdependence, but without a concurrent understanding as to the possible negative side effects. The consequence was the financial crisis, where the vulnerability of the regional states was exacerbated by the absence of a sufficiently responsive correct institution (such as APEC or ASEAN).[12] Moreover, the response to the 1997 Asian crisis seemed to suggest that non-regional states were pursuing their own agendas (such as forced openness of the regional market, more transparent corporate governance and financial institutions) under the guise of the financial support packages. Hence, the crisis made the regional states realise the need for common action, rather than mere rhetoric, to realise their ambition of increased regional cooperation in an age of greater interdependence.[13]

The importance of regionalisation to the social and economic well-being of East Asian states was further reinforced through their collective negative experiences with the IMF and World Bank. Against this background, they were compelled to realise much closer coordination in their financial and economic activities,[14] especially given their strong desire to prevent the recurrence of a similar crisis in the future. In other words, the growing interdependence of East Asia allowed regional states to take advantage of their 'geographic proximity and the relationship between economic flows and policy choices'.[15] In this situation, the goal of regional economic interdependence can no longer be exclusively concerned with the integration of economic flows, but needs to be expanded so as to encompass political collaboration and the creation of social safety nets.[16]

As a result of the increased political collaboration stemming from the 1997 crisis and the subsequent APT meeting, Korea became an enthusiastic supporter of regionalisation. During the Kim Dae-jung administration (1998–2002), East Asian regionalism became one of the major pillars of Korea's foreign policy. Korea's policy of regionalism during this era was predicated on the ideal that it offered a viable means to consolidate peace and prosperity in the East Asian region. This view was reflected in the guidelines for the mission statement of the EAVG, which was a Korean initiative.

Korea was particularly vocal in advocating regulatory frameworks for regional governance. It proactively assumed a leadership role in harmonising different policy opinions that surfaced naturally during political debates and negotiations at the meetings of these two groups. Under the leadership of the Chairman of the EAVG, former Korean Minister of Foreign Affairs Han Sung-joo, Korea was able to coordinate the EASG's policy recommendations of twenty-six points by breaking them down into three different time perspectives, short-, mid- and long-term. Moreover, Korea was active in organising and hosting related meetings on the agendas set forth by the EASG. However, President Kim Dae-jung's the close support for the EAVG and the EASG was a mixed blessing. With the subsequent change of leadership in 2003, support for their recommendations came to a virtual halt. Kim's successor, President Roh Moo-hyun would eventually remove governmental support from the groups, preventing the achievement of any substantial progress on the two action plans.

Despite this setback, regionalism became embedded in Korean foreign policy and was augmented by the participation of domestic interest groups. The expansion in the number of civil society organisations in Korea[17] since the beginning of the Sixth Republic has allowed a diverse range of opinions to be incorporated into policy-making processes at the national level.[18] The preferences and influence of these groups increased as consensus-based politics expanded domestically.[19] The increasing interaction between civil society organisations and the legislative and the executive branches of the government served as an additional check on the policy objectives of successive administrations. When a regional policy was deemed to be against domestic interests, these organisations were vocal in their opposition both at home and abroad.[20] At the 2003 WTO meeting in Cancoon, for example, a delegation of Korean farmers held a series of protests, one of them committing suicide before the international media.[21] A variety of Korean NGOs also went to Hong Kong in 2005 to hold demonstrations on the occasion of the WTO ministerial meeting.[22] While civil society acts as one of the domestic constraints on Korea's pursuit of globalisation, its active participation demonstrates that there exists broad social awareness in Korean society of the implications of the country's diplomatic discourse.

As long as Korea's economy remains export driven, it will continue to seek new opportunities for regional economic liberalisation, despite strong opposition from some domestic lobby groups. One salient example was the Korean farmers' opposition during negotiations on the Korea–US free trade agreement in 2006–2007. However, the actions of the opposition have, in turn, led to a somewhat contrary result. The result of domestic socio-political discussion of the costs and benefits associated with regional trade agreements, has been increased support for such international and regional arrangements.

Although institutional ties between Korea and the region are a relatively recent inclusion in its foreign policy, they have become an essential element of successive administrations' international modes of engagement. However, these same administrations have politicised the process to the extent that changes in government can lead to radical shifts in the level of commitment to regional engagement. Despite this, Korea has played an important role in various regional initiatives, such as the EAVG and the EASG. These efforts, and subsequent negotiations for regional trade agreements, have been underpinned by a strong domestic discourse on the merits (and otherwise) of regional engagement. Hence, while political enthusiasm may wax and wane, bureaucratic and civil society support continues to propel Korea's commitment to East Asian regionalism forward.

Korea's recent engagement in regional affairs

Beginning in 2003 with the administration headed by President Roh Moo-hyun, Korea's East Asian regional policy has deviated somewhat from that of previous administrations in terms of its scope and direction. Its core geographical focus shrank back to Northeast Asia, as the Roh administration announced its plan to transform the country into the centre of Northeast Asia, later to be envisaged as the 'Northeast Asian economic hub'.[23] This vision not only signalled a redirection of Korea's regional energies but also a new approach, with a stronger focus on bilateralism rather than on wider, regional multilateral efforts.

The most salient manifestation of this policy change in Korea's strategy for East Asian regionalism can be seen in its 2004 decision to give preference a ROK (Republic of Korea)-ASEAN Free Trade Area,[24] ahead of the broader East Asian Free Trade Agreement which it had earlier supported. This shift was Korea's response to the stalemate in regional power structures, arising from competing agendas and Sino-Japanese rivalry. Under these conditions Korea decided to pursue its own national interests in the region, rather than to place greater emphasis on the institutional development of the APT and its associated structures. Related to this is a perception on the part of Korean policy makers that there is still relatively little harmonisation of objectives across the APT dialogues. This seemingly growing division in the opinions and ideas of the regional players in areas of functional cooperation has undermined the Korean confidence in the matter of regional governance and the building of regional community.[25]

Reflecting similar attitudes to those of its two Northeast Asian neighbours, Korea has also deemed confidence building with ASEAN a necessary prerequisite for deeper engagement. To this end, in October 2004, it ratified the Treaty of Amity and Cooperation (TAC) with ASEAN.[26] The TAC is recognised as having a more than symbolic meaning, both sides seeing it as a necessary precondition for the deepening of their bilateral relationship.[27] Moreover, in commemoration of the fifteenth anniversary of the relationship, the Joint Declaration on Comprehensive Cooperation Partnership was ratified at the 8th ROK-ASEAN Dialogue in 2004.[28] Both parties were confident that the Joint Declaration confirmed and consolidated future directions for cooperation in a range of areas from politics to security, economics and culture.[29]

In addition to the Joint Declaration, Korea pledged its contribution to the ASEAN-ROK Special Cooperation Fund (SCF) and ASEAN-ROK Future Oriented Cooperation Projects Fund (FOCP) in 2005, which was considered to have cemented the strong bilateral commitment to the partnership.[30] In support of these funds, Korea offered funds amounting to approximately US $36 million between 1990 and 2007. The annual grant has increased since 2005 to US$3 million.[31] At the 7th ROK-ASEAN Dialogue (RAD) in April 2003, the ASEAN leaders also expressed their appreciation to the ROK for its commitment to the development of the Initiative for ASEAN Integration (IAI) adopted at the 4th Informal ASEAN Summit in 2000, and expressed of its full support to the implementation of the Vientiane Action Programme (VAP) to assist ASEAN in narrowing the development gap in information and communication technology (ICT) and accelerating regional integration as whole. As an indication of its commitment and support, the Korean government pledged to contribute US$5 million to facilitate the agreed projects in the IAI. Korea decided to play a constructive role in the 107 ongoing projects as of 2005, particularly in the development of human resources, infrastructure and ICT areas. Beyond 2005, Korea has agreed to provide 'USD 5 million over the next six years to fund 5 IAI projects in Infrastructure, Trade, and Information & Communications Technology'.[32]

Korea's support to IAI continues at the bilateral level. At the 9th RAD in 2005, leaders adopted the Korea–ASEAN Plan of Action, a roadmap for future cooperation to speed up the implementation of the Joint Declaration of 2004.[33] Korea and ASEAN's desire for the FTA was evidenced by the signing of the Framework Agreement on Comprehensive Economic Cooperation among the Governments of the Member Countries, which endorsed bilateral FTA negotiations and other cooperative measures.[34] In addition to the Framework, leaders of both parties urged that the FTA negotiations on goods be settled in early 2006, and on services and investment by the 10th RAD in 2006. Conforming to this demand, senior officials from Korean and the ASEAN states signed the Agreement on Trade in Goods at their 10th annual Senior Official Meeting (SOM) in August 2006.[35] Moreover, Korea and ASEAN went further to assure the implementation of the Plan of Action with the demand for the Executive Report on the Plan to be submitted at the next dialogue. At the 10th RAD in 2006, the Executive Report was submitted for review, and it was agreed that it should be submitted on an annual basis. Korea once again pledged to increase its support to the ASEAN in the areas of information technology (IT) and small and medium-sized enterprises, in particular.

In November 2007 at the 11th RAD in Singapore, leaders adopted the second Executive Report that reviewed the progress in implementing the 2005 Korea–ASEAN Plan of Action. According to the report, progress towards integration has advanced a step further, deeming it now appropriate for both parties to materialise the liberalisation of investment opportunities by ratifying an agreement by 2008, the last hurdle in the finalisation of the FTA negotiation. ASEAN acknowledged Korea's commitment to the Plan and requested that Korea play a greater role in such subregional cooperation frameworks as the Ayeyawady-Chao Phraya-Mekong Economic Cooperation Strategy (ACPMECS), the Singapore–Kunming Railway Link (SKRL), and environment-related projects, in addition to human resources development and information technology-related projects.[36] On this occasion, Korea and ASEAN also ratified the Agreement on the Trade in Services, an achievement recognised to have opened the market for communication, construction and marine transportation, which were highly regarded as being mutually beneficial.[37] A Memorandum of Understanding regarding the foundation of the Korea–ASEAN Centre in Seoul was also concluded, with both sides expecting the Centre to serve as a hub of cooperation in trade and investment as well as social and cultural exchanges between the two parties. They also discussed how to better address regional challenges such as transnational crimes, epidemics, calamities and the environment. For its part, Korea expressed its commitment to and full support for enhancing cooperation with ASEAN's development efforts, including IT and other high-tech projects. The Report also recommended enhancement of cultural and youth exchanges.[38]

So it can be seen that Korea has utilised both multilateral (ASEAN+3) and bilateral (ASEAN+1) venues to enhance and develop relations with the region. Through active engagement at both levels, Korea and ASEAN have made substantial progress with regional integration and free trade agreements. While Korea is viewed as making positive contributions to these processes with financial and technological support, ASEAN has reciprocated by being open and supportive. Active exchanges and contacts at various venues and levels have enabled both sides to identify their common interests for mutually beneficial outcomes. Increasing cooperation in the economic area has, in turn, led to deeper understanding in various regional security issues (such as terrorism and the North Korean nuclear crisis). Since the breaking of the second nuclear crisis of North Korea, ASEAN states have consistently expressed their concerns and remained supportive of a peaceful solution. Capitalising on the economic spillover effect on security cooperation, discussions on bilateral cooperation in the realm of anti-terrorism and maritime security have witnessed substantial progress in recent times.

Hence, Korea is becoming a partner more valued by ASEAN in both the economics and security areas, which Mely Caballero-Anthony identified in Chapter 2 as being two areas at the heart of ASEAN's desire for greater regional integration.

Korea's commitment to the region and its institutions will be most likely reinforced under new President Lee Myong-bak. According to the foreign policy doctrine he released while campaigning for the presidency in June 2007, Lee made it known that one of the primary objectives of his policy is to make greater contributions to regional and global causes, which would be commensurate with Korea's international profile. Lee's doctrine, also known as the 'MB Doctrine' (from his initials), asserts that it is time for Korea to broaden its diplomatic horizon by developing its relations with regions and states beyond the Korean Peninsula in particular, and the Asia-Pacific in general. In his doctrine, Lee dubbed this vision as a 'New Asia Diplomacy'.[39] His assertion comes from his own political philosophy of pragmatism. Lee portrays his foreign policy as being more pragmatic than that of his predecessors, with a greater orientation to the national interest. To realise this end, Lee has already specifically stated that Korea will expand its developing relations with Southeast, South and Central Asian states as well as with the Oceania states, including Australia and New Zealand. Moreover, it is now speculated that his foreign policy will evolve around making a greater contribution to global and regional causes. Cognisant of Korea's relatively low financial contribution in economic aid and low participation in peace-keeping/making operation, Lee wants to transform Korea into a more responsible state, a status that would fulfil the expectations of international society for the world's twelfth largest economy (in this respect, Korea is beginning to move towards the types of values and responsibilities most recently espoused by Japan, as mentioned in the previous chapter). As of 2006, for example, Korea's overseas development aid was only 0.05 per cent of its gross national income (GNI), below the 0.33 per cent averaged by the OECD members and far from the ratio of 0.9 per cent recommended by the UN.[40] Similarly, while Korea is the tenth largest financial contributor to the UN's Peace-keeping Operation (PKO) mission, it ranks thirty-eighth in the number of dispatched forces as of July 2007.[41] All of this is expected to be profoundly changed under the leadership of Lee's government in the coming years, thereby giving rise to the hope of seeing a Korea that is even more visible in regional activities.[42]

Balancing emerging issues and powers

The 1997 Asian crisis has proven to be a watershed in the evolution of East Asian regionalism. From the vantage point of the event and its aftermath, this evolution has been facilitated by changes in the regional structure and distribution of power. It does not necessarily imply that the event itself was the cause of regional evolution, rather that it was a consequence of the event. From the Korean perspective, a series of four key changes can be seen in the aftermath of the 1997 Asian crisis: (1) the emergence of China as a 'responsible power' in the region; (2) the relatively low level of commitment to its partners on the part of the United States after the 1997 crisis; (3) the reorganisation of economic (industrial, trade and financial) networks, and their loose 'spokes' arrangement around the Chinese hub; and (4) the diplomatic exploitation of these interdependencies by Beijing and Tokyo, as reflected in their competitive initiation of bilateral FTAs with ASEAN.

The first change with respect to China's changed profile to a responsible state was clearly demonstrated by its responsive endeavour in the wake of the 1997 Asian crisis. Not only did China offer to help the crisis-hit nations, but it also scored a public relations coup when it decided not to further devalue of its currency, thereby preventing further deterioration in the already volatile financial market. The second change is related to the reservation of the United States and other Western countries in taking immediate action on the crisis. Failure on part of Western-dominated international organisations (notably, the IMF and World Bank) and related fora (such as APEC) to undertake responsive measures raised doubts as to the nature of their commitment to the well-being of the East Asian economies. The rearrangement of regional economic networks has naturally flowed from China's willingness and Western hesitance in resolving the crisis. Since the 1997 Asian crisis, the economic dependency of regional states on China has further deepened, not only as a result of China's continued economic boom but also because of enhanced trust and confidence in China as a responsible regional actor. The third change was manifested in ASEAN's successive FTA announcements with their +3 partners, first with China and then with Japan.[43] Korea was the last of the +3 states, but realised its agreement a year earlier (2009) than Japan, whose FTA is due to start in 2010, again, a year earlier than China's.

An additional noteworthy change in the landscape of East Asian regional institutions is the launch of the EAS.[44] Against the seemingly lack-lustre progress of the existing regionalism, reflected most notably in the APT process, the EAS was founded with the hope of developing a new approach to the management of regional relations. Despite four summits between 2005 and 2008, this new approach has not yet distinguished itself in terms of achievements, as compared to other processes under the APT or ASEAN.

Regardless of this, the EAS is politically significant in its own right. The geographical range of East Asian regionalism has taken a new form, expanding to incorporate countries from South Asia (such as India) to Oceania (Australia and New Zealand). Even if the intention is to strengthen the region's economic position against deepening regionalisation in other parts of the world, the scope of its agenda is not limited to issues such as trade and investment. As stated by Filipino President Gloria Macapagal-Arroyo, the inclusive nature of the EAS and the possible formation of an economic bloc based on open regionalism by the East Asian states should be able 'to hold its own' position and advantages in bargaining with other similar blocs.[45] Since the first summit in 2005, its agenda has expanded to include security issues, poverty alleviation, economic ties and the joint development of energy capacities. It is expected to make a significant contribution to East Asian Community-building efforts so as to balance other regional groupings in the future; although, as pointed out in Chapter 1, whether it can do so is a very contested point.

As a result of the post-1997 changes – especially the creation of the APT and the EAS – East Asia is undergoing significant institutional changes in terms of the balance of power among member states which were the foundation of the regional security and economic networks. Amid these changes, one of the most affected states has been Korea, which witnessed a drastic curtailment of its profile and status as a regional actor following the 1997 Asian crisis. As a measure of its adjustment, Korea is today presented with a major challenge in balancing its relations between its closest ally – the United States – and its neighbouring states, especially China and ASEAN. This need for balance becomes particularly acute with respect to multilateral regional cooperation. Although Korea succeeded in concluding a free trade agreement with the United States in 2007, the agreement is bilateral in its scope and nature. As long as the United States remains cynical about the idea of multilateral cooperative frameworks in East Asia, Korea must become capable of balancing its competing interests. To achieve this end, Korea will have to further strengthen its relations with ASEAN and China, which have now become the focus of courtship by neighbouring regional states.[46] As discussed in the first two chapters in this volume, competition over ASEAN seems to have augmented that organisation's strategic standing and influence with respect to East Asian regionalism. As Cotton and Saint-Mézard note in Chapters 6 and 7, this is drawing in states that were previously ambiguous to the benefits of ASEAN-centred regionalisation, and not just for the EAS.

With this changing regional political and economic environment, Korea's involvement in East Asian institutions and networks is becoming a greater foreign policy challenge. Although it is clear that future expressions of regional governance will inevitably remain essentially centred around ASEAN, the rivalry between China and Japan for influence in regional institutions and norms further complicates Korea's strategic positioning.

Korea's position as the only state with that potential to assume an intermediate role between China and Japan suffered a setback with the economic damage inflicted by the 1997 Asian crisis. Soon after the crisis, China overtook Korea as the second-largest regional economy, not only in terms of its size but also as measured by its overall performance and capacity. A further deterioration in the relationship between China and Japan followed soon thereafter. Despite their showcased cooperation in developing and launching the APT, the rivalry between China and Japan over the economically vulnerable ASEAN states and Korea has only deepened further.

One of the most salient features of this rivalry is illuminated by their fierce competition for FTAs with ASEAN and the regional states at bilateral level as well as by their fervent desire to improve security ties. China and Japan's unwillingness to cooperate on regional affairs, coupled with an easily upset bilateral relationship, has pulled them in different directions with respect to the building of the East Asian Community (EAC). The fundamental level of their disagreements was revealed at the inaugural meeting of the EAS, when Japan insisted on – and China opposed – the membership of Australia and New Zealand.[47] Under these circumstances, it seems that the balancing role of middle powers such as Korea is more important than ever if the region is sincere about building the EAC.

Although Korea's capacity to play an intermediate role in East Asian regionalisation was significantly undermined by the 1997 crisis, this did catalyse its thinking as to the role and value of middle powers in Asia. With the core expression of East Asia seen through the lens of ASEAN, Korea has begun to view itself as a median state between the two Northeast Asian powers and the collective Southeast Asian states. This has prompted Korea to seek new ways to promote and strengthen policy coordination and cooperation with ASEAN. To an extent, the promotion of deeper ties with ASEAN (regardless of the government in power) was an inevitable choice for Korea, considering the creation of the APT and the EAS. Although the 'hub and spokes' structure of the APT may still place Korea on a equal footing with China and Japan as one of the spokes, there is a concern that Korea needs to proactively improve relations with ASEAN if its position is not to diminish in relative importance.

As such, it can be concluded that Korea is pursuing an active role in shaping East Asian regional governance. This is reflected in its continuous involvement in the creation of an institutional structure for regional integration. Korea's involvement not only serves the interests of an evolving region but reflects domestic policy shifts in its own perception of its regional profile and status.

Korea as a regional middle power and its norm articulation

Even though it has significant economic and other resources, as a middle power Korea does not have sufficient influence to unilaterally affect the outcome of the development of the region's normative structure. This is especially the case as it is situated in a region dominated by a number of greater powers, where its own norms and rules tend to be vulnerable to external influence. Given this, it can be suggested that ASEAN and Korea are after similar goals and objectives in constructing a regional system of governance. Moreover, it can be proposed that as a middle power it is more likely to seek alliances to further its aim and norms with like-minded actors whose influence is stipulated by the number in the alliance.[48] However, while Korea may be a regional middle power with a foreign policy that is developing an increasingly clear regional orientation, in practice it has yet to succeed in asserting itself as a middle power in the current regional process because it has failed to align its policy objectives clearly those of with other middle powers in the region.

Thus, a set of critical questions naturally arises with respect to Korea's status as regional middle power, namely, what constrains Korea from fully practising middle power diplomacy or displaying middle power leadership? Does it not have sufficiently coherent goals in relation to ASEAN that could facilitate enhanced interaction with ASEAN states as a key element in the creation of a regional normative structure? The answer to these questions could be inferred from its failure to assume so-called 'middle power leadership'. Regardless of the size of state, successful international leadership can be judged by whether or not a state succeeds in advancing the common interest of a group of states, since international leadership is exercised in a different setting (anarchical space), by different means (persuasion), a different motivation (self-interest) and a different basis (moral justification).[49]

Korea's leadership as a middle power, therefore, should be judged on whether or not it has successfully advanced the common interest of a group of states. In the light of regional integration theory, there are a few common interests that can be facilitated by successful international leadership. These interests encompass from consensus building to identity creation, from confidence building to institutional formation, and from peace and stability to development and prosperity. To advance these interests in the region, structural leadership based on national power is important. The common source for such power and activities is usually found in the leading states of a region. However, as the region has two antagonistic leader states (China and Japan) that remain too far apart for any chance of meaningful cooperation, East Asian regionalism may have to depend on middle-power actors to overcome the obstacle that this presents for the further institutionalisation of regional dialogues and norms.[50]

It is quite obvious that Korea has not been able to fulfil this role. There are several reasons that may account for this shortcoming, most of which lie in the rivalry between China and Japan, which has grown so out of proportion that it would be unrealistic to expect it to be mediated by any regional states, including Korea.[51] A lack of trust toward Japan notwithstanding, regional states are equally not in a position to side fully with China. The reason for this is simple: regionalism with the absence of either state will be incomplete and unsustainable. One option for a middle power like Korea – stuck between the two competing regional giants – is to be constructive in pursuit of regional endeavours by cooperating with other states in a collective way – through forming either a coalition or an alliance with other actors.[52] Such a framework will allow Korea – as a regional middle power – to pursue its own interests, despite the policy gridlock presented by great-power rivalry.

Against this background, Korea has embraced norms that have long been in existence, such as the 'ASEAN Way' or 'open regionalism'. It also embraces other regional norms such as equality, justice and the peaceful resolution of international conflicts. It is worth noting that, in terms of leadership affiliation, Korea's espousal of open regionalism places it much closer to Japan's set of norms than to China's. Korea's desire to preserve regional peace and prosperity was most clearly seen in its initiation of the EAVG, which held the aim of realising an 'East Asian community of peace, prosperity, and progress'.[53]

Korea has deemed that the normative values of peace and prosperity should be incorporated into any realisation of an East Asian Community, as they are perceived to be prerequisites for the effective functioning of the other extant norms. In other words, they are complementary and mutually reinforcing. While peace and prosperity will be attainable with the practice of equality, just and peaceful resolution, simultaneously, the latter will create an international environment conducive to the realisation of the former at the subregional level (the Korean Peninsula), in the regional arena (East Asia) and on the global stage. The logic behind this conviction was obviously seen in the foreign policy approaches followed by both Kim Dae-jung's and Roh Moo-hyun's governments. It was underscored by Kim's Reconciliation and Cooperation Policy (also known as the Sunshine Policy) and Roh's Peace and Prosperity Policy.

However, Korea's efforts towards the norm-building process have not been free of challenges. These challenges have stemmed from two sets of causes – domestic constraints and the fluid nature of East Asian regionalism to date. There are numerous domestic constraints at work. In light of regionalism, however, two factors deserve attention. One factor is deeply rooted in the elite politics of Korea's foreign policy. Traditionally speaking, Korea's foreign policy has long centred on its relations with major powers in general, and with the United States and Japan in particular. Notwithstanding the success in the development of relations with China and Russia, Korea's elite politics has hardly been attentive to the relationships with other regional states. The other domestic constraint relates to Korea's preoccupation with North Korea. Since North Korea presents a direct and immediate threat to Korea's security concerns, it has fewer resources that can be allocated to developing new relationships – either bilaterally or multilaterally.

One salient example that substantiates this point can be seen in the low levels of support provided for in Korea's Overseas Development Aid (ODA) programme. Although Korea was a beneficiary of US$33.1 billion in ODA from the international community during its economic miracle era (1960s-1970s), it has not been overly generous since establishing its own programme in 1991. As of 2007, Korea's total volume of ODA stands at a bit more than US$672 million, or 0.07 per cent of GNI, which places it at nineteenth (out of twenty-two countries) among OECD members in terms of the amount of assistance provided. This is far below the average rate of 0.1 per cent of the other OECD countries.[54] Despite this, it goes without saying that Korea targets its aid especially towards the Southeast Asian states, most of which are large recipients of its assistance.

Korea, however struggling, has been persistently making efforts not only to remain part of the ongoing process to realise an East Asian Community but also to contribute constructively to the building of regional governance at both governmental and non-governmental levels. Furthermore, Korea's policy towards this has also experienced substantial reorientations, according to the changing concepts of regionalism. When 'open regionalism' was at its peak in the first half of the 1990s, before its functionality and mechanism were greatly tested by the region-wide challenge of the 1997 Asian crisis, for instance, Korea made persistent efforts to embrace a broader identity so as to include non-APEC members, in the expectation that unilateral trade and economic liberalisation would have positive effects on a wider area of regional issues, such as security and the environmental matters.

Despite some early setbacks, Korea has continued to sustain this norm by launching more initiatives that engage with states outside the APT or EAS processes. Some examples of these initiatives include: NEACD, the Northeast Asian Conference on Environmental Cooperation (NEACEC)[55] and the Northeast Asia Regional Government Association (NEARGA), which was founded in 1996 to promote economic and political ties at local government level among the regional states of Northeast Asia.[56] Although Korea's desire for the further development of open regionalism in non-economic areas within the APT and EAS has yet to yield visible achievements, Korea still seeks out non-regional engagement as and when its needs and resources (and those of its partners) allow. Nonetheless, Korea's actions as a middle power have proved to be insufficient in unilaterally establishing any form of regional multilateral institution. In the absence of such achievements, Korea will need to continue working with other regional partners to foster any form of regional governance in Asia.

Conclusion

Despite these shortcomings, Korea has made a sustained effort to remain constructively engaged in the development of East Asian regional governance. Although its foreign policy is often constrained by domestic interests, the issue of North Korea and its immediate geopolitical environment, its focus on regionalism has continued unabated. Korea's numerous regional initiatives substantiate this position. This can be seen, for example, in its contribution to the EAVG and EASG processes. In addition, its proactive participation in regional governance-building meetings in both economic and non-economic areas has also allowed Korea to be an important actor, contributing to the progressive process of shaping regional governance. Moreover, Korea's role in East Asian affairs is slowly regaining the importance it once had in the early period of regionalisation in the 1990s, as the relationship between the leading regional powers, China and Japan, remains uneven and competitive. To further develop the East Asian Community, Korea, as a middle power, cannot rely on itself but will need to seek external support from other actors in a similar situation, who can be found in ASEAN.

It is safe to say that Korea now tends to share a similar ideational outlook with ASEAN, an outlook that has been developed since the launching of the APT in 1997.[57] Moreover, since the 1997 Asian crisis Korea has also been aligning itself with ASEAN's ideas as to the benefits of multilateral and regional cooperation, as witnessed in its leadership of the EAVG and EASG – although this was hampered by successive changes in Korea's foreign policy frameworks. Nonetheless, Korea has not followed through with this initial commitment. Besides its participation in fora such as the APT and the ARF, Korea has not been overly active in its pursuit of building a more wide-ranging relationship with ASEAN. In the economic realm, for instance, even though ASEAN (as a whole) is Korea's fourth-largest trading partner, the total volume it occupies in Korea's overall trade performance still remains very marginal.[58] Moreover, in the political realm, high-level diplomatic efforts (including summit meetings and other ministerial dialogues) are rarely conducted between the two parties. They are instead usually carried out as part of the extended meetings within the ARF, the APT or the EAS. Other than these occasions, Korea's bilateral diplomacy with ASEAN seems minimal.

As a middle power, Korea must cooperate better with ASEAN in building regional governance. Its interest in protecting and nurturing regional governance can only be realised once its engagement with ASEAN and ASEAN member states is better developed. Furthermore, a coalition with ASEAN based on the principle of cooperation would have a positive effect in coping with some of key issues confronting the region, such as the impact of future crises and evolving concepts of regional architecture.[59] Given the successful formation of a middle-power coalition, some of the major challenges confronting Korea's efforts with ASEAN (such as the risk of fragmentation, leadership and trust) could be resolved by the reconstitution of the coalition through including larger economies so as to enhance the middle powers' overall bargaining strength, thereby allowing them to exercise more influence in regional affairs – both across the region and in a variety of niches.[60]

To conclude, it can be said that Korea has enjoyed relatively little significant success in contributing to regional governance in Asia, despite numerous initiatives and extensive participation in the development of the regional architecture at both governmental and non-governmental levels. Reviewing the actions of the past administrations, it is clear that there is a growing awareness of the need to engage with the region in a more systematic and sustainable manner if Korea's vision for an East Asian Community is to be supported. One of the key obstacles Korea faces in articulating its vision is it political position as a middle power, bounded on either side by the two largest Asian powers, who are engaged in a constant process of rivalry and positioning for leadership. If Korea can enhance its relations with ASEAN, the resulting coalition may be able create to an alternative vision for the development of the region. However, Korea also must confront the additional challenge posed by the expansion of regional affairs under the EAS dialogue. Although the EAS may not replace the APT, and thus the APT will remain a basic framework for East Asian regional governance, as long as the EAS remains the titular pinnacle of regional institutions in Asia it will retain a degree of influence over the agenda-setting discourse. This provides Korea with additional motivation to actively seek out new ways of identifying common interests and policies for advancing East Asian regional governance.

Notes

1 Akaha, Tsuneo. 'International Relations in Northeast Asia: National Factors and Future Products', in Sumio Kuribayashi (ed.). *Rethinking Development Strategy in Northeast Asia*. (Tokyo: The Sasakawa Peace Foundation, 1993), pp. 25–46.

2 Oh, Gi-pyung. *Han'guk eui weogyoron: sin gukje jilseo wa bulhwaksilseong eui yiron* [Studies of Korea's foreign policy: New international order and uncertainties theory]. (Seoul: Oreum Publishing House, 1994), p. 253.

3 Han, Sung-Joo. *Korea in a Changing World: Democracy, Diplomacy, and Future Development*. (Seoul: Oreum Publishing House, 1995), pp. 15–16.

4 Adelman, Irma and Song Byung Nak. 'The Korean Financial Crisis of 1997–98', in Servaas Storm and C.W.M. Naastepad (eds). *Globalization and Economic Development: Essays in Honor of J. George Waardenburg*. (Northampton, MA: Edward Elgar, 2002), p. 87.

5 Kim, Suk H. 'The Asian Financial Crisis of 1997: The Case of Korea', *Multinational Business Review*. (Vol. 9, No. 1, April 2001), pp. 50–58. http://findarticles.com/p/articles/mi_qa3674/is_200104/ai_n8940217/print. Accessed 17 January 2008.

6 Kwak, Sung Yeung, 'Factors Contributing to the Financial Crisis in Korea', *Journal of Asian Economics*. (Vol. 9, No. 4, 1998), p. 618.

7 Haggard, Stephan. 'The Politics of Asian Financial Crisis', *Journal of Democracy*. (Vol. 11, No. 2, April 2000), pp. 135–138.

8 Kwak, Sung Yeung. 'Factors Contributing to the Financial Crisis in Korea', p. 616.

9 Adelman, Irma and Song Byung Nak. 'The Korean Financial Crisis of 1997–98', p. 88.

10 For a comprehensive analysis on the Korean government's failure to pass these reform bills because of domestic political factors, see Haggard. 'The Politics of Asian Financial Crisis', pp. 130–144.

11 The US manufacturing sector on average ranged between 0.62 in 1980 to 1.85 in 1992. Source: Adelman and Song, 'The Korean Financial Crisis of 1997–98', p. 90.

12 Haacke, Jurgen. 'The Concept of Flexible Engagement and the Practice of Enhanced Interaction: Intramural Challenges to the ASEAN way', *Pacific Affairs*. (Vol. 12, No. 4, 1999), p. 581.

13 For studies on APT nations' displeasing experience with lukewarm response form the US at the outset of the 1997 Asian Crisis see: Kurlantzick, Joshua. 'Is East Asia Integrating?', *The Washington Quarterly*. (Vol. 24, No. 4, Autumn 2001),

pp. 19–28; Ravenhill, John. 'A Three Bloc World? The New East Asian Regionalism', *International Relations of the Asia-Pacific*. (Vol. 2, No. 2, 2002), pp. 167–195.

14 Webber, Douglas. 'Two Funerals and a Wedding: The Ups and Downs of Regionalism in East Asia and Asia-Pacific after the Asian Crisis', *Pacific Review*. (Vol. 14, No. 3, 2001), p. 339.

15 Fishlow, Albert and Stephan Haggard. *The United States and the Regionalization of the World*. (Paris: OECD Development Center Research Project on Globalization and Regionalization, 1992).

16 Citing the work of Fishlow and Haggard, Mansfield and Milner explain that regionalisation is referred to 'the regional concentration of economic flows at intraregional level', whereas regionalism can be defined as 'a political process characterized by economic policy cooperation and coordination among countries.' See: Mansfield, Edward and Helen V. Milner. 'The New Wave of Regionalism', *International Organization*. (Vol. 53, No. 3, Summer 1999), p. 591.

17 As of 2006, the number of Korea's NGOs stood at 5,556. 'Lost 10 years-Korean NGO,' *Dong-A Ilbo*. 4 January 2008.

18 For a better understanding of Korean NGO's involvement in East Asian regionalism, see Jung, Ku-Hyun. 'Nongovernmental Initiatives in Korea for Northeast Asian Cooperation,' in Tsueno Akaha (ed.). *Politics and Economics in Northeast Asia: Nationalism and Regionalism in Contention*. (New York: St. Martin's Press, 1999), pp. 347–365.

19 Mansfield, Edward D. and Helen V. Milner. 'The New Wave of Regionalism', *International Organization*. (Vol. 53, No. 3, 1999), p. 604.

20 Yoo, Jae Won. 'The Changing Role(s) of Non-Governmental Organization in the Korean Policy Process,' *Journal of Public Administrative Studies*. (Vol. 42, No. 4, 2004), pp. 77–105.

21 Choi, Woo-suk. 'A Korean Farmer Kills Himself in Cancoon protest', *Chosun Ilbo*. 11 September 2003.

22 Yim, Sang-ho. 'Korean Protestors Puts on a High Sea Demonstration', *Yeonhap Television News* (YTN). 13 December 2005.

23 Yu, Hyun Seog. 'The Role of Korea in East Asian Regional Economic Cooperation', *East Asia: An International Quarterly*. (Vol. 20, No. 4, Winter 2003), pp. 77–98.

24 It was on this occasion that the Korean government announced its intention to launch its FTA earlier than that of either China or Japan. China's FTA with ASEAN is expected to be fully rolled out by 2011, whereas Japan's is due by 2010. However, Korea expects its FTA will do away with tariffs on 80 per cent of the commodities by 2009 and 90 per cent by 2010. See: 'President Roh to Attend ASEAN Summit', *Maeil Daily*. 13 December 2005.

25 Song, Eun-hee, 'Prospects and Feasibility of Korea-China-Japan FTA as Northeast Asia Economic Cooperation', *Korean Journal of Northeast Asia Studies*. (Vol. 23, 2002), pp. 3–20.

26 *Instrument of Extension of the Treaty of Amity and Cooperation in Southeast Asia by Republic of Korea*. http://www.aseansec.org/16625.htm. Accessed 13 January 2006.

27 Chairman's statement of the 8th ASEAN+Republic of Korea Summit: Deepening ASEAN-Republic of Korea Relationship (Vientiane: 30 November, 2004). http://www.aseansec.org/16743.htm. Accessed 13 January 2006.

28 'The ROK-ASEAN Dialogue was founded as a consultative body for discussions on ways to promote the ROK-ASEAN cooperation in different areas such as politics and economy. Since the establishment of the full dialogue partnership in 1991, the two sides have held 4 meetings biennially until 2001, the first meeting of which was held in Malaysia in May 1993. The meeting is being held annually

from 2002.' Source: The European Union Chamber of Commerce in Korea. http://eucck.org/site/news/government_news.htm?mode = view&num = 1312&page = 219&pCate2 = &pPart = &pKeyword = . Accessed 25 January 2008.

29 Jeong, Jae-wan. *Korea and ASEAN and the Joint Declaration on Comprehensive Cooperative Partnership.* (Seoul: Korea Institute for International Economic Policy, 2004).

30 Korean Ministry of Foreign Affairs. http://sub.mofat.go.kr/english/regions/intorganization/asean/index.jsp. Accessed 29 September 2007.

31 'President Roh Moo-hyun is to Attend the ASEAN+3, Korea-ASEAN and East Asia Summits in Singapore'. http://english.president.go.kr/cwd/en/pub/president/cnt0202011102.html. Accessed 24 January 2008.

32 *Initiative for ASEAN integration (IAI) Workplan for the CLMV Countries: Progress Report as at 15 May 2005.* http://www.aseansec.org/pdf/IAI-Article.pdf. Accessed 29 April 2008.

33 *Chairmans' Statement of the Ninth ASEAN-Republic of Korea Summit*, Kuala Lumpur, 3 December 2005. http://www.aseansec.org/18082.htm. Accessed 23 January 2008.

34 'Korea-ASEAN Framework Agreement on Comprehensive Economic Cooperation Inked'. http://english.president.go.kr/cwd/en/archive/archive_view.php?meta_id = en_dip_2005&category = 172&navi = president&id = 015568245c15adaa7039ea21. Accessed 24 January 2008). The contents of the Framework is available at http://www.aseansec.org/18063.htm. Accessed on 24 January 2008.

35 The Agreement on Trade in Goods is available at: http://www.aseansec.org/AKFTA%20documents%20signed%20at%20aem-rok,24aug06,KL-pdf/TIG%20-%20ASEAN%20Version%20-%2022August2006-final.pdf. Accessed 24 January 2008.

36 *Chairman's Statement of the 11th ASEAN-Republic of Korea Summit*, Singapore, 21 November 2007. http://www.aseansec.org/21141.htm. Accessed 24 January 2008.

37 The Agreement on Trade in Services is available at 'Agreement on Trade in Services under the Framework Agreement on Comprehensive Economic Cooperation among the Governments of the Member Countries of the Association of Southeast Asian Nations and The Republic of Korea'. http://www.aseansec.org/21111.pdf. Accessed 25 January 2008. See also: 'S. Korea, ASEAN sign FTA on services at annual summit', *Yonhap News*, 21 November 2007. http://english.yonhapnews.co.kr/national/2007/11/21/97/0301000000AEN20071121006900315F.HTML. Accessed 25 January 2008.

38 'Roh Emphasizes ASEAN's Continuous Support for the Construction of Permanent Peace System on the Peninsula', News release by the Korean Overseas Information Services, 21 November 2007. http://korea.kr/newsWeb/appmanager/portal/news?_nfpb = true&portlet_categorynews_2_actionOverride = %2Fpages%2Fbrief%2FcategoryNews%2Fview&_windowLabel = portlet_categorynews_2&_pageLabel = news_page_02&_nfls = false&portlet_categorynews_2newsDataId = 148642688&portl. Accessed 26 January 2008.

39 Sun, Kyung-cheol, 'Korea-ASEAN Free Trade Area within Sight', *Korea Portal News Services.* 21 November 2007.

40 Korean Ministry of Foreign Affairs and Trade. *Diplomatic White Paper.* (Seoul: Ministry of Foreign Affairs and Trade, 2007), pp. 136–138.

41 Korean Ministry of Foreign Affairs and Trade. *Diplomatic White Paper,* p. 99.

42 Joo, Jae Woo. 'Korea's New President Facing New Challenges: "Korea 747", "Pragmatism", "Reciprocity" and "New Diplomacy"', *EAI Background Brief No. 376.* (Singapore: East Asian Institute, 26 March 2008).

43 Terada, Takashi, 'Creating an East Asian Regionalism: The Institutionalization of ASEAN+3 and China-Japan Directional Leadership', *The Japanese Economy.* (Vol. 32, No. 2, Summer 2005), pp. 64–85.

114   *Jaewoo Choo*

44 The idea of the 'East Asian Summit (EAS)' was proposed by China and Malaysia during the 10th ASEAN Summit meeting in Laos in October 2004.
45 Cheow, Eric Teo Chu, 'New Challenges for Building an East Asian Community', *China Brief.* (Vol. 5, No. 2, 18 January 2005). http://www.jamestown.org, pp. 1–4.
46 Cheow, Eric Teo Chu, 'China as the Center of Asian Economic Integration', *China Brief.* (Vol. 4, No. 15, 22 July 2004). http://www.james town.org, pp. 3–5.
47 Terada, Takashi, 'Creating an East Asian Regionalism: The Institutionalization of ASEAN+3 and China-Japan Directional Leadership', pp. 76–78.
48 Mares, David R., 'Middle Powers under Regional Hegemony: To Challenge or Acquiesce in Hegemonic Enforcement', *International Studies Quarterly* (Vol. 32, No. 4, December 1988), p. 456.
49 Tang, Shiping, 'Institution-building under 10+3: Tackling the Practical Issues', *Global Economic Review.* (Vol. 31, No. 4, December 2002), pp. 3–16.
50 For an in-depth study on the reason why Korea should assume a role in undertaking a 'mission' to build a regional community of cooperation, Koo, Jung-Suh, 'Pan-Asianism for Primacy of East Asia', *Korea Focus.* (Vol. 3, No. 2, 1995), pp. 34–41.
51 One example of bizarre action by the Chinese official was the abrupt decision by the Chinese vice-premier and Minster of Commerce Wu Yi not to see Koizumi and to return to China without prior notification despite their appointment during her visit to Japan in May 2005. Cho, Joong-sik, 'PM Cancels Talks, Tensions in Sino-Japanese Relations Arises', *Chosun Ilbo.* 24 May 2005.
52 This view is widely shared by Rhee, Sang Woo, 'Japan's Role in New Asian Order', *Korea Focus.* (Vol. 4, No. 3, May/June 1996), pp. 22–36.
53 Soesastro, Hadi. 'Realizing the East Asia Vision', *CSIS Working Paper Series WPE 090.* (Jakarta: CSIS, February 2005). http://www.csis.or.id/working_paper_file/51/wpe090.pdf, p. 1. Accessed 27 January 2006.
54 Source: 'The nation's increased overseas development aid in line with its heightened national status', *KBS Global.* http://english.kbs.co.kr/news/issue/1517781_11780.html. Accessed 25 April 2008.
55 For a review of Korea's involvement in regional environmental cooperation in Northeast Asia at both governmental and non-governmental levels, see Lee, Shin-wha, 'Safeguarding the Environment: Regional Nuclear Cooperation in Northeast Asia', in Jae-Kap Ryoo, Tae-Hoon Kang, and Sung-Joo Kim (eds). *Bilateralism, Multilateralism and Geopolitics in International Relations: Theory and Practice.* (Seoul: Yejin, 1999), pp. 331–358.
56 The Association was initiated by a Korean local government in 1996, and has held a meeting once every other year. At its initiation, regional participation only came from South Korea, Japan, Russia and China. In 2002, its membership included all six states of Northeast Asia, including North and South Korea, China, Japan, Russia, and Mongolia, and 40 local NGOs and other related governmental organisations. Membership and participation are all represented by local governments of states. Details on the founding mission and the history of the development can all be referred to the home page of *The Association of North East Asia Regional Governments.* http://www.neargov.org. Accessed 26 May 2008.
57 Suk, Churl-Jin. 'Outlook for Asian Regional Cooperation: European Experience', in Guohua Pai and Zhang Xizhen (eds). *Dongya diquhezuo yu hezuojuzhi* [Regional cooperation and mechanism in East Asia]. (Beijing: Central Compliance and Translation Press, 2002), pp. 46–56.
58 However, Korean scholars like Chang-Jae Lee place a far greater value on the positive consequences of continuous discussion, as in the context of APT, on economic cooperation and major economic issues at regional level, and boldly predict it to have a positive influence on the regionalisation process. Lee, Chang-Jae.

'Northeast Asian Economic Cooperation: The Need for a New Approach', *NIRA Review.* (Autumn 2000), pp. 5–10.

59 The coalition could be formed in two ways: bloc-type coalition and issue-based alliances. While the former come together against a backdrop of ideational and identity-related factors, the latter are formed for instrumental reasons. Also, while bloc-type coalitions combine like-minded states and try to adopt collective positions across issue areas and over time, issue-based ones are directed towards specific threats and dissipate after the particular issue has been addressed. The debate as to which coalition is suitable to the interest of regional governance building and regionalism is outside the scope of this chapter, and therefore is not dealt here. For a detailed study on this particular issue, however, see Narlikar, Amrita and Diana Tussie. 'The G20 at the Cancun Ministerial: Developing Countries and Their Evolving Coalitions in the WTO', *The World Economy.* (Vol. 27, No. 7, July 2004), pp. 957–960.

60 Narlikar, Amrita and Diana Tussie, 'The G20 at the Cancun Ministerial: Developing Countries and Their Evolving Coalitions in the WTO', p. 954.

5 China's regional governance

Developing norms and institutions[1]

Nicholas Thomas

Introduction

As a rapidly modernising power China has attracted considerable attention from the international community with respect to its current intentions and future ambitions. Nowhere is this attention more apparent than with the countries of Asia, where there has been a long-running debate over whether China's rise constitutes a 'threat' or a 'promise' to the established regional order. Even though the current thinking appears to be favouring the 'promise' side, there is still a degree of wariness within regional policy communities as to China's intentions. This is a wariness fostered by historical memories of China's regional engagement as well as uncertainties over its longer-term intentions. A key objective of this chapter is to better understand the parameters of China's regional policy with its four peripheral regions: Southeast Asia, Central Asia, Northeast Asia and South Asia – so as to be able to evaluate the impact that China has on Asian regionalisation.

A useful way to understand this policy is through an examination of China's foreign policy norms and its involvement with regional institutions. To undertake this examination the chapter draws on the work of the governance school (presented in Chapter 1), but adopts the model so as to take into account specific cultural and historical nuances that are present in China's international relations. This requires the location of China's pattern of regional engagement in a longer historical perspective, taking into account domestic pressures on foreign policy development.

In doing so, this chapter will attempt develop a basis from which China's current regional policy can be understood and its implications for the development of regional governance in Asia be considered. To realise this, the chapter will first review China's modernisation, with specific reference to the development of its foreign policy. China's institutionalised and non-institutionalised engagement with surrounding Asian regions is the subject of the following two sections. China's engagement with Southeast and Central Asia and with Northeast and South Asia are analysed in tandem so as to highlight common patterns in the articulation of its regional policy, but contrasted so as to ensure that differences in approach are understood. The impact of China's engagement in the development of regional institutions and norms is considered in the fourth section, before some concluding remarks are made. As these sections are considered, it is important to note that this chapter seeks to understand China's role in the formation of regionalism and governance in Asia. While any foreign policy process is a complex undertaking, with a range of actors and pressures, the chapter is primarily concerned with Chinese international engagement at the regional level.

China's rise: from periphery to hub?

The establishment of the People's Republic of China (PRC) in October 1949 heralded the emergence of a major communist power in Asia. The ideological basis of the PRC guaranteed a worldview predicated on socialism's struggle against capitalism. However, almost from its inception, the applied nature of its socialist theory was tested, with China holding a different worldview from that of the Soviet Union. The Soviet Union under Khrushchev was committed to peaceful coexistence with the West, arguing that it would be economics that would decide the outcome, not conflict; while China under Mao 'argued for increased support for wars of liberation and national independence movements' to resist capitalist imperialism.[2] Relations between the two powers were further soured 'by Moscow's unilateral action during the Cuban Missile Crisis in 1962, its acceptance of a nuclear test ban treaty without consulting the Chinese, and by its refusal to support China in the 1962 border war with India'.[3] It was ideological and practical differences such as these that led to the great split between China and the Soviet Union.

Despite these differences, Western strategic thinking during this period was dominated by the concept of a monolithic communist bloc, stretching from East Berlin to Shanghai. Repeatedly during this period, terms used to describe the situation between Western and Eastern Europe – such as the 'iron curtain' – were transposed into an Asian context – becoming instead the 'bamboo curtain'. Another example, the domino theory, which was first used to describe the falling of Eastern European states under Soviet hegemony, was also used by American policy makers to describe a similar perceived threat in East Asia. Indeed, the concept that, if left unchecked, successive Asian states would fall to communism, was a major concern for Western and regionally allied powers. It is indicative of how far the region has progressed that former strategic and ideological adversaries can now meet as equals without hostility.

China's antagonism towards both the United States (US) and the Soviet Union was reflective of the political and strategic alliances in the territories surrounding China. To the east were the United States alliances with Japan, South Korea, Taiwan and – via the British – Hong Kong. To the west, Central Asia fell under Soviet control, while in the south India was also a Soviet ally. In Southeast Asia, the Association of Southeast Asian Nations

(ASEAN) was established with at least an implicit objective of halting the further spread of communism, and Vietnam leant towards the Soviet Union. It was a very hostile environment for such a young state and one that prevented the reconceptualisation of a Chinese periphery.[4]

Throughout the 1970s, this environment slowly changed as Sino-US ties began to improve. A series of bilateral sporting and cultural exchanges was followed by the normalisation of relations between the two countries in February 1972, and culminated in the United States' support for the PRC assuming the 'China seat' on the United Nations Security Council.[5] The restoration of Sino-US ties encouraged the adoption of a triangular foreign and strategic policy by China, one where Beijing balanced its needs against the competing demands of Moscow or Washington.

At the same time, the Chinese leadership changed, with the rise of an economic and technocratic elite led by Deng Xiaoping following the deaths of Zhou Enlai and Mao Zedong, and after the brief reign of Hua Guofeng. The primacy given to economic policy was not limited to agricultural and industrial modernisation programmes but also encompassed the Chinese military apparatus. The need to modernise the military was reinforced by the harsh lessons drawn from the 1979 Sino-Vietnam war, where an outdated Chinese military was able only to partially fulfil its objectives, at a ruinous cost.

The following decade saw an entrenchment based on the need for national economic development to provide for the stability and prosperity (and hence security) of China. Up until the brief isolation of China brought about by the events in Tiananmen Square, China gradually exposed its society and economy to global processes. China also began to consider its security more directly in terms of its relative power to the United States. This was aided by China's long-term economic development, coupled with the weakening of Soviet influence.

The modernisation of China in the 1980s laid the foundations for China's deeper engagement in international affairs. This was seen in political terms in March 1986 when Premier Zhao Ziyang outlined the main tenets of an independent foreign policy for China during the 4th Session of the 6th National Party Congress (NPC), which would allow it to engage with other states on an equal basis.[6] In economic terms this was later seen in 1992, when the 14th NPC shifted from a 'Socialist Planned Economy' to a 'Socialist Market Economy', and again in 2001 when China joined the World Trade Organisation (WTO). Along the way, China has embarked on a range of other multilateral initiatives, especially focused at the regional level. Indeed, over the two decades since the 14th NPC, China's engagement with other regional states has only accelerated. In particular, China has moved towards developing relations with Southeast, Central, Northeast and South Asian states. This period also witnessed a gradual shift away from a preference for bilateralism towards an acceptance of the utility of multilateral dialogues within regional and international organisations.

The period has also seen an expansion of both state and non-state actors involved in China's foreign relations. At the substate level, the provinces and municipalities have been playing an increasingly active role in developing external ties, with all provincial administrations forming a foreign affairs office [*waishi bangongshi*] to coordinate their affairs, 'under the dual leadership of the [Ministry of Foreign Affairs] and the provincial governments'.[7] Beyond a simple reiteration of Chinese foreign policy, these substate actors are able to take the lead in operationalising new projects (such as the Kunming Initiative, see below) or in maintaining relations with other states where state-level ties are not possible (as was the case in the post-Tiananmen period when Zhu Rongji – then Mayor of Shanghai – was able to visit countries that had otherwise suspended official ties with China).[8]

Outside of the state, the private sector and civil society organisations (CSOs) are also expanding their external linkages, with Chinese economic ties and investments rising most notably in all four regions. Indeed, in some smaller states (such as Uzbekistan, Myanmar or North Korea) China is now the leading trade partner, while it is a significant source of investment and trade in many others. China's CSOs have also been working with their regional counterparts in promoting social development issues, as was seen in China's CSO aid to Indonesia and Thailand after the 2004 tsunami (see Chapter 11 for more information on this topic).

In addition to the role played by civil society, the Chinese government is also actively promoting Chinese culture and language throughout the surrounding regions and internationally. By mid 2008, 238 Confucius Institutes had been opened around the world in 69 countries.[9] How these latest expressions of soft power are to be integrated into China's foreign policy is yet to be publicly articulated; nonetheless, China has a long history of using such mechanisms to promote its values and goals. As Gill and Huang point out, one way to measure the effectiveness of such actions is to look at the polling data for China's popularity. They noted that a BBC poll showed China was perceived to be a positive influence by a majority of people in 14 of 22 countries surveyed and that 'in no country did a majority of people have a negative view on China'.[10]

In seeking to understand how China engages with its peripheral regions a number of explanations have been put forth. There is an increasingly large body of work which explores China's growing engagement at the global and regional levels. Whether from a realist or liberal–institutionalist perspective, this collection locates this pattern of multilateral engagement as a recent phenomenon, one that has been witnessed since the early/mid 1990s. Kuik, for example, suggests that China's involvement in multilateral institutions – especially with respect to Southeast Asia – dates from the early 1990s as 'part of the country's "good neighbourliness" [*mulin zhengce*] policy that aimed at strengthening its ties with neighbouring countries in the wake of the Tiananmen Incident in 1989'.[11] Foot suggests that it was the post-1997 crisis period that marked the turning point in China's acceptance of multilateral institutions, where before bilateralism was the dominant approach.[12] Yahuda also identifies the mid 1990s as the beginning of multilateralism in Chinese foreign policy, but chooses to focus on China's signing of the Treaty on Deepening Military Trust in Border Regions in 1996, with the other members of the Shanghai 5 group as the first signs of this policy shift.[13]

Regardless of when it precisely began, in considering contemporary Chinese foreign policy it can be said that, since the 1990s, this trend towards engaging in multilateral dialogues at the regional level has only intensified. Not only is China now actively participating in regional security arrangements (such as the ASEAN Regional Forum (ARF)), but it has also initiated the creation of new multilateral dialogues (such as the Shanghai Cooperation Organisation (SCO)). Where the establishment of a formalised body has not been possible, China has still sought a leading role in informal regional security dialogues, such as in the six-party talks on the Korean Peninsula. Where such a role has not been possible, China has taken steps to upgrade its bilateral relations with specific regional states as a precursor to seeking involvement in wider regional dialogues, as can be seen in the case of South Asia. These deeper regional relations have created a zone of strategic alliances with less powerful states around the Chinese mainland. As Ong has noted, '[s]ince 1989, China has begun to focus on surrounding area (*zhoubian*) diplomacy, which entails establishing a broad range of relations with it neighbours'.[14]

The norms of Chinese foreign policy: from Bandung to the new security concept

> As the largest developing country in the world with a relatively low level of productive forces as a whole, China needs a long-term peaceful international environment and a good neighborly environment in particular to realize its modernization program through decades of arduous struggles. Even when China is developed, it will continue to adhere to the Five Principles of Peaceful Co-existence and treating others as equals. China will never seek hegemony. China will always be a staunch force in maintaining regional and global peace and stability.[15]

It would, however, be incorrect to assume that the norms which underlie this multilateralist outlook are new to Chinese foreign policy development. Rather, a core set of norms can be identified, which have been present in Chinese foreign policy since the early years of the PRC. These norms can be seen in the Five Principles of Peaceful Coexistence, which were first articulated during Sino-Indian negotiations in 1953–54, although they were based on earlier statements by Mao Zedong and Zhou Enlai with regard to China's foreign affairs. These principles include: (1) mutual respect for sovereignty and territorial integrity, (2) mutual non-aggression, (3) non-interference in each other's internal affairs, (4) equality and mutual benefit, and (5) peaceful coexistence. In April 1955, at the first Asia–African conference (hereafter the Bandung conference) Chinese Premier Zhou Enlai expounded on the Five Principles of Peaceful Coexistence, alongside the Ten Principles adopted by the Bandung conference. When analysing China's engagement with its peripheral regions it is useful to recall that of the twenty-nine states that attended the Bandung conference, twelve were from Northeast, Southeast or South Asia (in addition to China).[16] Hence, as China moves to develop ties with these regions, there is already an ideological congruence with many of the member states.

It should be noted that this argument of the Five Principles as a continuous stream of thought in Chinese foreign policy does have opponents. Kim has argued that the gap between the period when the Five Principles were first used (1955) and 1986, when China articulated an independent foreign policy, means that this cannot be seen as a continuous policy. Kim has further stated that the shift in Chinese foreign policy formulation from hostile/defensive to peaceful/engagement further reduces the functional relevance of the Five Principles.[17] However, as will be seen in the following two sections, despite this temporal gap and shift in worldview, these principles still remain central to the operationalisation of China's foreign policy. Moreover, it is in turn arguable as to whether or not the Five Principles did in fact lapse during this period. The global shift in diplomatic recognition from Taiwan to China that particularly occurred in the 1970s saw a reaffirmation of the Five Principles in the resulting joint communiqués as well as in China's statements when it joined the United Nations. Hence, it may be more accurate to state that the combined hostilities of the Cold War and the Sino–Soviet split limited the opportunities for the articulation of the Five Principles as the guiding norms in Chinese foreign policy.

The increase in political, economic and strategic ties between China and other states is reflected in China's latest foreign and security policy, the New Security Concept (NSC). As noted earlier, external insecurity is seen as having a direct bearing on the stability of the Chinese state, interfering with its ability to meet the needs of its peoples. The pacification of the Chinese periphery is thus a central concern in the management of China's foreign political and security relations. To achieve this requires China to engage with the surrounding states and regions in an effort to create a secure environment in which its development can take place. The diversity of threats from the Asian region, coupled and contrasted with the potential for a more politically secure and economic stable relationship, has required China to seek to operationalise this policy in a growing number of bilateral and regional fora.

The New Security Concept first emerged during the Shanghai 5 talks in 1996.[18] This new set of principles seeks to create a more refined framework for an Asia-centric policy to regional politics and security. While this approach is consistent with China's long-standing desire to secure the Asian region so as to provide a stable environment for its own development, it also is indicative of a growing resistance to the regional influence of other major powers, particularly the United States. In terms of norm articulation this opposition to Western influence can be seen in examples of foreign aid strategies adopted by China in Central, Southeast and Northeast Asia. In the case of Central Asia, China has been noticeably stepping up its trade and investment ties with regional states, even as the Western states and donor agencies withdraw from the area because of human rights violations. In Southeast Asia, the long-running campaign to halt trade and investment in Myanmar because of political and social abuses has led to China becoming its largest commercial partner, while in Northeast Asia China has continued to provide significant aid and support to North Korea. In all three instances, there is a split between two different sets of norms being operationalised. On the one hand, the Western countries and the donor agencies are expressing a set of universalist meta-norms of rights and freedoms that allow for a degree of international monitoring and enforcement (as described in Chapter 1). On the other hand, China holds to the principle of non-interference, reflecting its own set of norms that it sees as being encroached upon by the actions of these external powers.

Since 1996 the Chinese government has advocated the NSC principles in a wide range of other regional and international fora, such as the ASEAN Regional Forum, and the United Nations as well as in the multilateral talks over the future of the Korean peninsula.[19] In mid 2002, following the evolution of the Shanghai 5 grouping into the SCO in 2001, China promulgated a NSC position paper. This paper contained five key principles for the NSC. These principles covered:

> (1) To conduct cooperation on the basis of the UN Charter, the Five Principles of Peaceful Coexistence and other widely recognized norms governing international relations, and give full play to the leading role of the United Nations; (2) To peacefully resolve territorial and border disputes and other controversial issues through negotiations; (3) To reform and improve the existing international economic and financial organizations and promote common prosperity in line with the principle of reciprocity and mutual benefit and common development; (4) To place emphasis on non-traditional security areas such as combating terrorism and transnational crimes, in addition to the traditional security areas like preventing foreign invasion and safeguarding territorial integrity; (5) To conduct effective disarmament and arms control with broad participation in line with the principle of justice, comprehensiveness, rationality and balance, prevent the proliferation of weapons of massive destruction, uphold the current international arms control and disarmament regime and refrain from arms race.[20]

Although Kuik has argued that there is little 'new' about the NSC, as it simply 'repeats the basic themes that underline the Five Principles of

Peaceful Coexistence',[21] in terms of China's multilateral engagement the promotion of the New Security Concept does have a number of implications for the regional political and strategic environment. First, its articulation signifies that China's engagement with the wider region is part of a broader long-term strategy of *zhoubian* diplomacy, one where the lessons learnt from other surrounding states and regions can be used to measure the development of its regional relations. As such, a deeper understanding of these relationships may inform a broader understanding of Chinese foreign policy. Second, China is viewing the development of its relations in different regional institutions primarily through a lens of national self-interest to which region building is subordinated. Third, while foreign economic relations and trade agreements will help to create a more prosperous environment for China, political and strategic ties are essential in stabilising the peripheral regions without which China's internal economic development will be jeopardised. How China engages with its peripheral regions is discussed in the following two sections.

Institutionalised regionalisation

The security of the Asia-Pacific region is inseparable from that of each country in the region. If not every country enjoys security in the region, there is no region to speak of.

(Foreign Minister Qian Qichen, 17 August 1992)

In its surrounding areas, China has developed institutional links with two regions – Southeast Asia and Central Asia – through the ASEAN and the SCO. This section will explore these institutional links in turn, so as to understand how China has played a role in shaping regional governance and associated norms where an institutional arrangement is present.

The Association of Southeast Asian Nations

China has long historical ties with Southeast Asia. For hundreds of years Chinese traders have been actively seeking opportunities in Southeast Asian markets. With these seasonal traders came permanent settlements and a concomitant expansion of social and commercial networks. In more recent times, however, China was separated from most of Southeast Asia through the regional divisions of the Cold War. In this setting China was seen as a threat, through its adherence to a more confrontational variant of the communist ideology. This perception of regional threat was reinforced through its challenge to Taiwan, its domination of Tibet, its military role during the Korean War, its invasion of Vietnam and its unilateral acquisition of territory in the South China Sea.

The opening up of China in the early 1980s highlighted its economic potential. This potential gradually served to construct a very different image of China, one of promise rather than of threat. By the end of the Cold War both images coexisted uneasily in regional perceptions of China. In some countries (the Philippines or Indonesia, for example), the perception of threat was stronger. In other countries (such as Malaysia or Singapore), there was a greater willingness to see China's promise. However, despite these differences, with the end of the Cold War there was a perceived need to address the 'China question', so that the threat aspect could be diminished and the promise could be realised.

At the same time, China was also interested in reviving ties with Southeast Asia. This mutual interest led to Chinese Foreign Minister Qian Qichen attending the opening session of the 24th ASEAN Ministerial Meeting (AMM), as a guest of Malaysia, in 1991. Over the next five years the relationship gradually developed across a range of functional areas, including economic and trade cooperation and collaboration in scientific and techno- logical projects.[22] China also continued to attend the AMM and became a consultative partner of the ARF in 1994. The political and security rela- tionship reached a high point in 1996, when China's status within the AMM was upgraded to that of a full Dialogue Partner, with a similar status begin acquired within the ARF. While the involvement of China in the ARF could be seen as an example of its commitment to multilateralism with peripheral states, at least in the beginning Mack suggests that the ARF was rather 'an ASEAN initiative whose creation the Chinese were powerless to prevent. China joined the ARF not least so it could put a brake on initiatives that the Chinese saw as inimical to their interests and to try to keep other issues off the agenda.'[23] Hence, although China's involvement in the ARF did repre- sent the involvement of the PRC in an emerging regional institution, its commitment to the associated institutional norms is questionable.

The year 1997 was a watershed for China–ASEAN relations, with sig- nificant improvements in the economic as well as political fields. The 1997 financial crisis, while devastating for Southeast Asian economies, sig- nificantly advanced China's position in regional politics. China's decision not to revalue the yuan was welcomed by Southeast Asian states, not only for the economic benefits the decision was perceived to provide but also because it was interpreted as a significant statement of affinity with the regional states. This affinity was in stark contrast to perceptions of Western countries and international organisations such as the International Monetary Fund (IMF) during the crisis. It also stood despite China's aligning itself with the United States to oppose the Japanese proposal for an Asian Monetary Fund (AMF), which had the support of several Southeast Asian states. Indeed, from this point onwards, China has steadily cemented its place as ASEAN's key partner in East Asia, much to the dismay of Japan (as was noted in Chapter 3).

Towards the end of 1997 China also joined in the first informal meeting of ASEAN+3.[24] This new grouping linked the ASEAN states with the three key Northeast Asian states of China, Japan and South Korea. The formation of this group was due to ASEAN's recognition that Southeast Asia's future was irrevocably tied to that of Northeast Asia – a point reinforced by the financial crisis. Of the three sets of bilateral talks ASEAN held with its northern neighbours, the China–ASEAN meeting was the only one that based itself on both ASEAN and Chinese norms. Neither the Japanese nor the Korean bilateral discussions made any reference to such issues.[25] Paragraph 2 of the Joint Statement of the Meeting of Heads of State/Government of the Member States of ASEAN and the President of the People's Republic of China mentioned, in part, that both sides:

> affirmed that the Charter of the United Nations, the Treaty of Amity and Cooperation in Southeast Asia, the Five Principles of Peaceful Coexistence and universally recognized international law should serve as basic norms governing their relations. They reaffirmed in particular their respect for each other's independence, sovereignty and territorial integrity and the principle of non-interference in the internal affairs of other states.[26]

This norm agreement served as a far stronger basis for the development of China–ASEAN relations than was the case with either the Japan–ASEAN or Korea–ASEAN relationship.

In 1999 the ASEAN+3 group was further solidified with the first-ever meeting of all thirteen states, the three Northeast Asian states as well as all ten Southeast Asian states. Although this meeting is noteworthy for the decision to create the East Asian Vision Group, it is equally important to note that the Joint Statement on East Asian Cooperation (issued at the end of the meeting) once again included the Five Principles of Peaceful Coexistence as one of the key norms guiding the development of mutual relations.[27]

However, even as the ASEAN+3 group has expanded cooperation into a wide range of areas (see Table 5.1), it has been the China–ASEAN relationship that has remained the key axis for regional development. In the past five years this bilateral relationship has developed faster and further than either the Japan–ASEAN or Korean–ASEAN relationship. This rapid development of ties has also meant that the structures and norms developed in the China–ASEAN meetings have often become the basis for Japan and South Korea's institutional ties.[28]

As China has steadily taken the lead over Japan and South Korea, it has expanded cooperation with ASEAN in the political and strategic, economic and financial as well as social and cultural areas. In terms of political and strategic cooperation, the two sides have signed a joint declaration on cooperation in non-traditional security issues as well as a code of conduct on matters relating to the disputed areas in the South China Sea. At the Bali Summit in 2003, China became the first non-Southeast Asian state to sign ASEAN's Treaty of Amity and Cooperation. In 2002 China also became the first non-Southeast Asian state to reach an agreement with ASEAN on a

Table 5.1 Indicative scope of ASEAN+3 cooperation

Area	Year of establishment
Political and Security	2000
Economic, Trade and Investment	2000
Finance and Monetary	2000
Agriculture, Fishery, Forestry	2001
Labour	2001
Environment	2002
Tourism	2002
Culture and Arts	2003
Energy	2004
Health	2004
Information Technology and Communications	2004
Social Welfare and Development	2004
Transnational Crime and Counter-Terrorism	2004
Science and Technology (SOM only)	2001
Youth (SOM only)	2004

Source: Tanaka, Akihiko. 'The Development of the ASEAN+3 Framework', in Melissa Curley and Nicholas Thomas (eds). *Advancing East Asian Regionalism.* (London: RoutledgeCurzon, 2007), p. 66.

framework agreement to further bilateral economic cooperation towards the realisation of a phased free trade agreement, which became a reality in July 2005. This agreement is in addition to accords on transport, agricultural and ICT cooperation that have also been signed since the turn of the century. In social and cultural areas in mid 2005 the two sides agreed on an ASEAN–China Memorandum of Understanding on Cultural Cooperation, which will 'promote culture cooperation through artistic collaboration and exchange, joint research and study, exchange of information and people-to-people exchange and interaction'.[30] China and ASEAN senior officials and ministers for youth affairs have also been meeting since mid 2004.[31]

While these agreements could be dismissed as simply political statements with relatively little impact on regional governance or norms, it is necessary to consider the nature of some of the more recent agreements. The Agreement on Trade in Goods of the Framework Agreement on Comprehensive Economic Co-operation between the Association of Southeast Asian Nations and the People's Republic of China that was signed at the Vientiane Summit in 2004 is a good example of how far the bilateral relationship has developed and what impact it can have on regional governance and norms.

In contrast to earlier agreements, where interpretation was dependent upon a mutual understanding, the Framework Agreement has an associated agreement for the establishment of a dispute-resolution mechanism. When a dispute arises between any of the states covered under this agreement, an arbitration tribunal can be appointed to decide the issue. In two key departures from the mode of earlier agreements, not only is the decision of the tribunal binding but, in the event of a dispute over the composition of the tribunal, the Director-General of the WTO or his deputy acts as referee. This represents a significant step forward in the development of regional economic governance, as both sides will have to abide by the decision of a supranational institution. To do so will require the partial abdication of sovereignty in order to gain greater economic benefits. Although the significance of the dispute-resolution mechanism will only be known fully when it is tested (successfully or otherwise), its presence with the Framework Agreement does suggest that even as both sides uphold the norms of state sovereignty and non-interference they are prepared to modify these norms to fit in with the objectives of new regional institutions.

During 2005 China and ASEAN sought to upgrade their relationship with the convening of a bilateral Eminent Persons Group (EPG) to develop a blueprint for advancing the relationship over the following fifteen years. Beyond the usual commitments to political, economic and security concerns, the EPG report placed significant emphasis on developing multilevel institutional ties between subnational, municipal and civil society organisations, especially in the socio-cultural and functional cooperation fields. In terms of guiding norms, the EPG clearly placed the relationship within the 'purposes and principles of the UN Charter, the Treaty of Amity and Cooperation in Southeast Asia, the Five Principles of Peaceful Coexistence, and the Ten Principles of the Bandung Asian-African Conference'.[32]

The work of the EPG was further developed in 2006 during the ASEAN–China Commemorative Summit, when ten priority areas were identified for deeper and broader functional cooperation. These areas encompassed: 'agriculture, information and communication technology (ICT), human resource development (HRD), two-way investment, Mekong River Basin development, transportation, energy, culture, tourism and public health, as well as the signing of several Memoranda of Understanding (MoUs)'.[33] Cooperation on the environment was added to the list of priority areas the following year.[34] The outcomes from the 2006 summit can be seen throughout 2007, where the number of meetings in the priority areas increased, along with a concomitant rise in the number of agreements signed. Meetings on ports development, agreements on food safety and consumer rights, an MoU on inspection and quarantine cooperation as well as a new Centre for Promoting Trade, Investment and Tourism all signified the acceleration of the relationship.[35] At the bilateral summit in November 2007, both sides identified a further fourteen projects for formulation or implementation.[36]

The breadth and depth of the China's successful dealings with ASEAN has influenced its behaviour on multilateral relations, in general, and in regional organisations, in particular. Although not an explicit policy, this influence can be seen in China's conduct within the Shanghai Cooperation Organisation, which is the second example of China's engagement in an institutionalised region.

The Shanghai Cooperation Organisation

The Shanghai Cooperation Organisation (SCO) was formed in 2001, following the addition of Uzbekistan to the Shanghai 5 group of China, Kazakhstan, Kyrgyzstan, Russia and Tajikistan. This earlier group was an extension of Sino-Soviet talks and was a response by China to safeguard its interests in this area and along its northwestern border.[37] China's interests in this region included energy security (oil and gas) and political security (the separatist movement by elements of the Uighur minority in Xinjiang province) as well as regional balance-of-power considerations.[38] The SCO was also perceived by the member states as a useful mechanism for limiting the impact of the United States in Central Asia, an especial consideration after the terrorist attacks of 11 September 2001 and the subsequent relocation of US military and intelligence personnel into the region.

Since its inception, the SCO has rapidly expanded its institutionalisation into a number of sectors. The core interests of political and energy security remain paramount to the grouping. There are now defence and law-enforcement ministerial and senior officials meetings, in addition to meetings of both public prosecutors and law enforcement officials as well as the work of the SCO counter-terrorism centre. SCO economic ministers meet regularly, as do regional transport ministers.[39] Beyond these core interests there is also ministerial-level cooperation on culture and disaster relief management.[40] Complementing these meetings are a steadily growing network of bilateral accords, mainly between either Russia or China and the Central Asiatic states. Although originally it was conceived as an informal regional arrangement, the SCO Secretariat was officially opened in 2004.[41]

Although SCO documents do not collectively mention the Five Principles as guiding organisational norms, they nonetheless appear separately detailed in many of the speeches and joint statements.[42] Alongside the Five Principles, the SCO is also considered to embody the 'Shanghai Spirit', which encompasses the norms of 'mutual trust, mutual benefit, equality, consultation, respect for diverse civilisations and seeking common development',[43] many of which also appear in the Five Principles. If the identity of an organisation can be expressed through its members' adherence to a set of norms, then it can equally be expressed in terms of norms that its members oppose. As mentioned earlier, one of the forces behind the post-September 2001 development of the SCO was the desire of the regional states to check the influence of the United States in Central Asia. Declarations by SCO members – either multilaterally or bilaterally – have frequently expressed opposition to behavioural norms which they perceive the US as embodying. These have included: unilateralist (instead of multilateralist) behaviour, hegemonic (instead of consultative) practices and double standards (instead of mutual trust and equality).[44]

In 2005, the SCO underwent an enlargement process. India, Pakistan and Iran all joined the organisation as observer states. In India's case, in particular, this decision caps an extended period of diplomatic negotiation. China was unwilling to let India join the group, as it was concerned about a possible dilution of its influence, not least because of India's status as a major regional power and its close relationship with Russia. For that reason China insisted that Pakistan, a Chinese ally, join at the same time.[45] Iran joined at the behest of Russia. How this enlargement affects China's regional engagement with Central Asia remains to be seen, but due to the presence of both China and India it is unlikely that what occurs in the SCO will be completely divorced from China's regional strategy towards South Asia (see below). At the same time, the inclusion of Pakistan was also granted, not only due to China's support but also because it was seen – within the region – as a way to reduce the influence of the United States on Islamabad[46] – a view that could be interpreted as strengthening the prevailing set of regional norms and reducing the presence of opposing norms.

During 2005 the SCO also began to formalise its institutional arrangements, with permanent representatives from member countries appointed to the SCO Secretariat (similar to the new arrangements in ASEAN) as well as to the associated Regional Anti-Terrorist Structure (RATS).[47] At the same time the SCO began to expand its functional cooperation into new areas, such as the first annual meeting of the Heads of the SCO Supreme Courts being held in Shanghai.[48] Over 2006 and 2007, the SCO has sought to further deepen and broaden its institutional arrangements and networks. The fifth anniversary of the founding of the SCO was an opportunity for all members to consider new ways forward. Among these initiatives have been agreements for new transport networks from Russia to Kazakhstan and from Uzbekistan to China,[49] efforts to harmonise and integrate regional insurance markets,[50] as well as new pan-institutional networks being forged between the SCO and the Collective Security Treaty Organisation (CSTO).[51] Turkmenistan has also begun attending the SCO Heads of State meeting as a guest, adding greater weight to the SCO as a regional organisation for Central Asia.[52]

In the examples of East and Central Asia, China has helped to be develop new architecture that reflects – both implicitly and explicitly – China's values and overarching foreign policy ambitions. In the case of ASEAN, the China–ASEAN relationship has become the key relationship driving East Asian integration forward (as a model for ASEAN's other +1 relationships and the APT as well as in terms of necessitating closer ASEAN cooperation in order to address China–ASEAN concerns). In Central Asia, China has led the development of the SCO and strongly pushed for it to create mechanisms by which regional peace and prosperity may be supported. While these two regions represent possible successes for China in institutionalising its periphery, it has faced different challenges in Northeast and South Asia, where similar frameworks are largely absent or exclusionary to Chinese interests.

Non-institutionalised regionalisation

> A developing China needs a peaceful international environment and a
> favorable climate in its periphery.
>
> (*White Paper on China's National Defense*, 2002)[53]

Unlike China's involvement with ASEAN and the SCO, it has neither
developed a new regional institution in Northeast Asia nor has it managed
to become a full member of existing South Asian institutions. This section
will review China's policy towards these two areas to see how China has
sought to engage them and the impact this has had on regional behaviour.

Northeast Asia

Even though China engages with most Northeast Asian countries under the
umbrella of the various ASEAN+3 dialogues, it still faces a unique set of
issues with regards to this region. These issues encompass both bilateral
concerns (such as the tensions in the Sino-Japanese relationship) as well as
multilateral concerns (the resolution of the problems on the Korean Peninsula). Although these issues also spill over onto the Chinese policy agenda
when it works with other regional countries – either via the ASEAN+3 or
ARF processes – they are more intense within the context of China's
Northeast Asian relations. Moreover, the leading role that China plays in the
six-party talks argues for this region to be treated separately from that of
China's broader East Asian relations.

China, Japan and South Korea are the three largest regional economies.
Cooperation or conflict between them has a direct impact not only on
regional peace and prosperity but also on China's peripheral security.
Although China's decision to commence formal diplomatic relations with
South Korea in 1992 caused a minor upset in both countries' relations with
North Korea, in general these relations are stable and positive. Among the
issues that have caused problems for both sides are included the treatment of
Chinese workers in South Korean-run Chinese factories and questions of
historical identity and sovereignty.[54] However, these issues are relatively
minor when compared with the problems within the Sino-Japanese relationship. Within this dyad, issues of history, culture and identity clash with
struggles for regional influence and power. The problems posed by visits of
the Japanese leadership to the Yasukuni shrine and the portrayals of wartime
activities in Japanese high-school textbooks frequently cause bilateral fric-
tions. Indeed, as Yoo has noted, it is 'due to the Yasukuni conflict [that]
Beijing has refused to allow Japanese prime ministers to visit China since
2001'.[55] Although the visit by Japanese Prime Minister Fukuda in 2007 and
the reciprocal visit by Chinese President Hu Jintao in 2008 have helped to
stabilise the relationship, these problems remain serious issues of bilateral
concern.[56] It is also inescapable that China uses them to diminish Japan's

regional standing by allowing the diplomatic tensions to spill over into Chinese society.[57]

Above these bilateral relations, China works together with South Korea and Japan in developing trilateral modes of cooperation. Although the catalyst for these activities was the breakfast meeting of the three heads of state during the 1999 informal ASEAN summit in Manila, they have since evolved into a set of dialogues in their own right, not only to develop alternative avenues for discussing issues but also to overcome what Rozman has described as Northeast Asia's 'stunted regionalism'.[58] These trilateral meetings encompass economic and investment issues, energy and environmental cooperation, foreign affairs as well as youth and cultural issues.[59]

Overarching China's bi- and trilateral relations with Northeast Asian states is its leadership role in the six-party talks. These talks – first convened in August 2003 – in response to North Korea's ongoing uranium enrichment programme, bring together China, Japan, North Korea, Russia, South Korea and the United States.[60] China plays the lead role in these talks, due to China's ongoing support for (and perceived influence over) North Korea. Cheng has noted that, for China, the six-party talks represent 'a gradual transformation from a conservative acceptance of the regional balance of power to a more active, constructive approach to maintain and *shape* the balance'.[61]

As was also seen in the case of the SCO, China's efforts to shape this dialogue according to its own perceptions of international order are evidenced in both the mode of the talks as well as the various statements that result. As was seen in the case of the Shanghai Cooperation Organisation, while statements relating to the six-party talks do not mention the Five Principles of Peaceful Coexistence explicitly, various aspects of them are nonetheless contained in many of the documents released during the negotiations, as can be seen in the following phrases 'respect each other's sovereignty, exist peacefully together' [respect for sovereignty, peaceful coexistence], 'reflecting the spirit of mutual respect, consultation on an equal footing' [equality and mutual benefit].[62] Although such statements are not, in and of themselves, conclusive, they nevertheless reflect China's desire to shape the regional balance of power through an expression of a particular set of norms, which reaffirms the earlier-mentioned Chinese policy commitment that it is on the basis of the norms contained in the Five Principles that China approaches such regional dialogues.[63]

South Asia

China's engagement with the South Asian region, the subsequent development of institutions and corresponding transmission of norms is perhaps the most limited of the four peripheral regions. This is due to the existence of an established institution – the South Asian Association for Regional Cooperation (SAARC) – as well as the presence of another regional power – India – that is resistant to Chinese influence. In order to work around this issue

China has expanded its network of bilateral ties with South Asian states and developed its own Track-Two process of regional engagement. As will be seen, these efforts have begun to yield results in terms of China's involvement in regional institutions, but the nascent nature of these ties means that the issue of norm transference is – as yet – unclear, except in a deductive manner.

In the beginning, of all the South Asian countries, the PRC had the strongest relationship with India. Indeed, China participated in the 1955 Bandung conference at the invitation of India. However, the subsequent incorporation of Tibet by China and the resulting border problems led to a long-term deterioration in bilateral relations.[64] This deterioration led China to shift focus to Pakistan as its major regional partner. The tensions between India and Pakistan further froze Sino-Indian relations, which were also not helped by the Indian-Soviet alliance. In terms of the other continental South Asian countries, China developed good relations with Bhutan but, until recently, had only superficial ties with Nepal, which was under the Indian sphere of influence, while Bangladesh leaned more towards India than towards China. The resulting realpolitik meant that China did not have, until the turn of the century, a significant presence in South Asia, either bilaterally or in terms of membership of SAARC.

India's opposition to Chinese involvement in SAARC meant that China had to seek alternative means through which it could insert itself into regional dialogues. To this end it developed a new subregional process, the Kunming Initiative. This process began in October 1999 following a meeting of representatives from Bangladesh, China, India and Myanmar (BCIM) to explore ways to enhance economic cooperation between the four states. As the *China Daily* noted, 'such co-operation among the four countries falls in line with the Five Principles of Peaceful Coexistence and international practice'.[65] The subsequent BCIM conference has been held annually and, although limited in concrete outcomes, has become an important part of China's foreign policy apparatus. While the cooperative proposals that have arisen from the Kunming Initiative – principally revolving around the idea of a land corridor between the four countries – are useful in their own right, the Initiative has played a more significant role in allowing Chinese and Indian officials to develop a deeper understanding of each other that, in turn, has helped the development of new bilateral ties. Even with this development, it was only in late 2005 that the growth of China's bilateral ties and influence – coupled with a warming of Sino-Indian ties – meant that China was able to expand its regional presence.

These improved relations played a role in both countries' engagement with different regional organisations. As noted earlier, in mid 2005 India joined the SCO as an observer state. In return, later that year, China joined the SAARC as an observer state during the 13th SAARC Summit. The politics surrounding China's accession at this meeting revealed a changing regional landscape with respect to India's dominance and China's influence. In particular, Nepal's strong support for China's observer status – which it linked to

Afghanistan's membership – signalled a shift in regional influence, where three of the eight member states are now supportive of China's regional engagement.[66] Following the agreement for China and Japan to join as SAARC observers, Iran, South Korea, the United States and the European Union also expressed an interest in becoming observers.[67] All of these were eventually agreed upon, although it was the three Northeast Asian countries that signified the greatest commitment to the organisation in terms of both support and high-level representatives at the SAARC meetings.

At its first summit in 2007, China put forward a series of proposals to improve its bilateral relations with the region. These included a proposal 'to institutionalise the China–South Asia Business Forum to serve as a platform for discussion on economic co-operation and trade ... to discuss [the] establishment of a cooperative mechanism for poverty alleviation and [to] explore the possibility of setting up a joint mechanism for co-operation in disaster relief and mitigation'.[68] Japan and South Korea also sought to contribute to regional development with additional monies and new programmes in youth exchanges, 'economic cooperation, resolution of social issues, protection of the environment and disaster relief'.[69] While the support from Japan and South Korea were welcomed by all the SAARC members, China's series of proposals raised Indian concerns as to its long-term intentions towards the region, indicating that the wariness and mistrust that characterised earlier bilateral relations between China and India were still present.[70]

Had it not been for the problems in the Sino-Indian relationship, China's involvement in South Asian regional institutions could possibly have been one of its more successful attempts at peripheral diplomacy. India was one of the original supporters for the Five Principles of Peaceful Coexistence; it upholds consensus-based multilateralism; as a post-colonial state with key territorial and security challenges it is a strong supporter of sovereign norms and non-intervention in other states' affairs as well as the rule of international law. China would not have needed to project these norms of engagement as they were already in existence, albeit in a different cultural milieu. However, this was not the case. Instead, China and India find themselves as competitors for regional power. Although, this contest is one for which China far better positioned – both in current developmental terms and geographical position – nonetheless India's own modernisation process and the expansion of its ties with Southeast Asian, Central Asian and Northeast Asian states may act as a check on China's influence in regional institutions, as is further discussed in Chapter 7.

Impact of China on surrounding areas: Zhongguo redux?[71]

It is on the basis of the Five Principles that China has, through peace negotiations, resolved the boundary issues with most neighbors and maintained peace and stability in its surrounding areas.

(Premier Wen Jiabao, 28 June 2004)[72]

China as a status quo power

China's modernisation and the accompanying expansion of its economic and strategic capabilities have given rise to international and regional concerns as to the intentions underlying its Asian foreign policy. These concerns are specifically with regard to whether China will support the established regional order or whether it will seek to subvert it for its own ends. This 'threat' versus 'promise' debate has become particularly intense since the end of the 1990s, as China started to develop more comprehensive ties with regional institutions. Although the current thinking appears to favour the 'promise' side, there is still a degree of wariness within regional policy communities.

Insofar as China's interactions with existing Asian institutions can accurately reflect China's broader regional intentions, it can be concluded that it has definitely sought to play an active role. However, this has only been successful in the case of ASEAN. In the other example of SAARC, India has been quite successful in limiting China's integration with South Asia. Nonetheless, in terms of ASEAN+1 and ASEAN+3 processes, the ASEAN–China relationship has become the key axis around which the rest of the region revolves. This is also the case for ASEAN institutionally, as its engagement with China has required its members to develop common positions on a range of issues where such positions did not previously exist. In this way, the ASEAN–China axis also influences the development of the ASEAN–Japan and ASEAN–South Korea relationships, as ASEAN resists making changes to an agreed position. Given that Japan and South Korea's linkages with ASEAN are developing at a slower rate than that of China's ties, this shapes these two bilateral relationships into a reflection of the ASEAN–China relationship. By extension, this also means that as the ASEAN+3 process develops, it will reflect the policy position that emerges from ASEAN and ASEAN–China integration.

In considering the impact China has had on the maintenance or otherwise of regional norms it is first necessary to state that a coherent set of regional norms is problematic to compile. This is largely due to the wide disparities in social and political structures across the region. On the one hand, there are states – such as Japan, Thailand or the Philippines – that have backed policies that go beyond certain Westphalian ideals of state authority to support such issues as the establishment of the International Criminal Court, the Kyoto Agreement or broader remits for humanitarian interventions. On the other hand, there are states that steadfastly resist any form of international intrusion into their affairs (such as Malaysia, Uzbekistan or North Korea), regardless of whether it is by an international or regional organisation or simply another state. In terms of China's peripheral areas where there are regional organisations, none has sought to go beyond traditional models of states' rights. The sole exception to this may be ASEAN, whose organisational norms of consensus and non-interference are steadily changing towards a more flexible arrangement. However, even in the case of ASEAN, changes are only taking place in small steps and are confined to relatively uncontentious areas of cooperation, such as finance or economic integration.

In this respect China cannot be said to be promoting a set of meta-norms that go against the established meta-norms already present in regional organisations, nor do they represent a significant departure from the substantive norms that have been developed. Indeed, in the case of East Asia, China can be perceived as a conservative force in the evolution of localised norms and in the interpretation of internationally derived meta-norms. As noted above, this is evidenced by China's support for both Myanmar and Uzbekistan despite regional and international pressure to the contrary.

China's role in the development of regional institutions and norms would therefore suggest that it is largely a status quo power. As Morgenthau states, 'the policy of the status quo power aims at the maintenance of the distribution of power as it exists at a particular moment in history'.[73] However, the problems with this conclusion are twofold. First, it is essentially a static construction when the subject is constantly responding to an evolving regional and international environment. Second, the exact timing of that 'particular moment in history' is vague, although with an implied assumption of the 'now'. Chinese foreign policy views China as one of the poles in a multipolar world order. Inasmuch as China sees itself as having a natural competitor, it is the United States, the only remaining superpower. This would suggest that even though China supports a multipolar world order, it nonetheless envisages its potential place in that order as being at a relatively equivalent position to that of the United States – a position that it is yet to achieve.[74] Hence, while it can be concluded that China is a status quo power, its moment in history is yet to arrive.

China as a regional hegemon

> While some continued to remain optimistic, others became concerned that the disintegration of the Soviet Union and the potential withdrawal of the United States had created a power vacuum which would be filled by China, either as a new emerging super-power or as hegemon in the Asian region. The first of these contentions can be dismissed: Apart from trade, China has minimal global interests to protect, and minimal global reach by which to protect them. Regionally, it is otherwise.[75]

Related to the issue of whether or not China is a status quo power is the question of to what extent it can be considered to either be acting or seeking to act as a regional hegemon A narrow definition of a hegemon is provided by Mearsheimer, who claims that 'a hegemon is a state that is so powerful that it dominates all the other states in the system. No other state has the military wherewithal to put up a serious fight against it.'[76] More broadly, Wallerstein suggests that a hegemon is a state 'able to impose its set of rules on the interstate system, and thereby create temporarily a new political order'.[77] Wallerstein goes on to consider that a key representation of a hegemon is the construction of a hostile 'Other' and a supportive alliance network. 'The alliances are not constructed in order to combat the enemy but to control the allies. And that the point of the control of the allies is to make sure that they bend their immediate economic interests to those of the hegemonic power, thus creating that "extra" advantage which is the purpose and prerequisite of hegemony.'[78]

As to the how and why a hegemon acts the way it does, Gilpin proposed that a hegemon uses its power and influence to 'construct a hegemonic world order. Paradoxically, it does this by sacrificing its own interests for the greater good of all other states', which, in turn, derive a benefit that brings them closer to the hegemon's ideal order.[79] Cox takes a different view, namely that 'a hegemon constructs a hegemonic world order so as to maximise its own interests ... Hegemony is an ideological cloaking device, or a set of consensual norms, that enable the leading state to successfully maximise its power.'[80]

Drawing upon these definitions, it is difficult to argue that China is a hegemon, principally because it does not have the ability to 'impose' its norms on other regional states or institutions. As has been noted previously, there is a historical convergence of norm articulations in China, South Asia and Southeast Asia as well as an intersection in the articulation of some contemporary norms, such as those relating to consensus-driven politics. However, this is not the same as the imposition of China's interpretation of these norms on other regional nation-states.

Where China has begun to acquire certain hegemonic characteristics is in the way in which it is using its power and influence to construct a regional order conducive to its own economic and political priorities. The case of China and Southeast Asia provides the clearest example of China creating a regional order that has advanced its own interests as well as providing ASEAN states with a range of benefits, particularly stemming from economic and commercial cooperation. The example of China's engagement with Central Asia is also suggestive of a regional network of alliances where the threat of a hostile 'Other' (the United States) is used to bolster China's position more advantageously. To a lesser extent, the development of deeper ties in Northeast Asia between China, Japan and South Korea over the six-party talks process is also being pushed by China in response to its negative perceptions of US agendas.

In addition, China faces both extraregional and interregional limitations on any hegemonic expression. Extraregionally, the main limitation is the continued presence of the United States in the region. The United States' strategic and economic footprint in Asia ensures a constant alternative for Asian states. Although in some cases – such as Uzbekistan – regional states have chosen to significantly downgrade bilateral relations with the US in favour of those with China, in other cases – such as India and Singapore – regional states have expanded ties with the United States. China also faces a growing array of international organisations – such as the WTO or the International Criminal Court – which hold the potential to limit its ability to hold hegemonic sway over the other regional states.

The prime intraregional limitation on China acting as a hegemon is the current and foreseeable regional balance-of-power arrangements (here excluding the United States). In each of its surrounding regions, China faces other states or groupings of states opposed to Chinese domination. Russia and Japan act as restraining forces on China's influence in Northeast Asia; in Southeast Asia, Japan and India are both seen as states that balance the influence of China through the ASEAN+ dialogues; India and Japan also act as major checks on China's ambitions within South Asia; while in Central Asia, Russia is still the dominant actor, despite China's support for the SCO.

Shambaugh concludes that it 'remains far too early, however, to conclude that the regional order is becoming a modern version of the imperial "tribute system" or that China is becoming the dominant regional hegemon.'[81] Despite this, even senior Chinese policy makers see that something akin to the structure (if not the intent) of that earlier system is already re-emerging, with China at the centre of the region geographically, economically and culturally as well as playing an important role in regional political and security issues.[82]

Whether or not this regional structure will enable China to act as a hegemon will ultimately depend on its primacy in regional institutions and norm development. As was seen above, China is making a concerted effort to achieve that position. However, these institutions and norms are collages, formed by the interaction of the domestic and foreign policies of all participating states. Within such a complex and fluid environment, the potential for China's norms and influence to dominate regional affairs is likely to be less than hegemonic.

A peripheral hub?

This paper has painted a largely positive picture of China's engagement with its peripheral regions. As China has modernised it has been able to develop its regional relations, projecting itself (to varying degrees) into a variety of institutions and processes. In many cases, it has been able to do so in a way that is congruent with its own national and foreign interests, but has indicated a degree of flexibility in the articulation of those norms. In the previous sections it has been shown how China has developed good relations with Southeast and Central Asia and is constructing uneven but generally positive relations with the Northeast and South Asian regions. In interacting with these neighbouring areas, China has worked to transform itself into the hub of Asian regional integration, one of the world's major poles of power and influence.

The question is 'why?' It is the argument of this chapter that the process by which China has engaged these four regions is largely based on a long-standing policy of benign national interest – China believes that it requires a stable and prosperous periphery if it is to continue to develop. There is, however, another way to interpret this evidence, one that paints a decidedly less certain image of China's regional power. Consider the fact that, even as China has sought to develop its relations with these regions, it has done so – with the exception of Northeast Asia – with pre-existing or competing institutions. In Southeast Asia, ASEAN was established in 1967. In South Asia, SAARC was created in 1985. The five Central Asian states have been members of the Commonwealth of Independent States since it was created in 1991 and before that were part of the Soviet Union. More recently, Kazakhstan, Kyrgyzstan, Russia and Tajikistan were founding members of the Eurasian Economic Community (EEC) (with Uzbekistan joining in 2005). Kazakhstan, Kyrgyzstan, Tajikistan and Uzbekistan created the Central Asian Cooperation Organisation (CACO) in 2002 (with Russia joining in 2004),[83] while Kazakhstan, Kyrgyzstan, Tajikistan, Russia and Uzbekistan are members of the CSTO.

In other words, far from being the hub of regional activities, China has had to work to prevent itself from being marginalised by these surrounding regional bodies. With ASEAN, it has been able to shape the evolution of ASEAN+1 and ASEAN+3 dialogues and has played a key role in the formation of the East Asian Summit, but although these dialogues encompass a wide range of policy communities they are still peripheral to the core ASEAN meetings and processes. In other words, China can be seen as less of a 'hub' and more of a 'spoke', though this may change in the future. In Central Asia, China developed the Shanghai 5 group in 1996 and the Shanghai Cooperation Organisation in 2001. However, it does not have a role in the pre-existing CIS process, nor is it a member of the EEC, CACO or CSTO dialogues. In South Asia, China's Kunming Initiative was stalled by Indian suspicions of Chinese motivations, while in SAARC it has only just managed to acquire observer status – a move that has been limited by the simultaneous admission of Japan. In Northeast Asia cultural and historical issues as well as the additional involvement of Russia, Japan and the United States, further check China's capacity for engagement.

Thus, even after China's rapid and largely successful expansion of ties with its surrounding regions, its status as a regional hub is still fragile. Yet because of the ties it has developed, that have served to position it as a developing core, neither is it a periphery. It would be further inaccurate to describe it as a semi-periphery, as this implies an intermediate zone of transition between the two and the precise location of such regional poles is unclear at best. However, as China is yet to exert dominant influence over the Asian region or a collection of the four individual regions, it may be best characterised as a peripheral hub: a state which is developing into a hub yet still does not possess a hub's advanced political and economic capacity both for internal development and for external gain.

Conclusion

> China's governance challenges will also increasingly become the responsibility of China's neighbors, as well as other nations and international organizations. If they collectively fail, widespread unrest within China will result, which could then spill over China's borders and destabilize the regional order.[84]

In exploring the role of China in Asian regional processes it is necessary to consider China's unique set of national circumstances as well as the mechanisms which it has created to interact with its Asian neighbours. While China's modernisation has provided it with the capacity to enact a complex foreign policy based on bilateral and multilateral relations, it has only been in the last two decades that the regional and international situation has been conducive to a multilateralist policy being operationalised. The aim of this policy is *shishi quishi* – to make the outside world safe so that China's modernisation can proceed.[85] It is simultaneously a new policy as well as one rooted in Chinese antiquity, in policy objectives as well as geographical focus. In understanding the utilisation of the twin pillars of regional governance (institutions and norms) in Chinese foreign policy it is possible to place China within the regional order, both now and – to a certain extent – in the longer term.

In pursuing its foreign policy objectives, China has begun a series of dialogues with its four surrounding regions (Southeast, Central, Northeast and South Asia) in a bid to create a secure and prosperous periphery. The modalities of this engagement have depended on the regional environment with which China has been confronted. Underlying this engagement is a set of norms that China has developed to support these multilateral dialogues within the broader context of its foreign policy. While China has had such a set of principles since the early days of the PRC, they needed to be located with respect to a contemporary set of regional norms as well as the meta-norms of the international community.

Of the four regions, China has been most successful in expanding its ties with ASEAN, both in terms of realising its external goals as well as reinforcing its primacy in Southeast Asia's external relations, particularly with respect to Japan and South Korea. In Central Asia, China has also led the creation of the Shanghai Cooperation Organisation; although how this group develops in the future is uncertain, given the existence of other regional organisations and the presence of Russia. In Northeast Asia, China provides leadership in the six-party talks but lingering cultural and historical animosities as well as the presence of the United States have blunted the expansion of Chinese authority. South Asia is the fourth region where China is seeking to exert more influence. However, its recent accession to SAARC notwithstanding, India and its regional allies will most likely work to limit China's power.

The way in which China has engaged with these four regions has high-lighted a number of aspects of its foreign policy which are useful for evaluating China's intentions towards the governance of the Asia region. It has been shown that, while China supports the regional and international order, it does not necessarily see its position as fixed in the hierarchy of nation-states. This would suggest that even as China's internal modernisation is yet to reach a sufficiently developed status, so too its external power and influence are yet to be fully realised. This conclusion also suggests that, as its external authority grows, China will be faced with a foreign policy challenge as to how far that power and influence can be used within its current norm structure. A related point is that, while China's current exertion of authority is not hegemonic, it nonetheless bears certain hegemonic characteristics. However, any further development of those characteristics will require China to over-come resistance from its regional partners as well as from external powers with interests in Asia. Indeed, China may need the goodwill of its regional neighbours more than the current discourse would otherwise indicate – if the middle kingdom is to rise again.

Notes

1 This paper was first presented at the workshop on *Governance and Regionalism in Asia*, held at the University of Hong Kong, Hong Kong, 8–9 December 2005.
2 Hsü, Immanuel C.Y. *The Rise of Modern China*, 3rd ed. (Oxford: Oxford University Press, 1983), p. 682.
3 Ibid. p. 683.
4 A similar point is made by Bin Yu. See: Yu, Bin. 'China and Its Asian Neigh-bours', in Yong Deng and Wang Fei-ling (eds). *In the Eyes of the Dragon.* (Boulder, CO: Rowman and Littlefield, 1999), pp. 183–210.
5 Normalisation of Sino-US ties also spurred the normalisation of Sino-Japanese relations seven months later, further diminishing an antagonistic regional environment.
6 For a further discussion on the aspects of the independent foreign policy as expressed by Premier Zhao Ziyang during the 4th Session of the 6th NPC see: Cheng, Joseph. 'The Evolution of China's Foreign Policy in the Post-Mao Era', in Joseph Cheng (ed.). *China: Modernization in the 1980s.* (Hong Kong: Chinese University Press, 1989), pp. 161–202.
7 Cheung, Peter and James Tang. 'The External Relations of China's Provinces', in David Lampton (ed.). *The Making of Chinese Foreign and Security Policy in the Era of Reform, 1978–2000.* (Stanford, CA: Stanford University Press, 2001), p. 99.
8 Ibid. p. 105.
9 Confucius Institutes. http://www.confuciusinstitute.net/confucius_institutes. Accessed 1 May 2008.
10 Gill, Bates and Huang Yanzhong. 'Sources and Limits of Chinese "Soft Power"', *Survival*. (Vol. 48, No. 2, 2006), pp. 23–24.
11 Chwee, Kuik Cheng. 'Multilateralism in China's ASEAN Policy: Its Evolution, Characteristics, and Aspiration', *Contemporary Southeast Asia*. (Vol. 27, No. 1, 2005), p. 103.
12 Foot, Rosemary. 'China's Regional Activism: Leadership, Leverage, and Protection', *Global Change, Peace & Security*. (Vol. 17, No. 2, June 2005), pp. 141–153.

13 Yahuda, Michael. 'Chinese Dilemmas in Thinking about Regional Security Architecture', *The Pacific Review*. (Vol. 16, No. 2, 2003), p. 198.

14 Ong, Russell. *China's Security Interests in the Post-Cold War Era*. (London: Curzon Press, 2002). p. 3

15 Jiang Zemin. 'Towards a Good-Neighborly Partnership of Mutual Trust Oriented to the 21st Century', Speech Given at the 1997 Informal China-ASEAN Summit. 16 December 1997.

16 Actually there were 13 other regional states present as, in 1955, there were both the Democratic Republic of Viet-Nam and the State of Viet-Nam. However, for a contemporary-period analysis, these two states are counted as one.

17 See: Kim, Samuel. 'China and the Third World: In Search of a Peace and Development Line', in Samuel Kim (ed.). *China and the World: New Directions in Chinese Foreign Relations*. (Boulder, CO: Westview Press, 1989), pp. 148–178.

18 The five member states were China, Kazakhstan, Kyrgyzstan, Tajikistan and Russia.

19 Although He Xiangqi of the Chinese Foreign Ministry predates the development of the NSC to the early 1990s as a response to the end of the Cold War, the spread of globalisation and the emergence of non-traditional security threats. See: He Xiangqi. 'Cooperating for Common Security: China's Approach to Non-Traditional Security Issues', *China-ASEAN Occasional Paper Series No.7*. (Hong Kong: Centre of Asian Studies, The University of Hong Kong, 2005).

20 Source: 'China's Position Paper on the New Security Concept', 31 July 2002. http://www.fmprc.gov.cn/eng/wjb/zzjg/gjsgjzzyhy/2612/ 2614/t15319.htm. Accessed 10 November 2005.

21 See: Kuik, Cheng-Chwee. 'China's Participation in the ASEAN Regional Forum (ARF)', in James Chin and Nicholas Thomas (eds). *China and ASEAN: Changing Political and Strategic Ties*. (Hong Kong: Centre of Asian Studies, The University of Hong Kong, 2005), p. 156.

22 For a summary of some of these areas of cooperation see: *Joint Press Statement for the Meeting to Explore the Establishment of the Consultative Relationship with the People's Republic of China*. (Beijing, 13–14 September 1993). http://www.aseansec.org/5875.htm. Accessed 6 November 2005.

23 Mack, Andrew. 'Proliferation in Northeast Asia', *Occasional Paper No. 28*. (Washington, DC: Henry L Stimson Center, 1996), pp. 56–57. For more on China's intentions towards the ARF see: Alastair Iain Johnston. *Social States: China in International Institutions, 1980–2000*. (Princeton, NJ: Princeton University Press, 2007).

24 This was actually the second informal meeting, albeit the first informal meeting of the ASEAN+3 group. The first informal meeting was held in 1996 between the then six member states of ASEAN and the four non-ASEAN Southeast Asian states. For more information see: *Press Statement: The First Informal ASEAN Heads of Government Meeting*. (Jakarta, 30 November 1996). http://www.aseansec.org/5206.htm. Accessed 10 November 2005.

25 Respectively, see: *Joint Statement of the Meeting of Heads of State/Government of the Member States of ASEAN and the Prime Minister of Japan*. (Kuala Lumpur, 16 December 1997). http://www.aseansec.org/5224.htm. Accessed 10 November 2005; and *Joint Statement of the Meeting of Heads of State/Government of the Member States of ASEAN and the Prime Minister of the Republic of Korea*. (Kuala Lumpur, 16 December 1997). http://www.aseansec.org/5223.htm. Accessed 10 November 2005.

26 See: *Joint Statement of the Meeting of Heads of State/Government of the Member States of ASEAN and the President of the People's Republic of China*. (Kuala Lumpur, 16 December 1997). http://www.aseansec.org/5225.htm. Accessed 6 November 2005.

27 For more information see paragraph 4 of the *Joint Statement on East Asia Cooperation*. (Manila, 28 November 1999). http://www.aseansec.org/5301.htm. Accessed 6 November 2005.

28 Comment made by a senior ASEAN official during a visit to Hong Kong. 1 November 2005.

29 This table is sourced from: Tanaka, Akihiko. 'The Development of the ASEAN +3 Framework', in Melissa Curley and Nicholas Thomas (eds). *Advancing East Asian Regionalism*. (London: RoutledgeCurzon, 2007), p. 66.

30 For more information see: *ASEAN-China Memorandum of Understanding on Cultural Cooperation*. (Bangkok, 3 August 2005). http://www.aseansec.org/17649.htm. Accessed 6 November 2005.

31 Source: *ASEAN-China Dialogue Relations.* http://www.aseansec.org/5874.htm. Accessed 6 November 2005.

32 See: *Report of the ASEAN-China Eminent Persons Group.* Jakarta, ASEAN Secretariat, November 2005. http://www.aseansec.org/asean-china-epg.pdf. Accessed 1 May 2008.

33 *Joint Statement of ASEAN-China Commemorative Summit.* (Nanning, 13 October 2006). http://www.aseansec.org/China-Com-Summit.Doc. Accessed 1 May 2008.

34 *Chairman's Statement of the 11th ASEAN-China Summit.* (Singapore, 20 November 2007). http://www.aseansec.org/21105.htm. Accessed 1 May 2008.

35 See respectively: *Joint Statement on ASEAN-China Port Development*, (Nanning, 29 October 2007). http://www.aseansec.org/21000.htm. Accessed 1 May 2008; *Nanning Joint Statement*. (Nanning, 29 October 2007). http://www.aseansec.org/21022.htm. Accessed 1 May 2008 and *The Sixth Consultations between the ASEAN Economic Ministers and the Minister of Commerce of the People's Republic of China*. (Makati City, 25 August 2007). http://www.aseansec.org/20872.htm. Accessed 1 May 2008.

36 See: *Chairman's Statement of the 11th ASEAN-China Summit*. (Singapore, 20 November 2007). http://www.aseansec.org/21105.htm. Accessed 1 May 2008.

37 For more on the creation of the SCO see: Lukin, Aleksandr. 'Shanghai Cooperation Organization: Problems and Prospects', *International Affairs*. (Vol. 50, No. 3, 2004), pp. 31–40.

38 A useful summary of China's interests in this area is contained in: Chung, Chien-peng. 'The Shanghai Cooperation Organization: China's changing influence in Central Asia', *The China Quarterly*. (Vol. 180, 2004), pp. 989–1009.

39 For more on these meetings refer to the SCO website. http://www.sectsco.org/home.asp?LanguageID = 2.

40 For a report on the former see: 'Shanghai Group Culture Ministers Sign Joint Statement in China', *BBC Monitoring International Reports*. 13 April 2002.

41 See: 'Chronicle of Main Events of "Shanghai Five" and Shanghai Cooperation Organisation'. http://www.sectsco.org/html/00030.html for more information.

42 See, for example, comments relating to norms contained in the: *Tashkent Declaration of Heads of Member States of Shanghai Cooperation Organisation*. (Taskent, 17 July 2004). http://www.sectsco.org/news_detail.asp?id = 119&LanguageID = 2. Accessed 20 November 2005 and the *Statement by SCO Secretary-General Zhang Deguang during the High-level Plenary Meeting of the 60th session of the United Nations General Assembly*. (New York, 14–16 September 2005). http://www.sectsco.org/html/00521.html. Accessed 20 November 2005.

43 'China says Shanghai Cooperation Organization aids regional security, stability', *Xinhua*. 9 December 2002.

44 For example, see comments and analysis contained in: Saiget, Robert. 'China fearing US domination in post-Cold War world, analysts says', *Agence France Presse*. 16 December 2001; Bezlova, Antoaneta. 'China raises profile via Central Asian club', *Inter Press Service*. 8 January 2002; 'Shanghai Warning', *The Boston Globe*. 11 July 2005.

45 Radyuhin, Vladimir. 'India to join Shanghai group as observer', *The Hindu*. 5 June 2005.
46 Radyuhin, Vladimir. 'India to join Shanghai group as observer'.
47 *History of Development of Shanghai Cooperation Organisation*. http://www. sectsco.org/html/00035.html. Accessed 2 May 2008.
48 *Third Meeting of Heads of Supreme Courts due in Astana*. http://www.sectsco. org/news_detail.asp?id = 2117&Language ID = 2. Accessed 2 May 2008.
49 See: *SCO Special Working Group on Transit Potential meets in Tashkent*. http:// www.sectsco.org/news_detail.asp?id = 2099&LanguageID = 2. Accessed 2 May 2008.
50 'SCO seeking to harmonize, integrate members' insurance markets', *Russia & CIS General Newswire*. 25 April 2008.
51 'CSTO, SCO to sign Cooperation Protocol soon – Bordyuzha', *Central Asia General Newswire*. 31 July 2007. What is interesting about these two organisations is that – in terms of members – they are identical, except that China is not a member of the CSTO. The respective partners of both organisations, however, would extend the reach of the joint network from Armenia, Belarus and Iran in the West, Russia in the North, China in the East and India and Pakistan in the South; making it the largest regional organisation in the world in terms of geographical size and populations represented.
52 'Shanghai alliance interested in Turkmenistan membership – Russia', *UzReport. com*. 15 August 2007.
53 See: China's National Defense in 2002. http://www.china.org.cn/e-white/ 20021209/index.htm. Accessed 26 November 2005.
54 For an instance of the former see: 'China launches probe into poisoning of Korea-owned factory workers', *BBC Monitoring International Reports*. 12 February 2004. On the latter see: Seo, Hyun-jin. 'Skepticism lingers over history issue; Beijing pledges not to stake claim to Goguryeo in history textbooks', *The Korea Herald*. 25 August 2004; 'South Korea to File complaint with China over History Dispute', *BBC Monitoring International Reports*. 17 September 2004; and 'South Korea Cites Agreement With China over History Dispute', *BBC Monitoring International Reports*. 21 September 2004.
55 Cheong, Yoo. 'Northeast Asian Countries Locked in Multilateral Diplomatic Feuds', *Yonhap*. 26 August 2004. […] added for grammatical purposes.
56 For a report on these visits see: 'Japanese PM, Chinese FM agree to ensure success of Chinese president's visit', *Xinhua*. 18 April 2008. http://news.xinhuanet. com/english/2008–04/18/content_8005223.htm. Accessed 2 May 2008.
57 See, for example, the reports from the April 2005 protests in China that damaged Japanese businesses and diplomatic missions: Xu Ming. 'Protesters Harass Japanese Businesses in China's Shenzhen', *Ta Kung Pao* [as reported by *BBC Monitoring International Reports*]. 4 April 2005; 'Repair work begins on Mob-hit Japan Embassy Buildings in China', *Jiji Press Ticker Service*. 22 November 2005.
58 See: Rozman, Gilbert. *Northeast Asia's Stunted Regionalism: Bilateral Distrust in the Shadow of Globalization*. (Cambridge: Cambridge University Press, 2004).
59 See, for example: 'Japan, China, S. Korea aim to conclude investment talks in Nov', *Japan Economic Newswire*. 14 October 2005; 'S. Korea, Japan, China to Hold Ministerial meeting on Logistics', *Asia Pulse*. 14 July 2005; 'Japan, China, South Korea to hold trilateral talks', *BBC Monitoring Asia Pacific – Political*. 14 April 2005; 'Koike to attend trilateral environmental conference in Seoul', *Japan Economic Newswire*. 21 October 2005; 'China, Japan, ROK seek cooperation in youth exchanges', *Xinhua*. 18 July 2005.
60 A good summary of the current state of the six-party talks is contained in: Cotton, James. 'Whither the Six-Party Process on North Korea', *Australian Journal of International Affairs*. (Vol. 59, No. 3, September 2005), pp. 275–282.

61 Cheng, Joseph. 'China and the Korean Situation: The Challenge of Pyongyang's Brinkmanship', *East Asia: An International Quarterly.* (Vol. 20, No. 4, Winter 2003), p. 73. [Italics added]

62 *Joint Statement of the Fourth Round of the Six-Party Talks.* (Beijing, 19 September 2005). http://www.state.gov/r/pa/prs/ps/2005/53490.htm. Accessed 22 November 2005 and Wang Yi. 'New Consensus and New Steps', *Remarks on the Third Round of the Six-Party Talks.* (Beijing, 26 June 2004). http://www.fmprc.gov.cn/eng/topics/chlfht/ t141649.htm. Accessed 20 November 2005. For more such statements see: 'Six-Party Talks on the DPRK Nuclear Issue'. http://www.fmprc.gov.cn/eng/topics/chlfht/default.htm. Accessed 20 November 2005.

63 Most recently, comments from Chinese scholars involved in Track-2 processes have indicated that China is actively considering a proposal to institutionalise the six-party talks. Although it is unlikely that this proposal would be tabled and operationalised during 2008, if accepted by the other parties it may be realised in 2009/2010. (Personal communication). This would mean that China had contributed to the development of multilateral regional institutions in three of its four peripheral areas.

64 For more on these issues see: Garver, John. 'China's Decision for War with India in 1962', in Alastair Iain Johnston and Robert S. Ross (eds). *New Directions in the Study of China's Foreign Policy.* (Stanford, CA: Stanford University Press, 2006), pp. 86–130.

65 'Kunming Initiative Features Cooperation', *China Daily.* 5 October 1999.

66 Sources: Sridharan, Kripa. 'Beijing's role in Saarc expansion unsettles Delhi', *The Straits Times.* 23 November 2005, and 'Chinese Checkers', *Indian Express.* 15 November 2005.

67 'U.S. and S. Korea keen to get observer status in SAARC: Nepali Deputy PM', *Xinhua.* 29 June 2006; 'SAARC observer status for China, Japan, Korea, United States', *Hindustan Times.* 18 May 2006; and 'Japan, China, S. Korea ministers to observe SAARC summit', *Japan Economic Newswire.* 28 March 2007.

68 'China goes into overdrive', *The Statesman.* 4 April 2007. See also: 'SAARC invites five observers to summit meeting for first time', *Xinhua.* 3 April 2007.

69 'China goes into overdrive', *The Statesman.* 4 April 2007.

70 'China on a SAARC charm offensive, India cautious', *Indo-Asian News Service.* 4 April 2007; 'South Asia moving toward closer China relations', *Chinadaily.com.cn.* 3 April 2007; and 'China puts forward five proposals for cooperation with SAARC', *BBC Monitoring International Reports.* 3 April 2007.

71 Zhongguo is both the pinyin romanisation for China as well as a Chinese term literally meaning 'middle [zhong] kingdom [guo]'

72 Wen Jiabao. 'Carrying Forward the Five Principles of Peaceful Coexistence in the Promotion of Peace and Development', *Speech given at the seminar commemorating the 50th Anniversary of The Five Principles of Peaceful Coexistence.* Beijing, 28 June 2004.

73 Morgenthau, Hans. *Politics among Nations: The Struggle for Power and Peace,* 6th ed. (New York: Random House, 1985), p. 46.

74 For an excellent discussion of China as a status quo power and the impact its behaviour has on Sino-US relations and US policy approaches see: Johnston, Alastair. 'Is China a Status Quo Power?', *International Security.* (Vol. 27, No. 4, 2003), pp. 5–56.

75 Dreyer, June. 'Regional Security Issues', *Journal of International Affairs.* (Vol. 49, No. 2, 1996), pp. 391–411.

76 See: Mearsheimer, John. *The Tragedy of Great Power Politics.* (New York: Norton, 2001), p. 40.

77 Wallerstein, Immanuel. 'Three Hegemonies', in Patrick O'Brien and Armand Clesse (eds). *Two Hegemonies: Britain 1846–1914 and the United States 1941–2001.* (Aldershot: Ashgate, 2002), p. 357.

78 Ibid. p. 360.

79 See: Hobson, John. *The State and International Relations.* (Cambridge: Cambridge University Press, 2000), p. 130. See also: Gilpin, Robert. 'The Rise of American Hegemony', in Patrick O'Brien and Armand Clesse (eds). *Two Hegemonies: Britain 1846–1914 and the United States 1941–2001*, pp. 165–182.

80 Hobson, *The State and International Relations*, p. 130.

81 Shambaugh, David. 'China Engages Asia: Reshaping the Regional Order', *International Security.* (Vol. 29, No. 3, 2004), pp. 64–99.

82 Drawn from taped comments made by: Cui Tiankai. 'Regional Integration in Asia and China's Policy', *3rd East Asia Lecture.* (Hong Kong: Centre of Asian Studies, The University of Hong Kong, 4 February 2005).

83 For more on the other Central Asian groups see: Klimenko, Anatoly. 'Russia and China as Strategic Partners in Central Asia: A Way to Improve Regional Security', *Far Eastern Affairs.* (Vol. 33, No. 2, 2005), pp. 1–20.

84 Shambaugh, David. 'China Engages Asia: Reshaping the Regional Order', p. 98.

85 As quoted in Kim, Samuel. 'China and the Third World: In Search of a Peace and Development Line', p. 165.

6 Australia and Asian institutional networks

Bilateral preferences, multilateral gains[1]

James Cotton

In the end it's the substance of the relationship that we have with individual countries that really matters.

> (John Howard, interview 29 November 2004)

Let me stress, that innovations in institutional architecture must be kept in perspective.

> (John Howard, Asia Society address 12 September 2005)

A nation that has become a great force for good in its region and the world.

> (Kevin Rudd, Sydney Institute address 17 April 2008)

Introduction

For their meeting in Vientiane in November 2004, the ASEAN nations invited Australia and New Zealand to participate in the Southeast Asian Leaders' Summit to commemorate their thirty years as dialogue partners of the organisation. At the same time, negotiations (broken off by ASEAN in 2000) were resumed on an ASEAN-CER (Australia and New Zealand) trade arrangement. While in Vientiane, the ASEAN leaders resolved to establish an East Asian Summit (EAS) mechanism. In December 2005, Australia participated in the inauguration of the East Asian Meeting process with the attendance of then Prime Minister John Howard at the EAS in Kuala Lumpur. Yet this was the same Canberra administration that had expressed scepticism regarding the potential for Asian regionalism and that had long resisted taking the diplomatic steps which would make attendance in Kuala Lumpur possible.

This chapter is concerned with the Australian approach to Asian regionalism, and especially how it has changed in the last decade. Its main focus is official Australian policies towards ASEAN, the ASEAN Regional Forum (ARF) and the East Asian Summit as they were managed by the Howard government. It proceeds on the assumption that the Asia-Pacific Economic Cooperation (APEC) group is a transregional entity, though of course it is noteworthy that successive Australian governments have foregrounded the organisation as an essential part of their regional diplomacy. The argument is that during the Howard–Downer era the government, reasoning from realist premises, remained somewhat sceptical of the various institutional and norm-oriented embodiments of 'Asia', and evinced a decided preference for bilateralism (initially economic, but later strategic bilateralism). Nevertheless, it was prepared to make some contribution to the improvement of regional governance practices, despite such measures challenging the conventional realist view of state sovereignty. In the context of the continuing economic and strategic rise of China, and despite taking great trouble to facilitate mutually beneficial trading relations, the Howard government also oversaw the progressive institutionalisation of defence cooperation with Japan. Given the relentless impact of globalisation and the domestic change of federal government, it remains to be seen whether all of these foreign policies priorities will remain unaltered.

The partisan debate on Asian 'engagement'

The broader context of this chapter is the ongoing Australian debate on the extent to which the nation can or should align its policies with those of some Asian nations or with the region as a whole. Antecedents for this debate can be found in the nineteenth century,[2] and 'Asia' had been a preoccupation of Australian foreign policy makers since Federation. As early as the 1930s a small but prescient group of opinion leaders, including Latham, Eggleston, Crawford and Clunies Ross, could see that relations with Asia would be crucial for Australia's future but would pose difficult choices, especially between economic advantage and military security.[3] In the analysis of the post-war period the narrative was dominated by the perception of Asia as a location for military commitments (in support of great power allies), as a source of increasing economic linkage (at first principally with Japan) and also later as entailing an accommodation with the major regional powers, Indonesia and China, in an essentially post-colonial environment.

Discussing the evolution of Australia's embrace of regionalism involves making some reference to conflicting partisan claims as to its discovery and promotion. Former Labor prime ministers Paul Keating (1991–96) and Gough Whitlam (1972–75) both claim to have invented the idea of pursuing engagement or community in the Asia-Pacific region and both wrote books advancing their respective claims.[4] On the conservative side of politics, Percy Spender (Foreign Minister 1949–51) and R. G. Casey (Foreign Minister 1951–60, later head of state) paid great attention to diplomacy in the Asian region and also wrote books on this theme.[5] Nor is this a matter only of historical interest. In the 1990s, one feature of election rhetoric was the charge that one side of politics or the other could not be entrusted with government since it did not have regional credibility or, alternatively, could not advance Australia's regional interests without compromising important values. Echoes of this position could still be heard in the critiques of the Howard government offered by opposition foreign affairs spokespersons.

The widely accepted narrative version of Australian policy towards regional institutions and governance proceeds as follows. In the era of the Hawke and Keating Labor governments, the nation's policy makers sought to enmesh Australia in the developing web of Asian multilateral institutions. Australia was one of the founding members of APEC, and the impetus towards the formation of an Asia-Pacific equivalent of the CSCE/OSCE – realised in the ASEAN Regional Forum – was provided in part by the government advised by policy intellectuals.[6] Australian scholars and officials were also active participants in the efflorescence of 'Track-Two' organisations, notably CSCAP (Council for Security Cooperation in the Asia-Pacific).

The putative reasons for this trend to regional 'engagement' became a subject much debated in scholarly and policy literature. Economic, security and even social and cultural calculations informed this policy turn. The arguments ranged from the suggestion that growing economic complementarity (in some respects, a reprise of a trend first seen in the 1930s)[7] would bring a convergence of economic and even social systems,[8] to the proposition that Asian engagement was a desirable or even logical policy to follow once Australia had embraced extensive immigration from Asia and also multiculturalism. On the security front, the notion that Australia was moving from seeking security 'against' Asia towards pursuing a security relationship 'in Asia' or 'with Asia' was one of the (essentially rhetorical) arguments advanced for helping to establish a CSCE/OSCE mechanism in the region. Some proponents of this view also extended the analysis to anticipate an era when Australia's security bilateralism would be superseded by a comprehensive regional security system.

Yet this movement towards regionalism needs to be seen in context, lest the changes that became visible from 1997 be regarded as the product of a narrow political partisanship. This regionalism was always seen as ancillary to the more traditional alliance relationships, such as the Australia–New Zealand–United States (ANZUS) Treaty and the Five Power Defence Arrangements (the latter with the United Kingdom (UK), New Zealand, Malaysia and Singapore). Neither was it considered to contradict existing global obligations to the United Nations and the General Agreement on Tariffs and Trade (GATT)/World Trade Organisation (WTO). Further, the regionalism that was pursued was studied in its ambiguity. While the phrase 'our region' was embedded in many of Paul Keating's pronouncements, the precise geographical scope was ill-defined, though care was taken never to exclude the 'Pacific' wing (and thus, by implication, ties to the United States) of Australia's network of economic and security relationships. Bob Hawke's original experiment in the formation of APEC with a regionalism shorn of the US was not to be repeated.

Nevertheless, the regional issue became an element in the 'culture wars' of the 1990s. Aside from the supporters of the One Nation Party, who for a brief interlude held the power balance in domestic politics, no major participants in this dispute rejected the idea of 'engagement' itself. The debate was concerned, rather, with precisely what modalities were appropriate and how much, if at all, they should replace Australia's bilateral and global commitments.

The reality of Asia policy was thus less than fully partisan. Regarding this debate, Rawdon Dalrymple, in some respects a champion of a comprehensive national alignment with Asia, remarks 'there is not sufficient focus on and interest in East Asia by Australians to generate a dynamic of the kind required to support a policy thrust such as that which Paul Keating sought to implement'.[9] If Keating's enthusiasm for Asia was largely unqualified, it was also exceptional:

> There is an element of unreality about the debate between the two major political forces in Australia on this issue. Labor, the party of Curtin, Evatt, Hawke and Keating on the one hand, and the Liberal/National Coalition, the party of Menzies, Spender, Casey and Howard on the other, have both avoided publicly confronting the issue of Australia's relations with East Asia. Neither embraces an affirmative answer to the question 'Is Australia a part of Asia'? or 'Does Australia belong to East Asia'? Yet both have sought to have Australia included in the embryonic East Asian institutional framework. Both have wanted to engage with East Asia; but both have wanted very much to ensure that that could be done without prejudice to the security, political, cultural and ethnic links which present day Australia has with the United States and Europe.[10]

'Realism' and the preference for bilateralism

It is now apparent that one of the central themes in Australian foreign policy since 1996 has been an accentuation of bilateralism.[11] This predilection stemmed from several sources, including avowedly 'realist' assumptions, which will be enumerated here. It is important to note at the outset, however, that while over the past decade Labor figures in Australia have criticised bilateralism as inconsistent with and inferior to region-wide multilateralism, and thus as a retreat from the approach taken by the Hawke and Keating governments, this view is excessively partisan. It was certainly argued by the government and its supporters that in many respects the bilateral turn in Australian policy prepared the way for a more credible role in regional institutions.

Upon its accession to power in 1996, the Howard administration, in its approach to external issues, designedly adopted a tone crafted to differentiate it from its Labor predecessor. It described its philosophical position as 'realist' and defined its principal objective in this area as a pursuit of 'the national interest', defined in terms of the physical security of Australia and its citizens and their economic prosperity. In the words of the 1997 White Paper, *In the National Interest*:

Preparing for the future is not a matter of grand constructs. It is about the hard-headed pursuit of the interests which lie at the core of foreign and trade policy: the security of the nation and the jobs and standard of living of the Australian people. In all that it does in the field of foreign and trade policy, the Government will apply this basic test of national interest.[12]

Whereas in the Keating era republicanism was on the political agenda and aspects of the British inheritance and historical record were derided in favour of a new regional and historical identity, Howard rejected such re-evaluations as the 'black arm band' school of history. In a phrase that often occurred thereafter in public pronouncements and speeches he declared, 'we do not have to chose between our history and our geography' (a phrase in repetition modified only to include the preamble, 'time has only strengthened my conviction that … '). Though in foreign policy the Howard–Downer administration did not explicitly reject the idea of 'engagement' with Asia, it deemed this strategy as desirable only if it served 'the national interest' thus defined, and if it did not require or encourage the abandonment of essential values and traditions – understood in terms of transparency and the rule of law.

As the Coalition government, and the prime minister in particular, became more confident in the execution of foreign policy, references to the philosophical assumptions behind government thinking became more frequent and more extended. The most consistently expressed was a dogged adherence to an insistence on the primacy of the state in international affairs.

In a major foreign policy speech in early 2005, delivered at a time when Australian bilateralism had scored some notable successes but when a place at the East Asian Summit remained elusive, the prime minister reaffirmed his view of the primacy of the state and also of the limitations of regional institutions. On the former he said '[t]he need for strong, effective and accountable states is a theme that emerges again and again in thinking about our global future. Despite all we know about the importance of non-state actors in the international system, the nation state remains the focus of legitimate action for order and justice in our world.' On the latter, Australia apparently does not 'face a choice between multi-lateral institutions and alternative strategies to pursue our nation's interests', and while acknowledging that there was enhanced interest in regional institutions, John Howard expressed the view that 'this region can only fulfil its promise in the 21st century with an open and inclusive architecture'.[13]

As will be considered later, the decision to accede to the ASEAN Treaty of Amity and Cooperation (TAC) was not taken without considerable resistance. Following that decision, the government's declared position on the primacy of the state did not change. Speaking to the Asia Society in New York, Howard reaffirmed his view of the state, and declared that 'what matters most for our regional engagement is the substance of relations between countries, more so than the formal architecture of any diplomatic exchange'.[14]

At this time, the prime minister left specific comment on the EAS to Alexander Downer. Although he had come a long way from the somewhat condescending views of 2000 and 2001, and while he was careful to describe the Summit as 'a very significant step forward in our engagement with ASEAN, and with the nations of East Asia generally', Downer did not raise any great expectations regarding what this new process might achieve or portend. As he remarked in 2005, '[t]he EAS is not an end in itself but one means towards the objective of building more effective regional associations of practical benefit to the Asia-Pacific region'.[15] Downer then went on to refer to other regional and transregional mechanisms with which Australia had affiliations and placed these in the same category as alliance structures, thus suggesting that Australia, while welcoming the 'new sense of inclusive regionalism' was driven entirely by an ends-related pragmatism.

If the state is the pre-eminent building block of the international system, then bilateral arrangements with states sharing the same policy objectives are likely to prove the best way to advance the national interest. The most striking invocation of bilateralism by the Howard government was its animation of the treaty mechanisms of ANZUS in response to the 11 September 2001 terrorist attacks. Throughout the Howard–Downer administration the maintenance and strengthening of the relationship with the US was ostensibly the most important policy objective. The US was variously described as a country that shares many of Australia's national values, as the strongest economy in the world and as the dominant global military and security power. The most comprehensive and arguably the least advantageous of all the main trade and investment bilateral arrangements that were negotiated by the Howard government was that with the United States.[16] It was argued that the government's preparedness to invoke not only interests but also values in accounting for the breadth of ties with the US suggested that its 'realism' departed significantly from the conventional canons of that discourse.[17] It is from such premises that some analysts of alliance behaviour contended that national interest (alone) did not justify John Howard's decision to pursue the closest alignment with the US under the Bush administration.[18]

This fraternal view of the US accords, of course, with the traditional contention of the Coalition parties that they have consistently been the true trustees of the relationship with the US. It also reflected some specific attitudes regarding, on the one hand, the limitations of Asian multilateralism, and on the other, the extent to which regional bilateralism could deliver in areas of policy of central concern to the Howard government. On the latter point, as will be later elaborated, it is noteworthy that Howard and Downer pursued closer bilateral defence and security ties with Indonesia, Japan and India (although not with China).

If bilateralism is the preferred mechanism, then multilateralism must be a weaker and thus less desirable diplomatic modality. In the early years of the Howard–Downer administration there was a deliberate strategy of reducing the emphasis placed on the regional multilateralism that had been a distinctive feature of the Keating era. Thus, *In the National Interest*, the 1997 foreign policy White Paper, though it described the ASEAN Regional Forum as 'an important step forward towards the creation of a sense of strategic community', nevertheless was careful to state the limitations of the institution: 'The Government does not regard regional approaches to security as a replacement for strong bilateral security arrangements.'[19] While the development of ASEAN was discussed in terms of the growing global trend towards regionalism, and the organisation was described as likely 'to play a key role in the emerging regional order',[20] no specific Australian policy towards ASEAN was enunciated. This was entirely in keeping with the government's preference for bilateralism, which was expressed in the following terms:

> While foreign and trade policy strategies must deploy all three approaches – bilateral, regional and multilateral – effective bilateral relationships constitute the basic building block. The greater part of Australia's international efforts is bilateral. Within the framework of strengthening bilateral relationships, Australia develops and nurtures political and market access; exchanges information and intelligence; makes representations aimed at changing other countries' policies and practices which damage Australian interests; promotes commercial relations; negotiates bilateral treaties and agreements; and develops projects of practical cooperation in a wide range of fields.[21]

The 2003 White Paper, *Advancing the National Interest*, expresses a similar point of view regarding the pre-eminence of the state and thus bilateralism:

> The actions of nation states and their governments still have the greatest bearing on the world's security and economic environment. So Australia depends on the strength of its bilateral relations around the world to advance its national interests. The greater part of the day-to-day work of Australia's foreign and trade policy is bilateral advocacy – working to influence governments and others to take decisions that suit Australia's as well as their own interests.[22]

Accordingly, while the government was on record as seeking 'close cooperation with the ASEAN member states',[23] the document again delineated no policy towards the organisation as such, though it did discuss the advantages of an ASEAN-CER trade agreement. In the period since the first White Paper, security regionalism had made no significant advances, and thus was only of limited utility:

> In a region with little history of security cooperation, the ASEAN Regional Forum (ARF) is the principal forum for security dialogue in

Asia. It has made modest gains in building a sense of strategic community and has contributed to the region's counter-terrorism work. But efforts to develop tools of preventive diplomacy and conflict management have faltered.[24]

On the emerging greater East Asian regionalism, Australia would be pleased to be involved in the ASEAN+3 process,[25] though the document also noted a preference for open and inclusive relations that would complement the work of APEC and other regional initiatives.

These assumptions had an evident impact on policy. At most times the litmus test of any given diplomatic strategy is the question of its material contribution to national security, conventionally conceived. Following 11 September 2001, in Australia as elsewhere, security issues have taken on the greatest prominence in the national agenda. According to the Howard government, the most significant threats to Australian security were posed by transnational terrorism and by the proliferation of weapons of mass destruction. In describing the national strategy to deal with those threats, prominence was given to bilateral agreements and also to the role of Coalition operations. The negotiation of these mechanisms may be taken to illustrate the somewhat robust nature of the Howard government's fundamental assumptions in an era of complex international interdependence.

On the issue of terrorism, two government reports on the threat and measures to deal with it were released in 2004.[26] ASEAN, the ASEAN Regional Forum and APEC were all noted as having played a part in counter-terrorist activities, but bilateral efforts – especially between Indonesia and Australia, notably the establishment of the Jakarta Centre for Law Enforcement Cooperation (subsequently to involve other regional nations) – were given by far the greatest attention. Nevertheless, Australia co-hosted the Regional Ministerial Meeting on Counter-Terrorism in Bali in February 2004, and was prepared to participate in the declaratory diplomacy of the region, signing the ASEAN–Australia Joint Declaration for Cooperation to Combat International Terrorism on 1 July 2004. Regarding the problem of WMD proliferation, again the ASEAN Regional Forum received a brief mention, but global regimes and such ad hoc strategies as the Proliferation Security Initiative (PSI) provided the substance of the document. The most comprehensive statement of the Australian defence outlook was *Australia's National Security*, which was released in 2003 to update the previous White Paper, which had appeared prior to 11 September 2001. Though a whole section was devoted to what was described as 'a troubled region', neither ASEAN nor the ASEAN Regional Forum received a mention.[27] The 2005 recension of this document was more complimentary, noting 'the effectiveness of ASEAN as a force for change and the resolution of regional issues' and acknowledging the role of the ARF in confidence building.[28] The 2007 *Defence Update* only mentioned the organisation once, and only in relation to what were described as 'ASEAN partners'.[29]

Yet the Howard government's apparent preference for bilateralism in Asia was also in part a learned response. Almost immediately after taking office, the government had to grapple with developments in the region that over-turned many of the established assumptions of the foreign policy community. The Asian financial crisis that began in mid 1997 negated the widely shared expectation, as expressed in the 1997 White Paper, that an increasingly prosperous Asia would inexorably bring Australia into its economic orbit while compelling a more judicious and nuanced approach by Canberra to more self-confident and perhaps even more assertive and capable neighbouring powers.

Within the space of a few months, the relatively benign and predictable regional environment became profoundly disturbed. The political repercus-sions of the crisis, especially the attempted democratisation of Indonesia, inevitably subjected past attempts to build bridges with regimes and leader-ships in the region to new and critical scrutiny. However, it was not just previous relations with individual regimes that came under question. The backlash of Asian governments against perceived Western indifference to their financial plight, and the stimulus this gave to the creation of an East Asian identity, threatened to undermine Canberra's attempts at fostering regional organisations and good governance across the Pacific Rim.

The 1997 Asian crisis highlighted the ambivalence in the Coalition's approach to the region. On the one hand, the government rapidly responded by providing US$1 billion to each of the international relief programmes for Thailand, Indonesia and Korea. On the other, the crises provided an oppor-tunity for the government to point to the distinctiveness of Australia's eco-nomic and even social systems as an explanation for why the nation – not being genuinely embedded in the region – was immune from the regional contagion.[30] From being a pupil of the Asian dragons in the previous decade, Australia now volunteered itself as an instructor in the ways of reform. Australia's assumed role as tutor was not well received in many parts of the region. At the same time, the government was successful in managing a significant reorientation in Australia's trade outside of East Asia.

The events of 1997–98 therefore were interpreted as reinforcing the Coa-lition government's philosophical scepticism of multilateralism. Neither was the regional financial crisis the only area where regionalism was perceived to have failed. Despite serious and tangible costs to health, tourist revenues, agriculture and trade, the 'haze' produced by uncontrolled forest and plan-tation fires in Indonesia and East Malaysia depicted ASEAN at its most indecisive. None of ASEAN's many discussions and plans – the ASEAN Cooperation Plan on Trans-boundary Pollution, the Regional Haze Action Plan, the activities of the Haze Technical Task Force – had any real impact on the problem.[31] Neither did the enlargement of the group in 1997 show ASEAN in a favourable light. Not only did ASEAN's leaders appear to have no influence in the subsequent political crises in Phnom Penh and Yangon, but they were committed thereafter to defending both the soundness of their decision to extend membership and also the long-term democratic and developmental prospects of two of Asia's least competent states. In some respects, the crisis occasioned by the prospect of Yangon assuming the chairmanship of ASEAN in 2006 – a role the country was forced to relinquish after it became clear that many of ASEAN's partners would downgrade their diplomatic engagement with the group as a response – demonstrated that this negative assessment was not without foundation.

It should also be noted that a further outcome of the 1997 Asian crisis was new interest in the region, particularly on the part of Japan, Singapore and Thailand, in the negotiation of bilateral discriminatory trade agreements. After decades in which Canberra had opposed bilateral trade agreements in support of its preferred alternatives of multilateralism and open regionalism, the Howard government adopted this strategy. Bilateral FTAs were concluded with Singapore (2003), Thailand (2005) and Chile (2008) and similar packages were under contemplation in respect of China, Japan, Malaysia and the Republic of Korea. In a sense, Australia began a re-engineering of its 'entry' into Asia, this time through the door of bilateralism.

The debate on the Treaty of Amity and Cooperation

Given both its assumptions and its experience, as the pace of the movement towards Asian regionalism increased the Howard government was poorly placed to engineer a strategy shift. Perhaps the nadir of the Australian assessment of regional institutions was reached with the speech by Alexander Downer at the Asian Leaders' Forum in Beijing in April 2000. There he contrasted regionalism based upon 'common ties of history, of mutual cultural identity' with a regionalism that aims at 'practical goals', and characterised Australia's roles in APEC and the ASEAN Regional Forum and its association with ASEAN as examples of the latter.[32] This comment received a great deal of media attention and was taken to mean that Australia would only ever relate to emerging notions of regional governance on a pragmatic basis. Though the foreign minister never adverted to this formulation subsequently, he did speak plainly and thus undiplomatically on ASEAN's limitations. As he said in July 2001, 'ASEAN has a culture of working around problems rather than confronting them'.[33] The context for this remark was the failure at that time of the AFTA-CER (ASEAN Free Trade Area, Australia and New Zealand) trading negotiations to go forward as a result of a veto from Malaysia, a result he described as sending the wrong market signals for ASEAN but which he undoubtedly regarded as a rebuff.

In seeking to rebut the charge, frequently voiced by the opposition, that Australia had been excluded from regional multilateralism, Downer both emphasised Australia's participation in such bodies as APEC, the ASEAN Regional Forum and the ASEAN Post-Ministerial Conference (PMC), and then offered a low estimate of their relative importance: 'we do not see regional institutions as a test of whether or not we are somehow an accepted "part" of the region'.[34] Indeed, Downer's poor opinion of multilateralism in general was plainly asserted in the course of a speech delivered in 2003, when he said, 'increasingly multi-lateralism is a synonym for an ineffective and unfocused policy involving internationalism of the lowest common denominator'.[35] Yet within two years of that statement the Australian political leadership began the manoeuvre, belated but ultimately successful, that would lead to membership of the inaugural EAS. The process by which this occurred – and especially the circumstances under which Australia acceded to the Treaty of Amity of Cooperation – is immensely revealing of the Howard government's assessment of the effective power of regional norms.

The original TAC was intended exclusively for ASEAN member states. It was subsequently amended in 1987 and again in 1998 in order to allow other states to accede to the treaty. Indeed, it became an ASEAN objective to encourage its regional partners to take this step as an indicator of their regard for the goals of the organisation. The TAC gives expression to the principles that animate the organisation. It affirms mutual respect for sovereignty, independence, equality and territorial integrity, and the right for states to conduct their affairs free of external interference; in addition, the states party affirm that they will not engage in any activity that threatens the stability and well-being of another state and will avoid any use of force. As amended, the TAC also provides for the establishment of a High Council with dispute resolution powers.

There is one sense in which this is little more than a declaratory document. Its origins lie partly in an era when ASEAN states did engage in activities intended to have an impact on the domestic affairs of their neighbours. The desire to avoid another *konfrontasi* episode was one of the motivations for the formation of the organisation. Ironically, the origins of the MNLF/MILF (Moro National/Islamic Liberation Front) and also thus the Abu Sayyaf may be found in a plan, never executed, for Philippine-inspired subversion in East Malaysia.[36] The TAC has never been taken to infringe the rights of states to remain within military alliances, notably Five Power and the various arrangements the United States has with Thailand, the Philippines and Singapore. Neither does the treaty entirely remove the appeal to force in relations between the members of ASEAN. In 2005, for example, the territorial dispute between Malaysia and Indonesia in the Sulawesi Sea region led to the mobilisation by both sides of naval and air forces. Similarly, China's accession to the TAC has had no discernible impact on Beijing's plans to build multiple dams on the Mekong River, despite the deleterious effects this will undoubtedly have on water and thus on food supply in the downstream states of Laos, Cambodia and Vietnam.[37]

Nevertheless, if the document is read carefully, it may be taken to imply that the conduct within Southeast Asia of all signatories should be bound by its principles. In the case of Australia, ANZUS provides for concerted action with the United States in order to respond not only to armed attack but also to the emergence of (unspecified) mutual threats in the 'Pacific Area'.

Post-11 September 2001, the United States has affirmed its right to act uni-laterally against both terrorists and 'rogue states' and has perceived devel-opments in international terrorism in Southeast Asia as inimical to its interests. Australian lives have been lost due to terrorist attacks in Indonesia and Australian interests have been directly threatened by terrorist groups in that country and also in Singapore. In this context, in December 2002 the prime minister expounded a pre-emptive doctrine of his own. As he said in a media interview:

> [It] stands to reason that if you believed that somebody was going to launch an attack against your country, either of a conventional kind or of a terrorist kind, and you had the capacity to stop it and there was no alternative other than to use that capacity then of course you would use it.[38]

These comments produced a storm of denunciations in Southeast Asia, with Malaysian Prime Minister Mahathir threatening to withdraw from counter-terrorism cooperation with Australia, and a *New Straits Times* editorial describing Howard as 'Uncle Sam's Foremost Flunky'.

Though Howard and Downer offered various glosses on this statement, there was no reneging on its substance, and indeed to some extent it marked a restatement of a not dissimilar view expressed in 1999.[39] From that time it seemed that, being committed to a position, *in extremis*, of intervention, the Australian government could not contemplate signing the TAC. Thus, at the Vientiane Summit, when it was already clear that a number of ASEAN countries could see clear advantages in drawing Australia closer to the emergent Asian regionalism, and the Malaysian prime minister had even referred publicly to the possibility of Australia being invited to the EAS, in response to a question on the TAC John Howard described it as 'an agree-ment that has its origins, has particular origins at a time when Australia was not part of ASEAN and we just don't, for those reasons, think it's, at this stage, appropriate to sign it'.[40] At a joint press conference in early April 2005 with Prime Minister Abdullah Badawi, when his Malaysian counterpart was doing his best to downplay the pre-emption issue and behind the scenes was discussing the possibility of an invitation to Kuala Lumpur in Decem-ber, John Howard referred to the TAC as 'of a mindset that we've all moved on from'.[41]

According to press accounts and commentaries, by this time Downer had become convinced of the need to enter the TAC.[42] Meeting in Cebu in April 2005, the ASEAN foreign ministers acted to clarify the criteria that would provide entry to the EAS. Aspirant states would have to have substantive relations with ASEAN, be full Dialogue Partners, and accede to the TAC. Now that this requirement was formally stated, Australia would have to make a positive decision, otherwise an invitation would not be forthcoming. Downer was apparently able to persuade Howard of the advantages of accession. Only a week after the prime minister's dismissive comments, Downer made the following remarks on the TAC:

> we've got some problems with the treaty. I mean the thing is in this country we do interpret treaties and other legal documents very literally. I mean we take the words to mean what they say and so, you know, that is obviously a problem for us in terms of some of the language of the treaty. But I don't want to go into it in any more detail except to say two things. One, I'm very optimistic that Australia will be part of the East Asian Summit process and I think that is very good news for Australia in terms of its participation in regional architecture. In terms of the Treaty of Amity and Co-operation well, I've had discussions during President Yudhoyono and Abdullah Badawi's visits about this issue with my counterparts and further discussions last night with the Indonesian Foreign Minister, I think we can work our way through this issue.[43]

On 28 July 2005 a joint Australia–ASEAN communiqué announced Australia's intention to enter the treaty. By this time Korea and Japan, despite their similarly active alliance relationships with the United States, had themselves found it possible to accede to the TAC.

There is a further reason why Howard and Downer were for so long reluctant to countenance entry to the TAC regime. One of the criticisms made of the Keating administration was its readiness to enter international agreements independently of public or parliamentary scrutiny. Though very little criticism was voiced at the time, later on one of the complaints levelled at Keating related to the secrecy of his negotiation of the Agreement on Maintaining Security with Suharto's Indonesia, an accord (Keating was later candid enough to admit) that would never have passed the House of Representatives.[44] An early foreign policy reform of the Howard administration was the introduction of a parliamentary Standing Committee – the Joint Standing Committee on Treaties (JSCOT) – to scrutinise all new treaty commitments. If Australia were to enter the TAC regime a government statement would be needed on the national interest entailed in such a step and some of the very arguments made by government spokespersons for the last five years would have to be confronted. Moreover, given the ASEAN timetable, and especially the fact that a final decision on invitations to the EAS was to be made at the meeting of ASEAN foreign ministers in Vientiane, 25–27 July 2005, the government's late manoeuvre meant that its decision to accede had to be announced before the JSCOT could review the issue.

The national interest analysis prepared for JSCOT was instructive of the government's position. While Australia long satisfied the other conditions for participation in the EAS, the TAC posed a problem.[45] Following negotiations with his ASEAN counterparts, Alexander Downer wrote to the Lao foreign minister, Somsavat Lengsavad, outlining the position Australia had adopted on the TAC. Accession would not be 'inconsistent with Australia's treaty commitments, including on security matters', notably ANZUS and the FPDA. It would not place any limitation on Australia's rights and obligations as a member of the United Nations, nor would it have any bearing on Australia's relations with states outside of ASEAN. And the dispute resolution role of the High Council would only apply with Australia's express consent. The submission made a point of underlining the limitations that apply to accepting the 'renunciation of the threat or use of force' as required by Article 2 of the TAC by explicit reference to Article 51 of the UN Charter, which recognises the right of states to engage in self-help for their national defence.[46]

The limits of regionalism

The regional focus of this chapter is 'East Asia', an entity (or agglomeration) that is both clearly of immense importance for Australia in aggregate security and economic terms, and also an entity regarding which there has been continuing debate in Australia since the 1980s.[47] The extent to which there is any real concreteness to the region is vigorously disputed. The perception of the Howard government was that whatever or to what extent a single identity animates it, the region had been less than receptive to Australian overtures. Nevertheless, the Australian economy and civil society have become progressively more closely aligned to Asia's dynamics over the past several decades.

To what extent should East Asia be perceived by policy makers as a coherent entity? The country in that geographical region which generates much public and also professional attention is Indonesia. While this country is clearly Australia's most important neighbour, and was acknowledged as such by Keating, the Indonesian connection is undoubtedly unbalanced. In recent years, events have shown that while Indonesia is of great importance in security terms, for Australia the major players in respect of economic, security and even cultural power are China and Japan and – to a lesser extent – Korea. In fact it is often forgotten in Australia that the Korean economy alone is of almost the same dimensions as the aggregate economies of the original five countries of ASEAN. Now what is of concern to opinion leaders in Jakarta is frequently of very little interest in Tokyo, Beijing or Seoul. In short, there is limited value, as some policy makers have asserted, in discussing relations with Indonesia as part of a larger East Asian narrative.

The East Timor intervention is an important illustration of this principle. There is no doubting the fact that the International Force for East Timor (INTERFET) generated immense resentment in some circles in Indonesia. However, this resentment did not translate into a general ASEAN or East Asian unease, let alone regional rejection. Thus, Japan, after some initial bureaucratic hostility, first took the lead in organising the consortium of international donors to raise reconstruction funds for East Timor and then took the issue of security in East Timor so seriously that laws relating to the overseas deployment of the Japanese Self-Defence Forces were changed to facilitate a personnel commitment to the UNTAET/UNMISET military force in the territory. China, a power deeply sceptical of multilateral interventions, contributed civilian police to UNTAET and later constructed what is the largest diplomatic mission in the new nation. If we add reference to the Republic of Korea (a country with which Australian merchandise trade is almost three times that with Indonesia), President Kim Dae Jung's enthusiasm at the 1999 APEC Summit for INTERFET did a great deal to convince Southeast Asian nations – notably Thailand and the Philippines – that support for and direct participation in the anticipated intervention were warranted as a contribution to long-term regional stability. Beyond Indonesia and some of its immediate neighbours, therefore, the East Timor intervention did not have the deleterious effect on Asia-Pacific relations that was suggested at the time because in this – as in many other cases – the region must be disaggregated to comprehend the total response. Indeed, in respect of lessons for regional governance, the successful East Timor experience demonstrated that it was possible for Australia and other powers to construct an ad hoc crisis coalition with significant Asian participation.

This suggests a further question, which is to ask what the most vocal and committed proponents of 'engagement' understood that term to mean practically and, if it were achieved, how this would resolve the uncertainty of identity that critics such as Rawdon Dalrymple regard as a key national failing. Australia cannot now rely upon an emerging similarity of economic and social systems, what was referred to in the early 1990s as 'convergence' with East Asia, but must pursue a project more radical than that espoused by Keating in which Australia (in Dalrymple's phrase) 'must do most of the converging' if membership of the region is to be sustained.[48] If there was and is so little public support even for the limited engagement project of the Keating era, such a fundamental wrench could hardly be achieved without major social upheaval.

It is therefore evident that the debate in Australia on Asian engagement rests upon the tendency to hypostasise what is a less than substantial regional entity. Nevertheless, there are still those within the policy debate who are prepared to give 'Asia' concreteness. If Australia did seek not merely its security but its identity 'in Asia' what reception might the nation be given? Alison Broinowski's 2003 study, *About Face*, is a major contribution to an understanding of the Australian debate on this question. The evidence she assiduously assembled in her survey deserves very close attention, since no analyst has provided a more comprehensive consideration of what 'Australia' means to the various countries and cultures of the Asian continent. The material shows that Australia's 'image' has been enormously various, and that if there has been extensive stereotyping of 'Asia' among Australians, then in the countries of the continent the same applies in mirror image.

The latter may even be described as a species of 'occidentalism', as dependent upon reified identities as its orientalist sibling. Of Chinese perceptions Broinowski has written:

> For over a century, Australia has been represented as 'absent', negligible and boring by Chinese whose shared concern is to reinforce the superiority of their civilisation and to advance their national or personal standing, while others, who seek to reform China, selectively idealise Australia as an example. Those who prefer either to value the differences or detect the similarities between Chinese and Australians, including indigenous Australians, represent Australia positively. This pattern [is] ... repeated [in] ... other Asian societies.[49]

As to the issue of Australia's quest for 'membership' of the Asian region, it is Broinowski's view that 'Asian countries are now much more intimate with each other than with Australia'.[50] Over the last decade, official Asian pronouncements on the desirability of Australian 'membership' of the region have been decidedly equivocal, and consequently enthusiasm for this outcome is a product of the calculation that this 'maximises Asian countries' joint impact or serves their individual national interests'. Conversely, 'when *excluding* Australia is in their interests, Asian opinion leaders represent Australians as white, Western, British, American stooges who are anti-Asian and lack history and culture'.[51] At the extreme end of this spectrum of opinions, Broinowski also contends that the emergence of an increasingly negative image of Australia 'blew up in Australia's face' in October 2002 in the shape of the Bali bombing.

What could be done to promote a more positive image of Australia? Broinowski offers two specific prescriptions. The first entails behaving 'as an equal' in the region, thereby developing 'a record of performance that may eventually convince leaders that it would be more useful to have Australians inside regional organisations than outside them'. The second involves a more critical and independent approach to the US alliance, and especially the expeditionary military strategies that the alliance currently entails.[52]

In some respects, however, Broinowski's recommendations are not entirely consistent with her analysis. If Australia is sometimes chosen as a convenient whipping boy for what are perceived as 'western' positions on such issues as human rights, there is a limit to the actions that governments can take in practice to undermine that strategy. Further, to effect a change in the range of perceptions of Australia would require a response much bigger than that likely to be forthcoming from any government. Media, NGOs, tourists and even academics would all need to modify their behaviour, in some cases quite drastically. Whatever its merits and however it might be achieved, the attainment of regional 'belonging' would require considerable social realignment with likely and imponderable collateral social changes, for which there seems little public support. This finding is surely reinforced by the remarks of Singapore Prime Minister Goh Chok Tong and others at the 2003 ASEAN Summit where regional identity was defined in terms of race which, at least for the next fifty years, excluded Australia. Neither is there much sign of the political will that would be required for Australia to chart a different global course. Here it should be recalled that both the major political parties have supported the 'war against terrorism', and that the Opposition did not then have a clear alternative policy on Iraq. Whatever the truth of her larger claims, Broinowski's assertion that Australian participation in the coalition intervention in Iraq undermined rather than augmented the national security appears increasingly plausible with the apparent failure of the US programme of building democracy in that country. Such is the analysis of one of the most vocal supporters in Australia of closer alignment with Asia.

The Australian impact on regional governance

Notwithstanding the limitations considered in the previous section, there is plentiful evidence for the assertion that the Australian embrace of Asia is deepening with every year that passes. Being concerned explicitly with regional institutions, this chapter cannot consider in any detail the human and soft-power aspects of the Australia–Asia connection. Yet in some respects these are the bearers and essential animators of participation in Asian institutions, if that participation is to be sustained and credible. A few data items must suffice here to illustrate the dimensions of this foundation. Of the approximately 800,000 Australians who live abroad, there are some 10,000 in China, more than 50,000 in Hong Kong, 12,000 in Indonesia and over 12,000 in Japan.[53] There are more members of the Australian diaspora in East Asia than in North America. Data from the 2001 census show that – after 50 years – Chinese has now displaced Italian as the second language of Sydney. Around 200,000 students from East and Southeast Asia study in Australian educational institutions each year. In Malaysia alone there are more than 100,000 alumni of Australian educational institutions, including some in very senior positions. The largest ten source countries for short-term visitors to Australia (mostly tourists, business visitors and family movements) include six from East Asia, namely (in descending order of magnitude) Japan, Singapore, China, South Korea, Malaysia and Hong Kong. This picture is almost directly mirrored in the destinations of departing Australians.[54]

More familiar trade data illustrate a similar trend. Of all Australian merchandise exports, 53 per cent go to East and Southeast Asia, and by 2006 China had displaced the United States to become Australia's second-largest merchandise trading partner (though if service and investment flows are aggregated the US remains Australia's largest economic partner). China overtook the United States to become Australia's largest merchandise trading partner in 2007. China's rapid growth has been the most important determinant of the strong continuing performance of the Australian economy. Korea's POSCO is the largest single importer of an Australian commodity (coal). If interdependence brings with it mutual comprehension and, ultimately, some measure of convergence, the trend in Australia's regional alignment is clear. Indeed, data from the 2005 Lowy poll indicated that the Australian public was somewhat worried about current trends in US foreign policy while, at the same time, holding surprisingly more positive attitudes towards China than towards the United States.[55] To say that the Australian profile in regional institutions has not been prominent is only the start of the analysis of Australia–Asia relations.

Nor should more recent controversies obscure Australia's past contribution to such regional issues as human security. It should be recalled that 'from mid-1976 to mid-1983 the Liberal-National Party government admitted 76,248 Indochinese refugees under its Refugee and Special Humanitarian Programmes'. This amounted to the reception of around 'one refugee for every 800 Australians' and was achieved largely with bipartisan political support.[56] A greater contrast with the stance taken by the Coalition government from 2001 on 'border protection' is hard to envisage, and illustrates that – over the long term – Australia has been extremely receptive to people movements of all kinds from Asia, as from most other locations. Around 23 per cent of Australian citizens and permanent residents were born in another country (around 2,550,000 from ASEAN countries), a national proportion which is among the highest in the world.[57]

There have been many federal government initiatives over the past decade that have had a significant impact on the governance of Asian nations. Canberra initiated human rights training in Myanmar in 2000, continuing this programme until the re-detention of Aung San Suu Kyi in 2003. During the democratisation of Indonesia, considerable aid monies were expended to assist the conduct of free and fair elections. More recently, under the Australia–Indonesia Partnership for Reconstruction and Development, which was negotiated as a response to the December 2004 Indian Ocean Tsunami, A$1 billion in aid funds were donated for the reconstruction of Aceh. As the Australia–Indonesia Joint Declaration on Comprehensive Partnership of April 2005 notes, there is now extensive bilateral cooperation in a wide range of economic and technical programmes as well as in security. In 2005, Australia announced the funding of 600 new post-graduate scholarships for Indonesians students to study in Australia. And in 2005, the Australian Defence Force resumed joint training with Indonesia's Kopassus special forces as a counter-terrorism measure.

During this time the Pacific has become a particular focus of federal government programmes. Currently Papua New Guinea (PNG), the Solomon Islands and Vanuatu all have in operation improved governance programmes funded principally by Australia. In PNG there have been difficulties with the implementation of the Enhanced Cooperation Programme, but overall the sums of money involved are sufficient to have a real effect. In smaller states this is especially noticeable – the A$38 million provided to Vanuatu in 2006 to improve policing and the administration of justice doubled Australian aid to Vanuatu, Australia already being the principal source of aid to that country. The Centre for Democratic Institutions at the Australian National University, funded by AusAID, has been conducting training programmes for parliamentarians and officials not only from the Pacific, but also from Vietnam, Cambodia, Indonesia and East Timor.

As analysed by Michael Wesley, through a series of regional meetings he has labelled 'the Bali process', the Howard government attempted to promote a broader understanding of the problems posed by people smuggling and money laundering.[58] After patient preparation of the diplomatic ground, a considerable degree of policy convergence resulted, thereby to an extent bureaucratising and thus depoliticising what had been contentious issues. This opened the way for deeper functional cooperation between law enforcement, customs and immigration authorities. As the key partner in the process has been Indonesia, bilateral relations have also been significantly enhanced.

State and local governments as well as the private and NGO sectors have all had a deliberate impact upon governance in the Asia-Pacific region. In East Timor, Australian state and local governments have helped organise relief and reconstruction efforts designed specifically to improve human capital. In the case of China, these governance efforts have ranged from business and infrastructure development programmes to bilateral training schemes in health, education and energy cooperation.[59] In February 2006 the Lowy Institute launched the AsiaPacific Business Coalition, with major participation from Qantas and other business entities as well as AusAID. Its objective is to develop a longer-term and capacity-building approach to the prevention of HIV/AIDS in the region, especially in PNG, Vietnam and China. It is thus apparent that there is wide support for schemes to achieve practical improvement in governance standards in the region – in the process forging those horizontal 'transgovernmental networks' that have been discerned as augmenting and supplanting, to a growing extent, some of the traditional functions of conventional institutions of sovereignty.[60]

There have thus been important domestic drivers embedding Australia within regional dynamics just as the Howard–Downer administration, for all its commitment to the principle of sovereignty, has seen the logic of contributing to governance programmes consistent with the setting aside of that principle.

Going forward: bilateralism or regionalism?

To mark the thirtieth year of ASEAN–Australia dialogue in 2004, the Australian Department of Foreign Affairs and Trade released two studies, one devoted to an overview of the relationship and the other to an analysis of Australian aid to the group. On aid, the ASEAN Australia Economic

Cooperation Programme (AAECP), which was described by the ASEAN secretariat as 'the cornerstone of ASEAN–Australia dialogue relations',[61] had expended to that time over A$200 million, principally on technology transfer and training.[62] The emphasis in the programme, which included funds especially for expenditure in Myanmar, Cambodia and Laos, was on governance and on bridging the gap between the less-developed states and the original ASEAN membership. As a source of aid the AAECP, though undoubtedly useful and welcome, was not especially generously funded. To place its budget in perspective, in 2004–2005 Australian bilateral assistance to Indonesia, the Southeast Asia's largest recipient of Australian aid, stood at around A$151.7 million.

The official overview of the relationship recounted the many and varied trade, aid and education ties that bind Australia to the countries of Southeast Asia.[63] But the ties thus enumerated were overwhelmingly bilateral and largely (setting aside Five Power Defence Arrangement) economic. In addition to the development dimension already noted, the specific contribution of ASEAN as an organisation was restricted largely to its role as facilitator and chair of the ASEAN Regional Forum.

Bilateralism was the preferred option on the issues that count. The February 2004 regional meeting on counter-terrorism in Bali, co-hosted by Alexander Downer and Hassan Wirajuda, at which representatives from all ASEAN countries were present, was part of a concerted attempt to develop a network of issue-specific linkages. The Coalition government considered that the twelve bilateral memorandums of understanding negotiated on counter-terrorism – with Malaysia, Thailand, the Philippines, Indonesia, Brunei, East Timor and Cambodia, in addition to agreements with Papua New Guinea, India, Pakistan, Turkey and Fiji, as well as the stationing of Australian Federal Police (AFP) officers in the capitals of most of those countries – constituted the best available arrangement for international cooperation on this issue. And according to the Howard government's view, Australia's success in the region was pre-eminently to be measured by such indicators.

In 2006 Howard revisited what had originally been a stratagem associated with the Keating government, a bilateral security treaty with Indonesia. The 'Framework for Security Cooperation', subsequently referred to as the Lombok Treaty, was signed by the foreign ministers of the two countries on 13 November. For the most part, it brought together pre-existing initiatives, as could be seen by the fact that (under Article 6) the extant Indonesia–Australia Ministerial Forum was specified as the implementing mechanism. Indonesia did secure, however, a novel guarantee that Australia would not support or foster separatist movements in its territory, clearly a provision included with West Papua in mind. But as Downer noted in his remarks at the time, this measure would not obstruct freedom of speech or other freedoms recognised in Australia, so quite what would be meant by this undertaking in practice was not clear.[64] Given the unhappy history of the Keating-negotiated predecessor agreement, and also the government's expressed dislike of empty verbiage, it was noteworthy that the bilateralist preference was nevertheless pursued to this extent.

In a further departure with unprecedented historical resonances, the government entered into a bilateral arrangement for security cooperation with Japan in March 2007. While the existing US–Japan–Australia trilateral ministerial consultations were an indication of the extent to which the region's US partners were already self-consciously aligned, a joining of the spokes – to use the often-employed 'hub and spokes' analogy for the US-centred regional alliance network – was a new departure. The joint declaration incorporated a surprising amount of detail on objectives of especial interest to Japan, including the North Korea threat and the reform of the United Nations to bring Japan into the Security Council, but otherwise was short on specificity.[65] The fact that proposals for such arrangements in the past have excited criticism from Beijing was evidently not sufficient a disincentive to the adoption of this measure. It was ironic, nonetheless, that though this agreement was particularly associated with the personal objectives of Prime Minister Abe, as a result of major electoral reverses the government in Tokyo was under new leadership within six months.

Despite these other efforts, the standard set by the government for itself in respect of its Asian policy has increasingly been that with China. While maintaining the deepest engagement with the US and Japan, China was the recipient of a singular degree of attention. As John Howard often reminded his audiences, he had visited China more than any other country, and the simultaneous presence in Australia of Presidents Bush and Hu was something of a regional coup. From a time when he was a foreign policy ingénue, Howard had learned a great deal about Asia and had been especially well advised on China. The remarks contained in his most considered speech on foreign policy of 2005 illustrated that learning, while also showing that economic relations was his enduring theme:

> Asia is poised in coming decades to assume a weight in the world economy it last held more than five centuries ago. ... When we think about the future of Australia in the world, we inevitably think of a world where China will play a much larger role. Australia's relations with China have bulked large during my time as Prime Minister. China's rise is steadily reshaping our world. In the last two years, China has accounted for a quarter of world growth and a similar share of growth in global trade. ... Since my Government has been in office, Australia's trade with China has trebled – to the point where today it is our third largest trading partner. With the completion of our joint feasibility study on a free trade agreement, we now have an opportunity to strengthen this relationship further into a true partnership for prosperity. ... But I also want to assert that China will remain a large and growing partner for Australia whether or not we negotiate a Free Trade Agreement. Australia welcomes China's constructive approach to a range of security

matters in recent years – from the war on terror, to the Korean peninsula, to maritime security in South-East Asia. And in the context of our
one-China policy, we continue to urge restraint and a peaceful resolution
of issues across the Taiwan Straits.[66]

Here again could be seen the clear preference for bilateralism in general and
economic bilateralism in particular. Moreover, in other speeches and interviews in 2005 and 2006, Howard linked the diplomatic effort devoted to
relations with China to Beijing's express (if in reality qualified) support for a
role for Australia in the EAS. And given that one aspect at least of the
emergent multiple forms of regionalism remained a tension between the
three largest players, China, Japan and the US, his cultivation of Beijing may
be seen, if not as visionary, then at least as prudent. Nevertheless China
bilateralism had clear limits. Even though the 2007 *Defence Update* signalled
the possibility of cooperation with India (the two countries agreed to a
memorandum on defence cooperation in 2006), a security relationship with
China was not envisaged.

At the same time, there was latterly something of a rediscovery of the
transregional benefits of APEC. Though the goals of the organisation
remain diffuse, its representation includes the major parties from both sides
of the Pacific. As the prime minister remarked immediately prior to the
Busan meeting of 2005: 'The great value of a gathering such as APEC, particularly for Australia, is that it joins like no other forum those countries and
those parts of the world that are so important to our security, and so
important to our economic future.'[67] As the region's elder statesman, John
Howard acted as host for the 2007 APEC Summit in Sydney. While attempts
were made to refocus the group's strategy upon such issues as greenhouse
gas emissions, the continued US opposition to the adoption of mandatory
limitations forced Alexander Downer to defend the notion of 'aspirational
targets' regarding which, in connection with ASEAN's intramural processes,
he had previously been dismissive. By this time, however, Howard and
Downer were widely perceived as striving for domestic electoral advantage
rather than employing regional structures to address a major global problem. Bilateralism may have been the prime minister's preferred approach,
but the advantages of regionalism were subtly recognised.

A new direction?

The election of the Labor government under Kevin Rudd at the end of
2007 was the start of a new era in Australian politics – both domestic and
foreign. During the election campaign, much was made of the Labor leader's
Chinese-language skills and his background as a diplomat experienced in
regional affairs.

In a major policy address in April 2008 the new foreign minister, Stephen
Smith, outlined the new government's vision for Australia's foreign affairs. In

his address, the foreign minister clearly articulated a clear continuation of the former government's emphasis on bilateral relationships as the foundations of Australia's multilateral engagement, stating that the new government would seek to build 'on good bilateral relations to generate global outcomes through multilateral engagement'.[68] Underpinning this approach was a commitment to norms that fostered 'a stronger, rules-based order for the modern world' in which 'nation states can peacefully and peaceably pursue their own prosperity'.[69]

While the Labor government identified the bilateral relationships with Japan, India, Indonesia and South Korea and the importance of its multilateral involvement in the APT, EAS and APEC for Australia's international affairs, the Australia–China relationship was accorded a special place in the foreign policy milieu. This was clearly seen in the new prime minister's first overseas trip, which was solely to China. During the visit Prime Minister Rudd stated that 'A true friend is one who can be a "zhengyou", that is a partner who sees beyond immediate benefit to the broader and firm basis for continuing, profound and sincere friendship ... It is the kind of friendship that I also offer China today.'[70] Understandably, Australia's other regional partners were less impressed with its new relationship with China, feeling perhaps that it created a perceptible bias in broader regional affairs.[71] Hence, while the new government may have additional leadership skills that were absent in the pursuit of the Howard–Downer foreign policy strategies, its desire to strengthen a key relationship runs the risk of alienating other countries in the process. This is clearly a new foreign policy challenge for the Australian government in its engagement with the regional order.

Conclusions

What has driven the official Australian response to regionalism? The Coalition government's realist and bilateralist assumptions, the reinforcement of policy experience or learning, and the strong preference for trade and security ties with the United States have been the most obvious factors. This is not to suggest, however, that the government's policy was merely reactive. As Milner has observed, such bilateralism can be understood as a means to 'assist Australian participation in a broader regionalism' with the embrace, most notably if somewhat reluctantly, of the EAS.[72] In addition, while the bilateral relationship that has attracted most attention is that with the US, for some years the Howard government's calculations incorporated a realistic assessment of the rise of China to pre-eminence, if not hegemony, in East Asia. An awareness of this last point also accounts for the Asia orientation of some key subnational and market actors, from resource companies to service industries.

Changes in Australian policy are thus at least in part a result of major shifts in East Asian power relativities. In the 1980s Japan and Australia were the drivers of Western Pacific, growth-oriented regionalism.[73] With the economic emergence of China, Beijing has now become a major player, as much for strategic as for economic reasons. The different receptions of Australia and Japan are noteworthy in this regard. Japan–China enmity during the prime ministership of Junichiro Koizumi hampered Japan's ability to manoeuvre to best advantage in the new regional environment, whereas growing Australia–China economic complementarity and China's resource diplomacy have been factors in promoting Australia's inclusion in emerging institutions.

What impact has the more recent Australian approach to Asian engagement had upon regional governance? The post-1996 Australian government remained sceptical of regional norms, assessing them as declaratory rather than operative. Australian policy, nevertheless, had a significant impact on the trend to more open trade and investment, as well as encouraging more accountable government. Given the preoccupation with terrorism post-11 September 2001, there was, however, at least an implicit tension in protecting the national interest and fostering good governance, in light of the fact that the latter can be interpreted as consistent with order alone, as opposed to order reflecting justice.[74] Meanwhile, under the impact of domestic and global drivers, at many levels networks of governance have grown stronger and more complex even as Canberra's rhetoric continued to accentuate the claims of traditional sovereignty.

With the advent of a Labor government, national leadership passed to individuals who have embraced the notion of 'global governance' and have expressed strong criticism of the Coalition's priorities and of its neglect of the advantages represented by adept multilateral diplomacy. In particular, while in opposition, Kevin Rudd's qualified approach to Japan could be contrasted with his enthusiasm for a more comprehensive and longer-term China connection. It remains to be seen, however, to what extent the diplomatic momentum of the past decade is amenable to a significant course correction.

Notes

1 I would like to acknowledge Dr Nicholas Thomas and the Centre of Asian Studies, The University of Hong Kong, for the conference invitation that led to the writing of this chapter.
2 Stargardt, A.W. *Australia's Asian Policies: The History of a Debate 1839–1972.* (Wiesbaden: Harrassowitz, 1977).
3 Goldsworthy, David (ed.). *Facing North. A Century of Australian Engagement with Asia, Volume 1: to the 1970s.* (Melbourne: Melbourne University Press/ Department of Foreign Affairs and Trade, 2001).
4 Whitlam, E.G., *A Pacific Community.* (Cambridge, MA: Harvard University Press, 1981); Keating, Paul. *Engagement. Australia Faces the Asia-Pacific.* (Sydney: Pan Macmillan, 2000).
5 Spender, Percy. *Exercises in Diplomacy* (Sydney: Sydney University Press, 1969); Casey, R.G. *Friends and Neighbors. Australia, the US and the World.* (East Lansing, MI: Michigan State College Press, 1955).

6 Ball, Des and Pauline Kerr. *Presumptive Engagement: Australia's Asia-Pacific Security Policy in the 1990s.* (North Sydney: Allen & Unwin, 1996); Cotton, James and John Ravenhill. 'Australia's "Engagement with Asia"', in James Cotton and John Ravenhill (eds). *Seeking Asian Engagement. Australia in World Affairs 1991–95.* (Melbourne: Oxford University Press, 1997), pp. 1–16.

7 Tweedie, Sandra. *Trading Partners. Australia and Asia 1790–1993.* (Sydney: University of New South Wales Press, 1994).

8 Garnaut, Ross. *Australia and the Northeast Asian Ascendancy.* (Canberra: AGPS, 1989).

9 Dalrymple, Rawdon. *Continental Drift. Australia's Search for a Regional Identity.* (Aldershot: Gower, 2003), p. 141.

10 Dalrymple, *Continental Drift,* p. 108.

11 This topic is further discussed in: Cotton, James and John Ravenhill, '"Trading on Alliance Security": Foreign Policy in the post-September 11 Era', in James Cotton and John Ravenhill (eds). *Trading on Alliance Security: Australia in World Affairs 2001–2005.* (Melbourne: Oxford University Press, 2006), pp. 1–10.

12 Department of Foreign Affairs and Trade (DFAT) 1997, *In the National Interest. Australia's Foreign and Trade Policy.* (Canberra: DFAT, 1997), p. iii.

13 Howard, John. *Speech to the Lowy Institute.* 31 March 2005, http://www.pm.gov.au/news/speeches/speech1290.html. Accessed 20 October 2007.

14 Howard, John. *Interview.* 7 April 2005. http://www.pm.gov.au/news/interviews/2005/interview1312.html. Accessed 20 October 2007.

15 Downer, Alexander. *Interview.* 12 April 2005. http://www.foreignminister.gov.au/transcripts/2005/050412_sky.html. Accessed 22 October 2007.

16 Capling, Ann. *All the Way with the USA: Australia, the US and Free Trade.* (Sydney: University of New South Wales Press, 2004).

17 Smith, Gary and David Lowe. 'Howard, Downer and the Liberals' Realist Tradition', *Australian Journal of Politics and History.* (Vol. 51, No. 3, 2005), pp. 459–472.

18 Harries, Owen. *Benign or Imperial? Reflections on American Hegemony* (Sydney: ABC, 2004); cf. Garran, Robert. *True Believer: John Howard, George Bush & the American Alliance.* (Sydney: Allen & Unwin, 2004).

19 DFAT. *In the National Interest,* p. 38.

20 DFAT. *In the National Interest,* p. 66.

21 DFAT. *In the National Interest,* p. 53.

22 Department of Foreign Affairs and Trade (DFAT). *Advancing the National Interest. Australia's Foreign and Trade Policy White Paper* (Canberra: DFAT, 2003), p. 7.

23 DFAT. *Advancing the National Interest,* p. xv.

24 DFAT. *Advancing the National Interest,* p. 77.

25 DFAT. *Advancing the National Interest,* p. 85.

26 Department of Prime Minister and Cabinet, *Protecting Australia Against Terrorism.* (Canberra: Commonwealth of Australia/DPMC, 2004); Department of Foreign Affairs and Trade. *Transnational Terrorism: The Threat to Australia* (Canberra: DFAT, 2004).

27 Department of Defence. *Australia's National Security.* (Canberra: Department of Defence, 2003).

28 Department of Defence. *Australia's National Security. A Defence Update 2005.* (Canberra: Department of Defence, 2005), pp. 7, 13.

29 Department of Defence. *Australia's National Security. A Defence Update 2007.* (Canberra: Department of Defence, 2007), p. 21.

30 Wesley, Michael. 'Australia and the Asian Financial Crisis', in James Cotton and John Ravenhill (eds). *The National Interest in a Global Era. Australia in World Affairs 1996–2000.* (Melbourne: Oxford University Press, 2002), pp. 301–324.

31 Cotton, James, 'ASEAN and the Southeast Asian "Haze": Challenging the Pre-vailing Modes of Regional Engagement', *Pacific Affairs*. (Vol. 72, No. 2, 1999), pp. 331–351.

32 Downer, Alexander. *Speech*. 23 April 2000. http://www.dfat.gov.au/media/speeches/foreign/2000/000423_alf.html. Accessed 22 October 2007.

33 Downer, Alexander. *Speech*. 23 July 2001. http://www.dfat.gov.au/media/speeches/foreign/2001/0107.23_fa_asean_wish.html. Accessed 22 October 2007.

34 Downer, Alexander. *Speech*. 10 September 2001. http://www.dfat.gov.au/media/speeches/foreign/2001/010910_asia_aust_opp.html. Accessed 23 October 2007.

35 Downer, Alexander. *Speech*. 26 June 2003. http://www.foreignminister.gov.au/speeches/2003/030626_unstableworld.html. Accessed 23 October 2007.

36 Vitug, Marites D. and Glenda M. Gloria. *Under the Crescent Moon: Rebellion In Mindanao*. (Quezon City: Ateneo Center for Social Policy and Social Affairs, 2000).

37 Liebman, Alex. 'Trickle-down Hegemony? China's "Peaceful Rise" and Dam Building on the Mekong', *Contemporary Southeast Asia*. (Vol. 27, No. 2, August 2005), pp. 281–304.

38 Howard, John. *'Sunday' interview*. 1 December 2002. http://www.pm.gov.au/news/interviews/2002/interview2015.htm. Accessed 10 November 2007.

39 Brenchley, Fred. 'The Howard Defence Doctrine', *The Bulletin*, 28 September 1999; Lyons, John. 'The Howard Doctrine', *The Bulletin*, 28 September 1999, pp. 22–24.

40 Howard, John. *Interview*. 30 November 2004. http://www.pm.gov.au/news/interviews/Interview1162.htm. Accessed 10 November 2007.

41 Howard, John. *Interview*. 7 April 2005. http://www.pm.gov.au/news/interviews/2005/interview1312.html. Accessed 10 November 2007.

42 Kelly, Paul. 'The day foreign policy won Asia', *Australian*. 6 August 2005; Richardson, Michael. 'Australia-Southeast Asia Relations and the East Asian Summit', *Australian Journal of International Affairs* (Vol. 59, No. 3, 2005), pp. 351–365.

43 Downer, Alexander. *Interview*. 12 April 2005. http://www.foreignminister.gov.au/transcripts/2005/050412_sky.html.

44 Hartcher, Peter. 'How the Enemy Became an Ally', *Australian Financial Review* (Sydney). 4–5 July 1996, pp. 1, 18–19, 26–27.

45 Joint Standing Committee on Treaties (JSCOT). *Submission on the ASEAN Treaty of Amity and Cooperation*. 26 August. (Canberra: Parliament of Australia, 2005).

46 JSCOT. *Submission on the ASEAN Treaty of Amity and Cooperation*, para. 31.

47 This discussion draws on: James Cotton, 'The Near North, the East Asian Hemisphere, the Asia-Pacific: Seeking Direction in Australian Foreign Policy', *Australian Journal of International Affairs*. (Vol. 58, No. 1, 2004), pp. 143–155.

48 Dalrymple. *Continental Drift*.

49 Broinowski, Alison. *About Face. Asian Accounts of Australia*. (Carlton North: Scribe, 2003), p. 63.

50 Broinowski. *About Face*, p. 2.

51 Broinowski. *About Face*, pp. 228, 229.

52 Broinowski. *About Face*, p. 233.

53 DFAT. *Advancing the National Interest*; Fullilove, Michael and Chloë Flutter, *Diaspora: The World Wide Web of Australians*. (Sydney: Lowy Institute for International Policy, Paper 04, 2005).

54 Australian Bureau of Statistics (ABS) 2005. 'Short Term Visitor Arrivals: Esti-mates' (Canberra: ABS, 2005), http://www.abs.gov.au/Ausstats/abs@.nsf/e8ae5488b598839cca25682000131612/3218fb1c6dfdbea9ca256ddd0073a546!OpenDocument. Accessed 10 November 2007. See also Mackie, Jamie, 'The

Politics of Asian Immigration', in James E. Coughlan and Deborah J. McNamara (eds). *Asians in Australia. Patterns of Migration and Settlement.* (South Melbourne: Macmillan, 1997), pp.10–48.

55 Cook, Ivan, *Australians Speak 2005: Public Opinion and Foreign Policy* (Sydney: Lowy Institute for International Policy, 2005).

56 Dee, Moreen and Frank Frost. 'Indochina', in Peter Edwards and David Goldsworthy (eds). *Facing North. A Century of Australian Engagement with Asia, Volume 2: 1970s to 2000.* (Melbourne: Melbourne University Press/Department of Foreign Affairs and Trade, 2003), pp. 195–196.

57 See: Department of Immigration and Citizenship. *Fact Sheet 15 – Population Projections.* http://www.immi.gov.au/media/fact-sheets/15population.htm. Accessed 4 May 2008.

58 Wesley, Michael. *The Howard Paradox. Australian Diplomacy in Asia 1996–2006.* (Sydney: ABC Books, 2007), pp. 189–200.

59 Pitts, Liz. 'Collaborators, Business Partners, Friends: Australia-China Subnational Government Relations', in Nicholas Thomas (ed.). *Re-Orienting Australia-China Relations: 1972 to the Present.* (Aldershot: Ashgate, 2004), pp. 67–86.

60 Slaughter, Anne-Marie. 'Everyday Global Governance', *Daedalus* (Vol. 132, 2003), pp.83–90; Slaughter, Anne-Marie, *A New World Order* (Princeton, NJ: Princeton University Press, 2004).

61 'ASEAN-Australia Dialogue', Singapore, ASEAN Secretariat, 2004. http://www.aseansec.org/12974.htm. Accessed 14 November 2007.

62 AUSAID, AusAID, ASEAN and Australia. *30 years of Development Cooperation.* (Canberra: AusAID, 2004).

63 Department of Foreign Affairs and Trade. *ASEAN and Australia. Celebrating 30 Years.* (Canberra: DFAT, 2004).

64 Downer, Alexander. *Joint Press Conference with Indonesian Foreign Minister Dr Hassan Wirajuda.* 13 November 2006. http://www.foreignminister.gov.au/transcripts/2006/061113_wir.html. Accessed 14 November 2007.

65 Department of Foreign Affairs and Trade. *Australia-Japan Joint Declaration on Security Cooperation.* 13 March 2007. http://www.dfat.gov.au/geo/japan/aus_jap_security_dec.html. Accessed 14 November 2007.

66 Howard, John. *Speech to the Lowy Institute.* 31 March 2005. http://www.pm.gov.au/news/speeches/speech1290.html. Accessed 20 October 2007.

67 Howard, John. *Speech.* 21 October 2005. http://www.pm.gov.au/news/speeches/speech1644.html. Accessed 14 November 2007.

68 Smith, Stephen. *A Modern Australia for a New Era, Speech to the Australian Strategic Policy Institute National Security Dinner.* 9 April 2008, http://www.foreignminister.gov.au/speeches/2008/080309_nsd.html. Accessed 4 May 2008.

69 Ibid. The two quotes do not run sequentially.

70 See: Rudd, Kevin. 'Conversation with China's Youth on the Future', Speech at Peking University. 9 April 2008. http://www.pm.gov.au/media/speech/2008/speech_0176.cfm. Accessed 4 May 2008.

71 Sheridan, Greg. 'Region notices bias for Beijing', *The Australian.* 3 May 2008.

72 Milner, Anthony C. 'Comments on Michael Richardson's Article', *Australian Journal of International Affairs.* (Vol. 59, No. 3, 2005), p. 371.

73 Okita, Saburo. 'Pacific Regional Cooperation', in L.T. Evans, and J.D.B. Miller (eds). *Policy and Practice. Essays in Honour of Sir John Crawford* (Sydney: Australian National University Press/Pergamon, 1987), pp. 122–132.

74 Cotton, James. 'Southeast Asia after September 11', *Terrorism and Political Violence.* (Vol. 15, No. 1, 2003), pp. 148–170.

7 India and East Asia

Through the looking glass

Isabelle Saint-Mézard

Introduction

It could be seen as an irony of history that India – a country which nurtured intense interactions with its Eastern neighbourhood for centuries – had to embark on a policy of 'Looking East' to signal its return to the Asian fold. India's Look East policy was launched in 1992, as a conscious and deliberate attempt to link up to the emerging regionalism in East Asia. This opening up to East Asia was first and foremost a direct outcome of domestic developments, as New Delhi initiated a long-awaited process of reforms aimed at liberalising its economy in the early 1990s. Like the economic reform policy, the Look East policy has been pursued by successive governments in power in New Delhi. Due to these sustained efforts, India has now largely caught up with regional dynamics. India has substantially enhanced trade, financial and people-to-people interactions with East Asian countries. In terms of institutional integration, India became a full Dialogue Partner of ASEAN in 1996 and was admitted to the ASEAN Regional Forum (ARF) in recognition of its strategic significance to future regional stability. India's status was further elevated to that of summit-level partner of ASEAN in 2002. As a sign of its growing importance in regional developments, India was also invited to the first East Asian Summit in December 2005. However, despite its activism, this giant country is still slightly on the periphery of the regional integration of East Asia, as reflected in the fact that it is not part of the ASEAN Plus Three (APT) framework.[1] India thus appears as a giant neighbour slightly on the margins, but increasingly anxious to be fully integrated into East Asian regionalism.

As a backdrop to India's positioning in the regional integration of East Asia, the present discussion explores how the Look East policy may impact on governance modes in the region. In other words, this chapter tries to understand whether India has contributed to the development of regional governance in the context of its Look East policy. This general question leads to an engagement with the concept of governance, a sometimes broad and confusing notion, both in its theoretical definition and in its methodological applications. Generally speaking, the current interest in the governance concept has to be seen in the context of the declining authority of the state and its capacities of social intervention.[2] Nevertheless, it is not so much the withdrawal of the state as its new forms of action in face of market deregulation and economic globalisation that capture the interest of the governance literature. In the process, the state is seen as an actor among others and the traditional administrative model, which is based on a vertical, hierarchical and top-down kind of functioning, is increasingly challenged by new dynamics that are more inclusive and that nurture bottom-up processes. Thus, according to Krahmann, governance encompasses the multifaceted modalities by which a wide range of governmental and non-governmental actors with inter linked intents and interests participate in the collective exercise of authority, however dispersed and split that authority may be.[3]

Not surprisingly, the concept of governance has become pervasive in public policy studies. It has also permeated into the discipline of international relations and has successfully found a niche in the global studies field.[4] However, its application at the regional level has seemed to be more problematic and has mostly focused on the European experience and the process of multilevel decision making, as discussed in Chapter 1. In this scheme, states no longer have an exclusive role in terms of decision making, as a result of which they need to coordinate with different levels of authority, at both the supranational and infranational levels. Multilevel governance is thus conceptualised as a system of interdependencies within which 'state and sub-state, public and private, trans-national, and supra-national, actors all deal with each other in complex networks of varying horizontal and vertical density'.[5] In comparison to the European experience, studies of regional governance in the Asian context are still scarce. Moreover, with the trajectories of regionalism in Europe and East Asia being fairly distinct, the resulting governance modes can be expected to be unique to each regional context. Such an assumption raises the question of an Asian approach to regional governance. If, beyond its seemingly universal appeal, governance is to be contextualised according to regional settings, then the nuances of the Asian experience are yet to be exposed, both in their intellectual and normative interpretation and in their concrete practices.

At first glance, it seems that the architects of the regional integration project in East Asia have not yet fully and officially embraced the concept. For instance, broaching the question of governance in a speech, former ASEAN Secretary-General Ong Keng Yong admitted that the terminology of 'good governance' is not explicitly used by his organisation. He nevertheless suggested that governance was somewhat a de facto phenomenon in ASEAN, as reflected by its decision-making process, which features consensus building and consultations as well as interactions with the private sector and the NGO community. Ong also underlined that ASEAN's community-building enterprise, in particular the ASEAN Economic Community project, implies an evolution towards the rule of law and effective regulations, in addition to bridging the development gap between its members. He finally put the emphasis on the development of human resources as a critical dimension of governance, besides the empowerment of institutions.[6]

From an academic perspective, Jayasuriya defines regional governance as a political project reflecting a 'particular constellation of power and interests', and whose dynamics partake of the domestic political economy as well as the structures of the global political economy. Taking the 1997 financial crisis as a milestone in the evolution of East Asian regionalism, he observes the emergence of post-crisis governance mechanisms aimed at regulation and harmonisation of policies at the regional level. In his view, the new regionalism of the 1990s was driven by unilateral initiatives of trade liberalisation under the banner of the APEC and its open regionalism credo; by contrast, post-crisis regional developments partake of a political will to forge better coordination at the regional level through the setting up of legal structures and mechanisms that are more intrusive with respect to state sovereignty. Interestingly, regional integration has deepened in the financial and monetary spheres, which had until then been the exclusive realm of state sovereignty. Thus, if there is one point on which a practitioner such as Ong and an academic such as Jayasuriya seem to agree, it is that East Asia is entering an era of nascent governance characterised by greater concerns for a collective commitment to improving standards of coordination, rule of law, transparency and accountability.

From a methodological point of view, the present discussion considers three essential features of regional governance: (1) the specific code of conduct and behaviour, i.e. the norms and practices involved in policy making at the regional level; (2) the nascent institutional architecture that allows for greater regulation, harmonisation and coordination at the regional level, through multilevel and multidimensional arrangements, and (3) the full range of actors involved in the governing of the regional integration, in particular the emerging participation of subnational and private actors as stakeholders of the integration process. In other words, any methodological approach to the analysis of regional governance must encompass the study of norms and practices, the institutional structures as well as the varied stakeholders that are involved in the governing of the regional integration of East Asia.

Thus, this chapter attempts to explore the multifaceted relations between India and East Asia, while analysing their implications in terms of regional governance. It shows that the spectrum of India's approach to regional governance can be broken down into three broad patterns of behaviour: adjustment, emulation, innovation. 'Adjustment' refers to India's conscious efforts to abide by the specific norms and practices associated with ASEAN's policy making. 'Emulation' points to India's endeavours to be part of the web of new arrangements that have been developed in the post-crisis era and that steer regional integration towards new directions. 'Innovation' underlines India's inputs and specific contributions to the development of regional governance in East Asia, with a special emphasis on the role of civil society organisations and subnational actors.

Adjustments: abiding by prevailing regional norms

In the context of its Look East policy, India has taken due note of the specificity of the norms and decision-making modes prevailing in Southeast Asia. It thus has made an effort to adjust itself to the regional behaviour and practices in the policy-making area. Despite its different political culture, India has subscribed to a set of principles that ASEAN defines as its norms of governance: consensus, non-coercive means of resolving conflict, avoidance of direct confrontation and non-interference in the internal affairs of member states.

India and the 'ASEAN Way'

From the very beginning, economic preoccupations predominated in the new, open policy towards East Asia. To repeat, the Look East policy was initiated in the specific context of India's economic liberalisation, when the need to attract foreign capital and enhance trade relations with major economic poles in the world became a top-ranking foreign policy imperative. But, as India was slowly opening up to the world market, it felt a sense of isolation in face of the growing trend towards the formation of macro-regions the world over. India's fear of economic marginalisation was especially strong, as it had just lost one of its closest trading partners with the demise of the Soviet Union. Within the South Asian subregion, the South Asian Association for Regional Cooperation (SAARC) offered a rather unsatisfactory track record of regional cooperation as well as little prospect of transforming itself into a region with substantial economic weight in the near future. Consequently, India felt the urgency of associating itself with the prosperous and dynamic region that was emerging to its East. In that respect, the Look East policy could be seen as a strategy deployed by India to reposition itself in a world dominated by regionalist tendencies.

The main aim of the Look East policy was to integrate the Indian economy into the processes surrounding Asian regionalisation. In other words, into the structural process of intense socio-economic interdependencies that wove the regional fabric of East Asia. In a more political perspective, it was also to forge links with different institutions that were giving shape to East Asia. ASEAN was the number one target, as it stands at the heart of Asian regionalism. New Delhi was thus anxious not only to restore good relations with Southeast Asia but also to build up an atmosphere of confidence and comfort – on the basis that a sense of familiarity and closeness would make its counterparts more responsive to India's Look East policy. In so doing, India was faced with two challenges inherited from history. The first challenge had to do with recent history and the fact that India had neglected its relations with Southeast Asia since the early 1960s.[7] Ironically, New Delhi found itself knocking on ASEAN's door, some ten years after having ignored its invitation to a ministerial conference in 1980. In this connection, ASEAN had not forgotten that New Delhi had been a close ally of the USSR and a firm friend of South Vietnam, at a time when communism was their biggest threat.

Secondly, looking further back into history would reveal that India indulged in a type of cultural haughtiness in the earlier days of the nationalist struggles, and this past arrogance was not completely forgotten in the regional collective memory. From the 1920s onwards, India's nationalist awakening led to a rediscovery of its glorious past, including the influence of its ancient civilisation over the rest of the region through the pervasive spread of Hinduism and Buddhism. The magnified rediscovery of India's ancient contributions to the civilisations of Asia led to the theorisation of Greater India in the 1940s and 1950s, a narrative which was akin to the idea of an Indian cultural sphere of influence in Asia. As a result, India came to regard itself as the locus of Asian civilisations and this underlying assumption nurtured a sense of superiority that characterised its relationship to the rest of the region. In addition to its past grandeur, India came to be one of the first Asian nations to gain independence, which further strengthened its sense of destiny as the leader of the new Asia. Not surprisingly, such posturing was not well received by the nations of Southeast Asia, who had their own sense of pride and felt overwhelmed by India's self-importance.

Under the circumstances prevailing in the early 1990s, India realised that its past haughtiness was obsolete and counterproductive. Pragmatism and modesty became the order of the day. Fully aware of the discomfort that any invocation of its past glory was likely to provoke, India avoided any reference to Greater India. This low-profile diplomatic stand was taken in full recognition of Southeast Asian sensibilities and marked a change in India's foreign policy practices. New Delhi would only attempt to attract the goodwill of its eastern neighbours from then on. As a result, it played a prudent game and emphasised priorities more suited to the times: pragmatism, consensus, equal partnership and mutual respect – precisely the cardinal points of ASEAN's diplomatic functioning. The motto of India's policy towards ASEAN became 'quiet diplomacy' – a modest and discreet diplomacy aimed at building up a relationship on equal grounds. The first time India participated in a post-ministerial conference, then Foreign Minister I. K. Gujral stated that the new tenets of its foreign policy in Southeast Asia were that it would 'handle the [India–ASEAN] partnership with pragmatism and consensus orientation, taking a leaf out of the ASEAN book'.[8]

The days of Indian arrogance were over, with the country officially promising to comply with the ASEAN Way. According to Amitav Acharya, 'the "ASEAN way" consists of a code of conduct for interstate behaviour as well as a decision-making process based on consultations and consensus'.[9] The approach calls for a high degree of discretion, flexibility and pragmatism. Confrontations have to be avoided, thereby ensuring that more efforts are devoted to reaching a consensual solution. Indeed, the 'ASEAN Way' is akin to a socialisation process where national sensibilities are carefully dealt with and where the states save themselves the risk of delegating their sovereignty. Given these characteristics, it is easy to understand the posture of India, a country very concerned about the integrity of its sovereignty. India indeed could only find advantages in participating in regional mechanisms that would in any case safeguard its own sovereignty.

As a matter of fact, India adapted itself adequately enough to the style practised in Southeast Asia to satisfy ASEAN. In 1998, Singapore Foreign Minister Professor Jayakumar officially recognised that the Indo-ASEAN dialogue proved to be progressing 'at a faster and more constructive pace than some of our other dialogues'.[10] The success was largely attributed 'to the generous spirit of accommodation of the Government of India, which is working hard and in good faith to find fresh ways and means to add more value to the process'. Additional meetings between Indian and ASEAN high officials were gradually included in the agenda, so as to ensure 'a platform for discussing sensitive issues'.[11] The ASEAN premises were based on the fact that increasing the opportunities for meetings with Indian officials would 'build up confidence and comfort levels and nurture habits of co-operation'.[12] New Delhi and the ASEAN also agreed that their partnership should follow a prudent, step-by-step approach. Indeed, a learning process was to take place in the course of cooperation which would improve interactions as each partner was exposed to the other's concerns. For the ASEAN, the method also helped in putting New Delhi to the test, by ensuring that the country maintained a low profile and relinquished its traditional claims to pan-Asian leadership.

Nevertheless, it is of interest to note that India did not entirely give up cultural references. New Delhi was not shy of instrumentalising the notion of shared values with Southeast Asia in order to facilitate economic relations, as well as its admission into regional institutions. Thus, Foreign Minister I. K. Gujral observed that, given its cultural affinity with Southeast Asia, India was a natural partner of ASEAN: 'We are confident that with our common traditions of Ahimsa, Panchsheela and Samanvaya, of tolerance and gentleness, we can slip into the ASEAN culture easily.'[13] The notions of shared values and common historical experiences were also used to stress the fact that India was different from the other partners of the ASEAN and aspired to enjoy a privileged relationship.[14] Foreign Minister I. K. Gujral did not hide this fact, as he asserted that the age-old ties between India and Southeast Asia ought to be the 'emotive driving force' for the significant development of Indo-ASEAN relations.

An India–ASEAN convergence on the non-intervention principle: the Myanmar case

Another essential regional norm is that of non-intervention in the internal affairs of other member states. While this norm has been pervasive in ASEAN functioning, its prevalence has become particularly striking in the case of Myanmar. Indeed, the ASEAN approach has been to pursue a policy of constructive engagement towards the Burmese military junta, in the hope of initiating dynamics of internal change. This policy of conciliation and socialisation with the junta has provoked a bitter debate with the West. Not only have the European Union (EU) and the United States strongly criticised the misdeeds of the military junta in Myanmar, but they have also supported a policy of sanctions and isolation against the military regime. It was not surprising, then, that ASEAN's decision to welcome Myanmar as a full member caused an open confrontation with the EU and even threatened the future of their dialogue under the Asia–Europe Meeting (ASEM) framework (as is discussed more fully in Chapter 12).[15] Such is the prominence of the non-intervention principle that even proposals for a more nuanced approach by influential individuals from the region have failed. Indeed, towards the late 1990s, Thai Foreign Minister Surin Pitsuwan tried to promote the idea of 'flexible engagement', meant 'to promote greater political openness and transparency in ASEAN, both at domestic and regional levels'.[16] This proposal for a new governance norm proved unsuccessful, however.

Despite the fact that it has long subscribed to liberal democracy, India has proved to be very discreet with respect to its East Asian neighbours' political regimes. Its policy turnabout on the Myanmar issue stands as a case in point.[17] In the debate over defending democratic values and human rights versus the non-interference principle, India has clearly chosen the latter. In the process, it has also aligned itself with ASEAN by pursuing a policy of constructive engagement with the military junta and has, consequently, deliberately integrated some of ASEAN's specific modes of governance. India did not always side with ASEAN, however. Between 1988 and 1991, New Delhi actively backed the Burmese pro-democracy movement: it virulently denounced the measures of repression enforced by the Burmese state and welcomed Burmese refugees and several groups of pro-democracy students.[18] But, from the end of 1991 onwards, New Delhi started to actively re-engage Rangoon's military junta. India's relations with this authoritarian neighbour have since become extensive and multidimensional and they have resulted in India partly turning its back on the pro-democracy dissidents, led by Nobel Prize-winner Aung San Suu Kyi.

On account of its 'functional cooperation' with Rangoon, India, henceforth, aligned itself with ASEAN's policy of cooperation and inclusion. During its 1996 ministerial summit, ASEAN welcomed the Myanmar representative as an esteemed guest and a future member. India made the most of this event by underlining that, due to Myanmar's admission, it now had a land connection to ASEAN, a development that was bound to boost its economic relations with Southeast Asia. At the 1997 post-ministerial conferences, Indian Finance Minister P. Chidambaram clearly reaffirmed that India intended to develop close links with Myanmar, in order to 'give a new dimension' to Indo-ASEAN relations.[19] Indeed, in 1999 the government officially defined its policy with regard to Myanmar as that of 'constructive engagement', thereby modelling it on that of ASEAN.[20] Still more convincing is the case of Bangladesh, India, Sri Lanka, Thailand Economic Cooperation (BIMSTEC). Right from the creation of this regional organisation in June 1997, the founding members – India, Thailand, Bangladesh and Sri Lanka – announced that Myanmar's integration would be unavoidable. Despite Western pressures, Rangoon became a member of the organisation only six months after BIMSTEC was born, in December 1997. The BIMSTEC case was discussed in Chapter 5.

Indo-Burmese high-level exchanges have further accelerated since the early 2000s, culminating with the state visit of Senior General Than Shwe, Chairman of the State Peace and Development Council (SPDC) of Myanmar, in October 2004. Then, in March 2006, President A. P. J. Abdul Kalam's visit to Myanmar, the first by a head of state from India, marked a new milestone in bilateral relations. Concurrently, India has focused its energies on developing a land transport corridor linking up with Myanmar. In 2001, a road connecting the Indian border in the Northeastern state of Manipur to central Myanmar was inaugurated, while three new trade points were opened along the border. Since April 2002, Thailand, Myanmar and India have formed a troika aimed at exploring ways to develop a highway linking them. The urge to enhance economic interactions with Southeast Asia is one of the many incentives that account for India's approach to Myanmar. Another factor is that the internal situation in Myanmar has direct repercussions on India's law and order in the restive Northeast region. The fight against militancy, drug trafficking and arms smuggling along the border has led India to seek greater coordination with Rangoon. India's appeasement policy is also the outcome of mounting concerns regarding China's influence over Myanmar. Indeed, while relations with New Delhi continued to deteriorate during the 1980s, Rangoon entered a close relationship with Beijing. The nexus between China and Myanmar has since stood as a major security concern for India, accounting in many respects for its efforts to improve relations with Rangoon at all costs.

Without any doubt, there remains general sympathy in India for the pro-democratic movement, as borne out by the awarding of the prestigious Nehru Peace Prize to Suu Kyi in 1995.[21] Nevertheless, despite this general sense of sympathy, the Indian government reacted belatedly and in a rather subdued way to the incidents of September 2007 in Myanmar. Following the junta's use of force against civilian protestors and Buddhist monks, the Indian foreign ministry eventually expressed 'concern' at the incidents and called for peaceful and 'broad-based' political reforms. However, it opposed the possibility of UN-sponsored sanctions against Myanmar. Even more striking is the fact that India's Petroleum Minister, Murli Deora, visited Myanmar in late September 2007 even while the incidents confronting the military junta with the protestors were taking place.[22] This was followed by a series of high-level visits in both directions in early 2008 to discuss economic and energy cooperation.[23] Overall, India's reaction to the junta's crackdown and its continued commitments to closer ties point to an ingrained reluctance to comment on its neighbour's internal matters as well as a clear preference for a policy of engagement.

Emulation: entering into a web of new regional mechanisms

This section concentrates on what could be the forerunners of a post-crisis regional governance in East Asia. It first examines India's special positioning with respect to the APT, the structuring process of post-crisis East Asian regionalism. It then analyses India's endeavours to duplicate some of the new arrangements that are being developed in the region. It appears that India is increasingly integrated into the thickening web of regional and bilateral arrangements in East Asia, even while it is not part of the APT. The section has a final point, on the role of domestic coalitions in the Look East policy.

India's marginalisation from the nascent institutional architecture in East Asia

Since the 1997 Asian crisis, East Asian countries have been inclined to establish new cooperative arrangements that put the 'emphasis on the development of policy coordination and harmonization'.[24] As identified by Jayasuriya, this may herald a new trend of regional integration, in which regulatory initiatives will weave the regional fabric much more tightly than just trade liberalisation. The nascent surveillance and monitoring mechanisms at the regional level have been mostly related to monetary coordination and financial governance. For instance, in May 2000, the finance ministers from Southeast Asia, Japan, China and South Korea set up the Chiang Mai Initiative (CMI), a basic mechanism of crisis prevention and currency stabilisation based on a network of bilateral swap agreements. The finance ministers from the same thirteen countries agreed in May 2005 to enhance their network of currency swap agreements and significantly increased their US $39.5 billion swap programme under the CMI.[25] In May 2008, these ministers met again to agree to increase the size of the swap to US$80 billion.[26] There have also been renewed proposals for an Asian Monetary Fund, a concept which was originally put forward by Japan during the 1997 Asian crisis, and a common currency. Those developments point to an emerging governance architecture in East Asian regionalism.

India was not directly affected by the 1997 Asian crisis, thanks to its relatively insulated economy and its cautious approach to financial liberalisation. On the one hand, this has allowed India to profile itself more positively in the region as a stable economy with 'strong fundamentals' and with one of the highest growth rates in the region, along with China. On the other hand, India has been left on the periphery of the new initiatives taken at the regional level to address the crisis. As a result, India is not participating in the new regional systems of surveillance and regulation in East Asia: it is not part of the CMI and has not entered into bilateral swap arrangements with East Asian countries. India also does not participate in the Asian bond market. It is, however, of interest to note that ASEAN–India Vision 2020, a document which has been drafted by a network of think-tanks from India and Southeast Asia, clearly specifies that India should join the CMI, enter into its bilateral swap arrangements and participate in its finance ministers' meetings.[27] In this connection, India made a first step in August 2007 when it agreed to sign a basic bilateral agreement on currency swap with Japan. This agreement was finalised in March 2008, when the two sides agreed to create a US$3 billion currency swap facility.[28]

Moreover, the process of enhanced interactions between ASEAN and its three Northeast Asian partners has moved beyond the financial and mone-tary spheres. Since the informal meeting of 1997 between the heads of state of ASEAN and China, Korea and Japan, the APT process has progressively extended to new areas of cooperation, with the institutionalisation of regular consultation and cooperation mechanisms in the political, security, economy and socio-cultural sectors. As a result, the APT is now the driving force of East Asian regional integration. As for India, it was fairly quick to realise its marginalisation and tried to link up to the APT. In November 2000, it pro-posed to enhance its institutional cooperation with ASEAN by either joining the APT (which would thus become 'ASEAN Plus Four') or creating a separate ASEAN–India Summit, along the same lines as the APT. While ASEAN leaders judged that India's request for 'ASEAN Plus Four' was premature, they eventually agreed to the establishment of a separate summit with India in November 2001. This decision came as a clear indication of ASEAN's willingness to build a close relationship with India at the highest political level. The ASEAN–India Summit is now an annual event that is convened at the same time as the APT summits. Along with Japan, South Korea and China, India was at that time the only country among the ten dialogue partners of the ASEAN to interact at summit level.[29]

However, the advent of the ASEAN–India Summit is seen as a mixed success for the Look East policy, given that India has not been accepted into the collective process under the APT. In other words, India is not yet on an equal footing with ASEAN's closest partners in East Asia – China, Korea and Japan – which, besides their separate summit meetings with ASEAN, also take part in the collective dialogue held under the APT framework. In terms of regional policy coordination and harmonisation, India may find itself at a disadvantage. Interestingly, a compelling motivation in ASEAN's decision not to integrate India may be the underlying notion that APT is meant to promote an East Asia entity and avoid any dilution with South Asia. For instance, in his comments, former Malaysian Prime Minister Mahathir insisted that the ASEAN–India Summit shall be distinct from APT, which was to be 'East Asian' only.[30] In the same fashion, when New Delhi requested to have 'ASEAN Plus Four' in 2000, then Prime Minister

Goh Chok Tong explained to his Indian counterparts that 'it would be difficult to have an ASEAN+4 Summit. ASEAN+3 is more like an East Asian get-together'.[31] Geographical representations of South Asia as an entity distinct from East Asia have been pervasive since the 1960s and obviously remain an important structural factor shaping perceptions. So, it seems that while the ASEAN members are keen to build a close relationship with India, they tend to keep it as a second-tier partner vis-à-vis their nascent institutional architecture that has so far been based on the notion of an East Asian entity.

India's commitment to new institutional mechanisms

While India is not fully part of the institutional structure nurtured by the APT, it remains anxious to enhance integration mechanisms with East Asia. Interestingly, some of these new regional arrangements involve rule-binding commitments and new areas of cooperation and harmonisation. For instance, the proliferation of bilateral and regional trade agreements stands as a striking feature of post-crisis regionalism in East Asia, and India has fully acknowledged the importance of that trend, despite its traditional preference for multilateral trade arrangements under the World Trade Organisation (WTO). Thus, India concluded a framework agreement on a free trade agreement (FTA) with Thailand in 2003, and signed an ambitious Comprehensive Economic Cooperation Agreement (CECA) with Singapore in June 2005. Indeed, the CECA is one of the most advanced economic agreements ever concluded by India. It is a four-pronged project encompassing a free trade agreement, a bilateral investment promotion treaty, an improved double taxation avoidance agreement and an air services agreement. This is also the first time India has entered into a bilateral economic integration agreement in services. Singapore has indeed agreed to a mutual recognition agreement that will allow Indian-trained architects, accountants and doctors to practise in the city-state. Last, but not least, CECA provides for a dispute settlement mechanism with rule-binding powers.

Agreements such as CECA tend to develop new rules beyond those set by the WTO for the parties involved in the first place, as well as for other potential agreements, insofar as they propose a template for customised negotiations and arrangements. Therefore, India may be able to project CECA as a model while negotiating economic pacts with other states. Indeed, a number of countries from the region are approaching India, among them Japan, South Korea, China, Malaysia and Indonesia. Furthermore, at the First ASEAN-Indian Summit in November 2002, India offered to have a FTA with ASEAN in ten years. Then, the following year, at the second ASEAN-India Summit in October 2003, the leaders of India and the ASEAN signed the Framework Agreement for Comprehensive Economic Cooperation. It is of interest to note that the framework agreement was negotiated in only ten months, which reveals that India was anxious to show its political will and ability to deliver on its FTA proposals. The framework agreement plans for the setting up of a free trade area in goods, services and investments in ten years. ASEAN and India have agreed to an interim Rules of Origin for Early Harvest Programme. India will also extend special concessions to ASEAN's poorest member countries. Moreover, the framework agreement plans for a dispute settlement mechanisms, specifying that 'The Parties shall, within one year after the date of entry into force of this Agreement, establish appropriate formal dispute settlement procedures and mechanism for the purposes of this Agreement.'[32] India is also involved in another regional trade agreement with BIMSTEC, whose members concluded a framework agreement including trade in goods, services, investments and other sectors of economic cooperation (customs, standards, e-commerce and business visas) in 2004. Negotiations on trade, rules of origin and for a dispute resolution mechanism are ongoing.

In some respects, it seems that India tends to emulate China's initiatives towards the region. For instance, the Indian offer for an FTA with ASEAN in 2002 came just a day after China signed its own FTA with ASEAN. Then, at the ASEAN summit meetings in October 2003, India made sure to consent to the ASEAN Treaty of Amity and Cooperation (TAC) at the same time as China. In the same fashion, both China and India have been among the very first countries to sign overarching strategic partnerships, which are a commitment to deepening and enhancing cooperation with ASEAN. In 2003, ASEAN and China signed a Strategic Partnership for Peace and Prosperity. One year later, in 2004, an ASEAN–India Partnership for Peace, Progress and Shared Prosperity was concluded. In other words, India seems anxious to catch up with China's growing clout over regional arrangements. In so doing, India tends to duplicate and consolidate the template of regional governance that China is evolving in East Asia (this was also discussed in Chapter 5).

From the ASEAN viewpoint, this sense of emulation on the part of India has so far proved a rather positive development. In fact, ASEAN has followed a policy of keeping India engaged, as it is one of the few countries of the region that can help balance China's growing influence. Even if ASEAN is responsive to China's overtures, it would feel more comfortable with a balanced regional order. Consequently, India is increasingly seen as a key component in the regional architecture. This view transpired during the debate over the organisation of the East Asian Summit. The project was originally mooted by Malaysia, with the active support of China, with a view to enhancing the APT. However, when the question of the participants' line-up was raised, a debate ensued, with Singapore, Indonesia and Japan in particular strongly advocating the participation of India in the summit, while Malaysia and China opposed it. The inclusive version of the summit (the 'India supporters' camp') won over Malaysia and China and ASEAN announced in the early summer of 2005 that New Delhi would be invited to the summit. Thanks to its activism in catching up with regional development, India was able to meet all the requirements set by ASEAN: substantial relations with ASEAN, full dialogue partnership and to be signatory of the TAC. In many respects, India has become one of the most active 'external actors' to lobby for a broadening of the East Asian integration process. While still on the periphery, it may be increasingly difficult for East Asian countries to keep India as a second-tier partner in the overarching arrangements that are currently being established.

The Look East policy and domestic coalitions in India

From an internal point of view, it should not be ignored that some aspects of the Look East policy have been a battle ground for the various constituencies involved in the economic liberalisation debate. In particular, India's proactive FTA policy in Asia has sparked off a domestic controversy, with the issue of trade liberalisation and lowering of tariffs generating protectionist reactions among various sectors of Indian industry. In the political setting under the United Progressive Alliance, the constituencies in favour of the FTA policies have been Prime Minister Manmohan Singh, and high officials, especially in the Ministries of Commerce and External Affairs, along with some sections of the business communities. In many ways, these pro-reform stakeholders have used FTAs as an external strategy to wage an internal battle against protectionist constituencies. They have argued that India may be excluded from the wider aspects of Asian regionalism and fail to enter the future Asian Economic Community if it does not embark on a pro-active FTA policy and catch up with trade liberalisation efforts in East Asia. In so doing, they have pushed the agenda of trade liberalisation on the domestic front. Furthermore, by facing the domestic industry with the prospects of stiff competition from Asia, this pro-reform constituency has aimed to accelerate the agenda of economic modernisation and drive the industrial apparatus to adjust to higher competitiveness levels under conditions of globalisation. Thus, in a lecture in November 2005, Indian Prime Minister Singh admitted that his FTA agenda was not so much about trade liberalisation per se, as industrial restructuring: 'The new-found interest in regional arrangements is based not just on trade promotion but on exploiting the potential of efficiency-seeking restructuring of industry on a pan-regional basis.'[33] In that connection, the Indian case is a good reflection of Helen Nesadurai's analysis when she explains that 'regional arrangements are essentially political projects that cannot be understood apart from the approaches and priorities central to domestic economic governance'.[34]

Not surprisingly, India's FTA with Thailand, which was concluded in 2003, has been particularly controversial. Even the CECA with Singapore has been viewed with a degree of suspicion on the part of some sections of the business community. As Senior Minister Lee Kuan Yew stated when commenting on the difficulties faced in the process of negotiating the CECA and calling for state agencies to play the leading role over the business communities: 'When you leave the matter to the professional organisations, they want to protect their own professions. From the government side, we are going to push and make sure that they are on track.'[35] The negotiations for an FTA between India and ASEAN have provided a good example of the interplay between the various stakeholders of the Look East policy. While ASEAN put pressure on the Indian government to lower tariffs on a large number of imported items, the Indian government had to deal with stiff domestic opposition to the FTA project. The primary concern of the anti-FTA constituency was over the impact of liberal imports from ASEAN on agricultural products, but Indian industry was also worried about imports from Thailand and the possibility of Chinese goods entering the country through ASEAN nations. The issue reached such importance that it came to be raised by Congress president and chairperson of the ruling United Progressive Alliance coalition, Sonia Gandhi, in a letter to Prime Minister Manmohan Singh in April 2006. That such a powerful leader as Sonia Gandhi came to take up the issue personally against pro-reform Prime Minister is a reflection of the importance of the domestic coalition that formed in reaction to the Indo-ASEAN FTA project. Indeed, many of the anti-FTA sectors, such as farmers, are also quite powerful politically. Consequently, the issue of the sensitive list – the list of items that are exempted from tariff reduction – became one of the major hurdles in finalising the FTA, with India trying to protect the interests of its farmers and small-scale industry sector.

Despite the apprehensions expressed by Sonia Gandhi, the Prime Minister's Trade and Economic Relations Committee – a special unit directly under Prime Minister Singh – has given the green light to implementing the proposed free trade area with ASEAN from January 2007.[36] However, as of May 2008, negotiations between India and ASEAN had still not reached a positive conclusion, although reports suggest that an agreement is close.[37] It thus appears that India's FTA strategy is driven by conflicting dynamics: while some of the higher sections of the state apparatus are concerned with playing catch-up with China on the Asian strategic scene, a large portion of the business community is concerned about stiff competition from Southeast Asia and China. In other words, there seems to be a disjunction between the high officials who use FTA as a foreign policy tool, especially for their political and diplomatic implications, and large sections of domestic industry that fear to bear the brunt of an indiscriminate trade policy.

Innovation: India's original contributions to different levels of regional governance

India has taken a few initiatives on its own that may provide for better governance on various levels – at the subregional level and on a macro-level. These initiatives reveal the inputs of the academic community as well as the growing participation of subnational actors in the regional integration.

Improving Capacity building at the Subregional Level in the CLMV

ASEAN Secretary-Generals have repeatedly identified human resources development as a critical dimension of governance in ASEAN. In this connection, India stands as a worthwhile partner, which has supported cooperation in capacity building in the areas of information and communications technology, space technology, agriculture, and health and pharmaceuticals.[38] In a significant move, India has also undertaken to support the implementation of the projects under the Initiative for ASEAN Integration (IAI). The IAI was launched in 2000 as a set of specific policies aimed at bridging the development gap between the so-called 'ASEAN 6' and the newer – and poorer – members, namely Cambodia, Laos, Myanmar and Vietnam (CLMV). On account of its cultural and historical affinities with these countries, India has proved particularly keen on reviving ties with the subregion. It has put forward various initiatives in different areas: biotechnology, human resources development and agro-processing. In particular, it has committed to establish an Entrepreneurship Development Centre in each CLMV, aimed at promoting capacity building in the fields of entrepreneurship and skilled labour development. The first Centre was opened in Laos in 2004, followed by Vietnam and Cambodia in 2006.

In addition to its participation in the IAI, India has become a member of the Mekong-Ganga Cooperation (MGC), a subregional cooperation project that was launched in July 2000. MGC brings together India and five ASEAN countries of the Mekong River basin, namely Cambodia, Laos, Myanmar, Vietnam and Thailand. Besides the strong emphasis put on reviving close cultural links, the idea of MGC is that India's skills can contribute to the development of the CLMV in the transportation networks, tourism and education development sectors. ASEAN has welcomed the MGC initiative positively as it complements its own Initiative for ASEAN Integration. As a matter of fact, the MGC Summit meetings have so far developed under the ASEAN umbrella. While it will take time before this subregional project come to fruition, from an ideational perspective the MGC already stands as a noteworthy development because it transcends the symbolic boundary between South and Southeast Asia. Furthermore, India has understood that if it wants to be part of larger regional trends in East Asia, it has to be embedded in a matrix of different subregional schemes such as the MGC. Indeed, subregional cooperation provides a solid basis for wider regional integration. It helps develop intensified nodes of interaction between adjacent subnational zones, when transnational interaction between bigger entities such as nation-states prove to be difficult or slow processes to initiate. Subregional initiatives also allow for new avenues of cooperation and (perhaps) governance to be explored at a small-scale level.

As part of its aspiration to play a greater role in the Indochina subregion, India has also embarked on an original operation of awareness enhancement aimed at demonstrating its geographical contiguity with ASEAN. It organised an ASEAN-India Car Rally in November 2004 from Guwahati (Assam) to Batam (Indonesia). The rally is reported to have successfully helped generate public awareness of ASEAN-India relations, in general, and of the importance of connectivity between the two regions, in particular. The general objective of the operation was to draw peoples' attention to road transport and enhance trade, investment, tourism and people-to-people links between the ASEAN countries and India. India has even proposed to jointly organise the rally on a regular basis with ASEAN countries. Even if they may be modest in scale, India's initiatives can be seen as innovative contributions to the development of governance in the region, because they are concerned with awareness enhancement and capacity building, especially human resources development. More precisely, these initiatives are meant to launch a participatory process involving the civil societies in the CLMV.

Subnational Actors in India's Northeast

Many of the initiatives taken under the Look East policy highlight the centrality of Myanmar as well as India's Northeast. Accordingly, some in India's ruling elite have eventually realised that the remote, underdeveloped North-eastern region stands as the doorway to neighbouring Southeast Asia.[39] Furthermore, they are increasingly convinced that the resolution of the militancy and development problems in the Northeast implies an opening onto its neighbours. However, this new policy reorientation is still controversial as it runs counter to India's traditional approach of secluding these states from their neighbours. While the Indian Foreign Ministry tends to advocate a policy of transforming the Northeast into a subregional hub, the Home Ministry and Security agencies seem less than happy to open up a region notoriously prone to political unrest and of paramount importance to India's security. In any case, increasing sections of the Indian policy-making circles are finally realising that if their country is to further integrate into Southeast Asia, it has to substantially improve local governance in the North-eastern region.[40] Governance at the subnational level, especially in the border areas, thus appears as a critical parameter of India's future integration into the new regionalism in Asia. Concomitantly, the central government is slowly coming to terms with the fact that subregional cooperation could be an efficient way to improve local governance.

In this connection, it needs to be underlined that subnational actors are in a process of gaining a greater say in the decision-making process. Various stakeholders – whether they are political leaders or business representatives – from the Indian Northeast have become more vocal on the issue of opening borders to neighbouring countries. An interesting example of this nascent trend can be found in the domestic debate over the so-called Kunming Initiative (also known as BCIM). The Kunming Initiative was launched by China's Yunnan province in August 1999 as an informal process aimed at initiating subregional cooperation between China, India, Myanmar and

Bangladesh (This was discussed from the Chinese perspective in Chapter 5). In the general context of China's Western Development Strategy, the Yunnan authorities are indeed eager to reach out to the South Asian markets through Myanmar. Several conferences have already been convened, with the Yunnan Development Research Centre and the Yunnan Academy of Social Sciences as nodal agencies. The Initiative centres on the possibility of reviving the Stilwell Road, or Old Burma Road, a 1,043 mile long road, which used to link up Assam in India's Northeast to Yunnan in China via Myanmar. India's North-eastern states are particularly enthused by this project, as it could open new avenues for development. However India's prickly relations with Bangladesh and anxiety on China's strategic outreach in the region have so far acted as a stumbling block, with New Delhi responding in an overcautious fashion to Yunnan's overtures. Notwithstanding the central government hesitations, the BCIM is developing in its own way through an interesting combination of stakeholders that associate government agencies on the Myanmar and Chinese side to members of government and civil society – diplomats and researchers – on the Indian side. Future projects involve approaching international development agencies and establishing a business forum.

Another interesting case study can be found in Sikkim's economic agenda vis-à-vis China. For many years, Chief Minister Pawan Kumar Chamling has actively demanded the reopening of the trans-border trade route, through the Nathu La Pass. Indeed, the Nathu La ancestral route, linking Sikkim to Tibet, used to sustain the traditional industries of the local communities on both sides of the border before it came to be closed in the follow up to the Sino-Indian 1962 border war. Interestingly, Chamling's wish was realised in 2003 when Prime Minister Vajpayee and his Chinese counterpart announced the reopening of the Nathu La Pass to trans-border flow. Sikkim's business communities proved quite positive about this development as the reopening of the border trade point would allow for a revival of traditional industries and added economic activities for local communities on both sides of the border. However, security concerns at the federal level, especially on the part of the intelligence and defense agencies, delayed the reopening of the Nathu La Pass for three years (the pass was finally opened from 2006 onwards). The case of Sikkim thus shows how the security rationale of the federal state can run counter the improvement of governance at the local level and how different domestic agencies act to shape the regionalist agenda.

The Asian Economic Community: A Template for Macro-regional Governance?

At the macro-level, India is currently lobbying for a broadening of the regional integration, with its project of an Asian Economic Community – a broad economic grouping comprising ASEAN, China, South Korea, Japan and India (JICAK). The idea of an Asian Economic Community was first broached by RIS, a think-tank based in New Delhi. It has developed into a network of experts from India and East Asia, as well as the Asian Development Bank, holding annual or biannual meeting of a Track-Two nature. In many respects, JICAK is conceived as the logical outcome of the various FTA agreements that have been concluded or are under negotiations between ASEAN, Japan, China, South Korea and India. The idea posits that these various FTA agreements could be the building blocks of a larger economic grouping that could provide a framework to an Asian economic community in due course. Such a regional scheme would allow for a pooling of the various resources and endowments of its members, and provides for their optimal exploitation. One interesting dimension of the concept lies in its concern with issues related to regional governance, especially with 'appropriate regional institutional mechanisms' for 'addressing the common needs of the region'.[41] Among the proposed mechanisms, RIS has, for instance, explored the idea of creating a regional institutional infrastructure to pool some of the region's huge savings. It has thus suggested the establishment of an Asian Reserve Bank that would allow for investments in regional public goods, especially in transport, energy and information infrastructures.

What was originally an academic or policy research concept has been quickly endorsed by the Indian leadership. In his statement at the 2003 India-ASEAN Summit, former Prime Minister Atal Bihari Vajpayee mooted the idea of a broad Asian Economic Community, which would include the ASEAN-10, China, Korea, Japan and India: 'I put forward the idea that ASEAN needs to be more closely integrated with India, China, Japan and Korea. An Asian Economic Community, including the 14 countries of ASEAN+3+1, would more efficiently exploit our synergies'.[42]

As a sign of India's lasting interest in the JCIK concept, Prime Minister Manmohan Singh further elaborated on the proposition at the 2004 ASEAN-India Business Summit:

> Therefore, it is only inevitable that we seek to take the existing India-ASEAN relationship to a higher level, where we envision an Asian Economic Community, which encompasses ASEAN, China, Japan, Korea and India. Such a community would release enormous creative energies of our people. One cannot but be captivated by the vision of an integrated market, spanning the distance from the Himalayas to the Pacific Ocean, linked by efficient road, rail, air and shipping services. This community of nations would constitute an 'arc of advantage', across which there would be large-scale movement of people, capital, ideas, and creativity.[43]

Interestingly, some sections of the Singapore leadership have also shown some interest in the idea of an Asian Economic Community. In his keynote address at the 2003 East Asia Economic Summit, then Singaporean Prime Minister Goh Chok Tong observed: 'As India opens up, it will increasingly look East. India's long-term vision is an Asian economic community, comprising the ASEAN Plus Three countries and India. We should welcome this and embrace India. There is no reason to handicap ourselves by leaving out a new and highly promising growth centre'.[44]

One of the rationales behind the JICAK is also to challenge the consolidation of the East Asian Economic Community project, which would keep India in a peripheral position. Indeed the APT nurtures the long-term project of an East Asian Free Trade Area, and then later on, of an East Asian Economic Community – a pan-regional economic grouping between ASEAN, China, Japan and South Korea. In any case, both the East Asian Economic Community and the Asian Community are long term projects and they may look fraught with difficulties. What is of immediate interest is the 'battle of ideas', with 'competing regional concepts' that is taking place, and it seems that India has eventually understood the importance of broaching regional projects in which it is fully integrated. With its proposal for an Asian Community and even, an Asian Reserve Bank, India has actively engaged in the debate over the best mechanisms to be established in order to regulate and coordinate regional integration. In other words, India is putting forward new ideas and propositions that may contribute to the development of regional governance architecture.

Conclusion

Thanks to its sustained activism, in the realm of ideas as well as on concrete matters of policy making, India is emerging as an 'external actor' that the architects of the regional integration in East Asia find increasingly difficult to ignore. To recap, India has been so keen on catching up with the regional integration of East Asia that it has endorsed some critical norms, values and codes of conducts associated with the regional decision making as can be seen in the foreign policy challenges posed by Myanmar in 2007 and – more recently – by the Tibetan protests in 2008. Then, by imitation, it has sought to enter the web of bilateral and multilateral arrangements that give shape to the post-crisis governance modalities of East Asian regionalism. It has also tried to contribute to regional public goods, both in a concrete manner with capacity-building and awareness-enhancement projects targeted at civil societies, and in a more conceptual way as it enters the debate over the future of governance mechanisms in the region. It is to be expected that, as India pursues its Look East policy, it will increasingly seek to take the lead in matters of regional governance. The areas where it could make a special contribution in future may be diverse and include for instance capacity building, natural disaster management or maritime security. An additional dimension that is of interest to the issue of governance is related to that fact that the Look East policy has put so much emphasis on the rediscovery of

India's geographical contiguity with Southeast Asia, that border areas such as the Indian Northeast and Sikkim are now in the frontline, and subnational actors from these constituencies are bound to play a greater role in the general opening up of India onto its Eastern neighbourhood.

However, it should be underlined that India's approach to East Asian regionalism remains essentially driven by top-down dynamics. State agencies are the major actors of the rapprochement and the Look East policy is still striving to sustain a more participatory process. As a result, discrepancies have emerged between the trade preferences and protectionist inclinations of some domestic coalitions and the political approach of the pro-FTA constituency. An additional limitation is that governance in India's own subregion is not very advanced. While India has been quite sensitive to governance modes in East Asia, it has not been as supportive in its own subregion. As a result, much of South Asia (barring Bhutan, Sri Lanka, and the Maldives) continues to view New Delhi with suspicion. India's intractable conflict with Pakistan has been a cause of misunderstanding with East Asia, especially with the Muslim nations of Southeast Asia, such as Malaysia and Indonesia. It has also regularly disturbed the proceedings of the ASEAN Regional Forum since 1998. Pakistan's eventual admission in the ARF (with the consent of New Delhi) in 2004 confirms that, even in the East Asian regional context, India cannot expect to extract itself from the governance challenges that plague South Asia. Consequently, India's ability to address the need for governance arrangements in South Asia, notably through SAARC, cannot be separated from the ambitious Look East enterprise. This fact was clearly underlined by Prime Minister Manmohan Singh at the November 2005 SAARC Summit in Dhaka:

> It is important that we assess South Asia Regional Cooperation in the larger Asian context. Today, ASEAN is evolving rapidly into a truly integrated economic community. Parallel to this intra-ASEAN integration is the broader movement towards economic integration in the context of the proposed East Asian Economic Summit. We are clearly witnessing nothing short of an Asian resurgence based upon the rebuilding of the pre-colonial arteries of trade and commerce that created a distinct Asian identity in the first place. My question is – is SAARC prepared to be an integral part of this emerging Asian resurgence, or is it content to remain marginalised at the periphery? If our region wishes to be a part of the dynamic Asia, which is emerging in our neighbourhood, then we must act and act speedily and without any further loss of time.[45]

Indeed, as India increasingly integrates itself in the East Asian regional architecture and exerts a growing influence on governance developments in that part of the world, the need to substantially improve governance in South Asia will become an ever more urgent task.

Notes

1 As a sign of its peripheral position, India was denied membership of APEC in the mid 1990s and has still not been invited to this day. India was also denied membership of ASEM when it was created in 1996. It was eventually admitted in 2006.

2 Pierre, Jon. 'Introduction: Understanding Governance', in Jon Pierre, *Debating Governance: Authority, Steering, and Democracy.* (New York: Oxford University Press, 2000), pp. 1–10.

3 Krahmann, Elke. 'National, Regional, and Global Governance: One Phenomenon or Many?' *Global Governance.* (Vol. 9, No. 3, 2003), pp. 323–346.

4 Held, David and Anthony McGrew. *Governing Globalization: Power, Authority and Global Governance.* (Cambridge: Polity Press, 2002).

5 Payne, Anthony. 'Globalization and Modes of Regionalist Governance', in Jon Pierre, *Debating Governance: Authority, Steering, and Democracy.* (New York: Oxford University Press, 2000), p. 211.

6 Ong, Keng Yong. 'The Role of Good Governance in ASEAN', Keynote address at the ASEAN-EC Regional Symposium. (Bandar Seri Begawan, 28 November 2005).

7 Sridharan, Kripa. *The ASEAN Region in India's Foreign Policy.* (Aldershot: Ashgate, 1996). In 1980, ASEAN proposed that New Delhi become a dialogue partner. However India declined the offer as it was just about to recognise the Heng Samrin Vietnamese regime, installed in Cambodia. This decision amounted to a veritable affront, given that ASEAN's priority was to ostracise the regime.

8 Statement by the External Affairs Minister of India, I.K. Gujral, on the occasion of the ASEAN's post-ministerial conferences. (Jakarta: 24 July 1996).

9 Acharya, Amitav. 'Ideas, Identity, and Institution-building: from the "ASEAN way" to the "Asia-Pacific way?"', *The Pacific Review.* (Vol. 10, No. 3, 1997), p. 328.

10 Opening Statement at the Second ASEAN-India Joint Co-operation Committee Meeting in Singapore by the Minister for Foreign Affairs, Prof. S. Jayakumar on Tuesday, 28 April 1998.

11 Ibid. p. 2.

12 Ibid. p. 2

13 Gujral. op. cit., §. 9

14 Gujral. op. cit., §. 3

15 The EU opposed Myanmar's participation as a partner in its economic cooperation with the ASEAN as the European Parliament had imposed trade sanctions on the regime in Rangoon. At best, the country may be represented as an observer since it has been part of the Association since 1997.

16 Amitav, Acharya. 'How Ideas Spread: Whose Norms Matter? Norm Localization and Institutional Change in Asian Regionalism', *International Organization.* (Vol. 58, Spring 2004), p. 261.

17 In July 1989, the military regime adopted the official name of 'Union of Myanmar' (or *Myanmar Naingngan*, direct transliteration of the official name in the Burmese language). The country has changed its name several times. When it acquired its independence in 1948, the official name chosen was 'Union of Burma'. In 1974, the country opted for 'Socialist Republic of the Union of Burma'. In 1988, the former name 'Union of Burma' was put back in the agenda, before the new change in 1989.

18 The economic crisis that affected the country led to the formation of a movement of revolt against the autocratic regime of Ne Win in 1988. As of August 1988, the protest movement had reached the dimension of a pro-democratic movement. But the military junta fomented a coup d'état in September 1988 and formed the

State Law and Order Restoration Council (SLORC), while promising to hold multi-party elections. In May 1990, the National League for Democracy easily won the elections. But the SLORC refused to cede power and reduced the movement to silence. Aung San Suu Kyi, its leader, resided under surveillance. Suu Kyi was awarded the Nobel Peace Prize in 1991.

19 Statement of Shri P. Chidambaram, Finance Minister of India on the Occasion of the Post-Ministerial Conferences of ASEAN (9+1) Session, 29 July 1997, § 4
20 MEA. *Annual Report 1999–2000*, p. 7
21 MEA. *Annual Report 1995–6*, p. 5. This Prize was for the year 1993 'in recognition of her courageous, non-violent and inflexible struggle for liberty, democracy and human dignity'.
22 'India's engagement with Burma belies its image as a supporter of democracy', *The Nation*. 2 October 2007.
23 See, for example: 'India allocates funds to develop Burma port, border road', *BBC Monitoring Asia Pacific – Political*. 28 March 2008; and 'Myanmar general arrives in India on Wednesday', *Indo-Asian News Service*. 31 March 2008.
24 Jayasuriya, Kanishka. *Asian Regional Governance, Crisis and Change*. (London: RoutledgeCurzon, 2004), p. 7.
25 'China, Japan, South Korea, ASEAN agree on Wider Currency Swap Arrangements', *AFP*. 4 May 2005
26 'Asia finmins agree upgrade to $80 bln FX swaps fund', *Reuters India*. 4 May 2008.
27 Held, David and Anthony McGrew. *Governing Globalization: Power, Authority and Global Governance*. (Cambridge: Polity Press, 2002).
28 'India approves $3 bln currency swap pact with Japan', *Reuters India*. 27 March 2008.
29 ASEAN's other dialogue partners – Australia, Canada, EU, New Zealand, Russia and USA – do not have a separate summit meeting of this kind. Russia has, however, recently been elevated to the rank of summit partner.
30 Former Prime Minister Mahathir has been cultivating the idea of an East Asian region at least since the early 1990s, when he called for an East Asian Economic Group (EAEG) as an alternative option to the Asia-Pacific concept promoted by the US through APEC. This regional proposition is often seen as a precursor of the present ASEAN+3 and informs Malaysia's definite views on the regional identity.
31 Transcript of remarks by PM Goh Chok Tong to the media on the discussions at the fourth ASEAN Informal Summit, 24 November 2000.
32 Negotiations over the free trade agreement have already started. However, they are proving difficult because of Indian concerns over issues of rules of origin.
33 Singh, Manmohan. 'Time for a New Vision, New Commitment in South Asia', *Prime Minister Addresses Haksar Memorial Conference*. Press Information Bureau (India), 9 November 2005.
34 Nesadurai, Helen. 'Asia-Pacific Approaches to Regional Governance: the Globalisation – Domestic Politics Nexus', in Kanishka Jayasuriya (ed.). *Asian Regional Governance: Crisis and Change*. (London: RoutledgeCurzon, 2004), pp. 151–152.
35 Suryanarayana, P.S. 'We are seeing the renaissance of Asia led by China and by India', *The Hindu*. 16 January 2006.
36 Subramaniam, G. Ganapathy. 'Indo-Asean FTA set for Jan takeoff', *Times News Network*. 22 May 2006.
37 Bhuyan, Rituparna. 'India, Asean may ink free trade agreement by July', *Rediff News*. 16 January 2008.
38 *Chairman's Statement of the Third ASEAN-India Summit*. (Vientiane, 30 November 2004). http://www.aseansec.org/16745.htm. Accessed 8 May 2008.

39 Verghese, B.G. *Reorienting India: The New Geo-politics of Asia.* (New Delhi, Kornak Publishers, 2001).

40 Ramesh, Jairam. 'Northeast India in a New Asia', *Seminar.* June 2005.

41 Kumar, Nagesh. 'Towards a Broader Asian Community: Agenda for the East Asia Summit', *RIS Discussion Papers.* No. 100, 26 pp.

42 Press Information Bureau, New Delhi, Press Release (12 October 2003) as reported in *New Asia Monitor.* (Vol. 1, No. 1, March 2004). http://www.ris.org.in/newasia_mar04.pdf. Accessed 10 August 2007.

43 Singh, Manmohan. 'Indo-ASEAN Relationship should lead to an Asian Economic Community: PM Inaugurate India-ASEAN Business Meet', *Prime Minister's Office.* 19 October 2004.

44 Suryanarayana, P.S. 'Singapore PM backs India's long term vision', *The Hindu.* 14 October 2003.

45 *Statement by Prime Minister Dr. Manmohan Singh at the 13th SAARC Summit,* (Dhaka: 12 November 2005). http://www.meadev.nic.in. Accessed 20 December 2005.

8 The United States and regional governance in East Asia

The changing face of American power

Thomas G. Moore

Introduction

Much has been written about the declining influence of the United States (US) in East Asia, particularly in light of China's growing power and the rising profile of regional groups, such as ASEAN plus Three (APT) and the East Asian Summit (EAS), which exclude Washington.[1] Diplomatically, many observers point to the alienating effect that the US war on terrorism, the Iraq war and increased US unilateralism generally have had on East Asian countries. By contrast, China is often lauded for its nimble diplomacy and growing soft power. In terms of regional identity, moreover, the idea of 'East Asia' seems to have gained prominence at the expense of the 'Asia-Pacific' construction preferred by the US, as evidenced by the vitality associated in recent years with ASEAN-centred processes compared to the Asia Pacific Economic Cooperation (APEC) forum.[2]

Economically, the US is often seen as a player weakened by the erosion of its manufacturing base, mounting trade deficits and increased dependence on foreign borrowing to service its debt. By contrast, China has become the so-called workshop of the world, emerging as the world's third leading trading power and holder of the world's largest foreign exchange reserves. In a particularly symbolic development, China surpassed the US as Japan's leading trade partner in 2004 and is increasingly identified as a vital engine of East Asia's economic growth. Perhaps only in the military realm is Washington not seen as suffering from diminished influence. Even here, however, some observers see China's military modernisation and North Korea's nuclear capability as long-term threats to US military dominance in the region.

Questions are also often asked about the ability of the US to function effectively as a strategic actor, given the fragmented and increasingly divisive nature of the American political process, both within the government apparatus and in interactions between public and private actors. While executive–legislative conflict is hardly a new phenomenon in American politics, some observers see struggles between the White House and Congress over matters such as China policy as increasingly deleterious to US interests.[3]

Similarly, critics often point to a lack of coordination among executive branch departments. For example, the agencies involved in US economic policy include the departments of Agriculture, Commerce, State and Treasury, as well as the Office of the US Trade Representative, each of which has its own bureaucratic preferences and procedures. The issue of integrated strategy is further complicated by perceived deficiencies in the coordination of defence planning, economic policy and political–diplomatic relations. To some observers, for example, the Department of Defense's hard-nosed policies toward China – as expressed in documents such as the *Quadrennial Defense Review* (*QDR*) report and its annual report to Congress on *The Military Power of the People's Republic of China* – are out of step with the rest of the executive branch, to say nothing of the private sector's unrestrained embrace of commercial pursuits with Chinese partners.

This chapter examines the role of the US as an external actor in East Asia. As defined here, East Asia consists of China (including Hong Kong), Japan, South Korea, Taiwan and the ten members of ASEAN. The chapter begins by comparing and contrasting the concepts of regionalism, regionalisation and regional governance. Following an approach used elsewhere in this volume, the chapter then analyses US participation in East Asian governance in terms of norms, actors and mechanisms. Subsequent sections provide detailed examinations of the US role in and policies toward security and economic governance in East Asia. Finally, the chapter concludes with a preliminary exploration of how deepening interdependence between the US and East Asia affects governance arrangements among national, international and transnational actors that remain characterised by significant elements of American hegemony.

Regionalism, regionalisation and regional governance in East Asia

In thinking about the role of the US in East Asia, it is useful to distinguish among regionalism, regionalisation and regional governance. As used in this chapter, regionalism refers to the process whereby states within a particular geographical area construct collaborative agreements or otherwise coordinate activities at a multilateral level. As such, regionalism is associated with the conscious policy choices of states rather than the uncoordinated activities of non-state actors such as multinational corporations (MNCs). In this respect, regionalism is distinct from regionalisation, the process driven largely by private actors in which economic interaction, such as flows of goods and capital, increases faster among countries within a particular geographical area than flows between those countries and others outside the area.[4]

Regionalism is unquestionably an important subject in studying East Asia, both because state-led cooperation at a regional level was notably weak for most of the post-Second World War era and because regional initiatives in East Asia have begun to flourish over the past decade. Particularly through the ASEAN-centred processes of regional dialogue, which include APT, ASEAN Plus One, EAS and the ASEAN Regional Forum (ARF), regionalism has become a more important mechanism by which international relations in East Asia are managed. Furthermore, Washington finds itself excluded from groups such as APT and EAS. At the same time, the current trajectory of regionalism in East Asia should not be exaggerated, as the fruits of institutionalised cooperation achieved through ASEAN-centred processes – to say nothing of the Shanghai Cooperation Organisation (SCO) in Central Asia – remain modest at present. Indeed, a focus on Asian regionalism underestimates the influence of external actors such as the US by placing too much emphasis on the role of formal institutions.

Similarly, a narrow focus on regionalisation is equally misleading. As examined more fully later in the chapter, analysis of bilateral trade and investment flows can overstate the cohesiveness and independence of the East Asian economy vis-à-vis external actors such as the US. Although East Asia still accounts for about half of its own FDI inflows, the share from extraregional sources has increased over time. Moreover, while intraregional trade has grown to slightly more than half of East Asia's total trade over the past decade, seemingly validating the notion of accelerating regionalisation, this trend cannot be understood outside the context of globalisation (defined as increases in the density and speed of multicontinental flows).[5] The regional economy is perhaps becoming more integrated, but this does not necessarily come at the expense of extraregional ties. Indeed, this chapter argues that the impetus for regionalisation is owing to larger forces in the global political economy, including American hegemony. By focusing on private actors as the driving force in a largely market-driven process, the concept of regionalisation tends to understate the politics of regional-cum-global integration, including the role of state-based actors in creating the context within which regional integration occurs.

Unlike regionalism and regionalisation, regional governance captures the role of the US in East Asia more fully. As defined by Robert Keohane and Joseph Nye, governance is 'the processes and institutions, both formal and informal, that guide and restrain the collective activities of a group'.[6] As distinct from the concept of government, which focuses on 'policymaking arrangements and processes that centralise political authority within the state and its agencies', governance is typically conceived more broadly 'as the structures and processes that enable governmental and non-governmental actors to coordinate their interdependent needs and interests through the making and implementation of policies in the absence of a unifying political authority'.[7] As defined by the Commission on Global Governance, 'Governance is the sum of the many ways individuals and institutions, public and private, manage their common affairs.'[8]

As these definitions suggest, governance is a broad and perhaps even vague concept (as also noted in Chapter 1). For the purpose of this chapter, however, a governance approach is particularly useful insofar as it encompasses not only the individual and collective activities of governments but also the activities of non-state actors 'who resort to command mechanisms to make demands, frame goals, issue directives and pursue policies'.[9] Indeed, one of the strengths of the governance literature is its explicit acknowledgement that horizontal and vertical relationships of authority are increasingly 'fragmented among a multitude of governmental and non-governmental actors' who interact at local, national, regional and global levels.[10] Unlike regionalism and regionalisation, the concept of regional governance requires a comprehensive examination of how the interaction of governmental, quasi-governmental and non-governmental arrangements shapes outcomes.

As distinct from regionalism and regionalisation, therefore, regional governance focuses on the processes and structures – formal and informal alike – through which public and private actors manage regional affairs. Accordingly, governance arrangements can range from bilateral security alliances organised by an external power (the US-led 'hub and spokes' system in East Asia) to the organisation of cross-border manufacturing production through global commodity chains (such as networks controlled directly or indirectly by American MNCs).

Norms: the promotion of US values in East Asian regional governance

The values that Washington seeks to promote as norms for East Asian governance are captured well in the emphasis on freedom, democracy and free enterprise found in official documents such as *The National Security Strategy of the United States of America* (*NSS*). As President George W. Bush's introduction to *NSS 2002* explains, the US seeks 'to extend the benefits of freedom across the globe. We will actively work to bring the hope of democracy, development, free markets and free trade to every corner of the world.'[11] Indeed, the opening line of *NSS 2006* declares: 'It is the policy of the US to seek and support democratic movements and institutions in every nation and culture ... The goal of our statecraft is to help create a world of democratic, well-governed states that can meet the needs of their citizens and conduct themselves responsibly in the international system.'[12] With respect to East Asia, Bush used the major address of his November 2005 visit to the region, a speech delivered in Japan, to declare that the 'best opportunity to spread the freedom that comes from economic prosperity is through free and fair trade'. To affirm the strength of US–Japan relations, Bush pronounced that freedom 'is the bedrock of our engagement with Asia', asserting later in the speech that 'freedom is an Asian value – because it is a universal value'.[13]

One point of emphasis consistent across recent US administrations is the theme of 'good governance'. For example, in the wake of the Asian financial crisis US policy under both Bill Clinton and George W. Bush focused on the need for improved national governance, rather than improved regional or global governance. Consistent with the view that the crisis was caused mainly by so-called crony capitalism in East Asia, the US has strongly promoted the rule of law, anti-corruption measures and increased government transparency in the regulatory environment. In keeping with this position, the US Department of Commerce administers a 'Good Governance Programme' that seeks to 'increase market access and ensure a level playing field for US companies' by promoting norms such as transparency (including business ethics and corporate accountability), fairness in dispute resolution and protection of intellectual property rights (IPR).[14] Similarly, the US views the free trade agreements (FTAs) and bilateral investment treaties (BITs) it negotiates with other countries as mechanisms by which to 'encourage countries to enhance the rule of law, fight corruption and further democratic accountability'.[15]

As widely noted in the literature, the US has long sought to pursue a rules-based form of institutionalised cooperation in its dealings with East Asia. In APEC, as well as through FTAs and BITs, Washington has consistently promoted binding commitments to liberalise economic activity that have clashed with the preference of many East Asian countries for ad hoc, voluntary agreements and otherwise low levels of legalisation. Moreover, the US approach to decision making often puts it in conflict with the so-called 'ASEAN Way', which emphasises consultation and consensus.

Another area in which US governance norms encounter resistance is national sovereignty and conflict resolution. As embodied in the 'ASEAN Way', Asian norms place emphasis on non-coercive means of conflict resolution, non-interference in the internal affairs of other states and avoidance of direct confrontation. On issues such as how to handle Myanmar's international status and in cases involving human rights generally, the US position that human rights principles should trump the principle of non-intervention clashes with Asian sensibilities, especially as expressed in the engagement policies that ASEAN and China have historically adopted toward Myanmar. In the area of counter-terrorism and national security affairs generally, the US supports the notion of pre-emption, reserving its right to act unilaterally against terrorists and rogue states. Here, as well, US governance norms find themselves in opposition to the prevailing norms in East Asia.

Actors: the role of US public and private actors in East Asian regional governance

A wide array of public and private actors from the US is involved in various aspects of regional governance in East Asia. In economic and security affairs alike, the US federal government remains an important player unilaterally, bilaterally and multilaterally. This public sector engagement extends to subnational and municipal level actors, who are actively involved in forging substate ties across the region, whether this is in terms of sister/twinning agreements, trade agreements or advocacy networks. For their part, non-state actors are also important participants in regional governance. From human rights monitors and disaster relief specialists to environmental activists and labour groups, the US is home to a plethora of non-governmental organisations (NGOs) whose impact is felt in every corner of the earth. Other types of non-state actors critical to governance arrangements in East Asia include MNCs, financial ratings agencies, law firms and mutual fund managers.

For reasons of space, this section will focus on the role of MNCs and business coalitions as vehicles of US influence in East Asia, with particular emphasis on how these non-state actors shape US policy and participate in regional governance in East Asia. Given the importance of East Asia to the US economy, many of the most active and influential non-state actors are commercial associations such as the National Association of Manufacturers, the US Chamber of Commerce and the Coalition of Service Industries.[16]

In order to maximise their input on country or region-specific issues, MNCs and other organisations join associations such as the US–Japan Business Council, the US–China Business Council, the US–Korea Business Council and the US–ASEAN Business Council. In the case of FTAs, moreover, specific coalitions have been formed, such as the US–Korea FTA Business Coalition and the US–Thailand Free Trade Agreement Coalition, to organise the efforts of American corporate interests in shaping the process. Not surprisingly, this involvement begins well before the actual commencement of FTA negotiations. For example, the launch of US–Korea FTA negotiations in 2006 required that certain obstacles be overcome in advance, an objective that was achieved by securing commitments from the Korean government to change its policies on movie screen quotas, beef imports and assorted issues involving the automobile and pharmaceutical industries.[17] Months before Washington and Seoul officially announced their plans to pursue an FTA, the Korean trade minister met with US business leaders to discuss their concerns.[18] Similarly, a delegation from the US Chamber of Commerce met in 2005 with then Prime Minister Thaksin Shinawatra to discuss problem areas in stalled negotiations for a US–Thailand FTA.[19] Similar delegations – such as the US–Thailand FTA Coalition – have been active in pushing for a conclusion to the negotiations.[20]

These non-state actors are much more than simple lobbying groups, however. For example, the US Chamber of Commerce runs programmes in which its members and staff interact directly with national, provincial and local-level officials in China on matters such as IPR protection. Through activities organised by the Chamber, American business people and IPR experts participate in a variety of initiatives designed to improve the implementation of China's World Trade Organisation (WTO) obligations. From the standpoint of governance arrangements, what is especially notable about these capacity-building programmes is that the participants are subnational actors from the US and China. Nor are these programmes purely educational or consultative, as they sometimes result in memoranda of understanding between the Chamber and local officials on acceptable business practices.[21]

Mechanisms: US policy on East Asian regionalism

One major point of continuity in US foreign policy during the second half of the twentieth century was resistance to East Asian regionalism.[22] By most accounts, Washington actively impeded regionalism in East Asia throughout the Cold War, unlike in Western Europe where the post-Second World War order was designed to be multilateral.[23] Especially in the security realm but also in the economic arena, US bilateralism ensured that East Asia would be one of the least institutionalised regions of the world when the Cold War ended. In the 1990s Washington still sought either to block East Asian regionalism (e.g., the proposal to establish an Asian Monetary Fund in the wake of the Asian financial crisis) or to ensure that the US figured prominently in regional initiatives by promoting the 'Asia-Pacific' (with groups such as APEC) as an alternative conception to 'East Asia'.

While scepticism and caution still define US policy toward East Asian regionalism, the George W. Bush administration has not opposed regional initiatives – including those that exclude the US – as strongly as previous administrations. Some analysts have attributed this shift to a preoccupation with the war on terrorism, while others point to a more general neglect of East Asia policy born of ignorance. Another view, substantiated in interviews with US and East Asian officials, is that Washington no longer considers East Asian regionalism – at least as currently constituted – to be a major threat to its interests.[24] According to this argument, a number of recent developments have reassured the US that East Asian countries have neither the desire nor the capacity to pursue an exclusive regional bloc in the near future.

Although senior US officials now publicly acknowledge that it 'is entirely understandable that Asia is looking to strengthen its own regional institutions, just as other regional groupings in other parts of the world have done', they also continue to express concerns about whether regionalism is the most effective means of addressing East Asia's challenges.[25] For example, Christopher Hill, Assistant Secretary of State for East Asian and Pacific Affairs, suggested in a 2006 speech that the effectiveness of APEC and ARF was at risk of being diluted by 'proliferating regional fora'.[26] As a way of highlighting the importance of inclusive rather than exclusive arrangements, Hill further emphasised 'the question of how we can integrate pan-Asian and trans-Pacific fora ... The goal should be to achieve synergy and avoid redundancy.'[27] Washington may have grown more tolerant of East Asian regionalism, but it clearly prefers broader-based mechanisms such as the Free Trade Area of the Asia-Pacific President Bush has promoted within APEC to alternative proposals such as the Comprehensive Economic Partnership in East Asia under study by the EAS.

On security issues, in particular, US foreign policy attaches little significance to multilateralism in East Asia. With respect to ARF, for example, Washington uses it less as a mechanism by which to achieve US security objectives than as a venue to identify issues of concern and to garner support for its agenda.[28] Despite the expansion of ARF's focus from confidence building to preventive diplomacy, a step publicly supported by Washington, one source of ongoing US frustration with East Asian security multi-lateralism is its inability to respond effectively to specific problems and crises. On North Korea, for instance, ARF has accomplished little beyond provid-ing an international gathering at which Washington and Pyongyang can have dialogue. Similarly, resolution of territorial disputes in the South China Sea is not an issue on which ARF has made, or is likely to make, headway. Another problem of great US concern is Taiwan, but Taiwan does not par-ticipate in ARF and China refuses to discuss the Taiwan issue at ARF on the grounds that cross-Strait relations are a domestic matter.

As further evidence that East Asia has limited capacity to act collectively through multilateral institutions in addressing critical regional needs, US officials have repeatedly cited the case of the 2004 tsunami. In remarks to a 2005 ARF meeting, then Deputy Secretary of State Robert Zoellick noted how the tsunami demonstrated the continued importance of US bilateral alliances, arguing that they provided the mechanism that allowed Washing-ton to coordinate its massive military-led efforts at disaster relief.[29] More broadly, *NSS 2006* used the example of tsunami relief to underscore the superiority of 'results-oriented partnerships' as instruments of governance. In a section examining the national security implications of globalisation, *NSS 2006* declared: 'Existing international institutions have a role to play, but in many cases coalitions of the willing may be able to respond more quickly and creatively, at least in the short term. For example, US leadership in mobilising the Regional Core Group to respond to the tsunami of 2004 gal-vanised the follow-on international response.'[30] This point is supported by the analysis in the next chapter.

For its part, the *QDR 2006* made no references to multilateral institutions in East Asia, citing instead 'constructs' such as the Proliferation Security Initiative (PSI) as a model that can be extended to address other areas of security concern.[31] The US-led PSI, which was launched in 2003 to stem the flow of weapons of mass destruction, exemplifies the 'coalition of the willing' model touted in *NSS 2002* and *NSS 2006*. Like the Six-Party Talks on North Korea's nuclear weapons programmes, the PSI reflects Washing-ton's preference for ad hoc multilateralism, rather than a more institutiona-lised mechanism, in dealing with specific issues for which unilateralism or bilateralism are deemed insufficient.[32]

Security governance in East Asia

Another constant in US foreign policy for decades has been a desire to per-petuate the hub and spokes system of bilateral alliances in East Asia whose origins can be traced back to the San Francisco Conference of September 1951, at which the peace treaty officially ending the Second World War was signed. At best, multilateral security forums such as ARF are seen as playing a supplementary role to bilateralism in East Asia, which also accords with the Australian approach covered in Chapter 6. Not surprisingly, the US places even lower priority on multilevel security governance. Despite American participation in non-governmental 'Track-Two' groups such as the Council for Security Cooperation in the Asia-Pacific, the dominant US view is that security affairs are the preserve of sovereign nation-states.

The most authoritative statements of US security policy for East Asia include the *NSS*, the *QDR* and the Pentagon's annual report to Congress on *The Military Power of the People's Republic of China*.[33] The *NSS 2002* reaffirmed the centrality of America's bilateral alliance system to its security strategy in the post-9/11 era: 'The war against terrorism has proven that America's alliances in Asia not only underpin regional peace and stability, but are flexible and ready to deal with new challenges.'[34] Specifically, the *NSS 2002* cited US alliances with Japan, South Korea, Australia, Thailand and the Philippines, as well as close friendships with Singapore and New Zealand. *QDR 2006* emphasised that these 'long-standing alliance relationships will ... continue to evolve, ensuring their relevance even as new challenges emerge', further specifying that these alliances were prepared to 'address common security threats'.[35] In his speech delivered at the 2007 APEC Summit, President Bush declared that US bilateral alliances and defence relationships (citing Taiwan and Indonesia in the latter category) 'form the bedrock of America's engagement in the Asia-Pacific'.[36]

Space does not permit a detailed review of the individual bilateral security alliances the US maintains in the region, but it is important to note that Washington has sought to strengthen these relationships in recent years. The case of US–Japan relations is particularly noteworthy. Beginning with their 1996 Joint Declaration and 1997 Revised Defense Guidelines, Washington and Tokyo embarked on a strengthening and expansion of the bilateral alliance that led Secretary of State Condoleezza Rice to observe in 2005 that 'a relationship that was once only about the defense of Japan or perhaps about the stability in the region, has truly become a global alliance'.[37] This process, which included an agreement on the realignment of US forces in Japan (moving 8,000 marines from Okinawa to Guam) as part of a broader US–Japan Defense Policy Review Initiative launched in 2002, culminated with President Bush and former Prime Minister Junichiro Koizumi heralding a new US–Japan Alliance of Global Cooperation for the 21st Century at their final meeting in 2006.

In a related initiative, the US and Japan established a Trilateral Strategic Dialogue with Australia, beginning with low-level ministerial talks in March 2006 and culminating with a head-of-state trilateral summit in September 2007 during the APEC meeting in Sydney. To bolster this process Australia and Japan signed a Joint Declaration on Security Cooperation in 2007 that, while falling short of creating a military alliance due to Japan's constitutional obligations, will nonetheless facilitate intelligence sharing and defence cooperation. Less formally, India has begun participating with the US, Australia and Japan in a nascent quadrilateral dialogue touted as representing an 'Arc of Democracy' in Asia. Although the four countries have yet to hold ministerial-level meetings, officials did conduct security consultations on the sidelines of a May 2007 ARF meeting.[38]

Through processes such as the Future of the Alliance consultations and the US–Republic of Korea Security Policy Initiative, the US has sought to solidify its relations with South Korea by addressing base relocation issues and the redeployment of US troops from the Korean Peninsula. Equally important, Washington and Seoul signed an FTA in 2007, although in mid 2008 the pact still awaited ratification by the US Congress and the South Korean National Assembly.[39] By pursuing an FTA with South Korea, the US hopes that closer economic relations will solidify a bilateral relationship that has drifted, largely over the problem of how to handle North Korea.

Washington has been similarly active in its relations with Southeast Asia, signing an Enhanced Partnership Plan of Action with ASEAN in 2006, a five-year programme designed to bolster relations on a wide range of economic, political and security issues. Although the US has thus far refused to join the likes of China, Japan and India in acceding to ASEAN's Treaty of Amity and Cooperation (TAC), Washington has tried to strengthen ties in other ways. For example, the US and ASEAN signed a Trade and Investment Framework Agreement (TIFA) in 2006, opening the possibility of a US–ASEAN FTA in the long run. In addition, Washington announced in 2007 that it would create the position of US Ambassador to ASEAN in recognition of the deepening US–ASEAN relationship. That said, bilateral relations still dominate Washington's relations with Southeast Asian countries. In 2003 Thailand and the Philippines received 'Major Non-NATO Ally' status, and in 2005 Singapore was designated a 'Major Security Cooperation Partner' as part of a larger Strategic Framework Agreement.

The rising profile of India, as a TAC signatory, EAS participant and SCO observer, in the broader Asian strategic context has not escaped Washington's notice. For this reason, among others, the US signed a ten-year defence agreement with India in 2005 to enhance military cooperation through joint weapons production, technology transfer, maritime patrols and collaboration on missile defence. Although the bilateral relationship still falls short of a military alliance, Washington and New Delhi also signed a landmark agreement on nuclear energy cooperation, the US–India Civil Nuclear Cooperation Initiative. The stated goal of the US in taking these actions was, according to an unnamed senior State Department official, 'to help India become a major world power in the 21st century. We understand fully the implications, including the military implications, of that statement.'[40]

While the US accepts and apparently even embraces India's growing power, Washington's views on China's rise are decidedly more mixed. Although an in-depth analysis of the US debate over China policy is beyond the scope of this chapter, it should be noted that Washington still relies primarily on bilateralism to address China's currency policy, IPR violations, surging textile exports, trade surpluses, energy policy, military spending, Taiwan policy and most other areas of significant Sino-American contention. To this end, processes such as the Senior Dialogue and the Strategic Economic Dialogue established in 2005 and 2006, respectively, have become high-profile mechanisms for managing US–China relations. The Strategic Economic Dialogue, for example, brings together approximately ten US Cabinet-level officials and fifteen Chinese government ministers twice a year. In his September 2005 'stakeholder' speech in which China was encouraged to become a responsible world citizen, a theme repeated in *NSS 2006* and *QDR 2006*, Zoellick specifically cautioned Beijing against using regional multilateral institutions to 'manoeuvre toward a predominance of power'.[41] He then immediately cited ARF and APEC (groups in which the US holds membership) as appropriate avenues of multilateral diplomacy, omitting any mention of APT, EAS or SCO. Thus, while Zoellick acknowledged China's 'interests in the region' and recognised 'the useful role of multilateral diplomacy in Asia', the take-home message was decidedly bilateral in terms of East Asian diplomacy.

A strong argument can be made that the signature feature of US foreign policy toward East Asia during George W. Bush's second term has been a renewed emphasis on balance-of-power dynamics, particularly as regards China. *QDR 2006* declared that the US 'will seek to ensure that no foreign power can dictate the terms of regional or global security. It will attempt to dissuade any military competitor from developing disruptive or other capabilities that could enable regional hegemony or hostile action against the United States or other friendly countries, and it will seek to deter aggression or coercion.'[42] Lest there be any confusion about the country being referenced, this statement appeared immediately following a section on China's military modernisation which concluded that the 'pace and scope of China's military build-up already puts regional military balances at risk'.[43] In similar fashion, *NSS 2006* criticised China not only for its 'non-transparent' military expansion but also for its mercantilist trade efforts to 'lock up energy supplies' and 'direct markets rather than opening them up'.[44] It is no coincidence that the Trilateral Strategic Dialogue and the US–India nuclear agreement were both formalised in the same month that Rice characterised China as a 'negative force' in the region.[45]

Given the scope and depth of US commercial relations with China, not to mention areas of limited political–diplomatic cooperation, Washington's policy falls well short of containment. At the same time, increased US attention to balance-of-power dynamics in East Asia means that Washington's strategy relies on more than straightforward engagement in trying to get China to, in the words of *NSS 2006*, 'act as a responsible stakeholder that fulfils its obligations and works … to advance the international system that has enabled its success'.[46] In this respect, hedging is perhaps the most accurate characterisation of US policy toward China. Indeed, *NSS 2006* forthrightly declares that the US 'seeks to encourage China to make the right strategic choices for its people while we hedge against other possibilities'.[47]

One intriguing question raised by recent US policy is whether, in an effort to constrain China's strategic choices and otherwise shape its ambitions, Washington seeks (or at least will grow to tolerate) strong partners rather than subordinate allies – even if this means the erosion of its own pre-eminent strategic position. On the one hand, it appears that Washington's efforts to facilitate the emergence of alternative centres of power in Asia (Japan, India, ASEAN, Australia) are designed 'to allow the United States to retain its position as Asia's decisive strategic actor' by impeding China's rise.[48] On the other hand, some have argued that the US may seek (or, regardless of its intentions, will find itself having to accept) an emerging 'concert of Asia-Pacific democracies' in which Washington and its partners are relative equals.[49] Although the establishment of an 'arc of democracy' in Asia would be consistent with long-espoused US foreign policy values, the pursuit of a concert of powers system would represent an important conceptual break from the hub and spokes system that has constituted East Asia's primary security architecture for more than half a century. To this point, however, there is insufficient evidence to conclude that US strategy is actually shifting away from its traditional focus on maintaining bilateral alliances embedded in a hierarchical order.[50]

Economic governance in East Asia

Consistent with its approach elsewhere in the world, the US has pursued a strategy of so-called competitive liberalisation in East Asia. On the one hand, the US remains a staunch supporter of global multilateral organisations, such as the WTO, the International Monetary Fund (IMF) and the World Bank, as well as selected regional multilateral groups, such as APEC. In recent years, however, Washington has placed increasing emphasis on bilateral and regional agreements (such as the US–Morocco FTA and the Central American Free Trade Agreement) as instruments to advance its agenda of liberalisation in investment and trade flows. In East Asia, bilateral FTAs and BITs/TIFAs have rapidly become the primary means by which competitive liberalisation is pursued. As of mid 2008, the US has an FTA in effect with Singapore, an FTA with South Korea awaiting legislative ratification, and FTAs under negotiation with Malaysia and Thailand. (The US also has an FTA in place with Australia, although this chapter does not define Australia as being part of East Asia.) The Enterprise for ASEAN Initiative launched by Washington in 2002 requires that prospective partners sign a bilateral TIFA with the US before FTA negotiations can begin. As of mid 2008, the US has also concluded TIFAs with ASEAN, Brunei, Cambodia, Indonesia, the Philippines and Vietnam.

As a matter of practice, the terms of FTAs and BITs/TIFAs negotiated by the US are significantly more comprehensive and constraining for its economic partners than membership in the WTO.[51] For example, Washington's BITs/TIFAs take the WTO's Agreement on Trade-Related Aspects of Intellectual Property Rights (TRIPS), Agreement on Trade-Related Investment Measures (TRIMS) and General Agreement on Trade in Services (GATS) as a starting point for negotiations. Whereas TRIMS only affects trade-related investment, as its name suggests, BITs/TIFAs negotiated by the US typically include financial transactions such as the purchase of bonds and local equities as 'foreign investment'.[52] To the extent that Washington's BITs/TIFAs and FTAs include strengthened IPR protection, broadly defined investment provisions, and enhanced transparency in areas such as government procurement – in addition to the improved market access in goods and services that one might expect from an FTA – they represent 'important steps toward realising the long-sought objective of regulatory harmonisation'.[53] In this way, BITs/TIFAs and FTAs pursued by the US can be seen as encompassing governance issues – globally, regionally and nationally – that go beyond liberalisation per se.

Seen from this perspective, BITs/TIFAs and FTAs are instruments by which Washington seeks to intensify the restructuring of the global political economy. Specifically, BITs/TIFAs and FTAs are means by which US policy can facilitate the extension of cross-border production chains. As such, the US may be contributing to the acceleration of regionalisation without necessarily reducing its own role in, or impact on, East Asia.

For some observers, the current governance arrangements promoted by the US constrain the development strategies available to less advanced economies. Given the neo-liberal nature of BITs/TIFAs and FTAs, to say nothing of the WTO, IMF and World Bank, the main option for developing countries today is incorporation into transnational production networks. Strategic interventions such as the industrial policies associated with the success of developmental states (for instance, Japan, South Korea and Taiwan) in the second half of the twentieth century are increasingly difficult to achieve. According to this view, which is by no means universally held, the US is seen as protecting its own areas of comparative advantage by deliberating shrinking the developmental space available to less advanced economies.[54] Economic competitiveness can still be attained by developing countries, but it must be pursued mainly by exploiting existing comparative advantages rather than by trying to create new capacities.[55]

In this respect, the governance of global commodity chains becomes an important subject for understanding the developmental prospects of countries. Although private actors may play the defining role in determining how complex systems for production and distribution are integrated across borders, public actors such as the US government and international organisations such as the WTO shape the institutional context within which these networks or value chains are established and managed.[56]

For its part, the US has been a forceful presence in this process. With respect to its China policy, for example, Washington has been vigilant in pressing Beijing to converge with its preferred norms. In his 'stakeholder' speech, Zoellick called on Beijing to share responsibility in maintaining an open international economic system by living up to 'its commitments to markets where America has a strong competitive advantage, such as in services, agriculture and certain manufactured goods'. Moreover, Zoellick urged China to adopt 'market strategies' in dealing with 'its thirst for energy'.[57]

One development the US is particularly concerned about is the trend towards 'preferential' trade, in which FTAs shift the source of trade more than they liberalise trade. Washington's criticism, it should be noted, applies not only to FTAs involving China but also to FTAs concluded by countries such as Japan, Singapore and South Korea. US officials repeatedly emphasise that priority should be placed on achieving 'high quality' FTAs with rules of origin and other standards (for example, IPR protection or investment provisions) consistent with Washington's economic agenda.

Rising intraregional trade in East Asia: is the US economic shadow receding?

It is often observed that intraregional trade in East Asia has risen rapidly over the past twenty-five years, especially compared to the European Union (EU) and the North American Free Trade Agreement (NAFTA). Indeed, the share of intraregional trade in East Asia's overall trade rose from 34.9 per cent in 1980 to 52.2 per cent in 2006, far outpacing increases in the concentration of trade within the EU (57.3 per cent to 64.6 per cent) and NAFTA (33.2 per cent to 42.1 per cent) over the same period.[58] Not surprisingly, perhaps, this rise in intraregional trade is frequently cited as evidence that the importance of the US to East Asia as a trade partner has been declining. Consistent with this view, the US share of East Asia's overall trade decreased by 6 per cent between 1990 and 2005, from 21.6 per cent to 15.3 per cent. Interestingly, however, the share of East Asia's exports absorbed by the US decreased by only 1.5 per cent, from 22.9 per cent in 1990 to 21.4 per cent in 2005. By contrast, imports from the US fell by nearly half, from 15.9 per cent of East Asia's total imports in 1990 to 8.5 per cent in 2005.[59]

What the data show, therefore, is that East Asia's dependence on the US as an export market barely decreased (1.5 per cent) from 1990 to 2005 despite a substantial rise (11.4 per cent, from 41.2 per cent to 52.6 per cent) in the share of intraregional trade over the same period.[60] (Similarly, US dependence on imports from East Asia declined only modestly from 37 per cent of total US imports in 1990 to 34.4 per cent in 2005.)[61] In fact, there is strong evidence that the rise in intraregional trade in East Asia is closely related to production for export to extraregional markets. As one study concluded, 'the rise in intra-regional trade primarily reflects a shift in trade and production patterns rather than a change in the sources of demand for exports of final goods', noting that the US and EU remain important markets.[62] Another study reached a similar conclusion, finding that 'high intra-regional trade ... reflects rapidly expanding intra-regional trade in components. There is no evidence of rapid intra-regional trade integration in terms of final products.'[63] A third study concluded that 'intra-East Asian trade is more important as a source of imports than as a destination for exports. This finding indicates a trading pattern in which East Asian economies procure imports within the region and sell exports outside the region.'[64] As measured by an intraregional trade intensity index, moreover, the degree of economic integration in East Asia was essentially unchanged from 1990 to 2005, with the figure for 2005 actually falling slightly below average figures for the 1980s. By contrast, the comparable figures for the EU and NAFTA have risen slowly but steadily since 1980.[65]

Until recently, the study of East Asia's political economy was dominated by analytical perspectives, such as those focusing on developmental states, trading states, product cycles and flying geese, that emphasised national economies as the fundamental unit of analysis.[66] Today, however, such approaches obscure as much as they clarify. No longer is the world economy one in which trade can be understood primarily as 'an exchange of goods that are produced from start to finish in just one country'.[67] Because standard trade flow analysis does not distinguish between so-called fragmentation trade (trade in parts and components) and final goods trade, 'trade data are double-counted because goods in process cross multiple international borders in the course of their production sequence, generating international trade with each border crossing'.[68] Indeed, Prema-chandra Athukorala and Nobuaki Yamashita found that 'the share of component trade for East Asia as a group compares well with most other regions of the world'.[69] Consequently, standard trade flow analysis underestimates the continued importance of the US to the East Asian economy.

According to Athukorala and Yamashita, the share of intraregional trade in East Asia increased from 44.1 per cent in 1992 to 53.2 per cent in 2003.[70] What is most revealing, however, is the finding when trade in components is separated from trade in final goods. The intraregional share of East Asia's trade in components increased from 50.9 per cent to 67.3 per cent from 1992 to 2003, while the intraregional share of East Asia's final goods trade actually declined from 52.5 per cent to 47.6 per cent.[71] In a recent study, the World Bank found that non-Japan East Asia absorbed only 14 per cent of East Asia's exports once all double counting of trade was eliminated and the final destination of goods was determined. According to this research, Japan accounted for another 14 per cent, which means that 72 per cent of East Asia's market for final goods was extraregional.[72]

As summarised by Athukorala and Yamashita, 'when data on component trade are excluded from trade flows, our estimates suggest that extra-regional trade is much more important than intra-regional trade for continued growth'.[73] While they note that China's emergence as a major economy may alter this situation in the long run, Athukorala and Yamashita conclude that 'extra-regional trade is likely to remain the engine of growth of the region in the foreseeable future'.[74] In this sense, the rising levels of intraregional trade in East Asia reflect a deepening of globalisation rather than an independent process of regionalisation.

Intraregional investment in East Asia and the deceptively long arms of US economic actors[75]

Analysis of foreign direct investment (FDI) is difficult for several reasons, including substantial differences in how countries measure and report investment flows.[76] That said, the data can be useful in identifying trends. In East Asia, intraregional FDI has declined significantly since the early 1990s. According to Urata, East Asia's share of total FDI flows into the region shrank from 76.3 per cent in 1993 to 50.5 per cent in 2002. Although Urata focused on trans-Pacific FDI and therefore did not provide specific data on US investment, his research found that North America's share of FDI in East Asia increased from 10.2 per cent in 1993 to 15.7 per cent in 2002.[77] In another study, Kawai identified the US as the second leading source of FDI in emerging East Asia (i.e. non-Japan East Asia) from 1990 to 2002, trailing only the so-called Four Tigers (Hong Kong, Singapore, South Korea and Taiwan) and ahead of Japan and the EU.[78] Not only was the US an important investor, but its share of FDI also remained relatively steady over time.[79] By contrast, the share of emerging East Asia's FDI inflows absorbed from Japan and the Four Tigers has declined over time, consistent with Urata's data about the shrinking share of intraregional FDI in East Asia generally.[80]

In 2005 the US was the largest foreign investor in Malaysia, South Korea and Taiwan, while ranking second in the Philippines, Thailand and Singapore. For each of these six countries, approximately a quarter of FDI came from the US.[81] From 1995 to 2005, in fact, the US was the single largest source of cumulative FDI to the Four Tigers (as a group), Malaysia and the Philippines. Only in Indonesia, Thailand, Vietnam and China did the US rank third or worse.[82] Although the Four Tigers (as a group) invested more than twice as much as the US in non-Japan East Asia from 1995 to 2005, these figures understate the role played by the US. Specifically, the performance of the Four Tigers is greatly inflated by their overwhelming share (54 per cent) of China's FDI inflows, a share more than twice that of the US, EU and Japan combined.[83] One factor that helps to explain this disparity is Hong Kong's long-time status as the biggest investor in China. While Hong Kong companies have been an important source of investment in China, some of Hong Kong's FDI to China is the result of so-called 'round tripping': funds sent from the mainland to be rerouted back into China to take advantage of tax breaks and other preferential treatment available to foreign investors. Additional sums represent the proceeds of funds raised by Chinese companies in Hong Kong capital markets. These count as FDI when they are moved into China. Still other FDI registered from Hong Kong is actually capital originating from other countries (including the US) whose companies prefer to use Hong Kong as a conduit. The bottom line is that official data on China's FDI inflows do not always reliably identify the origin of investment, typically with the effect of overstating intraregional investment.

Even if more accurate data about the sources of FDI in East Asia were available, they would still yield an incomplete understanding of how broadly extraregional actors exercise control over the production decisions that give shape to national and regional economic life in East Asia. In this respect, the dominance of US and EU investment in the Four Tigers is particularly revealing. From 1995 to 2005, for example, the US alone accounted for the same share of cumulative FDI into the Four Tigers (17 per cent) as did Japan, the Four Tigers and ASEAN-9 (ASEAN minus Singapore) combined.[84] From this perspective, figures for FDI to East Asia as a whole obscure a dynamic in which the US and EU dominate investment in the Four Tigers (as well as Indonesia, Malaysia and the Philippines), while the Four Tigers in turn dominate investment in places such as China and Vietnam. In other words, investment patterns reflect the segmentation of production processes in East Asia.

In some cases, moreover, the long reach of extraregional actors may be felt even without investment. Breslin's analysis of how US companies retain a central role in the 'East Asian' computer industry without ownership or other investment illustrates this point well. Indeed, Breslin is worth quoting at length:

> Nearly three quarters of China's computer-related products are produced by Taiwanese companies, which are themselves dependent on OEM (original equipment manufacturing) contracts with Japanese and US companies. As such, these Taiwan-invested factories in China represent the end stage of a production process that spans the most industrialized global economies such as the USA and Japan, intermediate states such as Taiwan, and developing states like China. Bilateral investment figures will show Taiwanese investment in China. As the key components are sourced outside China, usually in Taiwan and Singapore and often exported to China via Hong Kong, one set of trade figures will show a Chinese deficit with regional states – but another set of trade figures will show Chinese exports to the major markets of the developed world.[85]

By setting industry standards and focusing on the highest value-added aspects of economic activity, such as research and development, innovation and marketing, US companies can remain at the forefront industrially and maximise profit without owning their suppliers or otherwise investing in actual computer production. As an illustration, Breslin cites how Microsoft and Intel 'effectively control access to the PC market without producing PCs themselves' through the near ubiquity of so-called Wintelism.[86]

In Breslin's example, the activity of Taiwanese-invested firms in China appears at first glance to buttress the argument that intraregional investment and trade flows are intensifying at the expense of extraregional relations. Underneath the surface, however, we see how MNCs operating in a world of post-Fordist arrangements can abandon much of the production process without relinquishing their position of dominance. As Breslin puts it, American companies have been 'much more engaged ... than the investment and trade figures suggest – albeit through third party actors' such as Solectron and Flextronics (two large contracting enterprises) that invest in China through regional hubs such as Singapore, on the basis of corporate strategies developed in the US.[87]

The United States and the governance of global commodity chains

At the risk of suggesting that East Asia lacks indigenous regional dynamics of its own, the preceding sections have sought to demonstrate how standard analyses of bilateral trade and investment flows understate the continued – and, in some product areas, even growing – significance of extraregional actors for economic governance in East Asia. One especially germane analytical framework is Gereffi's notion of buyer-driven global commodity chains, a concept that emphasises how global buyers, such as American MNCs, 'can and do exert a high degree of control over spatially dispersed value chains even when they do not own production, transport or processing facilities'.[88] To cite one such example, if the American retailer Wal-Mart were a country it would have been the world's seventh-largest importer of Chinese goods in 2004.[89]

Given how East Asia has become a focal point of manufacturing in industries such as electronics, any consideration of governance in the region must examine what Gereffi calls the 'coordination and control of global-scale production systems'.[90] Here, it should be noted that non-state actors are critical in forging the cross-border linkages of which global commodity chains are comprised. As Sasuga has documented for East Asia, relations between local firms and MNCs have been instrumental – albeit in conjunction with local governments and, to a lesser extent, national governments – in creating new forms of industrial organisation that constitute 'micro-regionalism'. Importantly, Sasuga emphasises that micro-regionalism in East Asia 'is not geographically self-contained but is sustained by certain crucial externalities ... and outside markets (especially those of the US and the EU)'.[91]

For the purpose of this chapter, it is most important to recognise how the US is contributing to the emergence of new structures of governance in cross-border economic life. Washington's promotion of neo-liberal globalisation has facilitated the extension and intensification of global commodity chains. For their part, non-state actors such as American MNCs have been important agents in this process. Within East Asia much emphasis has been placed, quite appropriately, on the role of Japanese FDI and the reform-minded economic policies of the Chinese government in restructuring the East Asian political economy. At the same time, the foundational role of the US should not be underestimated. In significant ways, the rescaling of global economic activity and concomitant transformation of industrial organisation over the past two decades can be traced back to the US.

In this sense, the US has also played an important – if sometimes indirect – role in the restructuring of governance arrangements among private firms, local governments and state-level actors in East Asia. The basic proposition is that the rising salience of global commodity chains means that the political economy of East Asia is best understood from the perspective of multilevel governance. Indeed, the concept of multilevel governance focuses our analysis on the formation of networks of decision making among public and private actors across national borders.

East Asian regional governance in an era of US-led globalisation

According to scholars such as Beeson, the United States has become an unwitting catalyst in spurring regionalism in East Asia since the end of the Cold War, especially since the Asian financial crisis. By virtue of both its overwhelming relative power and the specific nature of its policies, Washington has driven East Asian countries together into what Beeson calls 'reactionary regionalism'.[92] While there is evidence to support this position, reactionary regionalism is likely to be a limited phenomenon for several reasons, not least of which is the fact that US power and US policies constrain as well as fuel East Asian regionalism. Given its importance as an external actor, both as a critical economic partner and as the region's de facto security guarantor, the US remains an obstacle to East Asian integration. As this chapter has shown, US actors – governmental and non-governmental alike – continue to shape the economic, political and security context within which regionalism and regionalisation occur.

As Jayasuriya has argued, regional governance can be conceived as a 'political project' that reflects a particular constellation of power and interests operating interactively at the domestic and international levels. Rather than merely studying the 'governance of national economic units', Jayasuriya argues that we should examine how the political projects that constitute regional governance arrangements are 'rooted in particular structures of the global political economy'.[93] This, in turn, raises questions about the extent to which the US plays a fundamental role in shaping these structures. For example, by exerting pressure for neo-liberal forms of market governance, the US and US-dominated institutions such as the World Bank and IMF have facilitated the rise not only of a 'regulatory state' but also of what Jayasuriya calls 'regulatory regionalism'. According to Jayasuriya, the regulatory state:

transmits the disciplines of a globalised economy. This understanding underlines the critical point that the reproduction of the global economy requires the increasing harmonization of standards and codes such as corporate governance, transparency standards and broad macro- and micro-economic policies.[94]

In this way and others, US actors – public and private – push for the development of a global market economy, albeit one that has assumed a distinctly regional character during the first decade of the new millennium. For their part, non-state actors such as US MNCs, American bond-rating agencies and the US Chamber of Commerce push for the acceptance of standards, rules and practices broadly advantageous to American capital. At the same time, the US government pursues concerted bilateralism in East Asia and global multilateral initiatives such as the TRIPs and TRIMs agreements in the WTO. Taken collectively, these efforts seek to set the economic rules of the game. In this sense, the US wields what Strange called structural power: 'the power to shape and determine the structures of the global political economy within which other states, their political institutions, their economic enterprises and their scientists and other professional people have to operate'.[95]

Consistent with this view, the US strongly promotes regularisation and harmonisation in the conduct of world economic affairs, from the setting of industry standards such as Wintelism to IPR protection under the TRIPs agreement. In this way, the US pursues what Jayasuriya calls 'integration through regulation rather than simply through trade liberalisation'.[96] In the economic realm, therefore, the 'regionalist project' of East Asia has been substantially affected by what we might call the 'globalist project' of the US. This suggests that regionalism in Asia is more 'open' than 'closed', despite the efforts of some countries to develop architecture to the contrary. It also suggests that (in the economic sector at least) regional norms must take into account prevailing global norms when being developed or articulated.

Hegemony diluted? Growing interdependence in US–East Asian relations

This chapter has argued that US–East Asia relations continue to be defined in critical ways by American hegemony. Despite progress in developing institutions such as ARF and APT that may one day provide the basis for a functioning Asian security community, the US-led hub and spokes system remains the primary mode of security governance in East Asia. Similarly, US-based actors – public and private alike – remain integral to regional economic governance. In this sense, there are strong threads of continuity in US–East Asia relations. At the same time, the capacity of the US to change the behaviour of others or to act unilaterally in pursuit of its objectives is increasingly constrained by the deepening interdependence that characterises US ties to East Asia, especially but not only in economic affairs.[97] As defined by Keohane and Nye, interdependence 'refers to situations characterised by reciprocal effects among countries or among actors in different countries'.[98]

One of the most distinctive aspects of contemporary US–East Asia relations is the recycling of East Asia's massive foreign exchange reserves to offset huge imbalances in the US current account, a deficit which reached US$738.6 billion in 2007,[99] representing 4.9 per cent of US gross domestic product (up from zero in 1990).[100] The growth in Beijing's foreign exchange reserves, in particular, has received much attention, given the mounting bilateral trade surplus China enjoys with the US (US$256 billion in 2007).[101] Fuelled by growing exporting earnings, robust inward FDI and speculative capital flows, Beijing's world-leading reserves exceeded US$1.75 trillion by mid 2008. Also joining China among the world's top ten holders of foreign exchange reserves are (in descending order) Japan, Taiwan, South Korea, Singapore and Hong Kong. This 'East Asian Six' have invested their reserves largely in US dollar assets, such as Treasury securities and mortgage bonds issued by US government agencies. Beijing, for example, is estimated to have invested about 70 per cent of its burgeoning reserves in dollar-denominated assets in during the first half of the decade 2000.[102]

US data show that foreigners accounted for 98 per cent and 95 per cent of the growth in Treasury holdings in 2004 and 2005, respectively.[103] This means that the US budget deficit is being financed almost entirely by overseas money. Not all of this investment comes from East Asia, of course, but the East Asian Six (especially China and Japan) are the biggest players in a relationship with the US that is arguably dysfunctional as well as mutually beneficial. (China and Japan accounted for 46 per cent of US Treasury securities held by foreigners at mid-year 2007, with Hong Kong, Taiwan, South Korea and Singapore accounting for another 9 per cent.[104])

What happens, in essence, is that East Asian central banks lend the foreign exchange that they accumulate through trade surpluses and FDI inflows back to the US at low interest rates by buying US Treasury securities. As a result, the US can continue to buy more than it produces. Without this recycling of East Asia's foreign exchange reserves, the US would not have enjoyed the low interest rates that sustained its economic growth in recent years, primarily through consumer spending and the (now collapsed) housing boom. Nor, of course, would the Bush administration have been able to cut taxes and wage war simultaneously. According to one estimate, the US enjoyed interest rates in the first half of this decade that were between 1 per cent and 1.5 per cent lower than what would have prevailed if East Asian governments had not bought so many US Treasury securities and mortgage bonds.[105]

For their part, East Asian countries have allowed themselves to become significantly dependent on consumer spending in the US. Intraregional demand for final goods is not adequate to generate the level of economic growth necessary to maintain high employment rates. By enabling US profligacy, China, Japan and their East Asian neighbours are able to maintain a market for goods that they could not themselves consume.

Although the sustainability of this co-dependent relationship has been the focus of intense debate, governments on both sides of the Pacific seem inclined to pursue the status quo for as long as possible. As their behaviour has demonstrated, East Asian governments have an interest in stabilising exchange rates and subsidising American financial imbalances in order to maintain their own economic growth. Despite speculation to the contrary, there is little evidence that central banks are undertaking a major diversification away from dollars.[106] Although the current symbiotic financial relationship between the US and East Asia may prove unsustainable in the long run, it would be very costly for either side to break in the short run. This is why former US Treasury Secretary Lawrence Summers once characterised these governments as being caught in a 'balance of financial terror'.[107]

Rapkin and Thompson have characterised this situation as one of 'dissymmetric inter-dependence', arguing that disincentives for economic disruption are especially powerful in cases where complementary vulnerabilities among states allow unusually high stakes to cumulate.[108] That said, the greatest threat to financial instability might lie not in the behaviour of national governments but in the deeds of non-state actors. If, for example, dollar selling by currency speculators, MNCs, or other non-state actors were to become so pronounced that it overwhelmed the ability (or willingness) of China and Japan to buy dollars, foreign exchange markets would experience a dramatic correction.[109]

As this example illustrates, the interdependence of contemporary trans-Pacific relations is increasingly multifaceted. It is no longer only (or even primarily) the interdependence of national economies as captured by international political economy approaches that focus on state-to-state relations. There is also the interdependence created by the ongoing transnationalisation of production and investment, as captured by global political economy approaches that focus on non-state actors and multilevel, network forms of governance. While both perspectives offer insight, evidence that the nature of interdependence has broadened and deepened in ways illuminated by global political economy approaches is not difficult to find. As Ravenhill has pointed out, whereas a generation ago Japanese, South Korean and Taiwanese companies controlled their country's exports in a meaningful sense, today foreign companies control a staggering share of China's exports to the US and other leading markets.[110]

Even when US-based MNCs and other non-state actors exercise this kind of control, as they often do through the management of global commodity chains, trans-Pacific relations are still characterised by unprecedented interdependence. Like other countries, the US must adjust to the opportunities and challenges presented by the globalisation-cum-regionalisation of production and investment. While US-based actors may be important agents in this process, they are hardly immune from its effects, as public and private actors alike must respond to the realities of deepening interdependence. For example, even if American MNCs benefit disproportionately from the efficiencies achieved through global commodity chains, the US economy must still adjust to dislocating phenomena such as the infamous 'China price'. In this way, the US is increasingly constrained by the decisions of non-governmental as well as governmental actors, both at home and abroad.

Conclusion

The cross-border economic integration created by global commodity chains has important implications for regional governance. First, as discussed above, non-state actors are more influential in shaping the international context within which state-based actors interact. Consistent with Keohane and Nye's concept of complex interdependence, US–East Asia relations are increasingly characterised by multiple channels of exchange rather than by interaction primarily among states as unitary actors. Second, the globalisation-cum-regionalisation of production and investment has been propelled by – and, in turn, has transformed – domestic economic interests on both sides of the Pacific, in part by significantly expanding the number and kind of stakeholders impacted by this pattern of transnational collaboration.[111] New constituencies with wide-ranging interests on particular issues (e.g. Sino-American relations) have emerged in response to the proliferation of global commodity chains. In this sense, the domestic political context of US–East Asian relations has also changed with growing interdependence, not least in the US. Finally, some observers argue that transnational production via global commodity chains can have pacifying effects on international relations even more powerful than those associated with the bilateral exchange of finished goods.[112]

All told, networks of interdependence between the United States and East Asia are expanding and deepening in ways consistent with the concept of globalisation. As such, the effects of interdependence on the structures and processes by which actor interests are pursued, both domestically and internationally, are an important subject of study. Although interstate relations are still vitally important – especially in security affairs but also in economic affairs – governance increasingly reflects interaction among local, national, international and transnational actors. Consequently, a focus on interdependence is especially promising for how it emphasises that the role of the US in East Asia, while still critical, is changing in fundamental ways.

Notes

1 The ten members of ASEAN are Brunei, Cambodia, Indonesia, Laos, Malaysia, Myanmar, the Philippines, Singapore, Thailand and Vietnam.
2 Beeson, Mark. 'American Hegemony and Regionalism: The Rise of East Asia and the End of the Asia-Pacific', in Mark Beeson (ed.). *Bush and Asia: America's Evolving Relations with East Asia*. (London: Routledge, 2006), pp. 3–23.
3 The 109th US Congress, which was in session from January 2005 through December 2006, introduced more than two dozen pieces of legislation on matters related to East Asia, many of which represented direct challenges to the Bush

administration's handling of China policy. As of this writing, the 110th US Congress has introduced anti-China legislation at a pace far exceeding that of its predecessor.

4 The definitions of regionalism and regionalisation in this paragraph are consistent with those provided in Ravenhill, John. *APEC and the Construction of Pacific Rim Regionalism.* (New York: Cambridge University Press, 2001); and Mansfield, Edward and Helen V. Milner. 'The New Wave of Regionalism', *International Organization.* (Vol. 53, No. 3, 1999), pp. 589–627.

5 This definition draws on Keohane, Robert and Joseph S. Nye, Jr., 'Globalization: What's New? What's Not? (And so What?)', *Foreign Policy.* (No. 118, Spring 2000), p. 105.

6 Keohane, Robert and Joseph S. Nye, Jr., 'Introduction,' in Joseph S. Nye, Jr. and John Donahue (eds). *Governance in a Globalizing World.* (Washington, DC: Brookings, 2000), p. 12.

7 Krahmann, Elke. 'National, Regional, and Global Governance: One Phenomenon or Many?', *Global Governance.* (Vol. 9, No. 3, 2003), pp. 331.

8 Commission on Global Governance. *Our Global Neighbourhood.* (New York: Oxford University Press, 1995), p. 2.

9 Rosenau, James. *Along the Domestic-Foreign Frontier: Exploring Governance in a Turbulent World.* (Cambridge: Cambridge University Press, 1997), p. 145.

10 Krahmann. 'National, Regional, and Global Governance', p. 327.

11 *The National Security Strategy of the United States* (September 2002), hereafter *NSS 2002.* http://www.whitehouse.gov/nsc/nss.html. Accessed 29 April 2006.

12 *The National Security Strategy of the United States* (March 2006), hereafter *NSS 2006.* http://www.whitehouse.gov/nsc/nss/2006. Accessed 29 April 2006.

13 'President Discusses Freedom and Democracy in Kyoto, Japan'. http://www.whitehouse.gov/news/releases/2005/11/print/20051116-6.html. Accessed 3 March 2006.

14 The statement of purpose is available at US Department of Commerce. 'Good Governance Program'. http://www.ita.doc.gov/good governance. Accessed 3 January 2006.

15 *NSS 2006*, p. 7.

16 Other important groups include the Emergency Committee for American Trade, the Electronic Industries Alliance, the Telecommunications Industry Association, the Semiconductor Industry Association, the Information Technology Industry Council, the Biotechnology Industry Organisation, the Food Products Association, the Coalition Against Counterfeiting and Piracy, the Motion Picture Association of America, the Recording Industry Association of America, and the Entertainment Software Association.

17 US Chamber of Commerce. *The Asia Insider.* January/February 2006, p. 1.

18 US Chamber of Commerce. *The Asia Insider.* September/October 2005, p. 5.

19 Ibid. p. 1.

20 See: *US-Thailand FTA Business Coalition.* http://www.us-asean.org/us-thai-fta/. Accessed 8 May 2008.

21 US Chamber of Commerce. *The Asia Insider.* July/August 2005, p. 2.

22 Wesley, Michael. 'The Dog that didn't Bark: The Bush Administration and East Asian Regionalism', in Mark Beeson (ed.). *Bush and Asia: America's Evolving Relations with East Asia.* (London: Routledge, 2006), pp. 64–79.

23 See, for example, Beeson, Mark. 'Rethinking Regionalism', *Journal of European Public Policy.* (Vol. 12, No. 6, December 2005), pp. 969–985; and Hemmer, Christopher and Peter J. Katzenstein. 'Why is There No NATO in Asia?', *International Organization.* (Vol. 56, No. 3, Summer 2002), pp. 575–607.

24 Interviews with US and East Asian officials, June 2004, July 2005 and December 2005.

25 Hill, Christopher. 'The U.S. and Southeast Asia'. http://www.state.gov/p/eap/rls/rm/66646.htm. Accessed 11 September 2007.
26 Ibid.
27 Ibid.
28 Goh, Evelyn. 'The ASEAN Regional Forum in United States East Asian strategy', *The Pacific Review.* (Vol. 17, No. 1, March 2004), p. 59.
29 Zoellick, Robert. 'Remarks at ASEAN Regional Forum'. http://www.state.gov/s/d/rem/50411.htm. Accessed 29 April 2006.
30 *NSS 2006*, p. 48.
31 *Quadrennial Defense Review Report* (February 2006), hereafter *QDR 2006*, pp. 88–89.
32 Another example of Washington's preference for ad hoc multilateralism was the effort in 2004 to launch a Regional Maritime Security Initiative in which the US would have played a direct role in patrolling the Malacca Strait. Although Indonesia and Malaysia rejected the proposal, it did ultimately foster greater maritime security cooperation among Indonesia, Malaysia and Singapore.
33 In the 1990s, the Pentagon published four iterations of the *United States Security Strategy for the East Asia-Pacific Region*, also known as the *East Asia Strategy Report*. This report was discontinued in 1998.
34 *NSS 2002*, p. 26.
35 *QDR 2006*, pp. 87–88. http://www.defenselink.mil/qdr. Accessed 29 April 2006.
36 'Remarks by the President to the APEC Business Summit'. http://www.whitehouse.gov/news/releases/2007/09/20070906-9.html. Accessed 21 September 2007.
37 Rice, Condoleezza. 'Remarks with Defense Secretary Donald Rumsfield'. http://www.state.gov/secretary/rm/2005/55775.htm. Accessed 3 March 2006.
38 Although the Australian government under Kevin Rudd has signalled that this initiative no longer enjoys its support there remains strong pressure for it to reconsider its decision.
39 It is expected that the Korean National Assembly would ratify the deal following the April 2008 elections, but – as of May 2008 – this is yet to be seen. Similarly, the US was expected to ratify the deal by the end of 2008, but this is contingent on the outcome of the presidential election with the Democratic contender opposed to the FTA. See: 'Korea-U.S. FTA Unlikely to Pass U.S. Congress This Year', *English.Chosun.com*. 8 April 2008. http://english.chosun.com/w21data/html/news/200804/200804080013.html. Accessed 10 May 2008; and 'S Korean president: U.S. to ratify FTA with Seoul within this year', *www.chinaview.cn*. 21 April 2008. http://news.xinhuanet.com/english/2008-04/21/content_8020112.htm. Accessed 10 May 2008.
40 Omestad, Thomas. 'A budding relationship between U.S. and India', *US News & World Report*. 14 February 2006. http://www.usnews.com/usnews/news/articles/060214/14india.htm. Accessed 26 March 2006.
41 Zoellick, Robert. 'Whither China: From Membership to Responsibility?' http://www.state.gov/s/d/rem/53682.htm. Accessed April 29, 2006.
42 *QDR 2006*, p. 30.
43 Ibid. p. 29.
44 *NSS 2006*, p. 41.
45 Rice, Condoleezza. 'Roundtable with Australian, Indonesian and Latin American Journalists,' http://www.state.gov/secretary/rm/2006/62968.htm. Accessed 28 August 2007.
46 *NSS 2006*, p. 41.
47 Ibid. p. 42.
48 Twining, Daniel. 'America's Grand Design in Asia', *The Washington Quarterly*. (Vol. 30, No. 3, Summer 2007), pp. 80 and 89.
49 Ibid. p. 86.

50 Tow, William T. 'America's Asia-Pacific Strategy Is Out of Kilter' *Current History.* (September 2007), pp. 281–287.

51 Shadlen, Kenneth. 'Exchanging Development for Market Access?' *Review of International Political Economy.* (Vol. 12, No. 5, December 2005), pp. 750–775.

52 Ibid. p. 766.

53 Ibid.

54 Wade, Robert. 'What Strategies are Viable for Developing Countries Today?', *Review of International Political Economy.* (Vol. 10, No. 4, November 2003), pp. 621–644.

55 Shadlen. 'Exchanging Development for Market Access?'

56 Gereffi, Gary, John Humphrey and Timothy Sturgeon. 'The Governance of Global Value Chains,' *Review of International Political Economy.* (Vol. 12, No. 1, February 2005), pp. 78–104.

57 Zoellick. 'Whither China: From Membership to Responsibility?'

58 Kawai, Masahiro and Ganeshan Wignaraja. 'ASEAN+3 or ASEAN+6: Which Way Forward?', paper presented at the Conference on Multilateralising Regionalism, 10–12 September 2007, Geneva, Switzerland. Slightly different figures through to 2003 are presented in Masahiro Kawai, 'East Asian Economic Regionalism: Progress and Challenges', *Journal of Asian Economics.* (Vol. 16, No. 1, 2005), p. 31; and Gruenwald, Paul and Masahiro Hori. 'Intra-regional Trade Key to Asia's Export Boom', *IMF Survey Magazine.* 6 February 2008, http://www.imf.org/external/pubs/ft/survey/so/2008/CAR02608A.htm. Accessed 10 May 2008.

59 The figures in the previous three sentences were calculated by the author from data published by the International Monetary Fund (U.S.-specific imports and exports as reported by the US) and the World Trade Organisation (total imports and exports). The specific sources used were International Monetary Fund, *Direction of Trade Statistics Yearbook*, various years and World Trade Organisation, *International Trade Statistics, Statistics Database.* http://www.wto.org/english/res_e/statis_e/statis_e.htm.

60 For figures on intraregional trade share, see Kawai and Wignaraja. 'ASEAN+3 or ASEAN+6: Which Way Forward?', p. 30.

61 Calculated by the author from data presented in International Monetary Fund. *Direction of Trade Statistics Yearbook*, various years.

62 Zebregs, Harm. 'Intraregional Trade in Emerging Asia', *IMF Policy Discussion Paper.* PDP/04/1, p. 18.

63 Athukorala, Prema-chandra and Nobuaki Yamashita, 'Production Fragmentation and Trade Integration: East Asia in a Global Context', *North American Journal of Economics and Finance.* (Vol. 17, No. 3, 2006), p. 254.

64 Shujiro Urata, 'Emergence of New Type of Regional Economic Integration in East Asia', unpublished paper, May 2004, p. 9. http://fbweb.cityu.edu.hk/hkapec/Conference/Keynote/Shujiro%20Urata.pdf. Accessed 7 April 2006. See also Gaulier, Guillaume, Francoise Lemoine and Deniz Unal-Kesenci. 'China's Emergence and the Reorganization of Trade Flows in Asia', *China Economic Review.* (Vol. 18, 2007), pp. 209–243.

65 The index for 1990 to 2005 is available from the Asian Regional Integration Centre. http://aric.adb.org. Accessed 26 September 2007. For data going back to the 1980s and for comparisons with the EU and NAFTA, see Kawai. 'East Asian Economic Regionalism', pp. 31–32.

66 For descriptions and critiques of these approaches, see Rosecrance, Richard. *The Rise of the Trading State.* (New York: Basic Books, 1986); Woo-Cumings, Meredith (ed.). *The Developmental State.* (Ithaca, NY: Cornell University Press, 1999); Bernard, Mitchell and John Ravenhill. 'Beyond Product Cycles and Flying Geese', *World Politics.* (Vol. 47, No. 2, January 1995), pp. 171–209.

67 Athukorala and Yamashita. 'Production Fragmentation and Trade Integration: East Asia in a Global Context', p. 234.

68 Ibid.

69 Ibid. p. 241.

70 Ibid. For statistical purposes, Athukorala and Yamashita did not include Brunei, Cambodia, Laos and Myanmar as part of East Asia. This results in the slightly lower figure for intraregional imports (53.2 per cent versus 54 per cent in 2003) found in this study compared to Kawai, 'East Asian Economic Regionalism', p. 31.

71 Athukorala and Yamashita. 'Production Fragmentation and Trade Integration: East Asia in a Global Context', p. 247.

72 World Bank. *East Asia Update, Managing Through a Global Downturn.* (Washington: World Bank, 2006), p. 20

73 Athukorala and Yamashita, 'Production Fragmentation and Trade Integration: East Asia in a Global Context', p. 248.

74 Ibid. p. 254.

75 Data in this section stops at 2005 or 2006 depending on the figures, as this is the latest data usually available.

76 For a discussion of these issues, see United Nations Conference on Trade and Development, *World Investment Report 2005*, pp. 4–5. http://www.unctad/wir. Accessed 6 April 2006.

77 Urata, Shujiro. 'Changing Patterns of Trans-Pacific Trade and FDI Relations,' unpublished paper, May 30, 2005, p. 8. http://jri.inha.ac.kr/upload_/event/0530/ Session1_Urata.pdf. Accessed 7 April 2006. See also Urata, Shujiro. 'Emergence of New Type of Regional Economic Integration in East Asia,' unpublished paper, May 2004, pp. 11–12. http://fbweb.cityu.edu.hk/hkapec/Conference/Keynote/ Shujiro%20Urata.pdf. Accessed 7 April 2006. Urata also found that the share of East Asia's outward FDI that stayed in the region declined from 24.4 per cent in 1993 to 18.7 per cent in 2002.

78 Kawai. 'East Asian Economic Regionalism', p. 33.

79 In 1992, for example, the US share was 15.01 per cent. For the years 2000–2002, the average US share was 14.59 per cent. Calculated by the author from data presented in Kawai. 'East Asian Economic Regionalism', p. 33.

80 For example, in 1992 Japan and the four tigers accounted for 59.38 per cent of FDI inflows, compared to only 45.64 per cent in 2002. Calculated by the author from data presented in Kawai. 'East Asian Economic Regionalism', p. 33.

81 Wu, Friedrich. 'The Asian Myth', *The International Economy.* (Vol. 21, No. 2, 2007), p. 35. See also Department of State. 'Malaysia', http://www.state.gov/e/ eeb/ifd/2007/82336.htm. Accessed 10 May 2008.

82 Kawai and Wignaraja. 'ASEAN+3 or ASEAN+6: Which Way Forward?', p. 30.

83 Ibid.

84 Ibid.

85 Breslin, Shaun, 'Power and Production: Rethinking China's Global Economic Role', *Review of International Studies.* (Vol. 31, No. 4, 2005), p. 745.

86 Ibid.

87 Ibid. p. 747.

88 Gereffi *et al.* 'The Governance of Global Value Chains', pp. 82–83.

89 This figure was cited in remarks made by Assistant Secretary of State for East Asian and Pacific Affairs, Christopher Hill. See Hill, Christopher. 'EU–US Strategic Dialogue on East Asia', 23 May 2005. http://usinfo.state.gov/eap/ Archive/2005/May/27–523956.html. Accessed 8 March 2006. Other sources indicate that Wal-Mart, which stopped providing data on the dollar value of its imports from China after 2004, may rank even higher than seventh on China's list of export destinations.

90 Gereffi *et al.* 'The Governance of Global Value Chains', p. 81.

91 Sasuga, Katsuhiro. *Microregionalism and Governance in East Asia.* (London: Routledge, 2005), p. 165.

92 Beeson, Mark. 'ASEAN Plus Three and the Rise of Reactionary Regionalism', *Contemporary Southeast Asia*. (Vol. 25, No. 2, August 2003), pp. 251–268.
93 Jayasuriya, Kanishka. 'Introduction: The Vicissitudes of Asian Regional Governance', in Kanishka Jayasuriya (ed.). *Asian Regional Governance*. (London: Routledge, 2004), pp. 3 and 15.
94 Ibid. p. 8.
95 Strange, Susan. *States and Markets*. (London: Pinter Publishers, 1988), p. 23.
96 Jayasuriya. 'Introduction: The Vicissitudes of Asian Regional Governance', p. 9.
97 Ravenhill makes a similar argument, although he places less emphasis on continued US influence than does this chapter. See Ravenhill, John. 'US Economic Relations with East Asia: From Hegemony to Complex Interdependence?', in Mark Beeson (ed.). *Bush and Asia: America's Evolving Relations with East Asia*. (London: Routledge, 2006), pp. 42–63.
98 Keohane and Nye. 'Globalization: What's New? What's Not? (And so What?)', p. 105.
99 Bureau of Economic Analysis. 'News Release: U.S. International Transactions', *US International Transactions: Fourth Quarter and Year 2007 Current Account*. 17 March 2008. http://www.bea.gov/newsreleases/international/transactions/transnewsrelease.htm. Accessed 10 May 2008.
100 Moeller, Tom. 'U.S. Current Account Deficit Shrank in 2007', http://www.haver.com/comment/080317c.htm. Accessed 10 May 2008.
101 Morrison, Wayne. 'China–U.S. Trade Issues', *CRS Report for Congress*. 7 March 2008. http://www.committee100.org/media/media_eng/CRSChina-USTradeIssues_032508.pdf. Accessed 10 May 2008, p. 2.
102 Lague, David. 'China, a Trade Superstar, Accumulates Foreign Currency (and Anxiety)', *The New York Times*, 17 January 2006, Business Section, p. 4; McGregor, Richard and Andrew Yeh. 'China Plays Down Idea of Selling Off Its Dollars', *Financial Times*, 11 January 2006, p. 7.
103 Norris, Floyd. 'In Long-Term American Treasury Securities They Trust', *The New York Times*, 18 February 2006, Business Section, p. 3.
104 US Department of Treasury. 'Major Foreign Holders of Treasury Securities', http://www.treas.gov/tic/mfh.txt. Accessed 14 September 2007.
105 Wessel, David. 'Economic Imbalance Fuels Dollar's Big Drop,' *The Asian Wall Street Journal*, 3 December 2004, A1.
106 Rowley, Anthony. 'US$ diversification myth exposed,' *Business Times Singapore*, 16 February 2006.
107 Summers, Lawrence H. 'The United States and the Global Adjustment Process', www.iie.com/publications/papers/paper.cfm?researchid = 200. Accessed 12 September 2007.
108 Rapkin, David P. and William R. Thompson. 'Will Economic Interdependence Encourage China's and India's Peaceful Ascent?', in Ashley Tellis and Michael Wills (eds). *Strategic Asia 2006–07: Trade, Interdependence, and Security*. (Seattle: National Bureau of Asian Research, 2006), p. 359.
109 Cohen, Stephen D. 'The Superpower as Super-Debtor', in Ashley Tellis and Michael Wills (eds). *Strategic Asia 2006–07: Trade, Interdependence, and Security*. (Seattle: National Bureau of Asian Research, 2006), p. 53.
110 Ravenhill. 'US Economic Relations with East Asia', p. 55. According to Ravenhill, Wal-Mart alone accounts for one-eighth of China's exports to the US. Breslin has estimated that approximately '70 per cent of all of China's exports are made by or for foreign companies.' See Breslin, Shaun. *China and the Global Political Economy*. (New York: Palgrave Macmillan, 2007), p. 113.
111 Ravenhill. 'US Economic Relations with East Asia', pp. 56 and 62.
112 Brooks, Stephen G. *Producing Security: Multinational Corporations, Globalization, and the Changing Calculus of Conflict*. (Princeton, NJ: Princeton University Press, 2005).

9 The role of law in governing regionalism in Asia

Paul J. Davidson

Introduction

Good governance is essential to facilitate international economic activity. Over the last three decades, in particular, there has been a movement internationally to more of a rules-based framework to regulate international economic relations (rules-based governance), rather than relying on arrangements based on the personal relations of the actors (relations-based governance). In the course of economic growth and expansion of trade and investment, as an actor needs to work with less-familiar partners, there is a need for a shift away from relations-based and toward rules-based governance, so as to provide greater transparency and confidence.

International law plays an important function in rules-based governance. In the economic realm, international law provides the framework for regulating economic activity among the members of the international community and provides the international legal framework for rules-based governance. Laws and a legal system are important for economic development.[1] As Rajenthran has observed, 'increasingly, empirical evidence proves that efficient law and legal institutions promote and sustain economic activities. To this end, both create an ascertainable "structure of expectations"'.[2]

The spread of globalisation since the 1980s has been interspersed with the concomitant rise of regional associations. Although scholars remain divided as to whether these are two distinct processes or whether regionalism is simply a subset of globalism, there are a number of common characteristics, chief of which is the economic imperative for stability and prosperity. However, as the 1990s repeatedly showed, stability and prosperity are difficult to realise without the correct institutional architecture and norms. Economic development requires a stable system of inputs as well as checks and balances from a variety of actors – states, markets and supranational organisations – all of whom adhere to a common set of values. The crises of the 1990s – in Europe, Mexico, East Asia, Argentina and Russia – have fostered a concerted global push towards good economic governance as the essential component of international economic activities. Globally as well as in a number of regional organisations (such as the European Union or the North

American Free Trade Agreement (NAFTA) group), this governance is supported by a set of legal instruments that not only codify the values of the party states but also seek to ensure compliance with the norms agreed upon.

Almost all the member countries of the World Trade Organisation (WTO) also belong to a regional trade agreement,[3] and the Asia-Pacific region is currently undergoing significant changes with respect to its stance towards regional integration, with a number of countries actively considering the regional option.[4] The success of regionalism will depend to a large degree on the framework of rules, institutions and organisations that govern the conduct of economic activity. Formal and informal rules of behaviour, ways and means of enforcing these rules, procedures for settling conflicts, sanctions in the case of a breach of the rules, and organisations supporting market transactions are all important determinants in considering the governance system.

This chapter will consider the contribution of the existing mechanisms to the governance of regionalism in Asia and the need to create new rules, institutions and arrangements to more effectively govern economic relations in the region. Specifically, the discussion will focus on the role of law in economic governance and regionalism in Asia. There has been a move to 'rules-based' governance in international economic relations. Often 'rules-based' has been equated to the development of 'binding' rules and the development of dispute-settlement mechanisms to interpret and apply these rules. However, 'rules-based' comprises a wider range of 'rules', and 'legalisation' includes 'non-binding' ('soft law') as well as 'binding' rules ('hard law'). This chapter examines 'rules-based' governance in international economic relations, and the nature and role of international law (including the role of 'soft law') in 'rules-based' governance. In doing so, it seeks to answer the perennial question of whether or not a new governance order for Asia which may involve rules that do not fit existing definitions of international law is more appropriate for the region.

The next section of this chapter is a brief discussion of the concept of governance, particularly relations-based and rules-based approaches to governance, that builds upon the earlier models presented in the first two chapters of this volume. There has been a movement internationally to more of a rules-based framework to regulate international economic relations (rules-based governance),[5] particularly as manifested by the WTO legal framework. The WTO has made a valuable contribution to economic governance; governments have repeatedly shown a commitment to cooperation in the WTO. The WTO is perhaps the clearest example of the development of rules-based governance of international economic relations, with its rules for regulating international trade and its unified dispute-settlement mechanism, including its Dispute Settlement Body (DSB) and a standing Appellate Body to hear appeals on issues of law covered in the panel report and the legal interpretations developed by the panel. The WTO sets out the 'ground rules' for regionalism, and any discussion of the governance of regionalism requires a consideration of the rules and role of the WTO.

In contrast, within Asia, much economic cooperation has been achieved in the 'Asian Way', not through rules and regulations, but through discussion and consultation, and consensus (relations-based governance).[6] The 'Asian Way' relies to a large extent on the personal approach, in contrast to the Western way of dependence on structures and their functions. However, it has been stated that Asian countries must move away from this 'relationship-based' way of doing business and creating wealth to one that is more 'rules-based' and 'market-driven'.[7] In the course of economic growth, and expansion of trade and investment, as one deals with less familiar partners, there is a shift away from relation-based and toward rules-based governance. This section considers ASEAN and the WTO as examples of relations-based and rules-based governance and the movement within ASEAN to more of a rules-based approach.

Following the discussion of governance, the third section considers the movement internationally to more of a rules-based framework to regulate international economic relations and the role of international law in rules-based governance. Rules-based governance entails, in part at least, norm generation and dispute settlement, which are the function of a legal system in a society. Although a legal system is often thought of as comprising rules that create 'binding', enforceable obligations ('hard' law), rules-based governance comprises a much broader spectrum of legalisation, including 'soft law' or non-binding commitments. In considering a 'rules-based' legal framework it is important to consider the role of 'softer' legalisation, through 'non-binding' commitments. It may often be more appropriate to take a 'softer' approach to legalisation in rules-based governance of economic relations. 'Softer' commitments can be seen as a 'bridge' between 'rules-based' and 'relations-based' governance. The section includes a discussion of 'legalisation', and the role of 'soft law', particularly 'soft law' as practised by the Asia-Pacific Economic Cooperation (APEC) group. The chapter concludes with a consideration of how the foregoing discussion answers the question, 'Is a new governance order for Asia more appropriate that may involve rules that do not fit existing definitions of international law?'

Governance

'Since the 1980s, the concept of governance has increasingly been employed to describe policy-making in the national, regional and global arenas. Definitions and uses of *governance*, however, are as varied as the issues and levels of analysis to which the concept is applied ... Common to these notions is the changing locus of political authority.'[8] Governance is a broader notion than government.[9] Although a government is frequently established to administer these processes and systems, a 'government' is not essential to governance. Governance refers to a structure that both allows and constrains the behaviour of actors in interdependent relationships in the absence of an overarching political authority. In other words:

Governance is the sum of the many ways individuals and institutions, public and private, manage their common affairs. It is a continuing process through which conflicting or diverse interests may be accommodated and co-operative action may be taken. It includes formal institutions and regimes empowered to enforce compliance, as well as informal arrangements that people and institutions either have agreed to or perceive to be in their interest.[10]

In this chapter, the term is used to refer to the mechanisms which allow international economic activity to take place. International economic governance deals with the processes and systems by which states regulate economic activity *inter se.* Such governance may be regional (applying to a limited number of actors) or it may be global (open to the larger global community). 'Global governance ... refers to the complex of institutions, mechanisms, relationships, and processes between and among states, markets, citizens, and organisations to articulate collective interests on the global plane, establish rights and obligations, and mediate differences.'[11] '[T]he concept is typically ... used to describe the increasingly regulated character of transnational and international relations.'[12]

In theory, each state is free to regulate economic transactions which take place with it or within its boundaries as it pleases.[13] However, in practice, international economic relations are governed by an international framework which provides predictability or stability to a potential investment or trade situation. This framework is established through governance arrangements among the state actors. When reviewing these types of arrangements it is possible to identify two broad categories of governance, namely relations-based and rules-based. In considering their utilisation in global and regional practices it is worth briefly examining their main characteristics.

Relations-based governance vs. rules-based governance

'Relations-based' governance relies on the personal relationship of the actors to establish the parameters of their cooperation. Agreements are based on the mutual relations of the actors and depend on knowledge of and familiarity with each other. Formality is avoided and the maintenance of good relations is relied on for the 'enforcement' of commitments. 'Rules-based' governance relies more on structures and their functions. 'Rules-based' governance is more formal and normally involves the negotiation of more detailed, often binding rules to govern the cooperation among the actors, and the establishment of dispute-settlement mechanisms to resolve disputes in accordance with the rules. As Dixit has observed, 'The two systems can and do coexist. However, as the number of economic partners increases and as the economic activity becomes more complex, it becomes more difficult to engage in relationship-based governance because it becomes increasingly difficult to have the requisite knowledge of partners. Therefore, in the course of economic growth, and expansion of trade and investment, one should expect the mix to shift away from relation-based and toward rules-based governance.'[14]

Relations-based governance – the 'ASEAN Way'

The 'ASEAN Way' has determined ASEAN's approach to governance in the region. Norm building in ASEAN has been based on approaches determined by the 'ASEAN Way'. The underlying approach to decision making in ASEAN is the consensus approach embodied in the Malay terms *musyawarah* and *mufakat*, which relies largely on patient consensus building to arrive at informal understandings or loose agreements. *Musyawarah* is the process of decision making through discussion and consultation, and *mufakat* is the unanimous decision that is arrived at.[15] The concept involves processes including intensive, informal and discreet discussions behind the scenes to work out a general consensus which then acts as the starting point around which the unanimous decision is finally accepted in more formal meetings, rather than across-the-table negotiations involving bargaining and give-and-take that result in deals enforceable in a court of law. The 'ASEAN Way' relies to a large extent on the personal approach, in contrast to the Western way of dependence on structures and their functions.[16] This 'ASEAN Way' is in contrast to the formal legalism of most Western international institutions, and reflects a 'relations-based' approach to governance in the region.

Rules-based governance – the World Trade Organisation

The WTO is the principal international institution for the management and regulation of the process of economic globalisation.[17] The WTO framework provides the rules for international economic trade relations among its members. At its heart are the WTO agreements, which are the legal 'rules' for international economic trade relations. The WTO framework establishes rights and obligations – it guarantees member countries important trade rights and binds governments to keep their trade policies within agreed limits.[18] The WTO has evolved from its early, diplomatic relations-based origins in the GATT, to become perhaps the best-known example of rules-based governance of international economic relations. This is exemplified by its rules for regulating international trade and its unified dispute-settlement mechanism, including its DSB and a standing Appellate Body to hear appeals on issues of law covered in the panel report and the legal interpretations developed by the panel.[19] As Tarullo has suggested, 'the WTO represents the best extant case of what might be called a statutory/adjudicatory type of governance arrangement. Member countries negotiate and adopt reasonably detailed rules for state behavior ... The WTO has progressively refined its dispute settlement procedures into a quasi-adjudicatory process for applying those rules to specific state actions.'[20]

From relations to rules in ASEAN

At the time that the ASEAN was formed, the original individual member states (Indonesia, Malaysia, the Philippines, Singapore and Thailand) were hesitant to establish an organisation with strong powers over the members, as they wished to maintain a high level of individual sovereignty.[21] They were reluctant to be too 'legalistic' in their relations with each other, preferring to conduct relationships in the 'ASEAN Way'. This desire was reflected in the 1967 Bangkok Declaration,[22] which established ASEAN with a structure that was organisationally loose and avoided the trappings of a strong regional organisation.

ASEAN was initially formed with mainly political objectives. Although collaboration in the economic field was mentioned in its founding document, little was done in this area, as the member states concentrated on political concerns. However, with economic expansion in the region and closer economic cooperation among the members of ASEAN, objectives of economic cooperation became more prominent in ASEAN. With the development of closer economic relations, the need for a more legalistic framework to govern these relations has grown.[23] Furthermore, as cooperation has increased across a wide range of economic and financial sectors, the members of ASEAN have developed the need for more of a rules-based system to regulate their economic activity *inter se*.[24]

International trade and investment in the region are increasingly becoming subject to international regulation – one that is governed by a rules-based system and is accompanied by an evolving international legal framework able to regulate economic relations among trading partners. With this legal framework there has been a concomitant movement – albeit slowly – towards the development of greater institutional and organisational structure of ASEAN as an entity,[25] including creation of a more effective dispute-settlement mechanism (DSM) with powers to make legally binding decisions in resolving disputes over economic agreements among member states.[26] The formalisation of ASEAN's framework for economic cooperation can also be seen in the Regional Trade Agreements (RTAs) that ASEAN is entering into with its trading partners. These RTAs contain the rules for regulating trade relations between the member states of ASEAN and their trading partners. Importantly, they also contain settlement mechanisms to resolve disputes that may arise during the implementation of the agreements.

At the Eleventh ASEAN Summit in Kuala Lumpur in December 2005, the leaders of ASEAN signed the Kuala Lumpur Declaration on the Establishment of the ASEAN Charter, which noted, in part:

> [The] importance of having an appropriate institutional framework of ASEAN that is able to meet the challenges of realising an ASEAN community;

> [The] ASEAN Charter will serve as a *legal and institutional* frame-work of ASEAN to support the realisation of its goals and objectives.
>
> ... the ASEAN Charter will codify all ASEAN norms, rules, and values and reaffirm that ASEAN agreements signed and other instruments adopted before the establishment of the ASEAN Charter shall continue to apply and be *legally binding* where appropriate.
>
> ... the ASEAN Charter will confer a *legal personality* to ASEAN and determine the functions, develop areas of competence of key ASEAN bodies and their relationship with one another in the overall ASEAN structure.[27]

The foreign ministers of the Association of Southeast Asian Nations (ASEAN) reiterated the importance of moving to a rules-based organisation at the 40th ASEAN Ministerial Meeting in July 2007 in Manila, when they averred that:

> We stressed the importance of codifying the principles, values and norms of ASEAN into a Charter and in sustaining the momentum towards transforming ASEAN into a *rules-based organisation with a legal personality*, capable of performing a greater role in regional and international affairs.[28]

This development has been driven not only by the integration of the member states but also from ASEAN's desire to be seen as an attractive location for foreign investment. In order to attract foreign investment a state (or a region) must 'provide a legal framework to guarantee foreign investors' legal rights and commercial entitlements. In general, the more distance there is between the social, political and economic systems of the host country and those of the investing country, the more need for a highly developed legal framework',[29] in order to promote increased order and predictability in international transactions. As business partners are less familiar with each other, it becomes necessary to rely more on 'rules' and less on 'relations' in conducting transactions.[30] As Dixit has stated, once 'the system [rules-based governance] is established, one can deal with strangers'.[31]

However, although there has been a movement to more of a 'rules-based' approach, ASEAN has not completely abandoned the 'ASEAN Way'. While the ASEAN Charter contains more effective DSM with powers to make legally binding decisions in resolving trade disputes among member states, it is clear that there is a declared preference towards conducting regional affairs on the pre-existing basis. As Ambassador Manalo, the ASEAN Charter High Level Task Force (HLTF) Chair, stated:

> The general approach is consultation and consensus. That's the way of doing things in ASEAN. Up to every level possible before the heads of state, that is going to be applied ... You'll find that in the charter there are dispute mechanisms. That is totally different from sanctions ... This is because there may be states that in the exercise of their obligations

may only oblige halfheartedly or what you call token compliance which may give rise to disagreements.[32]

These developments within ASEAN are significant to the approach to governance in the broader East Asian region as much as they are for the governing of internal ASEAN affairs, because of the importance of ASEAN as a hub for regional activities in Asia. Although a detailed discussion of ASEAN's influence on regionalism in the area was already covered in the earlier chapters, mention can be made of ASEAN's role in the East Asian Summit (EAS). The first EAS was held in Kuala Lumpur in December 2005, following the Eleventh ASEAN Summit. As was noted above this led to the signing of the Kuala Lumpur Declaration on the Establishment of the ASEAN Charter, which contained calls for a move towards a rules-based organisation. This change was reiterated by the second EAS in Cebu in January 2007, when the Chairman's statement declared that the EAS members:

> welcomed ASEAN's efforts towards further integration and community building, and reaffirmed our resolve to work closely together in narrowing development gaps in our region. *We reiterated our support for ASEAN's role as the driving force for economic integration in this region.*[33]

Hence, as can be seen in the case of ASEAN, there is a clear shift towards the greater utilisation of rules-based governance in regional affairs. Given the close ties between ASEAN and the ASEAN+3 (APT) identified in the previous chapters, as well as between ASEAN and the EAS, it is reasonable to conclude that this normative change will gradually be transferred into other levels and areas of regional governance. However, it is also reasonable to conclude that this shift is not without its detractors, who prefer a more relations-based approach to regional governance. This is possibly one of the key tensions within the region as it continues to develop deeper forms of functional cooperation eventually designed to underpin an East Asian Community. As the previous three chapters noted, it is a tension that has been thrown into stark relief with the admittance of Australia, New Zealand and India into the EAS, all three of whom favour rules over relations in their regional affairs. Nonetheless, the region must not only resolve this tension intraregionally but – as observed above – must also resolve it with respect to the legal and normative regimes of the wider global community. This is the subject of the next section.

International law and rules-based governance

In many issue areas, the world is witnessing a move to law.[34]

> It would seem that the expanding number and the variety of international economic agreements, the new international economic organisations that

are being established to realize their objectives and the legislative, executive and judicial organs which have been set up under them are the significant aspects of a system (systems?) of international economic regulation which is evolving in response to a desire for a rule-oriented economic society.[35]

The shift towards a rule-oriented society in Asia is a reflection of the move to rules-based governance globally. Rules-based governance entails, in part at least, norm generation and dispute settlement. These are the function of a legal system in a society, which is reflected upwards into the behaviour of the international community. A legal system provides rules for the orderly interchange among members of the society, and provides a mechanism(s) for the settlement of disputes that arise among members of the society, concerning the rules established by that society, and for interpreting those rules.[36] International economic law provides the framework for regulating economic activity among the members of the international community and provides the legal framework for rules-based governance, which governs international trade in goods and services and foreign investment. Such a framework is necessary in order to promote increased order and predictability in international transactions.

Legalisation

Law is a necessary component of a rules-based governance system. As noted above, a legal system performs two primary functions in rules-based governance: (1) establishing rules and (2) settling disputes. The traditional approach to answering the question 'What is law?' has often been to look at whether or not the rule in question creates binding and enforceable obligations – in other words, 'hard law'. However, 'rules-based' does not necessarily require that the rules be binding. Although 'laws' and a 'legal framework' are often thought of in terms of 'hard law', rules-based governance comprises a much broader spectrum. Rules may vary from non-binding commitments to binding obligations, from vague to precise. The dispute-settlement mechanism may, for example, vary from a procedure for a diplomatic negotiation of a settlement, to a formal judicial system with a court.

Central also to the discussion of rules and legalisation is the issue of the 'enforcement' of the rules. It is often argued that the enforcement of the rules established by a system is necessary to consider the system as having a 'legal' framework. However, law is obeyed not solely because of force but because the members of society believe it should be followed for the good of the society. States 'obey' international law, not primarily because of its enforceability, but because it is of mutual benefit for all participants in the legal system. The essential constituent of law is an expectation that the commitments entered into will be taken seriously and given some measure of respect. The extent of 'compliance' with commitments, rather than the 'enforcement' of obligations is an indicator of the 'legalisation' of a framework. Moreover, compliance mechanisms may be informal or formal in their nature. Thus, the degree of legalisation may be illustrated as shown in Figure 9.1.[37]

Legalisation may be viewed as a three- (or four-) dimensional spectrum. Each of these dimensions is variable, and the degree of 'legalisation' ranges from 'hard' legalisation, where all dimensions fall to the right of the scale, through multiple forms of 'softer' legalisation. The possibilities of combinations across these extremes are multiple. On the one hand, hard law is not always attached to legal sanctions and it can often be vague. On the other hand, soft law, like standards, can be specific and detailed. There is no clear distinction between 'hard' and 'soft' law, but rather a continuum with various degrees of 'legalisation', from 'harder' to 'softer'.

Furthermore, the form of rules-based governance may be characterised according to the degree of legalisation. Rules-based governance utilising 'softer' legalisation may be characterised as 'diplomatic', while rules-based governance utilising 'harder' legalisation may be characterised as 'juridical', with different options available to the participants according to their agreements and needs.

Soft law

Generally, 'soft law' refers to a rule that is not law in the traditional sense. As defined by Craik:

> While there is no generally accepted definition of soft law, its essential characteristic is that, unlike traditional hard law sources, soft law does not create formally binding obligations. Instead, it records only the agreed-upon principles and objectives, and a considerable degree of discretion in interpretation and on how and when to conform to the requirements is left to the participants.[38]

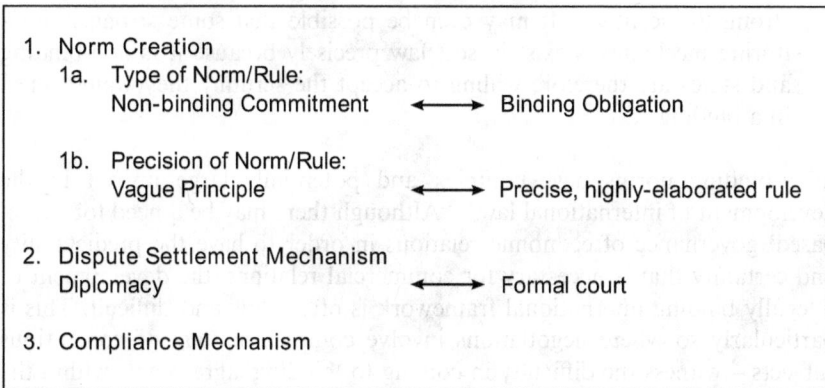

```
1. Norm Creation
   1a. Type of Norm/Rule:
       Non-binding Commitment    ◄──────►   Binding Obligation

   1b. Precision of Norm/Rule:
       Vague Principle           ◄──────►   Precise, highly-elaborated rule

2. Dispute Settlement Mechanism
   Diplomacy                     ◄──────►   Formal court

3. Compliance Mechanism
```

Figure 9.1 The degree of legalisation

Soft law is often distinguished from hard law through the use of such language as 'guidelines', 'declarations' or 'principles' to designate 'soft' law.[39] In order to be considered a valid form of law, however, the commitments must be complied with, despite the language used. According to Gold, 'The essential ingredient of soft law is an expectation that the states accepting these instruments will take their content seriously and give them some measure of respect.'[40] The ability of soft law agreements to meet these expectations is the ultimate test of their legitimacy. If actors expect compliance and, in fact, comply with commitments contained in soft law instruments as well as they do with norms contained in treaties and customs, then these agreements should also be considered part of the legal framework governing relations among those actors.

This leads to the question as to whether or not states tend to comply less with non-binding than with binding instruments or norms. The fact that 'soft' law commitments are 'non-binding' does not mean that they are complied with any less than 'hard' law mechanisms. Although it may be necessary to have a compliance mechanism to monitor commitments that are made on a voluntary basis, this does not necessarily mean that such a mechanism must be of the traditional hard law/enforcement type – namely, sanctions or other forms of coercion. Other mechanisms can be just as effective. Managing problems through supervision and incentives, for example, may be more effective. 'Managerial approaches suppose that states comply with rules in regulatory regimes out of enlightened self-interest and respond to non-coercive tools such as reporting and monitoring.'[41] While a binding legal obligation brings with it greater expectation of conforming behaviour and consequences for non-compliance, states are also demonstrating compliance with other forms of international commitment. As Shelton has further noted:

> Monitoring and publicly revealing non-compliance may be the most effective, if not the only, method of inducing compliance in the face of strong disincentives. It may even be possible that some stronger monitoring mechanisms exist in soft law precisely because it is non-binding and states are therefore willing to accept the scrutiny they would reject in a binding text.[42]

'Non-binding norms have complex and potentially large impact in the development of international law.'[43] Although there may be a need for 'rules-based' governance of economic relations in order to have the predictability and certainty that is necessary for commercial relations, the development of a legally binding international framework is often slow and difficult. This is particularly so where negotiations involve complex matters or contentious subjects – witness the difficulty in coming to 'binding' agreements within the current negotiations at the WTO. Soft law may be necessary to ensure consensus on sensitive issues or to mitigate conflict and build common positions and confidence. Soft law allows for vagueness of commitments where parties are prepared to enter into agreements but are unable to agree on the 'exactness' of their obligations. Indeed, hard law in the form of treaties often contains 'soft' obligations – in other words, soft law in a 'hard cover'. Consider, for example, the following statement: 'signatories will *endeavour* to … '.[44] It is not precise, yet expresses a commitment covered within a treaty and so is binding in nature, if not in fact. A distinctive characteristic of soft law, at least in relation to economic matters, appears to be the intended vagueness of the obligations that it imposes or the weakness of its commands. As Shelton stated:

> Soft law instruments often serve to allow treaty parties to authoritatively resolve ambiguities in the text or fill in gaps. This is part of an increasingly complex international system with variations in forms of instruments, means, and standards of measurement that interact intensely and frequently, with the common purpose of regulating behavior *within a rule of law framework*.[45]

Soft law can be useful in addressing the difficulties in reconciling the approaches of the 'East' and the 'West'. As Gold has observed:

> It is easy to be too condescending toward soft law, even if firm law would be preferable. Soft law can overcome deadlocks in the relations of states that result from economic or political differences among them when efforts at firmer solutions have been unavailing. A substantial amount of soft law can be attributed to differences in the economic structures and economic interests of developed, as compared with many developing, countries. Much soft law, therefore, is to be found in the law of universal international organisations, including the decisions of their organs, because the membership of these organisations is so diverse. The soft law of these organisations is the result not of a failure of will or technical skill on their part, but of the deep divisions among members.[46]

These economic and political differences often exist between the 'East' and the 'West'. However, the same statement can be equally applied to the deadlocks that arise from differences in the 'legal' approaches taken by Asian and non-Asian states.

'Softer' legalisation through 'non-binding' commitments can therefore be seen as a bridge between 'rules-based' and 'relations-based' governance. Soft law is rules-based insofar as it involves establishment of a framework (rules) for international cooperation on issues. It is also relations-based insofar as the compliance with the 'rules' depends on the relationship between the parties. 'Soft' law relies on mechanisms to encourage learning through regular interactions of relevant stakeholders. Depending on the issue, a soft law approach to economic issues may make good sense, instead of parties attempting to impose specific, binding rules.

Soft law may be increasingly utilised because it responds to the needs of the new international system, with its ever-increasing array of actors – not only states but also members of the private sector and civil society representatives. Ultimately, international law is concerned with international legal commitments – binding or non-binding – and their ability to prevent and resolve conflict and promote international relations. Soft law is playing an increasing and important role in this regard and, particularly in Asia, has become part of the regional governance structure. A good example of both the utilisation of soft law and the interaction between Asian and non-Asian states and economies can be seen in the case of APEC.

APEC and the utility of a soft law approach

Soft law, as practised by APEC, is particularly relevant to rules-based governance in the Asia-Pacific region. APEC has not sought to create binding rules but has advanced cooperation through non-binding commitments. Hence, discussions among members are not directed to achieving legally binding agreements. Commitments are framed as declarations of political will, rather than legal undertakings. They are expressed as being voluntary, non-binding commitments. Nevertheless, this soft law plays a role in the governance of economic relations among members of APEC. It also provides a flexible framework for assisting governments to identify good policies, not a rigid system that aims at a type of regional harmonisation that is enforced by a binding dispute settlement. It allows stakeholders to implement the rules when and as they are able. The specific content of regulation in each member economy may reflect national or local circumstances.

Much of this evolving framework is set out in APEC's soft law guidelines, namely, the Non-Binding Investment Principles (NBIP) and the agreement on a set of best practice principles for regional trade agreements and free trade agreements (FTAs). The 'APEC Best Practices for RTAs and FTAs' are intended to achieve high-standard FTA/RTA agreements in the APEC region and to ensure that RTAs/FTAs are consistent with the WTO. Although not 'binding' on the APEC members, these 'best practices' are influential and serve as a guide to some of the issues that need to be addressed by any new frameworks for regulating the economic relationship among members. Likewise, the NBIP provide guidelines for regulating investment among APEC members. These 'soft law' guidelines play an important role in the governance of economic cooperation among APEC members. Thus, in its operations APEC acts as a 'bridge' between the 'soft' and 'hard' legal approaches to regional governance.

As APEC is not a rules-based organisation it is not able to establish a formal, binding dispute-settlement mechanism. However, as noted above, although it may be necessary to have a compliance mechanism to maintain commitments that are made on a voluntary basis, this does not necessarily mean that such a mechanism must be of the traditional 'hard law'/'enforcement' type. Other mechanisms, such as managing commitments through supervision and incentives can be just as effective. One way that APEC accomplishes this is through its peer review process.

Although a detailed discussion of the peer review process in APEC is beyond the scope of this chapter, a few notes on the process are in order. There are two parts to the APEC peer review process. In the first stage, member economies develop and implement Individual Action Plans (IAPs) that include a comprehensive package of reforms and ongoing trade facilitation measures to implement their APEC commitments. In the second stage, these IAPs are reviewed every few years through a process that involves an assessment by independent experts who prepare a report which is then presented to the other APEC members, who then have the opportunity to question the member under review and evaluate its progress. This process lies at the heart of APEC's voluntary and consensus-based process. As APEC Secretariat Finance Director Geoffrey Woodhead stated:

> The review process is open and can be very frank if one economy feels another economy needs to improve their progress … While commitments are non-binding in a court of law, the peer review process ensures that if one economy does not appear to be honoring commitments there will be pressure for compliance.[47]

While useful, these peer reviews do have limitations. Currently, for example, most IAPs make only passing reference to preferential trading agreements (PTAs). If the peer review process is to be limited to a review of members' IAPs, PTAs should be included as an IAP chapter with specific reporting requirements on the planned actions of individual economies, so that members' PTAs are also subject to APEC peer review. Further study directed at the design and methodology of the peer review process is needed to strengthen the process and make it an effective component of the economic governance system for the region.[48]

If soft law is accepted as part of international law, then the evolving framework in APEC can be seen as part of the overall developing legal framework for governing regional and global economic relations. The growing complexity of the international legal system is reflected in the increasing variety of commitments adopted to govern international relations. International actors will create and attempt to comply with a range of international commitments, some of which will be in binding form, others of which will be contained in non-binding instruments. Such an approach may be especially necessary where diverse national legal systems necessitate different approaches. This approach is well suited to APEC. APEC is comprised of both Western and Asian members at various stages of economic development with a wide cross-section of legal and political systems. Thus, soft law may be increasingly utilised because it responds to the needs of the new international order. As Peng noted:

> The paradigm of APEC is essentially a mechanism based on voluntary consensus and peer pressure. This kind of 'soft' law, consisting of a set of commonly agreed skeletal principles stated in broad terms, is the preferred Asian way.[49]

APEC's approach is also significant for the development of a governance mechanism for international economic relations, insofar as APEC allows and encourages the participation of the non-government sector. An important consideration in 'modern' international law is the role of non-state actors. Where states once created and applied international norms through processes that lacked transparency, participation and accountability, non-state actors have demanded more transparency and participation in the process. Public participation is not only a goal but a reality in the development and implementation of international norms. In Chapter 2 of this volume, Caballero-Anthony referred to 'issues of participation and inclusion by non-state actors in the myriad regional processes that are taking place', and noted that 'attention to participation of other actors prompts us to probe further and examine whether the engagement of these society-based actors or civil society organisations have a significant bearing on how regional norms are translated into regional institutions'.[50] APEC emphasises the role of non-state participants in its governance process, for example, through its APEC Business Advisory Committee, a role that is possible only rarely in traditional law-making processes where states are concerned with creating *binding* obligations.[51]

The governance framework for Regional Trading Arrangements

Regional relationships are governed by the international legal framework regulating economic relations; Regional Trading Arrangements must conform to the international legal framework which constrains and shapes any economic cooperation among economic entities. Compliance with the framework is necessary to ensure that the formation of regional groups does not result in discriminatory practices, and that lack of uniformity does not severely hamper trade flows by the sheer fact of the costs involved for traders in meeting multiple sets of trade rules. The Asia-Pacific region has recently seen a surge in free trade agreements.[52] If these are to gradually develop into an Asia-Pacific Economic Community and not lead to fragmentation within the Asia-Pacific region, it is necessary to ensure that the formation and operation of these groupings conforms to an agreed framework governing the formation of RTAs.

Both hard law and soft law have a role to play in the formation of the framework governing RTAs. The 'hard' international rules are most

developed in the area of international trade, particularly in the legal framework comprised of the GATT and the other agreements administered
by the WTO. Of particular note to regionalism is Article XXIV of the
GATT, which makes provision for Free Trade Areas and Custom Unions.
Article XXIV of the GATT lists both substantive and procedural legal
requirements for WTO members to follow in order for an RTA to comply
with the WTO framework. More recently, Article V of the GATS makes
similar provisions for trade in services within RTAs. Of particular importance in regulating regional agreements among developing countries is the
Agreement on Differential and More Favourable Treatment, Reciprocity
and Fuller Participation of Developing Countries, which recognises tariff
and non-tariff preferential treatment in favour of and among developing
countries.

Soft law commitments – namely the APEC Best Practices for RTAs and
FTAs or APEC's NBIP – may also influence the development of these
agreements. The fact that the member economies of APEC have already
invested time and resources in negotiating these principles and that they
represent the consensus of the APEC economies, can influence new bilateral
negotiations between members. Although these 'Best Practices' and 'Principles' are non-binding in nature, they are evidence of a soft-law policy
approach and may be useful tools for the creation of other forms of regional
economic governance structures.

Soft law may be especially useful for establishing a framework to deal with
issues not currently regulated by the hard-law framework. There are a
number of areas of economic activity of concern in an RTA, for example,
which go beyond the requirements for liberalising trade as set out in the
WTO agreements and which are not regulated by the WTO or other international agreements or any other multilateral framework. A number of these
agreements deal with contentious issues which may be difficult to resolve by
conventional legal agreements, but could be dealt with by a 'softer'
approach; for instance, in regulating the investment aspects of an RTA. This
is supported by APEC Executive Director Heseltine, who suggested that 'a
lot of issues that are discussed have political sensitivities and negotiations are
likely to become bogged down if members are expected to sign on to binding
treaties or agreements'.[53]

In July 2007, APEC ministers responsible for trade reaffirmed that the
APEC model measures for RTAs/FTAs would serve as a reference for APEC
member economies to help them achieve comprehensive and high-quality
free trade agreements. They noted the progress in developing model measures for additional RTA/FTA chapters and instructed officials to accelerate
efforts to complete model measures for at least three additional chapters in
time for the APEC Ministerial Meeting in September 2007.[54] More recently,
in early 2008, APEC officials called for the RTAs between member economies to be expanded into an Asia-Pacific FTA. This Free Trade Area of the
Asia-Pacific (FTAAP) would seek to consolidate the trade outcomes from

existing agreements as well as generate new trade flows.[55] Any such FTAAP would need to draw upon the pre-existing soft- and hard-law approaches in order to obtain APEC members' approval.

Consolidating the ever-increasing number of RTAs into an Asia-Pacific Economic Community, or into a larger global community, 'may prove to be a very complicated task unless individual agreements are being designed towards convergence. This suggests the importance of developing guiding principles for the region.'[56] In some cases these principles may take the form of 'binding' obligations negotiated by the parties. However, in some cases it may be more appropriate/necessary to take a 'softer' approach to developing guiding principles. Although regionalism requires a strong international legal framework, this framework should not be restricted to 'hard' law, but should utilise 'soft' law where appropriate or necessary.

Conclusion

At the outset of this chapter, the question was posed, 'Is a new governance order for Asia more appropriate that may involve rules that do not fit existing definitions of international law?' As regionalism continues its rise, consideration should be given to the mechanisms for governance in the region. As Fidler noted:

> Framing the Asian century in terms of a governance challenge for world politics creates the need to discuss how governance of Asia's continued rise in power and prominence will be managed. Are existing governance mechanisms sufficient for the task, or will states in Asia and beyond need to create new institutions and arrangements to govern the power shifts taking place? Will the creation of new institutions require an expanded use of international law or other forms of law by Asian nations as they move to govern more effectively relations among themselves and with non-Asian states? These, and similar, questions can only be answered at a very general level; but even such general answers can be instructive in terms of how an Asian century might affect the role of international law in the governance of international relations.[57]

As observed above, the trend in Asia and across the Pacific has been the development of 'rules-based' governance to govern economic and other relations, of which a legal framework is an important component. However, if one continues to look at the evolving legal framework in Asia from the dichotomous viewpoint of 'binding' vs 'non-binding', 'law' vs 'non-law', then it will be difficult, if not impossible, to achieve development of the framework for governing relations.

Rules-based governance does not only comprise 'hard' law, but also 'softer' forms of legalisation, through a range of 'non-binding' commitments. The latter have an important role to play, particularly in an 'Asian' approach to governance. As Arner et al. note in the next chapter, in 'contrast to the rule-oriented WTO, the region's economic organisations and institutions are orientated towards dealings among participating states and are generally intended to have minimal impact on national sovereignty'.[58] Due to the economic and political differences within Asia, it may be more appropriate to develop a governance system which incorporates elements of 'soft' law rather than attempt to develop a legal framework which relies solely on 'binding' obligations. From an economic perspective, depending on the issue and other circumstances, a soft-law approach to certain matters instead of efforts to impose specific, binding rules for all situations may make good sense. A 'hybrid' system, comprising elements of both 'hard' and 'soft' law may be the preferred solution to governance of international economic relations in the Asia-Pacific region.

In such a 'hybrid' system of governance, soft law can contribute to the legal framework in two ways. First, soft law can be used to provide a degree of flexibility in the implementation of an agreed course of conduct that is otherwise established as 'hard law'. The agreed general principles provide a 'hard' framework to provide a certain degree of certainty and predictability, while allowing for flexibility in their implementation to account for such factors as levels of economic development or varying ways of achieving the same objectives. Such an approach may include a 'soft-governance' system of non-binding guidelines, periodic reporting indicators and a multilateral surveillance system to put pressure on parties to comply with their 'soft law' commitments and to allow for the imposition of sanctions if a party does not comply with the 'hard law' obligations.

Second, where parties are unable to agree to even general principles in a binding form, soft law may be used to reach agreement on the general principles of cooperation. Indeed, soft law may provide the only framework for cooperation. To reiterate what was discussed above, such an approach may include a soft-governance system of non-binding guidelines, periodic reporting indicators and a multilateral surveillance system to put pressure on parties to comply with their soft-law commitments.

International economic relations are becoming more complex and difficult, particularly where the parties have diverse economic, political and cultural backgrounds. The growing complexity is reflected in the increasing variety of forms of commitment adopted to govern international and regional relations. The evolving framework for economic cooperation may require an expanded use of international law to govern more effectively relations among economic partners. Soft law may become increasingly utilised because it responds to the needs of the new international system.

This approach may be particularly relevant within the Asia-Pacific region. Because of the economic and political differences within the Asia-Pacific economies, it may be more appropriate to develop (or continue) a governance system which includes a soft-law component. Such a governance system, although 'rules-based' from the viewpoint of developing norms to guide economic cooperation in the region, would maintain an 'Asian' approach in that it would allow flexibility and compromise, and rely on the use of non-adversarial and peer-pressure approaches for resolving disputes through policy dialogues, rather than via formal dispute-settlement processes.

A soft-law approach to governance offers a number of advantages, of which four in particular are relevant in the .context of the Asia-Pacific region. First, the utilisation of soft law allows for the possibility of differentiation in institutions involving a wide set of actors. Not all participants have to agree to be 'legally bound' to a course of action in order to move forward in respect of a certain matter. Closer cooperation among only a number of participants in the framework may be possible, with others joining as they are able/willing to do so.[59]

Second, a soft-law approach allows for flexibility and diversity. Binding harmonisation can be replaced by the non-binding coordination of policies and resources. As such, soft law allows states to adapt their commitments to their particular situations rather than try to devise a 'one size fits all' agreement. This allows for the accommodation of different economic structures and interests as well as providing scope for the renegotiation of agreements as circumstances change.

Third, soft law has lower sovereignty costs than legally binding agreements because states do not have the cost of the loss of authority of decision making in an issue area. This means that soft-law agreements are better able to promote cooperation while preserving sovereignty. As noted earlier, at the time that the ASEAN was formed, the original individual member states were hesitant to establish an organisation with strong powers over the members, preferring to maintain a high level of individual sovereignty, and established ASEAN with a structure that was organisationally loose and avoided the trappings of a strong regional organisation.[60] Indeed, as Chapter 1 noted, the challenges posed by suggestions of 'pooled sovereignty' and the tensions between regional states willing to adopt a more flexible form of governance and those that prefer to retain their full sovereign privileges are one of the key challenges currently facing the region. A greater utilisation of soft-law approaches would help to bridge this divide, while still moving the region towards deeper integration.

Fourth, soft law allows agreements to be made with parties that other parties to the agreement are not willing to formally recognise. APEC's soft-law approach, for example, created the situation whereby all 'three Chinas' – China, Hong Kong and Taiwan – were able to become members of the same organisation despite issues of status and conflict. As Hillgenberg has noted:

> It may be necessary to conclude a non-treaty agreement simply in order to reach an agreement at all … The fact that, when assessed realistically, the difference between a treaty and the binding 'political' effect of a non-treaty agreement is not as great to a politician as is often thought

may also play a role in the decision to opt for a non-treaty form of agreement.[61]

Finally, while it cannot be suggested that a 'soft law' approach is the better or preferable approach to regional governance, broadly, or economic governance, in particular, the above analysis does indicate that it should be considered as an alternative where appropriate, and that regional actors need not rush to the juridification of their activities as the only solution to the formation of rules-based governance. Both hard law and soft law have their place in the regulation of international and regional activity, and each has its unique advantages and disadvantages. As Bayne concluded, '[H]ard law and soft law are not alternatives. Rather, they serve different purposes and complement one another.'[62] When used together they can provide an effective solution to more efficient regional governance in Asia.

Notes

1 'The study found that law is certainly not, as some have argued, irrelevant to economic development in Asia', see Pistor, Katharina and Philip A. Wellons. *The Role of Law And Legal Institutions in Asian Economic Development, 1960–1995*. (New York: Oxford University Press, 1999), p. 15. The ASEAN law ministers have also noted that 'globalisation has revealed the close nexus between economic growth and legal systems such that a sound legal system and effective administration of justice is now seen as a key requirement for attaining economic and social growth.' See: *Joint Communique of the Fourth Meeting of ASEAN Law Ministers*. Singapore, 5–6 November 1999. http://www.aseansec.org/5662. htm. Accessed 29 November 2005.

2 Rajenthran, Arumugam. 'Indonesia: An Overview of the Legal Framework for Foreign Direct Investment', *Economics and Finance*. (No. 4, 2002). http://www. iseas.edu.sg/ef42002.pdf. Accessed 27 November, 2005.

3 'Regional Trade Agreements (RTAs) have become in recent years a very prominent feature of the Multilateral Trading System (MTS).The surge in RTAs has continued unabated since the early 1990s. Some 380 RTAs have been notified to the GATT/WTO up to July 2007. Of these, 300 RTAs were notified under Article XXIV of the GATT 1947 or GATT 1994; 22 under the Enabling Clause; and 58 under Article V of the GATS. At that same date, 205 agreements were in force.' WTO. 'Regional trade agreements', http://www.wto.org/english/tratop_e/ region_e/region_e.htm. Accessed 11 October 2008.

4 'Asian countries have traditionally been less enthusiastic about participation in RTAs ... However, the situation in Asia is changing rapidly.' Crawford, Jo and Sam Laird. 'Regional trade agreements and the WTO', *North American Journal of Economics and Finance*. (Vol. 12, No. 2, 2001), p. 195. For a look at trends relating to FTAs in East Asia, see: Japan External Trade Organisation (JETRO), *Prospects for Free Trade Agreements in East Asia*, (January 2003), http://www.jetro.go.jp/ en/stats/survey/studies/fta_eastasia.pdf. Accessed 18 November 2005. 'As of September 2006, there are an estimated 41 signed PTAs, 31 under negotiation, and 47 under discussion coming to a total of 119 agreements within the Asia-Pacific region.' Source: Scoles, Samuel and Linda Trutasnawint. 'Navigating Rules of Origin: A Look at ASEAN', in APEC. *The New International Architecture In Trade and Investment, Current Status and Implications*. APEC Human Resources

Development Working Group, Capacity Building Network, March 2007. http://www.apec.org/content/apec/publications/all_publications/human_resources_development.html. Accessed 4 September 2007.

5 See generally: Jackson, John. *The World Trading System – Law and Policy of International Economic Relations*, 2nd ed. (Cambridge, MA: MIT Press, 1997); and Trebilcock, Michael and Robert Howse. *The Regulation of International Trade*, 3rd ed. (New York: Routledge, 2005).

6 'If Europe and North America provide an implicit benchmark for high legalization, the Asia-Pacific region offers an important example of low legalization and possibly an explicit aversion to legalization ... More important, those regional institutions constructed with significant Asian participation remained highly informal and explicitly rejected legalization in their design.' Source: Kahler, Miles. 'Legalization as Strategy: The Asia-Pacific Case', *International Organization*. (Vol. 54, No. 3, 2000), p. 549.

7 Severino, H.E. Rodolfo C. Jr. 'Reforms and Integration in East Asia Could Strengthen Regional Stability', *Speech*. 14 August 1999.

8 Krahmann, Elke. 'National Regional, and Global Governance: One Phenomenon or Many?', *Global Governance*. (Vol. 9, No. 3, 2003), p. 323.

9 '"Governance" ... as opposed to "government", is the complex of more or less formalised bundles of rules, roles, and relationships that define the social practices of state and non-state actors interacting in various issue areas, rather than formal interstate organisations with budgets and buildings and authority to apply rules and impose sanctions.' Source: Kennedy, David. 'New Approaches to Comparative Law: Comparativism and International Governance', *Utah Law Review*. (No. 2, 1997), p. 548, fn. 4. This definition is supported by Snyder, who wrote: 'A multiplicity of other sites of governance complement, supplement, or compete with the State, hence the term "governance" instead of "government".' Source: Snyder, Francis. 'Economic Globalisation and the Law in the Twenty-First Century', in Austin Sarat (ed.). *The Blackwell Companion to Law and Society*. (Malden: Blackwell Publishers, 2004). http://www.blackwell reference. com/subscriber/tocnode?id = g9780631228967_chunk_g978063122896735. Accessed 12 May 2008.

10 Commission on Global Governance, *Our Global Neighbourhood* (New York: Oxford University Press, 1995) p. 2, as quoted in Burchill, Richard. 'International Law's Contribution to Democratic Multi Level Governance: the Position of Regional Intergovernmental Organisations', Paper prepared for conference on Multi-Level Governance: Interdisciplinary Perspectives, 28–30 June 2001, University of Sheffield, p. 2.

11 Weiss, Thomas G. and Ramesh Thakur. *The UN and Global Governance: An Unfinished Journey*. (Bloomington, IN: University of Indiana Press, forthcoming 2009).

12 Krahmann, 'National Regional, and Global Governance: One Phenomenon or Many?', p. 329.

13 The term 'state' is used here to include an economic entity which has control over the conduct of its economy.

14 Dixit, Avinash. 'Lawlessness and Economics: Alternative Modes of Economic Governance', Gorman Lectures – University College, London. (December 2002), p. 11. http://www.econ.ucl.ac.uk/ downloads/Lec1.pdf. Accessed 29 November, 2005.

15 For a more detailed discussion of the consensus model, see Thambipillai, Pushpa and J. Saravanamuttu. *ASEAN Negotiations – Two Insights*. (Singapore: ISEAS, 1985), pp. 10–13.

16 Solidum, Estrella. 'The Role of Certain Sectors in Shaping and Articulating the ASEAN Way', in R.P. Anand and Purificacion Quisumbing (eds). *ASEAN Identity, Development and Culture*. (Manila: UP Law Center and East West

Center Culture Learning Institute, 1981), p. 138. See also: Solidum, Estrella. 'An ASEAN Perspective on the Decision-Making Process in the European Community', in Purificacion Quisumbing and Benjamin Domingo (eds). *EEC and ASEAN: Two Regional Community Experiences.* (Manila: Foreign Service Institute and UP Law Center, 1983), pp. 127–131.

17 Van den Bossche, Peter and Iveta Alexovicová. 'Effective Global Economic Governance by the World Trade Organization', *Journal of International Economic Law.* (Vol. 8, No. 3, 2005), p. 667.

18 'The rules of the WTO can also be beneficial by reducing uncertainty regarding the policies that will be applied by governments – thus potentially helping to increase domestic investment and reduce risks.' Source: Hoekman, Bernard, Constantine Michalopoulos and L. Alan Winters. 'Special and Differential Treatment of Developing Countries in the WTO: Moving Forward After Cancún', *World Economy.* (Vol. 27, No. 4, 2004), p. 482.

19 Reich, Arie. 'From Diplomacy to Law: The Juridicization of International Trade Relations', *Northwestern Journal of International Law and Business.* (Vol. 17, No. 2/3, 1996/97), pp. 775–849.

20 'The WTO system rests on some well-known governance devices … The relative clarity of most rules, together with the surveillance and consultation procedures of the organization, facilitates the monitoring of compliance … An argument can be made for the proposition that the resulting system is more predictable and thus more effective in a heavily rule-oriented governance system.' Tarullo, Daniel K. 'Norms and Institutions in Global Competition Policy', *American Journal of International Law.* (Vol. 94, No. 3, 2000), pp. 487–488.

21 This feeling of the member states can be seen in an earlier statement of Ruslan Abdulgani, then Deputy First Minister of Indonesia: 'We fought to win the right to express and to develop our national identities. Must we now merge all this into a common denominator in our continuing struggle? I think we must not be so unrealistic … Our solidarity must not be allowed to mitigate against the fullest possible development of the national characteristics of each of our countries.' Source: Selo, Soemardjan. 'Introduction' in R.P. Anand and Purificacion Quisumbing (eds). *ASEAN Identity, Development and Culture.* (Manila: UP Law Center and East West Center Culture Learning Institute, 1981), p. xiii.

22 Joint Communiqué, 1st Ministerial Meeting, Bangkok, 8th of August 1967 – *The ASEAN Declaration*, as reproduced in Davidson, Paul J. *Trading Arrangements in the Pacific Rim.* (New York: Oxford University Press Oceana Publications Inc., 1995–) (hereafter *TAPR*), Document I.B.2.

23 This need was highlighted by H.E. Megawati Soekarnopoetri, in her opening statement at the Thirty-Sixth ASEAN Economic Ministers Meeting in Jakarta on 3 September 2004: 'in achieving the goal of an ASEAN Economic Community by 2020, much effort must be placed in realizing a *rules-based* economic system, where business activities will be guided by an adequate set of internationally accepted, transparent and consistent market-based investment and trading rules and practices.' Source: *The Thirty-Sixth ASEAN Economic Ministers Meeting Joint Media Statement.* (Jakarta: 3 September 2004). http://www.aseansec.org/16377.htm. Accessed 15 August 2007.

24 Severino, Rodolfo. 'Reforms and Integration in East Asia Could Strengthen Regional Stability', *Speech.* 14 August 1999. http://www.aseansec.org/golek.html. Accessed 20 November 2005.

25 While there is no doubt that the individual member states of ASEAN are recognised as sovereign states with full treaty-making powers, it is not clear in law that ASEAN, as an entity, currently represents more than an association of states that has no legal personality itself. However, this does not mean that ASEAN as an organisation has not developed any international legal personality

distinct from the international legal personality of its member states. More and more, other countries have shown and are showing an interest in dealing with ASEAN as a collectivity. For a fuller discussion, see, Davidson, Paul J. *ASEAN – The Evolving Legal Framework for Economic Cooperation.* (Singapore: Times Academic Press, 2002). The member states of ASEAN have recently taken steps to clearly transform ASEAN into a rules-based organisation with a legal personality, through the signing of the ASEAN Charter – see following discussion.

26 *ASEAN Protocol on Enhanced Dispute Settlement Mechanism*, 29 November 2004, http://www.aseansec.org/16754.htm. Accessed 20 November 2005. The new ASEAN Charter, Article 24, provides that disputes which concern the interpretation or application of ASEAN economic agreements are to be settled in accordance with this Protocol.

27 *Kuala Lumpur Declaration on the Establishment of the ASEAN Charter.* (Kuala Lumpur: 12 December 2005). http://www.aseansec.org/18030.htm. Accessed 9 May 2008. (Emphasis added).

28 *Joint Communiqué of the 40th ASEAN Ministerial Meeting (AMM), 'One Caring and Sharing Community'*, 29–30 July 2007. http://www.aseansec.org/20764.htm. Accessed 22 October 2007. (Emphasis added)

29 Yuan, Jing-dong and Lorraine Eden. 'Export Processing Zones in Asia: A Comparative Study', *Asian Survey.* (Vol. 32, No. 11, November 1992), p. 1045.

30 H.E. Rodolfo C. Severino, Jr. has pointed out that 'the financial crisis had convinced East Asian countries that they must move away from a "relationship-based" way of doing business and creating wealth to one that was more "rules-based" and market-driven.' See: Rodolfo C. Severino. 'Reforms and Integration in East Asia Could Strengthen Regional Stability', *Speech*, 14 August 1999.

31 Dixit, Avinash. 'Lawlessness and Economics: Alternative Modes of Economic Governance', p. 11. See also: Li, Shuhe. 'The Benefits and Costs of Relation-based Governance: An Explanation of the East Asian Miracle and Crisis'. http://ideas.repec.org/p/eab/govern/209.html. Accessed 19 November 2005.

32 Balana, Cynthia, 'Rights violators to be treated "ASEAN" way', *Inquirer,* 1 August 2007. http://services.inquirer.net/print/print.php?article_id = 79849. Accessed 13 June 2008.

33 *Chairman's Statement of the Second East Asia Summit.* (Cebu: 15 January 2007). http://www.aseansec.org/19302.htm. Accessed 9 May 2008. (Emphasis added)

34 Goldstein, Judith, Miles Kahler, Robert O. Keohane and Anne-Marie Slaughter. 'Introduction: Legalization and World Politics', *International Organization.* (Vol. 54, No. 3, 2000), p. 385.

35 Kohona, Palitha T.B. *The Regulation of International Economic Relations Through Law.* (Dordrecht: Martinus Nijhoff Publishers, 1985), p. 38.

36 These mechanisms can take a number of forms, ranging from more formal to less formal methods – litigation, arbitration, mediation, conciliation, negotiation. In this regard, it should be noted that it is not necessary to have a 'court' to have 'law'.

37 This characterisation of legalisation may be compared to that of Abbott, Keohane, et al., who consider legalisation as being characterised by three components: obligation, precision and delegation. 'These characteristics are defined along three dimensions: obligation, precision, and delegation. *Obligation* means that states or other actors are bound by a rule or commitment or by a set of rules or commitments. Specifically, it means that they are *legally* bound by a rule or commitment in the sense that their behaviour thereunder is subject to scrutiny under the general rules, procedures, and discourse of international law, and often of domestic law as well. *Precision* means that rules unambiguously define the conduct they require, authorise, or proscribe. *Delegation* means that third parties

have been granted authority to implement, interpret, and apply the rules; to resolve disputes; and (possibly) to make further rules.' See: Abbott, Kenneth, Robert O. Keohane, Andrew Moravcsik, Anne-Marie Slaughter and Duncan Snidal. 'The Concept of Legalization', *International Organization*. (Vol. 54, No. 3, Summer, 2000), pp. 401–419. (Italics in original).

38 Craik, A. Neil. 'Recalcitrant Reality And Chosen Ideals: The Public Function Of Dispute Settlement In International Environmental Law', *Georgetown International Environmental Law Review*. (Vol. 10, No. 2, 1998) pp. 551–580, as cited in Peng Shin-yi. 'The WTO Legalistic Approach and East Asia: From the Legal Culture Perspective', *Asian Pacific Law & Policy Journal*. (Vol. 13, 2000), p. 20. http://www.hawaii.edu/aplpj/pdfs/13-peng.pdf. Accessed 10 January 2008.

39 Gold, Joseph. 'Strengthening the Soft International Law of Exchange Agreements', *The American Journal of International Law*. (Vol. 77, No. 3, 1983), p. 443.

40 Ibid.

41 Shelton, Dinah. 'Law, Non-Law and the Problem of "Soft Law"', in Dinah Shelton (ed.). *Commitment and Compliance: The Role of Non-Binding Norms in the International Legal System*. (Oxford: Oxford University Press, 2000), p. 2.

42 Shelton, Dinah. 'Law, Non-Law and the Problem of "Soft Law"', p. 15.

43 Shelton, Dinah. 'Law, Non-Law and the Problem of "Soft Law"', p. 1.

44 See, for example, General Agreement on Tariffs and Trade (GATT). 'Article 37: Commitments', which states that: 'The developed contracting parties shall to the fullest extent possible – that is, except when compelling reasons, which may include legal reasons, make it impossible – give effect to the following provisions.' http://www.worldtradelaw.net/uragreements/gatt.pdf. Accessed 20 January 2008. p. 39.

45 Shelton, Dinah. 'Law, Non-Law and the Problem of "Soft Law"', p. 10. (Emphasis added).

46 Gold, Joseph. 'Strengthening the Soft International Law of Exchange Agreements', pp. 443–444. It is arguable whether 'firm law would be *preferable*'. In many cases it may be preferable to consider a more intensive examination of soft law as appropriate. A soft law approach might be a desirable alternative rather than simply a second-best solution. As Abbott and Snidal have also stated: '[I]nternational actors often deliberately choose softer forms of legalization as superior institutional arrangements. To be sure, soft law is sometimes designed as a way station to harder legalization, but often it is preferable on its own terms.' See, Abbott, Kenneth and Duncan Snidal. 'Hard and Soft Law in International Governance', *International Organization*. (Vol. 54, No. 3, Summer, 2000), p. 423.

47 See: 'IAP Peer Reviews: APEC Member Economies Make Progress', *APEC E-Newsletter*. (Vol. 12, March 2007). http://www.apec.org/apec/enewsletter/mar_vol12/onlinenewsa.html. Accessed 20 September 2007.

48 A peer-review process has also been used in APEC by the Sub-Committee on Customs Procedures. The SCCP Peer Review Process began in 2002 as a means to help assess the depth of implementation of the SCCP Collective Action Plan (CAP) items. Three peer reviews were completed by the SCCP Peer Review process; however, funding for the process expired at the end of 2006, and the United States recommended that this initiative be removed from the SCCP agenda after the SCCP meeting in January 2007.

49 Peng Shin-yi. 'The WTO Legalistic Approach and East Asia: From the Legal Culture Perspective', p. 13. This point is supported by Hiscock, who stated that: 'The APEC [non-binding Investment] Principles are an excellent example of the changed patterns of law making. They are best described as "soft" or "fuzzy"

law – a set of commonly agreed skeletal principles, stated in broad terms, establishing a minimum standard of treatment for foreign investors.' Source: Hiscock, Mary. 'Changing Patterns of Regional Law Making in Southeast Asia', *St Louis University Law Journal*. (Vol. 39, Spring 1995), p. 939.

50 Caballero-Anthony, Mely. 'Evolving regional governance in East Asia: from ASEAN to an East Asian community', Chapter 2 in this volume, p. XXX.

51 Regional economic governance within ASEAN also encompasses a set of actors beyond the state. The private sector in ASEAN also plays a formal role in economic governance through the ASEAN Business Advisory Council (ABAC), which has been mandated by the ASEAN Heads of State and Government as the official ASEAN linkage to provide private sector feedback and guidance to boost ASEAN's efforts towards economic integration, and to identify priority areas for consideration by the ASEAN leaders. The ASEAN Business Advisory Council was launched in April 2003 in Jakarta, Indonesia, and holds a regular ASEAN Business and Investment Summit just before the annual ASEAN Summit. This timing allows for private sector issues to be fed into the Summit discussions.

52 See supra, note 4.

53 Fang, Nicholas. 'Apec's Lack of Binding Powers Keeps It Useful', *The Straits Times*. 20 November 2007.

54 As the ministers stated: 'We took note of the concerns of the business community over possible complexities caused by the spread of RTAs/FTAs and the possibility of trade diversion. To this end we have instructed officials to examine, in close cooperation with the business sector, the scope for a rationalisation of preferential rules of origin and other relevant provisions of such agreements and to report to us when next we meet. The model measures for RTA/FTA chapters are a pioneering contribution by APEC to promote greater consistency and coherence among the RTAs/FTAs within the region ... Ministers reaffirmed that the model measures would serve as a reference for APEC member economies to help them achieve comprehensive and high-quality free-trade agreements and reiterated the nonbinding and voluntary nature of the model measures. We noted the progress in developing model measures for additional RTA/FTA chapters and have instructed our officials to accelerate efforts to complete model measures for at least three additional chapters in time for the APEC Ministerial Meeting in September.' Source: *Meeting of APEC Ministers Responsible for Trade*. (Cairns: 5–6 July 2007.) http://www.apec.org/content/apec/ministerial_statements/sectoral_ministerial/trade/2007_trade.html. Accessed 20 January 2008.

55 'Peru to Seek Creation of APEC Free-Trade Area', *Deutsche Presse-Agentur*. 18 February 2008.

56 Soesastro, Hadi. 'APEC's Trade Policy Challenges: The Doha Development Agenda and Regional/Bilateral FTAs', *Information paper prepared for SOM Policy Dialogue on RTAs/FTAs*. (Khon Kaen, 27 May 2003), APEC 2003/SOM II/RTAs/FTAs/008, p. 20.

57 Fidler, David P. 'The Asian Century: Implications for International Law', *Singapore Year Book of International Law*. (Vol. 9, 2005), p. 13.

58 Arner, Douglas W., Paul Lejot and Wei Wang. 'East Asian governance: implications for policy cooperation, regionalism and financial integration', Chapter 10 in this volume, p. XXX.

59 Compare this with the situation in the European Union where 'not all the Member States have to agree in order to move forward in respect of a certain matter'. Source: Senden, Linda, 'Soft Law, Self Regulation and Co-regulation in European Law: Where Do They Meet?', *Electronic Journal of Comparative Law*. (Vol. 9, No. 1, 2005). http://www.ejcl.org/. Accessed 20 December 2007.

60 See supra, at note 21.

61 Hillgenberg, Hartmut. 'A Fresh Look at Soft Law', *European Journal of International Law*. (Vol. 10, No. 3, 1999), pp. 501–502.
62 Bayne, Nicholas. 'Hard and Soft Law in International Institutions: Complements, Not Alternatives', in John Kirton and Michael J. Trebilcock (eds). *Hard Choices, Soft Law Voluntary Standards in Global Trade, Environment and Social Governance*. (Aldershot, England and Burlington, USA: Ashgate, 2004), p. 347.

10 East Asian governance

Implications for policy cooperation, regionalism and financial integration

Douglas W. Arner, Paul Lejot and Wei Wang

Introduction

The extent of financial integration among East Asia's newly industrialised and developing states matches neither the rhetoric expended in its support since the region's financial crisis of 1997–98, nor the degree of economic integration among the same states and with their highly industrialised neighbours, Australia, Japan and New Zealand. Regional trade flows and cross-border direct investment have long been greater and faster growing than other capital flows, while regional institutions that bear on financial markets are scarce or insubstantial. The interplay between national and international financial markets is limited, even among states that maintain relatively sophisticated financial systems, such as Korea or Singapore. No existing market can be considered regional: Asian actors freely enter global capital market transactions denominated in major currencies, but regional markets are underdeveloped and price-opaque. This dichotomy persists, despite several influences since the early 1990s that suggested that Asian financial integration would accelerate, and in apparent contradiction of the development of regional organisations such as the Association of Southeast Asian Nations (ASEAN) and of the enthusiasm of the region's states for the World Trade Organisation (WTO). Above all, it differs from post-crisis expectations that greater financial integration would help to guard against new shocks.

In reviewing the main elements of Asian financial integration to date, this chapter will suggest that two explanations relating to governance underpin the paradox of modest financial integration accompanying generally successful economic growth and economic integration. First, the long-standing cultural norms that have been expressed regularly within ASEAN and similar bodies which are characterised as the mild and quiescent 'ASEAN Way' have tended to militate against regional innovation in financial markets and systems, insofar as meaningful reforms in transnational institutions or organisations would represent sacrifices in state autonomy. This need for strict consensuality at best encourages incremental or pedestrian reform at a regional level. Second, similar cultural and socio-economic norms provide resistance to transparent market-oriented regional solutions, even when they may arise through cooperation among states. In particular, the primacy of banking systems within all East Asian national economies and close sym- biotic relationships between state and banking-sector actors have slowed the progress of regional financial integration, with neither group prepared to have its role in financial governance weakened by countervailing regional institutions or organisations.

Throughout this chapter, references to economic or financial integration are intended to signify no transnational political objectives unless stated. Shortly before the 1957 Treaty of Rome created the original European Eco- nomic Community, economic integration was regarded by one influential libertarian scholar as: '[T]he establishment of a condition which makes pos- sible the free and reciprocal flow of trade between the various national econo- mies',[1] requiring the free trade in goods and free movement of capital funds.[2] Thus, to assess integration by the permissiveness of cross-border regional trade and capital flows seems entirely fitting to contemporary East Asia.[3]

This chapter will show the extent to which economic and financial aspects of regional governance in Asia have become manifest mainly in transna- tional organisations and institutions and through 'functional cooperation' in national state policy,[4] especially in regional trade, dispute resolution, monetary cooperation and economic policy. The second section reviews the structure of East Asian financial integration in relation to issues of governance. The third section then identifies four factors that explain the extent of the region's current financial integration, while section four examines progress made in the specific fields of the trade in financial services, cooperation in monetary policy, and capital market development. After this the chapter asks whether Europe's path to financial integration may be a guide for future financial integration in Asia in ways more constructive and specific than implied by early theorists of regionalism. The chapter concludes with recommendations for future consideration. The chapter is directly concerned only with finan- cial integration and does not attempt to address the significance of standards of governance for financial market behaviour, for example, by influencing confidence or asset valuations. Financial governance in Asia is the concern of state or commercial actors and influenced only modestly by external official sources such as regional transnational organisations.

East Asian financial cooperation and structures of governance

Financial integration is associated with capital mobility, and is the extent to which a national economy's financial system is not shielded from or made distinct from other national and international capital markets.[5] Such inte- gration is difficult to identify consistently, because it can often be quantified only by proxy, and since its use was for long conflated with other forms of cross-border integration. Financial integration emphasises wholesale activity and examines only secondarily aspects of retail financial intermediation involving individuals, so that borders to the trade in retail financial services are well preserved, even in well-integrated regions such as the European Union (EU). Financial integration has been taken elsewhere to refer to price correlations of markets or systems, for example in securities or interest rates.[6] This is relevant to this chapter only in that arbitrage seeking to profit from such correlations may involve capital movements of the kind obstructed by Asia's lack of integration. Financial integration is taken as distinct from integration in commerce, economic policy, monetary policy or political cooperation.

Evidence of a direct relationship between financial integration and economic growth is inconclusive.[7] This is significant in terms of state norms in East Asia, given that national capital controls have often been regarded as anathema to transnational organisations such as the Asian Development Bank (ADB), International Monetary Fund (IMF) or the WTO. Capital controls became somewhat more favoured due to their use by states such as China and Malaysia that were relatively lightly affected by the 1997 Asian financial crisis.

Concepts of governance often abstract from thin material. While governance has been taken to involve a proactive state 'sustaining coordination and coherence among a wide variety of actors'[8] that may include transnational organisations, it may also represent the 'empirical manifestations of state adaptation to its external environment', or alternatively a 'theoretical representation of coordination of social systems'[9] by the state and others. Such conceptual inclusiveness allows a discussion of aspects of governance observed in East Asian regional financial integration to include instances where none exists, that is, an absence of governance analogous to the view of current Asian regionalism being a form of 'pre-governance',[10] as well as the roles taken by non-state actors, especially those prominent in the financial sector. The most appropriate approach for this analysis may be to regard governance as '[t]he processes and institutions, both formal and informal, that guide and restrain the collective activities of a group'.[11] Weakness in these institutions reflects an absence of regional governance.

Asian financial integration is modest, even though cross-border acquisitions, joint ventures and other forms of cross-border investment are well established and require substantial transfers of funding or capital goods.[12] That Asia's financial integration fails to match its considerable economic integration may appear inconsistent with the sophistication of certain national financial systems. The explanation may result from the influence of cultural norms operating at state and substate level that will be seen to govern behaviour within Asia's regional institutions and organisations. This influence is manifested in an elective aspect of state governance, that is, the primacy of certain national economic policies with which regional financial integration is commonly deemed inconsistent. Such norms are represented comprehensively by the 'ASEAN Way', stemming from ASEAN's founding declaration and succeeding first treaty and involving consensual decision making and commitments to mutual non-interference by member states. It was characterised during the 1997 Asian crisis by Singapore's then foreign minister as stressing 'informality, organizational minimalism, inclusiveness, intensive consultations leading to consensus, and peaceful resolution, of disputes'.[13] The nature of financial governance in Asia as revealed in the behaviour of its regional organisations and institutions is thus the result of weak regional norms competing with paramount national policy. Today's limited financial integration may be regarded as having been achieved in spite of such norms.

Founded in 1967, ASEAN is now the most conspicuous institution associated with regionalism in Asia, in part due to its having effectively expanded to include the dominant economies of Northeast Asia in China, Japan and Korea through the mechanism known as ASEAN+3 (APT). Throughout this chapter, ASEAN and APT are referred to as organisations or the products of institutional arrangements, since their existence is real if measured by actions or norms. It is less clear in law that either body represents at a non-trivial level more than an association of states without legal personality.[14] Were ASEAN to choose to make substantive agreements with third parties, for example in relation to trade with a non-ASEAN state, then each member would enter a separate treaty. ASEAN is thus more an expression of aims than a constitutional body, and this 'soft' personality constrains its capacity in regional governance.

ASEAN was for a long time unconcerned with financial sector issues, despite existing over a period of extended economic growth and integration among its members. However, it began exploring financial regionalism in the mid 1990s, influenced by the 1997 financial crisis, a consensual wish to see the region distinguished from elsewhere, and a surge in the growth of trade and direct investment with China. Thus, in 1995 ASEAN's heads of governments declared that it:

> shall move towards greater economic integration by building on existing economic cooperation activities, initiating new areas of cooperation, and promoting closer cooperation in international fora.[15]

ASEAN's first substantive venture in financial cooperation was made in early 1997, and the resulting understanding is a general framework for cooperation in banking, capital markets, customs, insurance, taxation, and human resource development, in each case through mechanisms provided by existing institutions.[16] The protocol encourages members to exchange views on macro-economic policies, improve policy and regulatory transparency, hold meetings among policy makers and regulators, and promote links between the state and commercial sectors. This is made subject to ASEAN's consensual approach with the proviso that two or more member states may engage in the 'implementation of programmes and projects' at their chosen pace rather than be delayed by others.[17] The qualification is less an advance in regional governance than an acknowledgement that financially under-developed states may lack the means or wish to engage in joint policies. Wholly new initiatives must be sanctioned by all members. The activities in which the states are exhorted to participate are stated briefly and without the 'functional specificity' held by early theorists of regionalism to be 'causally related to the intensity of integration'.[18]

More generally, the APT states have not been prepared to relinquish the high degree of national policy control that is a corollary of weak or non-existent regional institutions, organisations or markets. This may be distinguished from an absence of regional governance similar to the concept of 'pre-governance',[19] inasmuch as it represents deliberate choice rather than a formative period that will tend to give way to regional governance. It includes effective authority in governance given to certain non-state actors, in particular in national banking sectors. Thus, the extent of regional integration may be thought consistent with shared norms, whether deliberate as expressed in the consensuality and mutual non-interference of the 'ASEAN Way' and in making paramount other aspects of state policy, or indirect, such as the pivotal role in governance of commercial and banking interests. The organisation of Asian capitalism has been effective in this respect, characterised by close directional relationships between the state and leading commercial interests, including state enterprises.[20] It has been asserted, for example, that:

> authority structures in the Asia Pacific serve the interests of dominant actors and statebusiness [*sic*] coalitions, and that these actors are organized into informal networks of power, that is, particular informal modes of regional governance, serving private as well as public interests.[21]

This institutionalised involvement of non-state actors in Asian governance is distinct from the more general proposition that international economic activities of all non-state participants may contribute to governance.[22]

The most dramatic manifestation of regionalism being subsumed into national policy objectives is East Asia's rapid and substantial accumulation of international reserves since 2000, a consequence of the primacy of national exchange rate policy over financial integration or regional financial market development. Thus, the shared commitments and policies implicit in financial regionalism are constrained by national objectives. This is illustrated by the portion of APT international reserves pooled in a regional integration initiative representing only a small fraction of the aggregate.[23] The forcefulness of national policy has long been recognised in the context of regional integration:

> Organizations with an economic mandate short of creating a common market or free trade area have great difficulty in influencing the policies of their members.[24]

In this instance, the paradox for financial integration is that national post-crisis policies and risk aversion are similar and appear to be conducive to cooperation. While a relatively modest degree of integration might impact on existing arrangements for governance, it seems that greater connectivity and interdependence among both Asian states and substate participants do not imply greater financial integration, for regional institutions and organisations require shared objectives among their founders, as well as a mutual interdependence.[25]

Factors encouraging financial integration

Four particular factors have encouraged financial integration to become an overt aspect of governance, notably the 1997 financial crisis, but also economic integration, developmental issues and certain political imperatives.

Crisis imperatives

The 1997 Asian crisis has had a significant and enduring impact on national economies and on the stance of policy makers. The economic and social dislocation provoked in Korea and Southeast Asia by the exhaustion of confidence produced among state actors a concern that Asia lacked effective crisis remedies, either national or regional, since only non-Asian organisations such as the IMF could make available credit sufficient to stem the draining of external resources. More lastingly, it induced a profound risk aversion among policy makers anxious to protect against similar shocks. While this disposition initially helped to bring about limited financial sector reform, it has also prevented the introduction of significant regional solutions involving financial integration.

A further controversy arose soon after the crisis in the appraisal of external capital controls. During this period China and Malaysia maintained or introduced barriers to the flow of funds, contrary to the customary advice of the IMF and other transnational organisations. Each suffered lesser falls in output and financial market capitalisation after 1997, with the crisis felt most severely by states such as Indonesia, Korea and Thailand which had minimal controls on capital inflows. This is not to imply that free movement of capital will always induce external vulnerability, but these examples encouraged the perception in East Asia that the 'open' policies associated with the 'Washington Consensus' were deleterious to recovery.[26] National norms may have thus benefited at the expense of a more regional orientation. Capital mobility is entombed for policy makers as contributing to the severity of the 1997 crisis, making financial integration a low priority for APT actors.

The crisis signalled helplessness among Asia's regional organisations. This reflected the scale of its impact, added to a lack of prior attention to regional financial structure and resources. In 1997 no Asian organisation could provide even temporary help to any state, leading to the irony that Indonesia,

Korea and Thailand experienced an invasiveness towards national policy making and inappropriate credit restrictions that were contrary to all ASEAN precepts. Short-term IMF credit was essential, but was extended on output-reducing terms and without concern for non-interference in national state governance. Thailand first sought emergency liquidity from Japan in early 1997, but no mechanism existed to allow meaningful support and neither Japan nor the United States wished to abandon the conditionality of funding associated with IMF programmes, not least to protect their own influence. This impasse led to suggestions for new institutions, notably in Japan's proposals for an Asian Monetary Fund, but subsequent discussions on these issues have been obstructed by the US whenever possible.

Thus, the crisis revealed weaknesses in national financial systems while drawing attention to imperfect but well-established economic and financial linkages within the region that made each state vulnerable to contagion from any severe systemic shock. Its aftermath produced certain national reforms intended to bolster recovery and improve crisis avoidance. These sought to increase the visibility and effectiveness of national financial markets and alter the extent of state control of the financial system, but in most cases the scale of change was modest. State influence persists in financial market operations, and the startling results of national currency management have lessened the immediate incentives for domestic or regional financial reform.

Finally, the crisis led to the only attempt yet made to move away from ASEAN's doctrine of mutual non-interference. Thailand proposed in 1997–98 the adoption of 'flexible engagement' to signify active policy dealings among member states. The requirements and implications were not fully developed but it was clear that the change stemmed from a view that certain ASEAN members faced a common assault in the form of rapidly depreciating currencies and the withdrawal of international credit, which might be better resisted through cooperation more advanced than was contemplated by ASEAN precepts. The proposal received minimal support and was abandoned as unworkable. The consensus that rejected flexible engagement in 1998 was described as:

> the vision of ASEAN 2020 in which there will be a free flow of goods, services and investments, a *freer* flow of capital,[27] equitable economic development and reduced poverty and socioeconomic disparities. This closer economic integration will be achieved, among other strategies, by fully implementing AFTA [the ASEAN Free Trade Area].[28]

The suggestion that the movement of capital might eventually be 'freer' acknowledges the limits that states wish to set upon financial integration. Nothing in these remarks addresses the issue of the usefulness in crises of Asia's regional institutions. It is implicit in the stance that ASEAN will not engage in rule making. With APT now superseding ASEAN in high-level policy formation, it is unlikely that flexible engagement will revive, given

China's adherence to the existing approach and heightened nationalism in Thailand and elsewhere.

Economic influences

In the absence of national restrictions, growing trade and investment would be expected to increase the demand for financial instruments, in both scale and variety, most clearly in cross-border trade finance, funding for direct investment and the requirements of the commercial sector for treasury and cash management tools. While many Asian public and private sector users now have access to sophisticated financial instruments and applications, the extent of such activity within the region or denominated in local currencies is materially lower than is suggested by Asia's flows of trade and investment. This is the most visible result of relatively undeveloped financial integration. Thus the demand for financial instruments and systems associated with economic integration signals an array of impediments to regional and national financial market activity.[29] The fourth section of this chapter describes initiatives to address such impediments; none has seen full success. Problems remain at national level, for which a regional reform consensus could be valuable.

Developmental factors

Having the means to use regional resources to support regional development is an issue distinct from that of encouraging economic development through crisis avoidance. Part of Asia's post-2000 crisis response has been the precautionary acquisition of non-Asian financial assets, which has been closely connected to national currency management in the same period. Thus, state actors now control very substantial foreign reserves but the scale of their accumulation has prompted concern as to concentration of risk and the question as to whether a portion of these resources might be allocated to Asian assets and support development within the region.

Furthermore, most Asian economies have comparatively high rates of precautionary savings. Individuals tend to hold their savings as bank deposits, and high bank liquidity has often been associated with poor risk appraisal or indiscriminate lending. A development imperative thus focuses on encouraging deeper and more transparent financial markets, allowing broader uses of foreign reserves and applying savings to support economic development.

Political forces

Politics is a pervasive influence on the extent and character of financial integration, but beyond the direct scope of this chapter. The relative competitive positions and historic rivalries of states are significant in discussions on regional integration. The influence of China or India is encouraging other states to favour cooperation for defensive reasons, and similar interests may wish to counter the political-economic weight of the European Union and United States. At the same time, such efforts may be diluted by the increasing number of bilateral trade agreements within the region, notwithstanding the view that Asia's 'noodle bowl' network of such agreements may provide a foundation for universal free trade.[30]

Financial integration and development initiatives

Financial integration in Asia has been subject to considerable but equivocal attention, with results that reflect the paradox described in the opening sections of this chapter, of financial integration lagging behind economic integration. Asia's transnational organisations are important in this for two reasons. First, they represent, in part, extant regional institutions, and their limitations thus illustrate a chosen stance towards shared governance. Second, organisations such as the ADB and ASEAN have tended to provide support for states when they elect to conduct financial reform. State initiatives to encourage financial integration fall into three categories: trade in financial services, cooperation in monetary affairs and cooperation in finance, the latter marked so far by debt-capital market reform. This framework is similar to long-standing international financial architecture, with interest in monetary affairs, development and trade allocated to the IMF, World Bank and the WTO respectively. Note that Japan's strategies for financial cooperation, including reforming taxation through a web of treaties, are beyond the direct scope of this analysis.

There is no single view as to whether Asian financial development is more appropriately directed at domestic or regional issues. The 'Washington Consensus' traditionally saw domestic market development as contributing a greater benefit in utility and crisis prevention, and suggested that regional development is secondary. Asian policy makers may be more malleable, but the historical result of such differences has been for reform to arise in the forum of least resistance. Thus, APT has addressed regional development issues to which the US was opposed, while the Asia-Pacific Economic Cooperation forum (APEC) became a focus for proposals to which the US will lend support, including domestic financial development. For example, post-crisis proposals were mooted in APEC and by the ADB to capitalise a regional organisation to provide commercial credit enhancement in structured finance transactions, but lapsed due to the views of non-Asian participants or shareholders.[31] This chapter contends that both domestic and regional approaches to reform have value and may be mutually reinforcing.

Trade in financial services

Limited growth has occurred in the regional trade in financial services and improvements are likely to occur only slowly. This analysis examines one aspect of a proposed Asian Economic Community embracing APT, India, Australia and New Zealand, which may become the institutional framework for Asian economic cooperation.[32] The issue covers economic cooperation through financial services liberalisation, the structure of AFTA, and APEC's interest in the international framework for financial services liberalisation.

ASEAN Free Trade Area

AFTA began in 1992 as part of a wider ASEAN protocol on economic cooperation.[33] The breadth of the protocol's coverage means that, in common with other ASEAN initiatives, there is doubt as to whether it constitutes a treaty among members.[34] AFTA's legally substantive initiating institution is the 1995 Agreement on the Common Effective Preferential Tariff Scheme (CEPT) for AFTA, which sets objectives for members to eliminate tariffs and non-tariff barriers.[35] Later modifications set a goal for ASEAN members of the elimination of import duties by 2015.[36] Similar objectives have been adopted within APT and the China–ASEAN, Korea–ASEAN and Japan–ASEAN free trade areas that are under development.

AFAS financial service sector commitments

ASEAN's 1995 Framework Agreement on Services (AFAS) seeks to reduce barriers to trade in services, requiring members to negotiate on trade restrictions in specific sectors so as to expand upon their respective commitments to the WTO's General Agreement on Trade in Services (GATS).[37] Certain commitments were tightened in 2002–2003, making members agree to specific financial sector commitments in addition to those applying to all service sectors.[38]

Overall, ASEAN agreements and AFTA obligations differ little from specific WTO financial sector commitments, from which some are indistinguishable, including those of Brunei, Cambodia and Indonesia,[39] and the marginal access to foreign interests in most cases is limited. In contrast, China's accession commitments to the WTO to liberalise banking and insurance are more extensive than for many developing economies. China's influence within APT may eventually lead to broader financial services reform among ASEAN's developing members.

Table 10.1 shows how ASEAN protocols address the entry of foreign interests into designated markets.

APEC

APEC involvement in the trade in financial services is circumscribed. APEC policy formation preserves a hesitation against institutionalisation and the avoidance of binding rules. The group's diversity of interests ensures that

Table 10.1 ASEAN financial services sector commitments

	Market segment	*Future limits to foreign access*
Brunei	Financial advisory and ancillary services; insurance	Official approval required.
Cambodia	Lending and deposit taking	Permitted through licensed intermediaries.
Indonesia	Commercial banking	Non-banking financial service limitations will be eliminated by 2020; banking restrictions will be eliminated by 2010; foreign banks may establish or acquire domestic banks; foreign bank branches and joint ventures are subject to economic needs tests.
Laos	Lending and deposit taking; guarantees and unfunded commitments; provision and exchange of financial information	Foreign banks permitted only in Vientiane.
Malaysia	Insurance	Foreign shareholding not exceeding 30 per cent.
Myanmar	Loss adjustment	No restriction.
Philippines	Insurance, reinsurance and ancillary insurance	Foreign interests may control 60 per cent of domestic insurers (40 per cent of ancillary insurance ventures); no more than one-third of directors may be foreign nationals.
Singapore	Insurance	Foreign interests may control 49 per cent of domestic insurers; no restrictions on new insurance licences and representative offices.
Thailand	Lending and deposit taking; financial leasing; money transmission; guarantees and standby commitments. Securities trading and issuance; asset management; advisory, intermediation and other auxiliary financial services; financial information provision	No restrictions on bank representative offices; full market access limited to acquisitions of existing licensed companies but licenses may also be granted to new entrants; foreign interests may control the entire issued share capital of banks. There are restrictions on the number of non-Thai nationals allowed as directors of securities dealers, depending on the extent of foreign interests.
Vietnam	Bank guarantees	Foreign bank branches and joint-venture banks may issue guarantees in limited circumstances, covering mainly overseas interests or foreign-funded ventures in Vietnam.

informality is central in all proceedings. Such a governance vacuum inevitably lessens APEC's scope to contribute to financial integration.

APEC was thought to be an effective forum for economic concerns prior to the 1997 Asian crisis but has since been less successful. An emphasis on governance and resources has accordingly shifted to APT and the WTO. Meetings of APEC finance ministers began in 1993, prior to which Japan and the US resisted APEC giving attention to economic matters, preferring that economic policy coordination remain the domain of the Group of Seven (G-7) industrialised nations and the Organisation for Economic Cooperation and Development (OECD).

APEC stated views on a range of consensus financial matters in the approach to the 1997 Asian crisis, for example, supporting regional consultations in 1994 on banking and securities regulation. One year later its 'non-binding investment principles' contained guidelines based upon 'liberalisation and fairness', and in 1996 it endorsed regulatory cooperation and prudential regulation of financial markets in accord with international standards.[40] During the 1997–98 crisis, APEC statements supported the desirability of stable capital flows, domestic financial market development, efforts to promote financial stability, and work by the Basel Committee on Banking Supervision, the International Organisation of Securities Commissions (IOSCO) and the International Association of Insurance Supervisors (IAIS) to strengthen regulation of international financial intermediaries and increase cooperation among regulators to lessen global systemic risks. No principled objection can be made to these pronouncements other than to judge them a diversion of resources. It is clear that APEC's contribution to tangible financial integration has dwindled.

Monetary cooperation

Regional monetary cooperation is mainly evidenced by APT institutional arrangements for short-term credit lines. An Asian Monetary Fund was mooted during the 1997 Asian crisis when certain Asian states required credit to replace lost international reserves, but was dismissed upon intense US opposition. Nonetheless, the objectives of a putative regional fund were raised between APT members in 2006, with discussions of currency alliances and monetary union.

The 2000 ASEAN+3 Chiang Mai Initiative (CMI) seeks cooperation through the institution of bilateral currency swap agreements among central banks.[41] Today's network of sovereign[42] bilateral credit lines has two roots: collaborative foreign exchange swap lines set up by ASEAN's five original members; and a series of securities repurchase (repo) lines begun in the Executives' Meeting of East Asia-Pacific (EMEAP) central banks as a precautionary reaction to the collapse of the Mexican peso in 1994.[43] These origins reveal two aims, the first political, in showing the group's robustness, and the second assisting economic policy.

ASEAN's arrangement began in 1977 as a modest US$100 million set of foreign exchange swap lines, facilitating simultaneous spot sale and forward purchases of local currency for US dollars among five central banks to assist a member in temporary need of external liquidity. Such lines are a form of credit that become loans in the event of non-payment at maturity. Conforming with commercial practice, swaps may extend for up to 90 days and be renewable once with counter-party consent and the absence of need from a second member. The spirit of the arrangement was foreshadowed in fictional France, the group agreeing to pool commitments equally for any line usage.[44] The scheme was extended, expanded, and may have been used once each by Indonesia, Malaysia, the Philippines and Thailand between 1979 and 1981, and on a second occasion by the Philippines in 1992, in each case for modest amounts.[45] The arrangement's limited size and conditionality account for its failure to be used at any time in 1997, when all the members' external positions came most under pressure.

With these swap arrangements came a series of bilateral repurchase lines among EMEAP members, the first introduced in late 1995. Japan was active in their creation, partly due to its interest in promoting regional blocs distinct from those involving other G-7 members. The lines allowed a participant to raise major currency liquidity for intervention or other purposes by discounting – with a fellow member – high-grade securities held as international reserves, most commonly US government securities. Market practice knows several contexts in which the use of repurchase lines is prolific, involving both the commercial sector and central banks, but EMEAP's repurchase lines are analogous to the conduct of money-market operations by central banks seeking to influence domestic liquidity, including cases where a central bank becomes lender of last resort for a financial intermediary and accepts collateral in the form of prescribed securities. Usage of EMEAP lines has no direct consequence for domestic credit expansion. The amounts of these lines were made public only for those involving Japan, each being of US$1 billion.[46]

Excluding those involving Australia and New Zealand, two sets of lines thus evolved into more complex agreements heralded by the CMI.[47] This spurred ASEAN members (by now a group of ten) to raise their total swap arrangements to US$1 billion (later US$2 billion) and to China, Japan and Korea each pledging to maintain bilateral credit lines among themselves and with each ASEAN member, allowing currency swaps and securities repurchases.[48] The initiative is not an agreement but an expression of intent, making APT the catalyst to bilateral arrangements customary among developed economies.

The CMI's results blend purposeful display with practical confusion.[49] First, most of the bilateral lines established by China, Japan and Korea[50] entail contractual terms that make IMF sanction mandatory for most swaps. It is not enough to merely satisfy a set of conditions to those customarily demanded by the IMF.[51] It would have been identical impossible for the

CMI's expanded lines to have been drawn in the Asian crisis prior to an applicant agreeing terms for IMF support, by which time any need would have become redundant. In a similar instance in mid 1997, Thailand may have used a precursor swap line with Japan.[52] If so, this failed to influence markets intent on selling the baht, since drawing from a finite source could only encourage the seller.

Second, although the post-CMI lines provided by China, Japan and Korea allow for securities repurchases, this is now seen by all participants as outmoded and given little attention compared to the swap provisions. The largest non-cash component of Asia's international reserves is held in US government securities, an archetypal broad and deep bond market. Critics suggest that the liquidity available through repurchases could not compete with so profound a source.[53] More attention is now paid by participants and commentators to swap operations and availability. However, this approach neglects shocks not focused on Asia, as in October 1987, when, for a week following sizeable equity market losses, the US treasury market was highly illiquid, frequently closed to foreign participants and useable only by negotiation among primary dealers.[54] Asian repurchase lines could have insulatory value in such circumstances by promoting non-domestic liquidity, despite the region's reserves being concentrated in US dollar assets. Prevailing conditions have changed markedly with the substantial accumulation of reserves in APT vaults. That the 1995–97 repurchase lines were barely used, if at all, in the 1997 crisis was due to a scarcity of collateral or to the participants' simultaneously suffering similar problems not amenable to mutual resolution.

The outcome of the CMI is said by APT to be regional, but its facilities are entirely bilateral in creation and use, despite involving a gesture towards harmonisation and shared views of crisis avoidance. ASEAN ministers declared in 1999 that it:

> shall adopt a more proactive role at various international and regional fora to ensure that its interests and priorities are given due consideration in any proposal to reform the international financial architecture.[55]

Market practitioners see the post-2000 CMI swap line framework as inconsequential and its significance as solely political. History suggests that using swap lines other than to dampen prevailing volatility will at most delay the impact of selling pressure and may give confidence to the seller. It is ironic that CMI's co-option of IMF conditions makes credit line usage unlikely, as some participants perhaps intended, and that the older repurchase lines are neglected, despite their usefulness in crises. While CMI's profile has little relation to its modest impact in form and scale, it may provide an institution to support the creation of a currency pact similar to that adopted in Europe in the 1970s (the 'snake') or a foundation upon which to lay an Asian Monetary Fund. Following their increase at the ADB's 2005 annual meeting, these arrangements have been ambiguously labelled 'Asian Monetary Facilities' or AMF.

Most recently, APT finance ministers have endorsed in principle the augmentation of the CMI by creating a new multilateral agreement for the pooling of additional international reserves.[56] This arrangement would involve administrative resources separate from those within participating states and their respective central banks, and is intended to command at least US$80 billion in commitments, with China, Japan and Korea together providing 80 per cent of the total and ASEAN members the remainder. The arrangements would 'supplement the existing international financial arrangement',[57] but in the event that a participating state sought temporary liquidity it is as yet undecided whether conditions for drawings would differ from those of existing multilateral organisations, notably the IMF. The ministers stress that usage would be subject to 'rigorous principles',[58] and there is no sign that the APT is inclined to develop distinct conditions for its members. The realisation of this proposal would represent the first truly regional arrangement related to monetary cooperation.

Capital market development

Post-crisis regional attention to capital market development initially focused on the bond and money markets but has recently begun to consider equity market reforms. Work on bond market development comprises three collaborative efforts: the APT Asian Bond Market Initiative (ABMI), APEC's efforts in developing securitisation, and work by members of the Asia Cooperation Dialogue (ACD). It also includes the EMEAP banks' 2003–2005 pooling of international reserves in two Asian bond funds (a third fund may follow). By contrast, equity market development has begun only recently in APT, mainly examining cooperation among exchanges and regulators with a view to encouraging cross-border portfolio flows. Success in debt-market reform has been limited, due to the reluctance of state actors to cede national governance in order to create regional policy capital. This is visible in the supremacy of national currency policies over cooperative market reform, resulting in the constraining of initiatives on regional trade in financial services and monetary cooperation. Only modest effort has to date been made in allowing non-bank investment intermediaries to hold foreign regional assets, although they often enjoy far greater freedom to acquire OECD investments.

APT, APEC and ACD

APEC's regional bond market initiative began in 2003, exploring the merits of regional market development and specific institutions to encourage financial activity.[59] APEC established teams to examine aspects of market development, one of which sought recommendations for securitisation and credit enhancement mechanisms to improve the credit risk quality of Asian bonds.[60] APEC asked whether securitisation could provide a continuous fundraising mechanism in the region and assist in the recycling of non-performing financial assets. The work was led by officials from Hong Kong, Korea and Thailand, the first two having experience of using policy measures and legislation to promote large scale structured finance.

Soon afterwards, APT commissioned research similar in scope to APEC's as part of its ABMI, with six working groups housed at the ADB and provided support from ADB resources. They investigated the following subjects:

- Using securitisation to increase the supply of debt instruments;
- Enhancing local currency credit quality through credit guarantees and other transaction structures;
- Improving national clearing, custody and settlement systems;
- Developing domestic credit rating agencies and encouraging the dissemination of information;
- Harmonising market regulations to international best practice; and
- Eliminating legal and regulatory impediments to cross-border bond investment.

The final group's work ended prematurely, in an example of conflict between national and regional policy objectives among state actors. It was charged with exploring cross-border local currency bond issuance by multilateral agencies, governments and their agencies, and regional companies. Yet China, as the group's convenor, allowed it to examine the mechanics of issuance only by multilateral agencies. After inaugural domestic bond issues in China and Thailand by the ADB and International Finance Corporation the group concluded that it had completed its mission and was dissolved in 2004, leaving many omissions from APEC's original reform agenda.[61]

In terms of their contribution to governance, the projects adopted by ASEAN generally constitute functional specificity that is 'so trivial as to remain outside the stream of human expectations and actions vital for integration'.[62]

Last, in 2002 Thailand initiated the ACD among APT, India and fourteen other Asian states to explore regional cooperation so as to encourage capital market activity. The group's visibility declined after the end of Thailand's APEC chairmanship in 2004.

Pooled reserves: Asian bond funds

The EMEAP central banks comprise ASEAN's founding five members and Australia, China, Hong Kong, Japan, Korea and New Zealand. Its non-Japan Asian members are the nominal sponsors of collaborative ideas developed by senior Hong Kong and Thai officials, and implemented in 2003–2005 as the two Asian Bond Funds (ABF1 and ABF2). The funds are poolings for fund management of a small portion of international reserves.

The plan had two roots: criticism of Asia massing reserves in non-Asian risk assets, and the proposition that active capital markets could provide a stabilising resource in times of heightened volatility. The project had start-up assistance from the Bank for International Settlements (BIS), which was a politically important aspect of governance, given the absence of a viable regional or shared infrastructure. Assigning this nominal role to the BIS eliminated any national hierarchy among participating banks and dispensed with the contentious need for a new regional institution to organise or manage the funds. Ironically, the principal fund managers for the project are of British or American domicile.

Both funds are indexed and managed passively. The project's ceiling represented less than 0.15 per cent of the subscribers' aggregate reserves at inception, but it is innovatory in several respects. While the fund cannot directly contribute to liquidity it departs from traditional reserve-management practice by including sub-investment grade EMEAP sovereign risks. ABF1 is a US$1 billion pooling of core currency Asian bonds held by EMEAP's Asian member central banks.[63] The later ABF2 is a US$2 billion fund holding local currency issues. Families of single currency exchange-traded funds and regional index funds will each acquire and hold sovereign and quasi-sovereign Asian securities. Hitherto, proposals to create regional bodies have been ambitious and not easily implemented,[64] so if the more complex ABF2 is successful it may become a platform for more regional cooperation in financial structure. ABF2 has so far prompted the introduction of Asia's first bond-related exchange-traded fund, caused two domestic markets to allow the creation of local currency exchange-traded funds, and opened dealing in China's domestic inter-bank bond market to approved foreign investors.[65]

ABF2's single-currency and regional-index funds provide a means to lessen problems associated with direct investment in local currency instruments by most offshore investors and certain domestic investors, including those affecting custody, enforcement of rights, reliability of transfer, and taxation.[66] If the plan succeeds, it will do so not overtly, but by encouraging the removal of legal and regulatory constraints that currently make its objectives impossible to achieve. The test of the project must be whether it generates liquidity and induces new participants to issue, invest or trade. Yet, in its first six months the sums raised from non-EMEAP sources amounted to US$200 million,[67] a figure that had merely doubled by April 2006.

This scheme is demanding because it seeks to circumvent pervasive problems of investor access, custody, enforcement, transfer and taxation that exist for non-bank investors throughout the region, but in so doing will be self-limiting as to its external impact on market development. Indeed, pre-establishment announcements suggested that this might be intentional in that ABF2 would 'accelerate market reform', but no commitments to this effect have been disclosed.

Transnational organisation factors: the role of the ADB

The ADB mixes regional interests and supraregional governance. While its operations focus purely on development activity in Asia, eighteen of the bank's sixty-five shareholders are non-Asian OECD members who together account for 34.75 per cent of votes in the bank's supervisory board of governors. Members of the G-7 group hold 39.9 per cent of board of governor votes. The governors also elect a twelve-person board of directors, four of whom represent non-Asian members. China, Japan and the US each nominate a director to serve their sole respective interests. As in certain other Asian organisations, the regional interests of ADB policy may not coincide with the aims of shareholders.

At the same time, the ADB has given material support to financial sector cooperation. It became involved in a coordinating function with the CMI in 2005, and policy makers may welcome its efforts because of a lack of resources and institutional weaknesses in ASEAN and APEC. The ADB established six working groups to support market development at the same time as APT began its ABMI in 2002,[68] making provision for loans, technical assistance and funding. The bank regards its own local-currency bond issues as developmental, although they rely more on the structuring resources of private law than reforms in national policy. The ADB encourages transparency in these initiatives and in widening investor access to market information through a web-based portal, AsianBondsOnline, which disseminates data and links more comprehensively than many commercial or national sources but which as yet has a limited life.[69]

More significantly, a new Office of Regional Economic Integration (OREI) seeks to promote economic cooperation and integration among the bank's developing members and to contribute to the region's 'harmonious economic growth'. This is an initiative of current ADB president Kuroda, emphasising regional integration, financial integration, and providing resources for research, technical assistance projects and investment. A successful OREI may ameliorate the ADB's lack of coherent objectives when compared to the World Bank, which has a focus on domestic markets and engaging with the commercial sector. A 2007 study by an ADB Eminent Persons Group found agreement with these reforms.

Europe's experience of financial integration

Financial integration among EU states is the most developed of any region. This reflects the adoption of serial objectives since the 1950s, leading ultimately to the creation of a single internal market in financial services.[70] Advances in integration have transformed markets among professional intermediaries, but Europe's trade in retail financial services remains fragmented and subject to only fractional regional competition. This is the result of strong national socio-economic norms that reform and regulation find difficult to overturn, although the introduction of the euro may have induced greater similarities in national retail financial markets.[71]

EU founding treaties provide for free movement of goods, services, workers and capital, and freedom of establishment. In theory, investments may be made without restriction across national borders. A high level of integration has been achieved in each of these dimensions, partly due to supportive rulings of the European Court of Justice (ECJ), and markets have become considerably harmonised,[72] so that national legislation covering certain market segments reflects developments initiated regionally. Member states must adhere to certain EU precepts so that decisions and legislation passed at EU level will directly affect those in individual states, while national governments may be liable to damages for failing to implement EU legislation to the detriment of their citizens. No such treaty obligations exist elsewhere in a regional setting. Nonetheless, in a more technical sense EU experience shows how financial integration may encourage the adoption of sound principles and practices. The concept of mutual recognition and a system providing a single regulatory licence for financial intermediaries now allow EU directives to set minimum norms without hindering competition.

An influential 1966 study addressed impediments to the functioning of Europe's national markets and their openness to foreign borrowers,[73] identifying a home bias towards national governments and other domestic borrowers achieved through regulations on permissible investment by banks and insurers. Few companies were listed outside their domiciles. These conditions generally reflect how Asia's markets function some forty years later. It has long been controversial to draw generic lessons from EU experience as to conditions or prospects for regionalism,[74] but the approach taken elsewhere to specific technical aspects of financial integration may be helpful in discussing the obstacles that Asia confronts.

The EU legislative framework for financial markets seeks equivalence among disparate regulatory and legal systems, so that regional initiatives recognise national legal and regulatory regimes.[75] Rule harmonisation proved impossible to achieve for many activities and so the European Commission made a tactical shift towards new principles, first outlined in a 1985 White Paper[76] and enshrined in the subsequent Single European Act.[77] This stipulated a common internal market based upon mutual recognition and common minimum standards, made applicable by EU directives and effected through domestic law.[78] Member states would thenceforth recognise each other's law, regulation, authorities and standards, enabling the freeing of the trade in goods and services without need for prior harmonisation.[79] The system also uses minimum regional requirements to limit competitive deregulation by state actors and regulatory arbitrage by commercial parties.

National financial regulation in Europe has developed significantly since the early 1990s, due to a combination of the needs of government and pressure from harmonisation, access deregulation, and prudential re-regulation inherent in the process of market opening developed under the Maastricht

Treaty objective of free movement of capital. The EU framework for financial services provides minimum standards for financial intermediaries, securities regulation, accounting, company law, and regulation of institutional investors, based on the principles of financial intermediation unfettered by national borders or restrictions on activity, and an open internal market. However, the harmonisation approach means that the framework is incomplete, since it augments rather than replaces existing national laws.

The single market is manifested in single 'passport' directives,[80] by which an authorised intermediary may be able to sell its services overseas without maintaining a permanent presence in its target market.[81] The passport's aim is to promote competition and allow intermediary firms to adopt their most cost-effective means of product delivery.[82] Passport directives in financial services define the intermediary to which they apply, its activities or market segment, the conditions for initial and continuing authorisation, the division of regulatory responsibility between the home (domicile) state and the host (target) state,[83] and aspects of dealings with non-EU member states.[84]

The free movement of capital needed to facilitate European monetary union became effective through the Maastricht Treaty in 1994. This provided an impetus for EU states to implement prior financial services directives and led to members other than Ireland and the UK adopting legislation that was foreign to their traditional financial markets. Prior to this degree of political consent, commercial interests may have encouraged financial integration, if only among professional intermediaries. For example, the early 1990s saw Europe's offshore markets in loans and securities rival the long-established and varied national markets. This led to negotiations between industry representatives and regulators that resulted in offshore activity infiltrating national markets and subsuming local practices. The process became entrenched with the introduction of the euro. There is little near-term chance of Asia following this precedent, regardless of whether the offshore European markets of the 1970s and 1980s were part of a trend towards financial integration or relied upon institutional barriers to be effective.

One contemporary source saw the Eurobond market as a substitute for financial integration, given that capital mobility was only a secondary EU goal until the 1990s.[85] Others referred to the Eurobond market relying on an 'asymmetry' between local and foreign targeted national capital controls.[86] Similarly, the official 1966 Segré report was prescient of the potential for financial integration or how officially inspired integration might be confounded by commercial interests. If a capital market can be established anywhere, then what need is there for formal integration unless and until monetary integration is also an objective?[87]

Conclusion: governance and financial integration

Europe's protracted experience in forming a single regional financial market indicates the scale of obstacles to Asian financial integration. Policy

attention given since the mid 1990s to Asian market development has led
to two tangible results. The first, a repurchase line construct, is discounted;
the second, ABF2, is constrained from directly affecting liquidity. Yet that
these steps have been attempted suggests that practical objectives could be
employed to guide all national and regional reforms. If regionalism is
construed as the results of a large-scale conception, for example:

> From a 'global' perspective, regionalism constitutes a trans-nationalization
> of economic and political activity, which implies the transcendence of
> state boundaries in the interests of ensuring cooperation and reducing
> the potential for conflict.[88]

Alternatively:

> From a 'bottom-up' perspective, the formation of a regional bloc is
> concerned with various dimensions of state-building. The rationale for
> regionalism is invariably that there are common goals which can best be
> pursued in concert with other states or actors.[89]

It would seem that the transnational model of regionalism has no application in Asia but that the more practical functionalism implicit in the second
alternative is, in the context of financial integration, a limited objective
which APT members may become willing to accept.[90] This in turn suggests
that Asia can gain insight from EU experience in certain technical respects:

> [T]he principle of minimum harmonization together with mutual recog-
> nition principles underlines the potential for leaving integration to
> market forces once national legal and regulatory frameworks share
> common minimum standards.[91]

The second section of this chapter showed why the EU's goal-setting
regionalism process is infeasible in today's Asia. At the same time, elements
of European regionalisation may eventually assist the process of Asian
financial cooperation and development, notably, mutual recognition, harmonisation to common minimum standards and shared commitments to
reform. Initiatives adopted within APT and EMEAP may increase accountability, transparency and the extent of participation in reform by commercial
actors in ways which could become generally beneficial to economic development. This is conceptually similar to ASEAN's existing approach and
accords with the ADB's identifying accountability, predictability, participation
and transparency as principles of necessary financial governance.[92]

Cooperation in financial policy among Asia's newly industrialised and
developing economies has a short history and slender results, even though
Asia's need for market reforms is associated with substantial tasks in
national and multilateral policy making. Past regional initiatives on financial

issues have lacked practicality, or foundered when confronted by competing interests from China, Japan or the United States,[93] leading to doubts as to the effective influence on financial policy formation of Asia's multiplicity of regional bodies.[94] To the extent that material results now exist, their value may rest in the fact of completion. At the same time, there have been long-standing examples of the adoption by national authorities of like external financial policies, most clearly seen in currency management in the five years prior to 1997.

Asia's economic and financial integration lacks an institutional and legal framework set within the region. In contrast to the rules-oriented WTO, the region's economic organisations and institutions are orientated towards dealings among participating states and are generally intended to have minimal impact on national sovereignty. More generally, greater financial integration requires a new approach to several aspects of governance:

- States would recognise shared interests in protecting regional competitiveness. This might imply the acceptance in due course of certain political consequences, for example in reconsidering whether external mercantilism need be paramount in national economic policy.
- The commercial sector has been included in Asian financial integration only as a residual matter and, in contrast with the EU pattern, in no transparent governance role. Financial integration may require 'multi-level governance' that involves many actors, rather than Asia's state-centric tradition.[95]
- Since Asia's prevailing regional financial institutions are weak or constrained by state-orientated governance, the outcome for future financial integration and development is a function of the nature of the actors involved in their instigation, whether they represent national, commercial or other interests.

During the 1997 crisis, Asian state actors failed to find regional solutions, through financial integration, to regional problems of contagion. Time would not be any more accommodating in a future shock. Without devoting resources to governance to improve regional financial integration, those states will continue to rely heavily on risk-averse portfolio management by holding high reserves, to the detriment of their own financial markets and the wider East Asian region.

Notes

1 Röpke, Wilhelm. 'Economic Order and International Law', *Recueil des Cours.* (Vol. 86, No. II, 1954), p. 251.
2 Ibid. p. 252.
3 Röpke's description of the European Payments Union (1950–1958) is of an arrangement in functional cooperation (see n. 5 below) resembling the APT web of central bank payment lines explained in the fourth section of this chapter.

With the European Coal and Steel Community (1952–2002), this is held to be one of 'two great international actions ... to further Europe's economic integration', ibid. p. 258.

4 See n. 20 below.

5 It is thus the antithesis of the Bretton Woods international financial system that prevailed for almost thirty years after World War II. Bretton Woods required the separation of national markets to support fixed exchange rates, independent national monetary policies and general stability, see Arner, Douglas. *Financial Stability, Economic Growth and the Role of Law.* (Cambridge: Cambridge University Press, 2007), pp. 91–125. The system paradoxically allowed the creation of the offshore regional Eurobond market in the 1960s. Until the mid-1980s this was a permissive institution that relied on the circumvention of national rules. Without a web of national obstructions the market would have been unnecessary and infeasible. No such regional market exists today in Asia.

6 Cowen, David and Ranil Salgado. 'Globalization of Production and Financial Integration in Asia', *IMF Working Paper No. 06/196*, 2006.

7 See Schularock, Moritz and Thomas Steiger. 'Does Financial Integration Spur Economic Growth? New Evidence from the First Era of Financial Globalization', *CESifo Working Paper No. 1691*, 2006. http://www.ssrn.com/abstract = 884434. Accessed 21 May 2008, suggesting that developmental benefits associated with financial integration require prior domestic institutional reforms, in particular the maintenance of adequate property rights. The indeterminate general result may signify empirical problems in specifying integration, which is most commonly observed in the ratio between capital flows and national income or represented by a binary indicator for cross-border capital controls, see Lane, Philip and Gian Maria Milesi-Ferretti. 'International Financial Integration', *IMF Working Paper No. WP/03/86*, 2003. This is contextually important in Asia in that if modest financial integration is linked to high net national savings, then the disutility of recent reserve accumulation is compounded by developmental effects, see Lane, Philip and Sergio Schmukler. 'The International Financial Integration of China and India', *Institute for International Integration Studies Discussion Paper No. 174*, 2006. http://ssrn.com/abstract = 925872. Accessed 21 May 2008.

8 Pierre, Jon. 'Introduction', in Jon Pierre (ed.). *Debating Governance.* (Oxford: Oxford University Press, 2000), p. 3.

9 Ibid.

10 Payne, Anthony. 'Globalization and Modes of Regionalist Governance', in Jon Pierre. *Debating Governance.* (Oxford: Oxford University Press, 2000), pp. 214–215.

11 Keohane, Robert and Joseph Nye. 'Introduction', in Joseph Nye and John Donahue. *Governance in a Globalizing World.* (Washington, DC: Brookings Institution, 2000), p. 12.

12 Kaminsky, Graciela and Marco Cipriani. 'A New Era of International Financial Integration: Global, Market, and Regional Factors', *School of Economics & Finance Workshop Discussion Paper No. 534.* (Hong Kong: Hong Kong University, 2006).

13 Jayakumar, Shanmugam. 'Stick to Basics', *Speech to ASEAN ministerial meeting.* 24 July 1998. http://www.aseansec.org/3924.htm. Accessed 22 August 2007. See also Acharya, Amitav. *Constructing a Security Community in Southeast Asia: ASEAN and the Problem of Regional Order.* (London: Routledge, 2001), pp. 47–79.

14 A proposal for ASEAN to assume a legal personality may be discussed at an ASEAN heads of state summit in late 2007 as this book goes to press. This follows recommendations of an ASEAN 'Eminent Persons' study convened under a 2005 initiative named Vision 2020 to revise ASEAN's Charter.

15 *Bangkok Declaration*. December 1995. http://www.aseansec.org/5189.htm. Accessed 21 May 2008.
16 *Ministerial Understanding on ASEAN Cooperation in Finance*. http://www.aseansec.org/1939.htm. Accessed 21 May 2008.
17 Ibid. Art. 5.
18 Haas, Ernst. 'International Integration: The European and the Universal Process', *International Organization*. (Vol. 15, No. 3, 1961), p. 372.
19 See Payne, Anthony. 'Globalization and Modes of Regionalist Governance'.
20 See especially Redding, Gordon. *The Spirit of Chinese Capitalism*. (Berlin: W. de Gruyter, 1990). The developmental state was associated first with Japan, see Johnson, Chalmers. *MITI and the Japanese Miracle: the Growth of Industrial Policy, 1925–1975*. (Stanford, CA: Stanford University Press, 1982).
21 Söderbaum, Fredrik. 'Modes of Regional Governance in Africa: Neoliberalism, Sovereignty Boosting, and Shadow Networks', *Global Governance*. (Vol. 10, No. 4, 2004), pp. 419–436.
22 Nye, Joseph and Robert Keohane. 'Transnational Relations and World Politics: an Introduction', *International Organization*. (Vol. 25, No. 3, 1971), pp. 329–349.
23 See the fourth section of this chapter. By contrast, several states have committed very sizeable amounts to sovereign wealth funds.
24 Haas, Ernst. 'The Study of Regional Integration: Reflections on the Joy and Anguish of Pretheorizing', *International Organization*. (Vol. 24, No. 4, 1970), p. 616.
25 Keohane, Robert. 'From Interdependence and Institutions to Globalization and Governance', in Keohane Robert. *Power and Governance in a Partially Globalized World*. (London: Routledge, 2002).
26 Williamson, John. 'What Washington Means by Policy Reform', in John Williamson (ed.). *Latin American Adjustment: How Much Has Happened?* (Washington, DC: Institute for International Economics, 1990), Ch. 2. A World Bank official, Williamson later criticised the consensus on financial integration, arguing that 'the policies these institutions advocated in the 1990s were inimical to the cause of poverty reduction in emerging markets in at least one respect: their advocacy of capital account liberalization', see Williamson, John. 'What Should the World Bank Think about the Washington Consensus?', *World Bank Research Observer*. (Vol. 15, No. 2, 2000), p. 257.
27 Emphasis added.
28 Jayakumar. 'Stick to Basics' (see n. 13 above).
29 Arner, Douglas, Paul Lejot and S. Ghon Rhee. *Impediments to Cross-border Investments in Asian Bonds*. (Singapore: Institute of Southeast Asian Studies, 2006).
30 Baldwin, Richard. 'Multilateralising Regionalism: Spaghetti Bowls as Building Blocs on the Path to Global Free Trade', *NBER Working Paper No. 12545* (2006). http://www.nber.org/papers/w12545. Accessed 22 August 2007; idem, 'Managing the Noodle Bowl: The Fragility of East Asian Regionalism', *CEPR Discussion Paper No. 5561* (2006). http://www.ssrn.com/abstract = 912265. Accessed 21 May 2008, p. 2.
31 APT also failed to support the proposal, but for the reasons outlined in the second section. Note that a regional guarantor would compete with commercial monoline insurers, most of which are US domiciled.
32 This issue is also discussed in Chapter 2.
33 *Framework Agreement on Enhancing ASEAN Economic Cooperation*. http://www.aseansec.org/12374.htm. Accessed 21 May 2008. One of fifteen clauses deals with AFTA.
34 Pelkmans, Jacques. 'ASEAN and APEC, A Triumph of the "Asian Way"?', in Paul Demaret, Jean-François Bellis and Gonzalo García Jimenez (eds). *Regionalism*

and Multilateralism after the Uruguay Round: Convergence, Divergence and Interaction. (Brussels: European Inter-University Press, 1997), p. 211.

35 See: *Agreement on the Common Effective Preferential Tariff Scheme for the ASEAN Free Trade Area.* http://www.aseansec.org/12375.htm. Accessed 21 May 2008.

36 Brunei, Indonesia, Malaysia, the Philippines, Singapore and Thailand intend to do so by 2010. However, all members may retain tariffs on goods they deem 'sensitive'.

37 See: *ASEAN Framework Agreement on Services.* http://www.aseansec.org/6628. htm. Accessed 21 May 2008, Art. IV.

38 See: *Protocol to Amend The ASEAN Framework Agreement on Services.* http://www.aseansec.org/AFAS_Amendment_Protocol.pdf. Accessed 21 May 2008.

39 The financial services commitments of Brunei and Indonesia appear in WTO documents GATS/SC/95 and GATS/SC/43/Suppl.3, respectively, see http://www.wto.org/english/tratop_e/serv_e/ finance_e/finance_commitments_e.htm. Accessed 21 May 2008. Cambodia's WTO accession schedule for financial services commitments appears in document WT/ACC/KHM/21/Add.2, see http://www.wto.org/English/thewto_e/acc_e/completeacc_e.htm. Accessed 21 May 2008.

40 This is covered in more detail in the preceding chapter.

41 See *Joint Ministerial Statement of the ASEAN+3 Finance Ministers Meeting.* (Chiang Mai: 6 May 2000). http://www.aseansec.org/635.htm. Accessed 22 August 2007.

42 Counterparty risk is taken here as sovereign, whether it involves a central bank or finance ministry.

43 Reported in Moreno, Ramon. 'Dealing with Currency Speculation in the Asian Pacific Basin', *Federal Reserve Bank of San Francisco Economic Letter.* (Vol. 97, No. 10–11, April 1997), pp. 1–3. See also the fourth part of this chapter.

44 "'And now, gentlemen,' said d'Artgagnan, … ' All for one – one for all, this is our motto is it not?'" Alexandre Dumas, *The Three Musketeers*, Ch. IX.

45 See Henning, Randall. *East Asian Financial Cooperation.* (Washington, DC: Institute for International Economics, 2002), p. 14, citing unnamed Thai sources. A United Nations Economic and Social Commission for Asia and the Pacific (UNESCAP) report claims that the arrangement 'has been extensively used' but this is unsupported and implausible, see Wang, Seok-dong and Lene Andersen. 'Regional Financial Cooperation in East Asia: The Chiang Mai Initiative and Beyond', *Bulletin on Asia-Pacific Perspectives 2002/03.* UNESCAP, Bangkok 2003, p. 90.

46 See Moreno. n. 43 above.

47 See n. 41 above. CMI is subject to no public agreement to which all its adherents are party.

48 Implementation of the agreement by Cambodia, Laos, Myanmar and Vietnam has to date been waived.

49 This view has support in official circles in China and Japan (for example, Japan Finance Ministry Institute for International Monetary Affairs. *Report Summary of Studies on Toward* [sic] *a Regional Financial Architecture for East Asia.* (Tokyo: 29 March 2004). http://www.mof.go.jp/jouhou/kokkin/ASEAN +3research.htm. Accessed 21 May 2008.

50 Totalling US$39.5 billion equivalent as at end of April 2005; source, Japan Ministry of Finance. http://www.mof.go.jp/english/if/if.htm. Accessed 21 May 2008.

51 In May 2005 ASEAN+3 raised the portion available unconditionally under post-CMI swap lines from 10 to 20 per cent of the total 'in order to better cope with sudden market irregularities', but stressed this represented no contradiction that 'the international financial arrangements and other disciplined conditions would be firmly maintained'. See: *Joint Ministerial Statement of the ASEAN+3 Finance Ministers Meeting.* 4 May 2005. http://www.aseansec.org/17448.htm. Accessed 21

May 2008. It is arguable that IMF compliance would be demanded for usage even if had it not then made credit commitments to a hopeful user.

52 *The Economist.* 10 May 2001 (cited by Randall, n. 45 above).

53 For example, Randall, n. 45 above, p. 22.

54 Similar acute illiquidity affected certain interbank and securities markets in mid-2007 following a collapse of confidence in high-risk US sub-prime home mortgage lending.

55 *ASEAN Finance Ministers Joint Ministerial Statement.* 20 March 1999. http://www.aseansec.org/742.htm. Accessed 22 August 2007.

56 See: *Joint Ministerial Statement of the 11th ASEAN Plus Three Ministers Meeting.* (Madrid: 4 May 2008). http://www.aseansec.org/21502.htm. Accessed 21 May 2008.

57 Ibid. s. 6.

58 Ibid.

59 *Joint Ministerial Statement, Tenth APEC Finance Ministers' Meeting.* (Phuket: 4–5 September 2003). www/apec.org/apec/ministerial_statements/sectoral_ministerial/finance/2003_finance.html. Accessed 21 May 2008.

60 Securitisation is a structured finance technique involving the irrevocable transfer of defined financial assets by their originator, funded by the simultaneous sale to third party investors of new securities issued by the asset buyer, which is an insubstantive vehicle in the form of a company or trust.

61 Many remaining impediments are listed in Lejot, Paul, Douglas Arner and Liu Qiao. 'Missing Links: Regional Reforms for Asia's Bond Markets', *Asia-Pacific Business Review.* (Vol. 12, No. 3, 2006). Table 2, pp. 11–13.

62 Haas. 'International Integration', (n. 18), p. 372.

63 Many central banks trade liquid foreign currency debt securities but the assets held by ABF1 are generally illiquid and represent the fund's feasible investment universe.

64 For example, currency cooperation pacts discussed at intervals by APEC and ASEAN.

65 Yam, Joseph. 'The Euro: Lessons for European and Asian Financial Markets', *Speech at a conference sponsored by the European Commission and the Hong Kong Monetary Authority.* (Hong Kong: 24 February 2006).

66 See Lejot *et al.* 'Missing Links' (op. cit. note 61 above).

67 'Pan Asia Fund Fails to Excite Investors', *Financial Times.* 13 June 2006.

68 Pholsena, Khempheng, ADB vice president. *Speech at seminar on Local Currency Bond Issuance by Foreign Multinational Corporations.* Shanghai, 5 August 2004.

69 Asian Bonds Online: An ASEAN+3 Initiative, http://asianbondsonline.adb.org. Accessed 21 May 2008.

70 Op. cit., note 4 above.

71 See for example Sørensen, Christoffer Kok and Josep Maria Puigvert Gutiérrez. 'Euro Area Banking Sector Integration: Using Hierarchical Cluster Analysis Techniques', *European Central Bank Working Paper No. 627,* 2006, pp. 7–8.

72 Tertak, Elemer, Director, European Commission financial institutions directorate. Speech: *The Euro: Lessons for European and Asian Financial Markets,* Hong Kong, 24 February 2006.

73 European Economic Community. *The Development of a European Capital Market,* 1966. Cited by Kindleberger, Charles. *A Financial History of Western Europe.* (Oxford: Oxford University Press, 1993), pp. 438–439.

74 Haas, Ernst. 'Turbulent Fields and the Theory of Regional Integration', *International Organization.* (Vol. 30, No. 2, 1976), pp. 173–212.

75 See Steil, Benn (ed.). *The European Equity Markets: The State of the Union and an Agenda for the Millennium.* (New York: Brookings Institution, 1996), p. 113.

76 European Commission, *Completing the Internal Market: White Paper from the European Commission to the European Council.* Com (85)310 final (1985).

77 Single European Act, 1986 O.J. (L 169) 1 (1987). http://eur-lex.europa.eu/en/treaties/index.htm. Accessed 21 May 2008.
78 Ibid.
79 See Steil, note 75 above.
80 Passport directives in financial services include two banking coordination directives (1BCD and 2BCD); one Investment Services Directive (ISD); one directive on collective investment schemes (UCITSD); three life and three non-life insurance directives; and a proposed Pension Funds Directive.
81 See Fraser, Innes and Paul Mortimer-Lee. 'The EC Single Market in Financial Services', *Bank of England Quarterly Bulletin.* (Vol. 33, No. 1, 1993), pp. 92–97.
82 Ibid.
83 The home state will generally be responsible for the supervision of intermediaries and their branches and the fitness and properness of managers and major shareholders. The host state will be responsible for a conduct in its jurisdiction. Ibid. p. 93.
84 Ibid.
85 Richebacher, Kurt. 'The Problems and Prospects of Integrating European Capital Markets', *Journal of Money, Credit and Banking.* (Vol. 1, No. 3, 1969), p. 337.
86 Genillard, Robert. 'The Eurobond Market', *Financial Analysts Journal* (Vol. 151, March–April 1967). The article concluded that the Eurobond market was a 'fine example of the benefits of international collaboration by bankers in a fully competitive climate.'
87 EEC Commission. *The Development of a European Capital Market: Report of a Group of Experts Appointed by the EEC Commission* (Brussels, European Economic Community, 1966). pp. 195 and 202. The experts argued for harmonisation of non-retail national markets in ways later encouraged by the Eurobond market.
88 Philips, Nicola. 'Governance after Financial Crisis: South American Perspectives on the Reformulation of Regionalism', *New Political Economy.* (Vol. 5, No. 3, 2000), p. 386.
89 Ibid.
90 See Acharya, Amitav. 'How Ideas Spread: Whose Norms Matter? Norm Localization and Institutional Change in Asian Regionalism', *International Organization.* (Vol. 58, No. 2, 2004), pp. 239–275. Acharya uses a similar argument in the context of cooperative regional security.
91 Jordan, Cally and Giovanni Majnoni. 'Financial Regulatory Harmonization and the Globalization of Finance', *World Bank Policy Research Working Paper 2919* (2002), p. 9. Furthermore, 'in a financially integrated world, size matters both for regulated entities and for the regulators and the same set of rules may not be efficient and equitable for both large and small players', pp. 9–10.
92 ADB. 'Improving Governance and Fighting Corruption: Implementing the Governance and Anticorruption Policies of the Asian Development Bank', Manila, 2006.
93 For example: Baker, James. *The Politics of Diplomacy: Revolution, War, and Peace, 1989–1992.* (New York: G.P. Putnam's Sons, 1995), pp. 609–611. The former US Secretary of State notes his determination while in office that 'any move towards economic integration in East Asia include the United States', such that notably, in 1991, he did his 'best to kill' an East Asian Economic Group then proposed among APEC's East Asian members.
94 Sceptics include Bisley, Nick. 'The End of East Asian Regionalism?', *Journal of East Asian Affairs.* (Vol. 17, No. 1, 2003); and Ravenhill, John. 'APEC Adrift: Implications for Economic Regionalism in Asia and the Pacific', *Pacific Review.* (Vol. 13, No. 2, 2000). Others see policy success in the creation of bilateral central bank repurchase and credit lines, especially their expansion under CMI

(Thomas, Nicholas. 'An East Asian Economic Community: Multilateralism Beyond APEC', presentation to Asia-Pacific Economies: Multilateral vs. Bilateral Relationships Conference, City University of Hong Kong, May 2004). http://www.cityu.edu.hk/cityu/events/APEC.htm. Accessed 21 May 2008. Yamagake, Susumu. 'The Construction of an East Asian Order and the Limitations of the ASEAN Model', *Asia-Pacific Review*. (Vol. 12, No. 2, 2005), pp. 1–9, suggests that Asia's regional model body may inherently conflict with collective policy initiatives.

95 See Payne. 'Globalization and Regionalist Governance' (op. cit. note 10), pp. 211–212.

11 Regional governance and disaster response

Alain Guilloux

Introduction

This chapter explores regional responses to disasters in Asia and the implications for the development of regional governance mechanisms. Disasters are traditionally categorised as either natural or man-made. Natural disasters include, in particular, floods, earthquakes, typhoons and volcano eruptions, while man-made disasters include violent conflicts and the forced displacements of populations that they usually cause.

Regardless of the cause of a disaster, the subsequent relief action is concerned with the alleviation of suffering of those affected. Its first imperative is to treat the sick and the injured, to feed and shelter the survivors at risk. A primary indicator for assessing the severity of a crisis is the daily mortality rate (DMR). It is generally accepted that an emergency response is warranted if the DMR exceeds 1/10,000 in a given population. The focus of this chapter is on the emergency response to disasters rather than on crisis prevention or post-disaster reconstruction. The purpose of emergency responses, usually referred to as rescue and relief operations, is to return mortality and morbidity rates to pre-crisis levels.

Asia's response to disasters is worth exploring, as it has evolved rapidly in recent years. Whereas the region was long on the receiving end of assistance, state and non-state organisations have, during the two decades since the early 1990s, become significant players and provided relief in the aftermath of both natural and man-made disasters. From Afghanistan to Myanmar, from Kashmir to Sri Lanka, Asia faces long-lasting, violent conflicts and forced displacements of populations. These man-made disasters have severe consequences in terms of mortality and morbidity, not to forget the ongoing situation in North Korea. It is further estimated that 'nearly 90 per cent of the people affected by natural disasters between 1975 and 2002 were from Asia, due both to its large population and to its high population density'.[1] Of deaths caused by natural disasters worldwide, 70 per cent occur in Asia and the region 'has suffered from approximately 43 per cent of all natural disasters in the last decade, costing the region about USD 360 billion between the years 1991 and 2000'.[2]

While the burden of disasters remains high in the region, a growing number of Asian organisations, both state and non-state, have become aid providers. In particular, South Korea, Taiwan, Hong Kong and Singapore have become donor states as they grew more affluent. Private sector groups have also provided financial support for various aid programmes initiated by states and non-state actors. Beyond funding, regional states are also becoming more willing to commit military forces in disaster relief operations. China, India and Japan, in particular, along with other Asian states, have become significant actors in peace-keeping operations since the turn of the century.

For various reasons, the international activities of Asian civil society organisations (CSOs) were, until recently, limited. In Japan, it took the Kobe earthquake in 1995 to challenge the view that only government could deal with disaster relief.[3] Colonial or authoritarian regimes have also long restricted civil society initiatives, especially in their international links. In Hong Kong, Taiwan and South Korea, this was compounded by sensitive political and strategic concerns. In this context, the sustained interest of Asian individual donors and volunteers in faraway emergencies is all the more remarkable. Established international aid agencies have channelled part of this response, but Asian-based aid groups have become increasingly active.

In short, Asian states and civil society organisations are becoming increasingly active players in response to regional disasters. This raises a number of questions. Will the increased capacity of Asian state and non-state organisations to respond to disasters pave the way for regional institutions and mechanisms? Will it lead to a coordinated regional response or set of responses? Are disasters in Asia likely to be addressed in terms of regional governance? To answer these questions, the issue of Asian responses to disasters is examined within a governance framework. ASEAN's response to the December 2004 Indian Ocean tsunami is used as a case study for the issues raised. Following the analysis and conclusions raised by the main case study, the chapter will briefly consider some of the preliminary issues for regional disaster governance generated by the May 2008 tropical cyclone Nargis in Myanmar.

Governance and disaster response

Humanitarian relief actions in response to man-made and natural crises have become an important component of international relations in the post-Cold War period. International humanitarian law, as defined by the 1949 Geneva Conventions and the 1977 additional protocols, specifies the requirements, in terms of protection of and assistance to, civilian populations and wounded soldiers, for which warring parties and occupying powers are held responsible. In addition, the laws of war prohibit certain methods and means of warfare. The Geneva Conventions also define the principles and modalities of action that apply to humanitarian organisations. These organisations must be independent – in other words, free from other affiliations and influences. They must independently assess needs, distribute relief items and monitor relief operations. In addition, humanitarian organisations must not take sides in a conflict or discriminate between victims. Finally, aid must be provided in proportion to needs.

In addition to international humanitarian law, responses to disasters are informed by other norms, including sovereignty and human rights. In line with the principle of sovereignty enshrined in the United Nations (UN) Charter, states have the primary responsibility to respond to disasters that affect the territory and population under their control. If other state or non-state actors want to intervene in response to a disaster, they must seek the consent of the affected state, unless the situation represents a threat to international peace. In such a case, the issue may be referred to the UN Security Council.

Since the 1990s, however, the sovereignty norm has been increasingly challenged.[4] In particular, emphasis has been put on 'humanitarian interventions'. High-profile, direct military involvement, with or without UN approval, has been deemed necessary by a state or group of states to stop massive human rights violations and/or restore democracy, in addition to other tasks such as the delivery of emergency relief supplies or the protection of refugees and internally displaced people.[5] The emerging norm of humanitarian intervention challenges the principle of state sovereignty, on the one hand, and the principles of international humanitarian law, on the other. The response to life-threatening crises is thus characterised by a tension between competing norms: international humanitarian law and humanitarian intervention. More recently, relief or reconstruction operations deemed to be an important component of the war on terror have been portrayed as humanitarian, in particular in Afghanistan and Iraq. This has added to the confusion between humanitarian, political and military objectives in responding to crises.

The three main types of actors involved in disaster response are state organisations, inter-governmental organisations (IGOs) and non-governmental organisations (NGOs). The private sector has also become a significant provider of monetary and of in-kind support.

The main operational inter-governmental agencies involved are the specialised agencies of the UN. They include the UN High Commissioner for Refugees (UNHCR), the World Food Programme (WFP), the World Health Organisation (WHO) and United Nations Children's Fund (UNICEF). In addition, the Office for the Coordination of Humanitarian Assistance (UNOCHA) disseminates information about crises. In line with the UN Charter, all these organisations must obtain the consent of the governments of the countries and territories where they operate or from the UN Security Council. The International Committee of the Red Cross (ICRC), the first modern humanitarian organisation, is a private, Geneva-based organisation.

However, it is also accorded formal recognition by states and mostly funded by them. In addition, national Red Cross (or Red Crescent) Societies are affiliated with the International Federation of Red Cross and Red Crescent Societies (IFRC).

Many humanitarian organisations are small-scale groups which operate locally and often focus on a single issue. However, a few groups have become global players and are active or represented in many countries. These include, in particular, private non-profit organisations such as Oxfam, Médecins Sans Frontières (MSF), International Rescue Committee (IRC) or Cooperative for Assistance and Relief Everywhere (CARE). Other civil society organisations involved in disaster relief assistance include church-affiliated organisations such as Caritas, World Vision, the Joint Distribution Committee and several important Islamic and Buddhist organisations.

There is no clear-cut distinction between domestic and international crises. One important dimension is the scale of the disaster. Another is the capacity of a government to respond, coupled with its willingness to allow external actors to be involved in the relief efforts. Exceptionally, a natural disaster may affect several countries simultaneously, as in the case of hurricane Mitch in Central America in 1999 or the 2005 earthquake in South Asia. However, even a large-scale disaster may not always elicit an international response. Although at least 250,000 people died in the 1976 Tangshan earthquake in China, the outside world did not respond, as it was neither informed of the disaster nor did the Chinese government request assistance. The response to a natural disaster is coordinated by the government of the country where it occurs. Appeals for international aid are often launched by resource-poor countries in the case of large-scale disasters.

In conflict areas, excess mortality among civilian populations most often results from population displacements in resource-poor areas. UN relief agencies and leading international NGOs usually operate in such situations. NGOs have played an increasingly important role in the UN system,[6] although the cooperation between both types of actors is not always easy.[7] States may decide to intervene militarily on various grounds, and sometimes fail to respond. In addition, it was shown that in some cases assistance was withdrawn or provided by states to force warring parties to comply with peace agreements.[8]

Competing norms, the rising number of actors and the complexity of the processes involved have led to numerous concerns regarding the relevance of the processes, outputs and outcomes of the aid system.[9] For the region, these questions were especially highlighted in the context of the relief effort in response to the December 2004 tsunami, which is considered next.

The response to the 2004 tsunami

The December 2004 Indian Ocean tsunami was unquestionably one of the major disasters in recent history. On 26 December 2004 an earthquake of magnitude 9.2 on the Richter scale triggered off a series of tsunamis that affected twelve countries around the Indian Ocean. The earthquake was the most powerful in four decades. Although the tsunami reached as far as Southern Africa, the most severely affected countries were Indonesia, Sri Lanka and India. More than 240,000 people died, while 50,000 are still missing and over one million people were displaced.[10]

Few natural disasters have been so devastating in living memory. A cyclone killed 300,000 people in Bangladesh in 1970. The earthquake in Tangshan, China, killed at least 250,000 people in 1976. Hurricane Mitch in 1998 brought devastation to several countries in Central America, but over a much smaller area. In addition to its geographical extent, the number of victims and the number of countries affected, the tsunami was also exceptional because of its global nature due to developments in global communication technology and tourism patterns.

As is usually the case in natural disasters, the rescue phase was short, with work being primarily carried out by residents of the affected areas. Family members, neighbours and local authorities accounted for the bulk of the rescue efforts. As Singh has noted with respect to Indonesia:

> Despite the tendency of foreign media to focus on what their respective forces and agencies have done, the affected countries have played important roles as well. In Indonesia's case, the Indonesians did a lot of ad hoc relief work even before foreign agencies arrived. The Indonesian Armed Forces had done a good job in coordinating emergency relief work.[11]

In addition, many regional state and non-state organisations responded swiftly to the disaster. It would be difficult, if not impossible, to acknowledge all the efforts undertaken and ascertain all the contributions, as a very large number of people and organisations were involved.

The Singaporean contribution was one of the most recognised of all the ASEAN countries. Over 1,200 military and defence personnel from the Singapore Armed Forces (SAF) were involved. In fact, the Singapore military were the first outsiders to reach the most affected area of Aceh Province in Indonesia. This did not happen by chance, but was the result of a prior focus. 'The SAF's defence diplomacy helped facilitate the relief missions. The SAF had joined the Indonesian Navy over the years in combined civic projects (dental care, repairing community facilities) around Meulaboh.'[12] The SAF deployed three amphibious vessels in the area. Singapore also sent emergency relief supplies and teams to Thailand, Sri Lanka and the Maldives. In addition, the Singapore government provided significant grants bilaterally and through the International Federation of Red Cross and Red Crescent Societies. The largest was a US$4.4 million grant for post-tsunami reconstruction projects in the Maldives.[13] The Singapore government also spent S$1 million to help the Singapore Red Cross launch an appeal for public donations.[14]

Malaysia was in a different situation initially, as the country was affected by the tsunami, though not severely. However, the Malaysian government quickly deployed a team of 179 Special Malaysian Rescue Team (SMART) and relief workers to Aceh. In addition to emergency supplies and search and rescue equipment delivered by helicopter, ship and aircraft, the Malaysian government donated around US$2.5 million in cash. Interestingly, the corporate sector is reported to have given nearly US$3.35 million.[15] Lastly, MERCY Malaysia, a Malaysian medical relief organisation, sent volunteers to Aceh and Sri Lanka. MERCY Malaysia claims it was one of the first NGOs on the ground, as its doctors and volunteers were sent to Aceh the very next day after the tsunami.[16]

The reported contributions from other ASEAN countries were more symbolic. In particular, Laos gave Indonesia, Thailand, India and Sri Lanka a US$25,000 cash contribution each, and a US$100,000 grant through FAO for 'comprehensive fisheries environment and livelihood impact assessments'.[17] The Philippine Red Cross contributed US$65,528 through IFRC and the government sent a 'humanitarian contingent',[18] but as no system was set up to record donations across the region, many more contributions doubtless went unnoticed.

However, whereas aid was massively provided on a bilateral, multilateral or non-governmental basis, regional processes were limited. ASEAN leaders convened a special meeting, held in Jakarta less than two weeks after the disaster. The meeting was described as an opportunity to strengthen the response to the tsunami in terms of emergency relief, rehabilitation, reconstruction and future prevention. At the same time, it was short on precise regional input. The tsunami aid summit's declaration emphasised, under the heading 'Prevention and Mitigation', the agreement of participants to:

a   Support ASEAN's decision to establish regional mechanisms on disaster prevention and mitigation, inter alia:
    The utilisation of military and civilian personnel in disaster relief operation and an ASEAN Humanitarian Assistance Centre, as provided for in the ASEAN Security Community Plan of Action;
    ASEAN Disaster Information Sharing and Communication Network, as provided for in the ASEAN Socio-Cultural Community component of the Vientiane Action Programme;
    A regional instrument on disaster management and emergency response.
b   Establish a regional early warning system such as Regional Tsunami Early Warning Center on the Indian Ocean and the Southeast Asia region.[19]

This suggests that ASEAN's response to the disaster was seen as an opportunity to upgrade the region's capacity to respond in the future and to reaffirm decisions made earlier by the institution. This quite narrow response can be seen as stemming from shortcomings in both ASEAN's institutional capacity to address the needs of its members in a timely manner and the limitations placed on the organisation in terms of new operating procedures and norms. In other words, even as different Southeast Asian states were dispatching coalitions of state agencies and civil society organisations to the disaster sites, the body charged with ensuring 'active cooperation and mutual assistance' for stability and prosperity was effectively sidelined – as was also the case with the 1999 intervention in East Timor. This implies a repeated failure of governance at the regional level, implying that the region is less institutionally cohesive and its actors instead behave more as a coalition of like-minded states rather than as a nascent community.

Much of this failure can be related to the way in which ASEAN responds to disasters – in terms of mechanisms and norms – as well as the way that ASEAN relates to civil society organisations, whose role in these situations is so critical. In disaggregating this failure, four main factors can explain ASEAN's limited response, apart from the diplomatic efforts that led to the Jakarta conference. The two primary factors are the prevailing regional security environment and ASEAN's institutional basis for disaster response. In addition, ASEAN over-relied on the role of the UN, which failed to deliver relief efforts in a timely manner, while regional civil society organisations faced constraints in their efforts to respond to the disaster.

The regional security environment

The tsunami struck one of the sensitive regions of the world in terms of security concerns. It affected an area from the Straits of Malacca, in the east, to Sri Lanka, in the west. The Straits is one of the busiest sea lanes in the world and an essential route for global trade. In particular, it is a vital passage for energy supplies for many East Asian countries. Any disruption to these trade flows could cause significant disruption to the global political economy. Beyond the Straits, the Andaman Sea and the Indian Ocean are equally sensitive areas, despite a long history of confidence-building measures between naval forces that have taken place. Moreover, countries in the region have civil insurgencies in affected areas, especially Indonesia and Sri Lanka.

In response to the human tragedy in this sensitive area a rapid intervention was called for, for which only the militaries of a few countries were immediately equipped to substantially provide across all the affected areas. The infrastructure required for the relief operation was quickly made available from the naval forces of various countries. In particular, the US Navy deployed an aircraft carrier battle group to Indonesia within days. The Indian Navy reached Sri Lanka and the Maldives within two days of the disaster, in addition to assisting the severely affected Andaman and Nicobar Islands on its own territory. Military helicopters were extensively used to ferry supplies to communities that could not be reached by other means.

As the naval forces of various countries converged towards the areas affected by the tsunami, US President George W. Bush announced that a core group of nations would lead the response to the tsunami. The US initially called on India, Japan and Australia to take the lead in that response jointly with the US 'as it became clear that Australia, Japan and India had relief capabilities as well as military forces in the region, even though India was itself a major victim'.[20] Within days, though, the core group was dissolved and the UN was officially put in charge of the coordination of the relief effort. As then US Secretary of State Colin Powell noted, 'The core group helped to catalyze the international response ... But now having served its purpose, the core group will fold itself into the broader coordination efforts of the United Nations.'[21]

The distribution of power capabilities across the region restricts the ability of Southeast Asian nations to provide a significant input in response to regional disasters. In particular, the military capabilities of ASEAN countries in general, and their naval capabilities in particular, are no match for the United States, China and India. However, capabilities alone fail to account for ASEAN's low profile during the emergency phase. In this instance, one could argue that a different thinking could have led to the development by ASEAN navies of significant capabilities to respond to the tsunami. After all, an adequate response did not necessarily require the induction of an aircraft carrier battle group, as helicopters and amphibian vessels or other landing craft constituted the bulk of the hardware specifically needed in this case.

The issue here is that the development of such capabilities by the navy of one ASEAN country or another would likely arouse suspicion by other countries in the region as to the motives behind it. As observed in Chapter 1, issues of trust and sovereignty remain obstacles to deeper regional integration. Where mutual trust is low and sovereign concerns are high, the use of military personnel from regional countries in disaster relief remains limited. This in turn points to the fragility of the regional security framework in Southeast Asia, even though regional processes are certainly more advanced in Southeast Asia than in any other region of Asia.

In addition, the security context in Asia is marked by fluid, evolving alliances among the major powers involved. The US–Japan and US–Australia alliances are the exception, and have been strengthened since the turn of the century. In the same period the US has – in stark contrast – come to regard China as a strategic threat. The Indo-Russian alliance of the Cold War has gradually dissolved and, in its place, a steadily growing and wide-ranging partnership between the US and India has developed, while China and Russia are becoming increasingly close in a wide range of areas.

In this environment, it is difficult to anticipate coordinated political or military responses to current and future crises at a regional level. In the absence of sufficient trust and understanding to provide a responsive security framework, it is unlikely that the public goods (such as the physical instruments and coordination processes) required to respond effectively to a large-scale disaster can be provided. This does not mean that such public goods are created simply to respond to disasters, whether natural or man-made, but once these capacities are created, the marginal cost of ensuring their versatility is low, while the returns can be high.

The US armed forces have pioneered this integration of disaster-relief capabilities in their doctrine and equipment. It was noted in particular that:

> While the numbers of forces dedicated to the relief effort and the extent of aid they provided were impressive, the most invaluable U.S. contribution focused around another Defense Department unique capability: command, control, communications, and coordination. These attributes, critical in wartime, proved equally critical in ensuring an effective, coordinated response.[22]

This response system evolved as a result of past interventions, in particular a disaster relief operation by the US First Marine Expeditionary Force in 1991 in the aftermath of a typhoon in Bangladesh. As Cossa has observed:

> Since then, the Pacific Command has put great emphasis on developing its crisis response capabilities, to include its Military Planning Augmentation Team (MPAT) program, which has created a cadre of professionals who are accustomed to working together on a multinational basis to respond to crisis. As Deputy Secretary Wolfowitz observed, 'MPAT experience was put to good use in response to the tsunami crisis.'[23]

The restrictions caused by shortcomings in the regional security environment have significant implications for the development of regional systems for disaster relief management as well as for the ongoing development of regional governance in Asia. The mechanism that responded to the tsunami was neither regionally located nor formally based. The call for a core group came from outside the region and there was no formal security agreement linking the four participants. In this type of environment, the question that then arises is whether or not ASEAN could have played a more significant role in responding to the disaster.

ASEAN and disaster responses

In security issues, ASEAN has traditionally focused more on confidence-building measures (CBMs) and preventive diplomacy (PD) than joint crisis response. The 'ASEAN Way' – with its emphasis on consensual approach to security issues and the principle of non-intervention in the internal affairs of sovereign members – may have precluded a more decisive regional intervention. The focus is primarily on crisis prevention through confidence-building measures and preventive diplomacy. Most measures concentrate on crisis prevention rather than on crisis response.[24] Whereas there have been calls for more effective capacity building through joint exercises in response to threats such as piracy, terrorism or illegal immigration, the pace of implementation remains problematic. As was noted above, 'the Asia-Pacific region contains numerous flashpoints and ongoing conflicts where crisis-time responses could be called for'.[25]

Nonetheless, in the ASEAN Security Community (ASC) Plan of Action adopted at the Ninth Summit in Bali (2003), ASEAN leaders identified specific policy directions in the sensitive area of responses to conflicts.[26] These covered the use of both military and civilian personnel in disaster-relief operations and the sharing of member countries' experiences in peace-keeping operations 'with a view to establishing an ASEAN arrangement for the maintenance of peace and stability'.[27] In addition, under a sub-section titled 'Post-conflict Peace Building: Strengthening ASEAN Humanitarian Assistance', the following objectives were spelled out:

a Providing safe havens in conflict areas;
b Ensuring the delivery of basic services or assistance to victims of conflict;
c Orderly repatriation of refugees/displaced persons and resettlement of internally displaced persons;
d Ensuring safety of humanitarian relief assistance workers;
e Promoting the role of humanitarian relief assistance organizations;
f Considering the establishment of an ASEAN Humanitarian Assistance Centre; and
g Intensifying cooperation with the United Nations and other organizations/ donor countries.[28]

This list of objectives calls for several comments. First, even though it would otherwise indicate a commitment to a cooperative, engaged process, the norms underpinning the 'ASEAN Way' still largely hold – meaning a high degree of sensitivity to matters that may impinge on state security or legitimacy. Second, the ASC Plan of Action does not explicitly refer to principles and norms. This may be due to the fact that there is a diverse range of opinions held by ASEAN members towards humanitarian intervention, although most remain wary of advocating or supporting humanitarian interventions.[29] That said, 'the role played by the Philippines and Thailand in East Timor peace-keeping efforts suggests that some ASEAN countries are more positive about humanitarian intervention than others'.[30] On the other hand, there is also no explicit reference to international humanitarian law in ASEAN's Security Community Plan of Action, although member states are signatories to the Geneva Conventions. In addition, while the focus is on the repatriation of refugees and resettlement of displaced people, there is no reference to refugee law and the right of asylum. These absences suggest a lowest-common-denominator approach by regional states to the ASC, one that provides maximum flexibility to signatory states.

Third, while humanitarian organisations are mentioned, it is not clear how ASEAN states plan to interact with them. The concern for the safety of aid workers apparently points to a protection role. However, the framework for the interaction between humanitarian organisations and security forces is not defined here. It is also not clear on what basis ASEAN plans to promote humanitarian relief assistance organisations. Finally, it is also not clear who would be responsible for organising the safe havens mentioned in ASEAN's plan. In particular, it is not explained under what circumstances and for whose benefit such safe havens would be established.

ASEAN's main achievement so far is that there has been no war between member countries since the organisation was established. The organisation has, overall, been more effective in crisis prevention than in crisis response. However, ASEAN was also involved for many years in the Cambodia issue. Although major powers played a decisive role, ASEAN was nonetheless credited with a significant input to the solution of the crisis. In particular, ASEAN was 'unwilling to accept state sovereignty as an excuse to ignore national-level conflict and so "interfered" in Cambodia and legitimised that interference'.[31] The main bargaining chip was ASEAN's decision to conditionally admit Cambodia as a member. However, ASEAN did not repeat this success with Myanmar and has since been timid and slow in addressing the Myanmar issue, notwithstanding calls from some regional states and civil society organisations for more constructive engagement.

ASEAN was also involved in the East Timor crisis, although the crisis was first discussed within the Asia-Pacific Economic Cooperation (APEC) framework. But in the emergency phase the organisation's response was rather weak and limited.[32] ASEAN member countries 'did not feature strongly in the initial intervention by the multinational force led by Australia in September 1999',[33] even though some states sent troops and support personnel to East Timor.

Little has been done by ASEAN with regard to the involvement of security forces in emergency responses to man-made or natural disasters. One reason may be that, barring Singapore, the armed forces of ASEAN member countries have had an important role in maintaining order within their own boundaries. Another is that there is no common understanding between ASEAN member countries with regard to threats. As a result, ASEAN has not developed – at a regional level – the capacities required to respond effectively to large-scale disasters. The critical issue here is that, because ASEAN members are wary of interference or intervention in the internal affairs of other countries, they have not developed the military capabilities that would enable them to respond to large-scale disasters in the region, whether natural or man made.

Limited attention has been devoted by ASEAN to non-traditional threats such as epidemics, natural disasters or refugee influxes, although:

> The need for ASEAN cooperation on natural disasters and calamities was among the first envisioned by ASEAN leaders and was enunciated in the ASEAN declaration on Mutual Assistance on Natural Disasters

in 1976. In 1996, the development of an ASEAN Regional Program on Disaster Management was first proposed at the 9th AEGDM Meeting in Manila.[34]

Nevertheless, a positive step was achieved in 2002 with the establishment of the ASEAN Regional Programme on Disaster Management (ARPDM) document as 'a framework for cooperation among ASEAN Member Countries on disaster management'.[35] In particular, the programme outlined regional strategies and priorities in disaster management, focusing on capacity building, the sharing of information and resources, public education, awareness and advocacy. The disasters that called for technical cooperation included 'earthquake vulnerability reduction; flash flood, landslide, sea and river erosion preparedness and mitigation; dissemination of flood early warning; safety of children in flood-prone areas; typhoon and cyclone preparedness; and early warning system for forest fire management'.[36]

ASEAN went further and called for the establishment of a Response Action Plan, with a view to enhancing the response capacities of member countries, and joint simulation exercises for disaster relief.[37] A fresh impetus was given at the 38th ASEAN Ministerial Meeting in July 2005 in Vientiane, where an Agreement on Disaster Management and Emergency Response was signed.[38] The creation of 'mechanisms to mitigate the impacts of natural and human-induced disaster and serve as a joint response to disaster emergencies'[39] was in particular welcomed by the Red Cross, as the lack of regional structures and legal arrangements had previously hampered efforts to respond to disasters.

In addition, ASEAN organised its first-ever 'Regional Disaster Emergency Response Simulation Exercise' (named ARDEX-05) in September 2005. The exercise was designed to test the joint response capacities of Malaysia, Singapore and Brunei to a serious earthquake in peninsular Malaysia. An evaluation meeting and a workshop followed to incorporate the lessons learned into the ASEAN Standby Arrangements and Standard Operating Procedures under the ASEAN Agreement on Disaster Management and Emergency Response.[40] However, the scope of this exercise was limited to a search and rescue operation on a cluster of high-rise buildings. The operation only mobilised eighty rescue workers from Malaysia, six special squad members of the Brunei Fire Services Department and an undisclosed number of personnel from the Singapore Civil Defence Force.[41]

The establishment of a Response Action Plan at the 38th ASEAN Ministerial Meeting and the organisation of a 'Regional Disaster Emergency Response Simulation Exercise' may be seen as positive outcomes of the tsunami, along with the call for a regional tsunami warning system. However, the ARDEX-05 exercise was on a limited scale and certainly not one that would enable ASEAN to respond on its own to future large-scale disasters in the region. Notwithstanding the difficulties the African Union faces in Sudan, ASEAN clearly trails the AU and other regional organisations in its capacity to organise a regional military component in response to a disaster.

At the 40th ASEAN Ministerial Meeting in July 2007, it was noted that 'the EAS has carved for itself an important niche as a Leaders-led forum for dialogue on broad strategic, political and economic issues of common interest'.[42] Natural disaster mitigation was listed as one of the priority areas, which suggests that ASEAN may prefer to address the issue in a geographically broader framework, with increased input from the 'periphery'. On this point, India offered to host an EAS meeting on disaster management in November 2007 in New Delhi during the 2nd EAS.

An adequate military response from ASEAN to a large-scale disaster is unlikely in the foreseeable future, given the regional security constraints and ASEAN's relatively timid approach. In this context, could the push for a more assertive regional response come from other players? The role of the UN and that of civil society organisations is discussed in the following sections.

ASEAN and the UN: exploring an integrated framework for disaster response

In its Regional Programme on Disaster Management, ASEAN mentions external partnerships, in particular with international agencies such as the United Nations.[43] The United Nations was open early on to the idea of regional efforts in support of peace-keeping and other relief efforts. In particular, it was hoped that countries from a given region would be more knowledgeable about a crisis in the neighbourhood and more willing to contribute troops and other resources to respond to such a crisis. However, there were also fears that a peace-keeping or other relief effort with a regional focus might jeopardise the impartiality that the United Nations is mandated to uphold. In practice, however, these regionally based operations have not been a success.

The situation is complicated by the fact that the UN agencies involved in disaster response are not organised along a regional focus. None of these agencies has strong regional offices except the WHO, whose directors of regional offices are elected by member countries from the region. But whereas some ASEAN countries (Indonesia, Myanmar, Thailand, Timor-Leste) are under the WHO Office for Southeast Asia, others (Brunei, Cambodia, Laos, Malaysia, the Philippines, Singapore and Vietnam) are under the WHO Office for the Western Pacific. In any case, the WHO has only a limited operational role in disaster-response efforts, except in addressing subsequent epidemic outbreaks.

In contrast, the main operational agencies of the United Nations involved in disaster relief (UNICEF, UNHCR and WFP) do not have strong regional offices. They work primarily on a bilateral basis with the countries that require their support, and decision-making processes are centralised in Geneva, New York and Rome. Conversely, regional governments do not contribute significantly to these UN agencies. Japan stands out and has been for a long time the second-largest contributor to all international agencies specialised in disaster response. Besides, the WFP is the only UN agency involved in disaster relief which draws significant contributions from other Asian governments. In addition to Japan, China, India and Korea also rank among the top twenty-five contributors to the WFP.

In the aftermath of the tsunami, few observers concluded that the UN did a good job in terms of coordination. One participant, from CARE Emergency Group, noted that:

> With more than a dozen UN agencies in Banda Aceh competing for their turf, coordination went into overdrive, with 72 coordination meetings per week in Banda Aceh alone ... It was often not clear if the purpose of meetings was to share information, build consensus or make operational or policy decisions. Senior staff often spent more time on coordination than implementation.[44]

The UN was also criticised for its slow response, bureaucratic ways and limited ability to deliver in the emergency phase, which stood in contrast to the assistance deployed by the naval forces of various countries. The Indonesian minister of defence noted that 'the US Military there has been the backbone of the logistical operations providing assistance to all afflicted after the disaster'.[45]

ASEAN members have clearly sought increased interaction with the United Nations. At the 40th Ministerial Meeting in Manila, they declared:

> We welcomed the conferment of observer status to ASEAN at the UN General Assembly and other main bodies in December 2006. We recalled our decision during our ASEAN Foreign Ministers Retreat in Siem Reap in March 2007 to explore the possibility to upgrade our relations with the UN.[46]

But beyond the diplomatic rhetoric, the level of engagement and collaboration between regional organisations and UN agencies specialised in response to disasters remains low. This suggests that in developing disaster-response mechanisms the region will either have to rely on Asian-based institutions or depend on ad hoc coalitions of individual states with the requisite capacity, trust and willingness to assist as needed. However, if regional organisations remain timid and intergovernmental organisations specialised in disaster relief show little interest for the concept of regional governance, can non-governmental organisations provide a regional impetus?

ASEAN and humanitarian organisations

Asian humanitarian organisations, like their counterparts from around the world, faced difficult issues in the aftermath of the tsunami. Natural disasters are conceptually and legally regarded as separate from conflict situations, and usually call for distinct responses. But it quickly became clear to all that the main affected areas, in Sri Lanka and Aceh, were also war zones. In particular, the Aceh province of Indonesia, the most affected region of all, had not been under firm state control for many years. When the tsunami struck, Aceh had been a battleground between the Indonesian armed forces and the Free Aceh Movement for nearly thirty years. The province was under martial law for more than two years and closed to foreigners.

This had two main consequences. First, physical constraints in the form of restriction on the free movements of aid workers in Aceh, or threats of such restrictions, were repeatedly mentioned. The policy, as explained by an Indonesian general, was that 'a foreign medical team has to be working with a team from the Indonesian Department of Health, and together they will be accompanied by the Indonesian military on everything outside Banda Aceh and Meulaboh'.[47] The security context remained volatile and led to several incidents. In addition, questions arose about the meaning of impartiality in such a context, as people displaced by the tsunami reportedly received more attention than their neighbours displaced by war.

In fact, there is not much that humanitarian organisations can do in such situations. As mentioned earlier, the bulk of the rescue work was carried out by the affected communities themselves and local/national authorities. Contrary to the apocalyptic predictions of UN officials, there was little that outsiders could do to support tsunami survivors. Water, sanitation, food and shelter were provided where needed. Expatriate doctors and nurses were sent to help run medical facilities where local staff had been killed by the tsunami – even as the affected countries moved quickly to send their own medical workers to the affected areas, as their capacity to respond was not seriously reduced at the national level. In short, this required a relatively modest, targeted and short-term effort. As the emergency phase was short and a large number of other agencies joined in, leading international humanitarian organisations quickly scaled back their operations and refocused on acute operational priorities at the time, including Sudan/Darfur and Niger.[48] However, the aid system as a whole, including UN agencies and numerous NGOs, was once again the target of harsh criticism. Lessons learned in previous emergency operations, including after the Rwanda genocide and in Kosovo, were forgotten. Shortcomings included 'the quantity and quality of international personnel; inappropriate methods and tools; and weak engagement in or management of coordination'.[49] They also included poor communication with the beneficiaries and the local authorities, and 'supply-driven, unsolicited and inappropriate aid.'[50]

While dealing with the same issues, Asian relief organisations faced additional difficulties. Civil society organisations have developed remarkably across the region since the mid 1990s. However, three limitations come to mind if Asian humanitarian organisations are to contribute significantly to the setting up of a regional disaster relief framework, namely, levels of state–society cooperation,[51] state tolerance for civil activism,[52] and institutional capacity for humanitarian organisations.

Civil society organisations are still regarded as nuisances in many Asian countries. Constraints in terms of registration, restrictive operating conditions and criteria in terms of membership, legislation curtailing the public activities of CSOs or their ability to receive funding from outside the country have thwarted the development of civil society organisations in many countries across the region. In the past few years, the situation has gradually improved, although not everywhere.

More specifically, Asian states are likely to remain wary of civil society involvement in international activism. In the past, various governments have sought to co-opt international NGOs active in disaster response in pursuit of their own foreign policy agendas. Japan and Taiwan, in particular, have been noted as adopting this approach.[53] In contrast, most Asian states, whether aid providers or recipients, have sought to restrict civil society involvement in sensitive disaster relief activities. In particular, overseas relief activities by Singapore-based charities are hampered, as they are required by law to spend at least 80 per cent of the donations they receive in Singapore itself. Information about disasters in China was regarded as state secret until very recently and disclosure of such information was a punishable offence.[54]

It can be argued that such sensitivity is understandable, as groups pursuing self-determination have sometimes linked up with international NGOs and tried to recast their struggle in terms of human rights violations and the need for humanitarian assistance, in particular in East Timor, Aceh, Tibet and Myanmar.[55] In contrast, it has been argued that some ASEAN governments tend to cast the struggle as Asian versus Western values and ignore the fact that NGOs from within the region were also vocal in defending human rights.[56] Throughout the 1990s efforts by civil society organisations from ASEAN countries attempting to publicise the situation in East Timor or to invite East Timorese representatives to regional conferences were repeatedly thwarted by their governments.[57]

Finally, Asian humanitarian organisations still have a limited pool of staff and/or volunteers with experience in emergency operations, as it takes a long time to build such teams. Specifically, it was noted in the aftermath of the tsunami that, while Asian humanitarian organisations initially sent experienced workers and volunteers, they were struggling to replace them with equally experienced staff in a second phase.[58] In addition, independent humanitarian action remains constrained by several factors, including the expansion of state humanitarianism. Addressing these issues and adjusting to a rapidly changing environment has been an ongoing challenge even for humanitarian organisations with a long international experience. This is all the more true for Asian humanitarian organisations, as they have less experience and expertise in overseas relief operations.

This does not mean, though, that Asian humanitarian organisations are reluctant to respond to disasters on a regional basis. In fact, thirty regional

CSOs met in February 2002 to discuss the issue of regional cooperation in this field and created the Asian Disaster Reduction & Response Network (ADRRN) with the following objectives:

- To develop an interactive network of NGOs committed to achieving excellence in the field of disaster reduction and response;
- To raise the relevant concerns of NGOs in the Asia-Pacific region to the larger community of NGOs globally, through various international forums and platforms;
- To promote best practices and standards in disaster reduction and response; and
- To provide a mechanism for sharing reliable information and facilitating capacity-building among network members and other stakeholders.[59]

However, the issue here is that there is little interaction between NGOs and ASEAN overall, although it was argued that 'the future of the Association may depend as much on the activities of NGOs as on those of ASEAN's governments and private enterprises'.[60] It was mentioned in particular that 'there is also discussion on an ASEAN coalition of NGOs in disaster relief'[61] and that 'there are 58 NGOs registered with ASEAN and several are related to the social sector'.[62] However, the scope for regional interaction between governments and NGOs appears to remain highly restrictive, especially as one of the conditions spelled out is to 'promote the formulation of an ASEAN consensus at international forums'.[63] In comparison, the EU has established a specialised office (ECHO) to respond to disasters outside Europe, which distributes more than half of its €500 million annual budget through the nearly 200 NGOs from EU member countries with which it has a partnership agreement.[64] Given the constraints identified above, it is unlikely that Asian civil society organisations can be a driving force behind the establishment of a regional response to disasters in Asia or any of its subregions in the foreseeable future.

Conclusion

The December 2004 tsunami in the Indian Ocean was the first regional natural disaster of the modern period. However, disaster-response efforts were primarily driven by major powers, not by regional actors. In South Asia, India took the initiative and the lead, but on a bilateral basis. In Southeast Asia, ASEAN was diplomatically active – it hosted the Jakarta conference – but was conspicuously absent from the core group set up by the United States. There was no effective response at a regional level. Tying its fate to the UN around an ill-defined regional paradigm neither enhanced ASEAN's institutional capacity to respond nor allowed the institution to retain any significant degree of control over the processes involved.

The response of Asian states to future disasters is unlikely to be driven by a regional governance paradigm. Since its inception ASEAN has been successful in achieving peace between member states, but it is still timid when a situation calls for swift and decisive action. ASEAN's reluctance to intervene in the internal affairs of a sovereign country restricts its capacity to act and, in particular, to respond to crises. Furthermore, military cooperation between ASEAN member countries remains limited, as trust between ASEAN states remains low. With only three ARDEX operations in the field of disaster response between the tsunami and May 2008, the same pattern of outside intervention and regional irrelevance is likely to be repeated the next time a large-scale disaster strikes the region.

In this environment, Asian humanitarian organisations have to deal with the dilemmas that other humanitarian organisations face. In particular, they must position themselves as independent actors in an environment where military forces increasingly play a high-profile role in disaster-response efforts, at least in the initial stages, as was the case in Kosovo, in Afghanistan or after the tsunami. In addition, they cannot yet rely on a large pool of staff and volunteers with experience in emergency response, and positive interactions with the region's governments remain limited.

In conclusion, even though responses to disasters in Asia draw upon numerous linking arrangements between actors at the state and non-state levels – with private sector organisations relied upon for some funding support – the crisis-management response remains dominated by those states with the greatest capacity. In the absence of a guiding international framework for managing regional cooperation in this area, and without the development of a similar capacity within ASEAN or ASEAN+3, regional states will remain dependent on ad hoc arrangements and outside intervention rather than jointly act as members of a developing East Asian Community. Hence, although the regional governance model may be a way to build capacity in this area, the low level of trust between Asian states makes it unlikely that it will be embraced as a way forward in the foreseeable future.

Postscript: tropical cyclone Nargis

As this volume was going to press, tropical cyclone (TC) Nargis made landfall on 2 May 2008, in the Irrawaddy Delta of Myanmar. Initial estimates of human casualties were low, but quickly rose. While the final figure may never be accurately known, a mid-range estimate places the death toll at approximately 100,000 persons, with many more displaced or injured. In terms of regional disaster governance, the response to TC Nargis is extremely relevant to this chapter and volume, especially as it supports the preceding analysis regarding the 2004 tsunami.

As with the tsunami, the humanitarian disaster caused by TC Nargis in Myanmar quickly highlighted failures of governance – at both the national and regional levels. At the regional level, ASEAN's response showed that it remains – in this area, at least – a collection of states unable to forge transnational policies or actions that compel actions by member states. In the aftermath of the 2004 tsunami, ASEAN members signed the ASEAN Agreement on Disaster Management and Emergency Response (ADMER), which provides the governing framework for the region to respond to disasters.[65] This was the latest in a long series of agreements – stretching back to the 1976 ASEAN Declaration on Mutual Assistance on Natural Disasters – that attempted to bind the region closer together in the event of calamities.

The ADMER contains a number of objectives for its signatories, of which the first two are most relevant for this discussion, namely: to 'co-operate in developing and implementing measures to reduce disaster losses', and to 'immediately respond to a disaster occurring within their territory'.[66] In both objectives, Myanmar and ASEAN have failed to demonstrate a commitment to disaster governance. Myanmar's response – both internally and regionally – has been the subject of sustained criticism from the international community. First, even though it was informed a week beforehand of the danger posed by TC Nargis by the Asian Disaster Preparedness Centre (established for exactly this purpose following the tsunami) and then by the Indian Meteorological Department, the Myanmar government failed to prepare its population.[67] Although, in the period immediately following landfall, the low surplus organisational capacity of the Myanmar state, coupled with the preparations for the general referendum on political reform, may have accounted for the regime's inaction, this was not a conclusion that could be sustained over the following three weeks. Indeed, despite the severity of the cyclone it was not until four days later that the regime formally requested help. When it did so, it was Canada, Thailand and the United States that were the first to respond with aid.[68]

ASEAN's response has been hamstrung by another passage within the ADMER which ensures that the 'sovereignty, territorial integrity and national unity of the Parties shall be respected … [and that] offers of assistance shall only be provided upon the request or with the consent of the affected Party' as well as by the general weakness of the organisation with respect to its individual members.[69] As with the 2004 tsunami, it fell to individual ASEAN members to respond – insofar as they were allowed – to the crisis. The first emergency ASEAN meeting was only held on 19 May, nearly three weeks after TC Nargis made landfall.[70] In the interim, regional and international diplomats worked to pressure the Myanmar government into allowing access for the necessary aid and the technical support staff. They were supported by aid agencies, especially those with staff already in the country.[71] ASEAN's inability to respond in a timely fashion to the crisis posed by TC Nargis and to assist Myanmar in recognising the scale of the disaster, supports the earlier conclusions reached on the tsunami – that, at present, ASEAN is unable to effectively implement regional disaster governance, with the responses falling to the level of its member states (some of which are coordinated multilaterally and others of which are unilateral initiatives), international civil society organisations and the wider international community. The fact that this is still the case over three years since the tsunami, shows how slowly substantive policy reform can occur in contentious areas in ASEAN. Meanwhile, it is the people of the region who suffer.

Notes

1 Arakida, Masaru. 'Information Sharing for Effective Disaster Management', presentation at the World Conference on Disaster Reduction (WCDR). (Kobe: January 2005). http://www.fao.org/documents/show_cdr.asp?url_file = /docrep/007/ae541e/ae541e05.htm. Accessed 12 September 2005.
2 United Nations Economic and Social Commission for Asia and the Pacific (UNESCAP) and the Asia Disaster Preparedness Centre (ADPC). 'International Day for Natural Disaster Reduction', Bangkok, undated. http://www.unescap.org/unis/Front/Disaster.asp. Accessed 27 September 2005.
3 Shaw, Rajib and Katsuihciro Goda. 'From Disaster to Sustainable Civil Society: the Kobe Experience', *Disasters*. (Vol. 28, No. 1, 2004), pp. 16–40.
4 See Deng, Francis M. 'Dealing with the Displaced: A Challenge to the International Community', *Global Governance*. (Vol. 1, No. 1, 1995), pp. 45–57, and Thomas G. Weiss. 'The Politics of Humanitarian Ideas', *Security Dialogue*. (Vol. 31, No. 1, 2000), pp. 11–23.
5 For a comprehensive discussion of the various options and controversies, see Ramsbotham, Oliver and Tom Woodhouse. *Humanitarian Intervention in Contemporary Conflict*. (Cambridge: Polity Press, 1996), pp. 106–164. See also Weiss, Thomas G. 'The Sunset of Humanitarian Intervention? The Responsibility to Protect in a Unipolar Era', *Security Dialogue*. (Vol. 35, No. 2, 2004), pp. 135–153.
6 See, for instance, Willetts, Peter. 'From "Consultative Arrangements" to "Partnership": The Changing Status of NGOs in Diplomacy at the UN'. *Global Governance*. (Vol. 6, No. 2, 2000), pp. 191–212. Alger, Chadwick. 'The Emerging Roles of NGOs in the UN System: From Article 71 to a People's Millennium Assembly', *Global Governance*. (Vol. 8, No. 1, 2002), pp. 93–117.
7 Donini, Antonio. 'The Bureaucracy and the Free Spirits: Stagnation and Innovation in the Relationship between the UN and NGOs', *Third World Quarterly*. (Vol. 16, No. 3, 1995), pp. 421–439. Smith, Edwin M. and Thomas G. Weiss. 'UN Task-sharing: Towards or Away from Global Governance?', *Third World Quarterly*. (Vol. 18, No. 3, 1997), pp. 595–619. Duffield, Mark. 'NGO Relief in War Zones: Towards an Analysis of the New Aid Paradigm', *Third World Quarterly*. (Vol. 18, No. 3, 1997), pp. 527–542.
8 Weissman, Fabrice. 'Sierra Leone: Peace at Any Price', in Fabrice Weissman (ed.). *In the Shadow of 'Just Wars': Violence, Politics and Humanitarian Action*. (London: Hurst, 2004), pp. 60–61.
9 For a discussion of the response of the aid system to famines, see de Waal, Alex. *Famine Crimes: Politics and the Disaster Relief Industry in Africa*. (Oxford: James Currey, 1997), pp. 1–6. For a discussion of the response of the aid system to the tsunami, see: Telford, J., J. Cosgrave and R. Houghton. *Joint Evaluation of the International Response to the Indian Ocean Tsunami*. (London: Tsunami Evaluation Coalition, 2006); and Guilloux, Alain. 'The Changing Environment of Disaster Response: Challenges for Humanitarian Organizations', paper presented at the 4th ISTR/Asia-Pacific Conference. (Bangalore: 16–18 November 2005).
10 United Nations, General Assembly: Economic and Social Council, 2005. 'Strengthening emergency relief, rehabilitation, reconstruction, recovery and

prevention in the aftermath of the Indian Ocean tsunami disaster', *Report of the Secretary-General*. A/60/86-E/2005/77.

11 LTC (Ret) Singh, Deep. 'Singapore's Humanitarian Assistance Efforts in the Aftermath of the Indian Ocean Tsunami', *Pointer Journal*. (Vol. 31, No. 1, 2005). http://www.mindef.gov.sg/safti/pointer/back/journals/2005/Vol31_1/4b.htm. Accessed 1 December 2005.

12 Ibid.

13 United Nations Office for the Coordination of Humanitarian Affairs (UNOCHA) Financial Tracking Service. 'Indian Ocean – Earthquake/tsunami – December 2004. List of all commitments/contributions and pledges as of 14 September 2007'. http://ocha.unog.ch/fts/reports/daily/ocha_R10_E14794_07091407. pdf. Accessed 14 September 2007.

14 Ibid.

15 Ibid.

16 Mercy Malaysia. *Annual Report 2004*. http://admin.mercy.org.my/functions/ar_reports/ar-04.pdf. Accessed 4 December 2005.

17 UNOCHA Financial Tracking Service. 'Indian Ocean – Earthquake/tsunami – December 2004. List of all commitments/contributions and pledges as of 14 September 2007'.

18 Ibid.

19 'Jakarta Tsunami Aid Summit's Declaration', *The Jakarta Post*. 6 January 2005. http://www.thejakartapost.com/tsunami_declaration.asp. Accessed 30 September 2005.

20 'In Efforts to Organize Aid, Powell and Governor Bush Will Tour Ravaged Areas', *The New York Times*. 31 December 2004.

21 'Annan Nudges Donors to Make Good on Full Pledges', *The New York Times*. 7 January 2005.

22 Cossa, Ralph A. 'South Asian Tsunami: U.S. Military Provides "Logistical Backbone" For Relief Operation'. http://usinfo.state.gov/journals/itps/1104/ijpe/cossa.htm. Accessed 30 November 2005.

23 Ibid.

24 Institute of Defence and Strategic Studies. 'A New Agenda for the ASEAN Regional Forum', *IDSS Monograph No 4*. A report on the IDSS project on the future of the ASEAN Regional Forum. (Singapore: ISDS, 2002).

25 Ibid.

26 More on the ASEAN Security Community is discussed in Chapter 2 of this volume.

27 *ANNEX for ASEAN Security Community Plan of Action (2004)*. http://www. aseansec.org/16829.htm. Accessed 14 September 2005.

28 Ibid.

29 See Severino, Rodolfo C. 'Toward Expanding the Frontiers of International Humanitarian Law', Remarks at the opening of the Regional Seminar on the National Implementation of International Humanitarian Law of the Southeast Asian Countries. Jakarta, 12 June 2000. http://www.aseansec.org/3223.htm. Accessed 14 September 2005.

30 Watanabe, Koji. 'The Debate on Humanitarian Intervention', in Koji Watanabe (ed.). *Humanitarian Intervention: The Evolving Asian Debate*. (Tokyo: Japan Center for International Exchange, 2003), p. 17.

31 Tay, Simon C. and Sukma Rizal. 'ASEAN', in Koji Watanabe (ed.). *Humanitarian Intervention: The Evolving Asian Debate*. (Tokyo: Japan Center for International Exchange, 2003), p. 114.

32 Hill, Cameron J. and William Tow. 'The ASEAN Regional Forum: Material and Ideational Dynamics', in Mark Beeson (ed.). *Reconfiguring East Asia: Regional Institutions and Organizations after the Crisis*. (London: RoutledgeCurzon, 2002), pp. 176–177.

33 Tay, Simon C. and Rizal Sukma. 'ASEAN', in Koji Watanabe (ed.). *Humanitarian Intervention: The Evolving Asian Debate.* (Tokyo: Japan Center for International Exchange, 2003), pp. 114–115.
34 Asian Disaster Preparedness Center. 'Partnerships for Disaster Reduction in South East Asia (PDR-SEA) Updates. Regional Workshop for the Development of the ASEAN Regional Program on Disaster Management', *Asian Disaster Management News.* (Vol. 8, No. 2, 2002). http://www.adpc.net/irc06/Newsletter/2002/04–06/program3.html. Accessed 16 September 2007.
35 Ibid.
36 Asian Disaster Preparedness Center. 'The 12th ASEAN Experts Group on Disaster Management Endorses the ASEAN Regional Program on Disaster Management', *Asian Disaster Management News.* (Vol. 8, No. 3, 2002). http://www.adpc.net/irc06/Newsletter/2002/07–09/program3.html. Accessed 16 September 2007.
37 Ibid.
38 'ASEAN Mounts First Regional Disaster Emergency Response Simulation Exercise'. http://www.aseansec.org/17734.htm. Accessed 20 September 2005.
39 'Red Cross Welcomes ASEAN Disaster Relief Pact'. http://www.aseansec.org/afp/128.htm. Accessed 20 September 2005.
40 'ASEAN Mounts First Regional Disaster Emergency Response Simulation Exercise'. http://www.aseansec.org/17734.htm. Accessed 20 September 2005.
41 Ibid.
42 'Joint Communique of the 40th ASEAN Ministerial Meeting (AMM)'. http://www.aseansec.org/20764.htm. Accessed 10 September 2007.
43 Asian Disaster Preparedness Center. 'The 12th ASEAN Experts Group on Disaster Management Endorses the ASEAN Regional Program on Disaster Management', *Asian Disaster Management News.* (Vol. 8, No. 3, 2002). http://www.adpc.net/irc06/Newsletter/2002/07–09/program3.html. Accessed 16 September 2007.
44 Völz, Carsten. 'Humanitarian Coordination in Indonesia: An NGO Viewpoint'. http://www.fmreview.org/FMRpdfs/Tsunami/11.pdf+carsten+voelz+aceh+un&hl = en. Accessed 5 December 2005.
45 Press conference by Deputy Secretary of Defense Paul Wolfowitz and Republic of Indonesia Minister of Defense Juwono Sudarsono. (Jakarta: 16 January 2005). http://jakarta.usembassy.gov/press_rel/ Wolfowitz-Jakarta-Jan05.html. Accessed 1 December 2005.
46 *Joint Communiqué of the 40th ASEAN Ministerial Meeting (AMM).* http://www.aseansec.org/20764.htm. Accessed 10 September 2007.
47 'Indonesia Puts Curbs on Relief in Rebel Areas', *The New York Times.* 12 January 2005.
48 For a discussion of these issues, see: Alain Guilloux, 'The Changing Environment of Disaster Response: Challenges for Humanitarian Organizations', paper presented at the 4th ISTR/Asia-Pacific Conference. Bangalore, 16–18 November 2005.
49 Telford, J., J. Cosgrave and R. Houghton. *Joint Evaluation of the International Response to the Indian Ocean Tsunami.* (London: Tsunami Evaluation Coalition, 2006), p. 17
50 Ibid.
51 For a discussion of this issue across the region, see in particular Shigetomi, Shinichi (ed.). *The State and NGOs: Perspective from Asia.* (Singapore: Institute of Southeast Asian Studies, 2002).
52 See Luna, Emmanuel M. 'Disaster Mitigation and Preparedness: The Case of NGOs in the Philippines', *Disasters.* (Vol. 25, No. 3, 2001), pp. 216–226.
53 He, Baogang. 'Transnational Civil Society and the National Identity Question in East Asia'. *Global Governance.* (Vol. 10, No. 2, 2004), pp. 227–246.
54 'Veil Lifted on Natural Disaster Death Tolls', *South China Morning Post.* 13 September 2005.

55 He, Baogang. 'Transnational Civil Society and the National Identity Question in East Asia', *Global Governance.* (Vol. 10, No. 2, 2004), pp. 227–246.
56 Aviel, Joann F. 'The Growing Role of NGOs in ASEAN', *Asia-Pacific Review.* (Vol. 6, No. 2, 1999), pp. 84–87.
57 Ibid.
58 Telephone interview with a Red Cross official. 7 November 2005.
59 Asian Disaster Reduction and Response Network. http://html.adrc.or.jp/dbs/new/aboutus.asp. Accessed 4 December 2005.
60 Aviel, Joann F. 'The Growing Role of NGOs in ASEAN', *Asia-Pacific Review.* (Vol. 6, No. 2, 1999), p. 78.
61 ASEAN. *Remarks by Mr Ong Keng Yong Secretary-General of ASEAN Plenary Session on "Civil Society and Regional Cooperation"*, 31st International Conference International Council on Social Welfare. (Kuala Lumpur: 18 August 2004). http://www.aseansec.org/16324.htm. Accessed 4 December 2005.
62 Ibid.
63 Ibid.
64 See ECHO website. http://europa.eu.int/comm/echo/statistics/echo_en.htm. Accessed 5 December 2005.
65 See: *ASEAN Agreement on Disaster Management and Emergency Response*, (Vientiane: 26 July 2005). http://www.aseansec.org/17579.htm. Accessed 13 May 2008.
66 Ibid. Article 4.
67 See: Goodspeed, Peter. 'Junta had 48-hour Warning Before Nargis Made Landfall', *National Post.* 8 May 2008. See also: Ghosh, Nirmal. 'A Vulnerable Nation Unprepared for Disaster', *The Straits Times.* 8 May 2008.
68 Aung, Hla Tun. 'Junta Makes Rare Plea for Aid as Death Toll Hits 15,000', *The Gazette.* 6 May 2008.
69 ASEAN Agreement on Disaster Management and Emergency Response, Article 3 (1).
70 'ASEAN Ministers to Discuss Aid for Cyclone-hit Myanmar Next Week', *Japan Economic Newswire.* 12 May 2008.
71 'Aid Getting to Survivors Despite Regime, Says Agencies', *New Zealand Press Association.* 12 May 2008.

12 Asia/Europe and the construction of regional governance

Stephanie Lawson

Introduction

Global and regional governance in the contemporary period are both attuned to a policy agenda requiring a certain convergence in behaviour among states around the goals of a liberal world economic order. As is pointed out in the introductory chapter, this implies a certain universalist orientation. However, while 'global governance' may be understood in application to multilateral mechanisms that transcend interstate relations on a worldwide scale, 'regional governance' obviously narrows the scope of these activities to a particular geographical space in which state actors may find 'a more concentrated sharing of norms and histories'.[1] How any particular region is defined, whether in geographical, economic, social or political terms, and on what basis it assumes a distinctive identity within the broader global sphere, thus become issues in any discussion of regional governance.

It seems equally obvious that regional governance implies some measure of regional integration. The latter, however, needs to be scrutinised further, for it envelops two closely related dimensions: regionalisation and regionalism. These terms are often used synonymously, but at least some observers have posited a distinction that takes the former as denoting activities consisting largely of region-centred economic pursuits emanating from a relatively uncoordinated set of private sector actors. Regionalism, on the other hand, is understood to denote self-conscious political activities that give rise to formal political initiatives and agreements, although these are by no means unrelated to economic activities.[2]

This chapter suggests a different distinction between the two terms, at least for the purposes of the present discussion. First, regionalisation can be taken to refer to processes that generate a structure or order for which rules (formal or informal) of governance are established by authoritative actors within a certain geographic space, as defined by the participants. These processes may be driven by economic and/or political considerations and are to be regarded as dynamic rather than static, meaning that they are continually subject to contestation, negotiation and revision. Regionalism, as with virtually any term ending in 'ism', can refer to a set of beliefs and values surrounding invocations of 'region' and the processes, activities and institutions that are built around it.

To the extent that regional governance is itself understood as a set of practices and processes with a political institutional dimension that is held together by commonly accepted values and beliefs, it is underpinned by both regionalisation and regionalism and is subject to the same dynamic forces. This, however, says little about the role of external forces and the dynamics of interregional relations. Gilson points out that regionalisation and region-alism, taken together, involve overlapping processes and pressures on regio-nal entities which serve to shape ideas of self and others as 'regions' and which are thrown into sharper relief in region-to-region interaction.[3]

A principal argument of this chapter is that wherever one finds a construct such as a region, one will find that 'values and beliefs' are based on various motives, agendas, interests, assumptions and aspirations. These are always at work, as well as the promotion of various identities, representations, 'reali-ties', prejudices and so forth.[4] A distinction between regionalisation as a description of processes of increased economic, political (and perhaps social) integration on the one hand, and regionalism as an ideology and a political project that is pursued by various influential actors on the other,[5] is therefore difficult to maintain. Both are invariably underpinned by the same complex of assumptions, interests and motives. Thus, regionalisation as a process is no less subjective than regionalism. Nonetheless, it is commonly understood that region*alism* refers to a set of ideas rather than processes, and that it generates a search for some kind of regional identity based on common characteristics. As a former Secretary-General of Association of Southeast Asian Nations (ASEAN) has remarked, regional integration – meaning that member countries of ASEAN need to 'work more closely together and act more strongly as one' – requires a 'heightened sense of regionalism and of a Southeast Asian identity'.[6]

Here it should be noted that 'values and beliefs' are not usually depicted as being based on instrumental interests and prejudices. They are much more commonly understood in terms of 'culture' – a concept that acquired increased salience in the post-Cold War period with the demise of the bipo-lar world order and its ideological underpinnings. Certain culturalist ideas in regions such as the Asia-Pacific had already gained some resonance as part of a broad post-colonial discourse from an early stage in the post-Second World War period, but rapidly changing conditions following the collapse of the Cold War, along with strong economic growth in some areas, saw cul-tural politics move to centre stage. This may be understood partly as a reaction to globalisation which implies, almost by definition, the transcending of cultural/national spaces.

As suggested above, however, regionalisation and regionalism imply the clustering of cognate entities. Culturalist approaches to regionalisation emphasise internal cohesion and a certain homogeneity, therefore tending to exclusiveness.[7] Opponents of Turkey's inclusion in the European Union

(EU), for example, often invoke cultural difference along with Turkey's geographical location. Former French president Valery Giscard d'Estaing is one proponent of the idea that 'they' are simply not like 'us'. Apart from pointing out that Turkey's capital and 95 per cent of its population are outside Europe, he argued that Turkey is 'a different culture, [has] a different approach, and a different way of life', adding that Turkey's accession to the EU would effectively signal 'the end of Europe'.[8]

In Southeast Asia, the 'ASEAN Way', understood as a specific set of diplomatic and security norms, has been strongly oriented to cultural regionalism. Although the cultural component has lost some of its edge, especially in the wake of the Asian financial crisis of the later 1990s, implicit culturalist assumptions still underpin important ideas about identity and governance in the region.[9] The 'ASEAN we' which emerges from the articulation of certain common norms, values and orientations is therefore formulated to assert that its collective identity makes it 'not like' some other grouping. This highlights the relational dimension that attends virtually any exercise in identity construction and without which the very idea of 'identity' is almost meaningless.

The present discussion is primarily concerned with elucidating certain aspects of regional identity formation in Asia and some of the implications for regional governance. Due to the fact that the relational aspects of identity in this broad region almost invariably involve a contrasting image of 'the West', it is essential to consider this aspect of identity formation as well. This is illuminated through an account of the Asia–Europe Meeting (ASEM) process in which 'Asia' is posited in contrast with 'Europe' – the latter representing the original heartland of what is today understood as 'the West'. An account of certain aspects of the ASEM process to date, especially with respect to human rights, democracy and state sovereignty, highlights some key issues for regional governance in the contemporary period, especially in terms of how ideas about 'cultural values' continue to feature in the broader dynamics of contemporary politics in the Asian region.

It is important to note from the start that the culture concept itself has had – and indeed continues to have – a 'political career', and is therefore not a concept that can simply be taken for granted in terms of encapsulating a straightforward set of beliefs, practices, norms and values that underpin certain communities, whether constructed on a subnational, national or regional basis. Another preliminary point to note is that this discussion is not concerned with the 'set-piece debates' between realist, institutionalist and constructivist approaches identified by Jayasuriya.[10] Moreover, while the term 'construction' appears in the title, this should not be taken to imply that the present discussion follows a conventional constructivist line, especially in view of the fact that so much constructivist literature – although rightly emphasising the importance of norms and other 'ideational' constructs which give meaning to the material world – takes the concept of culture as given rather than subjecting it to critical scrutiny.[11]

Culture and international order in the contemporary period

The concept of culture most often used in international politics derives from an anthropological conception developed in the late nineteenth and early twentieth centuries, which is taken as an essential marker of difference between various communities. The concept is widely used in inscriptions of distinctive identities, often determining who belongs and who does not belong in or to specific political communities and what those communities stand for.[12] When it is asserted that 'they' are not like 'us', and vice versa, it is an anthropological notion of culture that is generally taken to constitute the *essential* differences. This is also where the culture concept and the idea of 'nation' intersect, since the latter is usually defined not simply as a political community characterised by a particular culture, but as a political community *by virtue of* its possession of a particular culture.

Regional 'identities' have usually been based on similar ideas, with national components subsumed within a broader structure defined by overarching cultural or civilisational elements. 'Europe' as a regional entity, especially as represented by the EU, is certainly understood as possessing an identity based on certain cultural/civilisational properties, while the 'Asia' of the 'Asian values debate' as well as constructs such as the 'ASEAN Way', both of which continue to inform ideas about regional identity, have been constructed at least partly in opposition to the 'cultural values' of 'Europe' and, more generally, 'the West'.[13] The latter obviously includes the United States (US), Canada, Australia and New Zealand. Less obviously, it has occasionally included Japan too, thereby introducing an interesting contradiction into the dynamics of cultural regionalism.

World politics has moved on since the heyday of 'Asian values'. The 1997 Asian crisis dampened Asianist discourses considerably, although it did not necessarily eliminate the essential anti-Westernism that underpinned them. Indeed, for Dr Mahathir, then Prime Minister of Malaysia and longtime purveyor of anti-Western Asianist rhetoric, the crisis served to highlight the predatory nature of Western interests and their neo-colonial projects in the region. A few years later, however, the events of '9/11' and the subsequent 'war on terror' saw much of the explicit anti-Westernism of the Asianist rhetoric dropped in the interests of presenting more of a united front against terrorist organisations. Even so, the entity 'Asia' is still defined in terms of the rather vaguely formulated 'cultural' values that characterised the discourse of 'Asian values', embracing norms such as 'consensus', 'harmony' and 'respect for authority'. These have been held as more or less constant despite the enormous variety of social and religious practices throughout the region. In order to construct the region as distinctive and give it greater coherence, however, these values are necessarily contrasted with those of another cultural/regional entity. For 'Asia' it has always been 'the West' rather than any other civilisational categories. 'Asian' values, for example, have never been constructed in contrast with 'African' or 'Latin American' values.[14]

Despite the fact that 'the West', like 'Asia' is itself irreducibly diverse, it has nonetheless been described as constituting a 'specific historic and/or cultural community'. The values associated with liberal democratic forms of governance, especially, are seen as peculiarly Western. One important aspect of the communitarian critique of (liberal) democracy, as developed in relation to East Asia, uses the language of historical contextualism and cultural specificity to drive a firm dividing line between East and West on the issue of values, especially those relating to democracy and human rights:

> Liberal democratic ideals and institutions command almost universal allegiance in Western societies, a phenomenon to be understood in the light of the West's shared history and culture[15] ... a liberal democratic political system, informed and justified by the ideals of equality and freedom ... is a culturally distinct, historically contingent artefact, not readily transferable to East and Southeast Asian societies with different traditions, needs and conceptions of human flourishing.[16]

This is a form of cultural and historical contextualism that has found its way into both popular and elite political discourses. It is expressed primarily through the lens of a communitarian normative theory that dichotomises and relativises 'Asia' and 'the West' while supporting an implicit cultural determinism. But it is enormously problematic. As has been argued elsewhere, it tends to stereotype the members of each regional category implying, for instance, that notions of freedom and political equality are valued only by 'Westerners' and that illiberal or authoritarian ideas are more congenial to Southeast and East Asian people. This not only misrepresents many people in the latter category; it also overstates the extent to which 'Westerners' are freedom-loving individualists imbued with a normative commitment to liberal principles. Further, its historical perspective is severely truncated, for it fails to mention that liberal democratic ideas and institutions have only recently become widespread in the West itself. Sixty years ago, democracy was in very short supply in Western Europe. Indeed, even three decades on it was still only a dim prospect in parts of Southern Europe, let alone Eastern Europe.[17]

As suggested above, the anti-Westernism of the old Asian-values debate has necessarily been muted at a time when a much more united front against terrorist organisations operating under the banner of religious fundamentalism is required. Furthermore, some of the more vociferous exponents of the kind of anti-Westernism that underpinned Asianist discourses in the 1990s, such as Dr Mahathir, have departed from office. A new generation of politicians, less committed to the old rhetoric and with other concerns to pursue, is now making its presence felt, introducing new dynamics into the ongoing project of regionalism and methods of governance. This is partially demonstrated by the inclusion of Australia and New Zealand in the East Asian Summit process since December 2005.[18] Nonetheless, it would be a mistake to dismiss the cultural conservatism that characterised past discourses in terms of a 'politics of difference' as irrelevant to current regionalist developments, as will be seen in the next section.

The emergence of ASEM

ASEM's emergence as a formal dialogue between Europe and Asia – therefore requiring an overarching framework of governance for interregional relations – can be at least partly attributed to the perception by actors, in both locations, that the post-Cold War economic order was dominated by forms of regional association linked directly to the US and that other new linkages needed to be established. Apart from an EU–ASEAN link – formally established in 1980 and strengthened in 1994 by the EU's participation in the first ASEAN Regional Forum (ARF) – and a network of bilateral arrangements and activities, there was nothing in the way of formal interregional relations.[19] Described by former Singaporean Prime Minister Goh Chok Tong as the 'missing link' in a tripolar world, the relationship between Europe and Asia was one in need of fortifying in a globalising world.[20]

On the European side, there was also a rather belated recognition that Asia had become a significant locus of economic power. This led in the first instance to the commissioning by the EU of a report on a 'new Asia strategy' in the mid 1990s. This document foreshadowed a strategy framed largely in terms of the economic opportunities that Europe should grasp without delay.[21] Just three months after the release of the report, the initiative was seized by former Prime Minister of Singapore Goh Chok Tong, who proposed that a summit meeting be held in Bangkok. Indeed, it is largely due to Singaporean international activism that the other members of ASEAN,[22] as well as Japan, China and South Korea, were persuaded to support the project. At this stage, it was to some extent within the power of key ASEAN countries to define the 'Asia' that would initially participate, while on the European side, 'Europe' was automatically assumed to consist of the EU.

The inaugural Bangkok meeting evidently produced an enthusiasm for further development of the meeting process, with the leaders committing themselves 'to develop a common vision of the future, to foster political dialogue, to reinforce economic cooperation, and to promote cooperation in other areas'.[23] As vague and platitudinous as these may seem, the willingness to engage in a 'political dialogue' was significant, for it moved the process into areas of potential sensitivity usually avoided by at least some key countries in the Asian region. Since Bangkok, the ASEM summits have become a biennial event, meeting in London in 1998, Seoul in 2000, Copenhagen in 2002, Hanoi in 2004 and Helsinki in 2006, with the next scheduled for Beijing in 2008. The ASEM process has also spawned a huge number of other gatherings, including meetings of foreign ministers, senior officials, finance ministers and an annual Asia–Europe Business Forum as well as many other ad hoc ministerial conferences and meetings.[24]

Parallel activities and meetings conducted by NGOs have been drawn together under an Asia–Europe People's Forum (AEPF), which receives formal funding and an official presence at the biennial ASEM summits. Its aim is to build networks between European and Asian civil societies, with a particular focus on the effects of neo-liberalist globalisation on citizens' lives and issues relating to security and militarisation. The AEPF also 'aims to establish a channel for the representatives of civil societies to influence the official ASEM process'.[25] NGOs and the kind of 'civil society' they represent are usually tolerated rather than positively welcomed. In providing for their official presence and support, however, ASEM has perhaps pre-empted at least some of the dissent often voiced by NGOs. Indeed, the latter have risked being co-opted into the very structures they often purport to challenge.[26]

The other major forum for non-state activity is the Asia–Europe Foundation, established in 1997 with the mission to 'promote greater mutual understanding between the peoples of Asia and Europe through closer intellectual, cultural, and people-to-people exchanges'.[27] Since its inception, it boasts of having implemented more than 310 projects involving some 13,500 participants. Its flagship programmes include the Asia–Europe Environment Forum, the ASEM Informal Seminars on Human Rights, the Asia–Europe Museum Network (ASEMUS), the ASEF University Programme (AU) and numerous 'dialogues on cultures and civilisations of Asia and Europe.'[28] The concept of 'culture' embraced by both the AEPF and ASEF is actually a very open one, including not just non-controversial expressions embodied in dance, drama, music and the arts more generally, but politically sensitive issues of human rights and democracy as well. In the broader arena of ASEM, these latter issues have inevitably produced tensions, most notably in terms of membership issues.

From the beginning, the expansion of the EU and/or ASEAN held the potential for more serious controversy in the future, and this is precisely what occurred with the expansion of both ASEAN and the EU in the late 1990s and early 2000s. The nub of the difficulties has centred on Myanmar, which joined ASEAN, along with Laos and Vietnam, in 1997 (with Cambodia joining in 1998). Nothing happened in the first few years because ASEAN's new members did not immediately apply to join the ASEM process (noting that it was individual countries rather than ASEAN members as such that were originally included in ASEM). However, the EU expansion in May 2004 to include ten new members changed this position. In the lead-up to ASEM V in Hanoi in 2004, the EU proposed that its new members join the meeting process. This gave ASEAN the green light to insist that its four most recent members also join. Due to the EU's policy towards Myanmar,[29] the scene was set for a diplomatic struggle that was embedded at least partly in identity politics and which drew attention to issues of 'cultural regionalism'. These diplomatic and political issues surrounding regional expansion will be considered shortly, but first the latter phenomenon must be examined.

The politics of cultural regionalism

Cultural regionalism is generally taken to be more exclusive than regionalism based on economic/geographic criteria. According to Wesley, the latter support a functional rationale, while cultural regionalism finds support among those concerned with internal cohesion and homogeneity and who see these as essential to the prospects of a regional bloc playing a 'coherent international role'.[30] In Europe, despite its rather obvious cultural diversity – manifest in religious, linguistic and ethnic differences throughout the region – there is nonetheless strong support for a certain socio-cultural 'Europeaness'.[31] This is assumed to be embedded in a set of shared cultural values and concerns contributing to a political identity that is portrayed as modern, rational and secular and which upholds basic principles underpinning human rights and democracy. One can argue about how the reality matches up to the ideal but, at the very least, the EU possesses an *official* political culture[32] – based on a set of broadly articulated values in support of universal human rights and democratic governance, and its stated values inform issues of both membership and foreign policy as part of its more general governance provisions. Aspirants for membership must demonstrate their credentials with respect to these values, and countries with noticeably poor human rights records, such as Myanmar and Zimbabwe, have been subject to EU sanctions.

The basic principles in support of human rights and democracy are enshrined in certain key instruments and form the basis for official policies underpinning the EU's form of regional governance, which now includes the EU's Common Foreign and Security Policy (CFSP). The following statements illustrate some of the implications for EU governance as well as for its external relations:

A considerable step in integrating human rights and democratic principles into the policies of the European Union was taken with the entry into force of the Treaty on European Union (TEU) on 1 November 1993. The treaty considers as one of the objectives of the Common Foreign and Security Policy of the European Union the development and consolidation of *'democracy and the rule of law, and respect for human rights and fundamental freedoms'*. At the same time the new title on development cooperation includes a second direct reference to human rights and democratisation: *'Community policy in this area shall contribute to the general objective of developing and consolidating democracy and the rule of law and to that of respecting human rights and fundamental freedoms'*.

The Treaty of Amsterdam, which came into force on 1 May 1999, marks another significant step forward in integrating human rights into the legal order of the European Union. This treaty inserts a new article 6 in the Treaty on European Union, which reaffirms that the European

Union *'is founded on the principles of liberty, democracy, respect for human rights and fundamental freedoms, and the rule of law, principles which are common to the Member States'.* Member States violating these principles in a 'serious and persistent' way run the risk to see [*sic*] certain of their rights deriving from the application of the Union Treaty suspended.[33]

With respect to its moral authority, the EU claims that since all EU member states are democracies espousing the same treaty-based principles in their internal and external policies, this 'gives the EU substantial political moral weight'.[34] The same document points to the EU's commitment to the abolition of the death penalty not only as a requirement for countries seeking EU membership, but as 'a high profile policy that the EU pursues in international fora and in dialogue with *all* countries, regardless of the nature of the EU's relationship with them'.[35] This is worth mentioning because it means that the US, which has also nurtured an identity in international relations as a protector and promoter of human rights, would not be permitted membership of the EU precisely on the grounds that it does not measure up to EU human rights standards because of the death penalty.[36]

Examining some of the reasons behind the EU's stance on human rights and democratisation sheds some light on more general issues to do with history, culture and context. Although one can be highly critical of theories based on historical determinism, as argued earlier, some of Europe's shared historical experiences have certainly contributed to the identity that Europe – as represented by the EU and its predecessor organisations – has forged since 1957. Whereas analysts usually emphasise Europe's shared historical experience with democracy, it can also be agreed that it has much more to do with its shared history of violence. This has not only provided the basis for the EU's official support for democratic and rights protective regimes in the post-war period but also for the weakening of national sovereignty in favour of supranational institutions of governance. Portes and Vines note that for the founders of contemporary Europe, who created the European Steel and Coal Community in the 1950s, their explicit purpose was to internationalise – and therefore immobilise – the primary means of waging war: 'This lesson was connected with a reading of European history which claims that the existence of the nation state is a major explanation of Europe's wars, and a deeply held view that moves to enmesh the nation state in wider structures would erect bulwarks against future conflict.'[37] In summary, it is not so much shared practices of 'civilisation' that has given Europe much of its present unity, but rather a history of horrendous warfare and outright barbarity among and between many of its constituent members.

Turning to the Asian region, one is hard pressed to identify shared 'cultural' or 'civilisational' characteristics here as well. Of his own subregion, Singapore's Prime Minister Lee Hsien Loong said that: 'Far more than European countries, Southeast Asia is characterised by political, economic and cultural diversity rather than natural coherence.'[38] Yet a more common claim, first purveyed by his father, Lee Kwan Yew – and pushed vigorously by a number of other leaders over the years – is that there is a certain cultural bond that has given rise to a common and unique set of values in practically the entire East/Southeast Asian region that are qualitatively different from those of Europe or 'the West'. The implicit notion of the 'Asian values' described earlier has certainly underscored the identity of 'Asia' as a participant in the ASEM process.[39]

Just as one can point to a set of post-war experiences in Europe that produced a political consensus, one can identify shared experiences in the Asian region that have contributed to the development of certain values. One significant experience that most Asian countries have shared – and which has a profound influence on issues of identity in the present – is that of colonisation by European powers.[40] Without going over a great deal of fairly obvious ground on this point, it can be said that the memory of the colonial period sustained a continuing resentment against 'Europe', partly manifest in the 'Asian values' debate as well as in the broader phenomenon of 'Asianism'.[41] It is also evident in the commitment to the doctrine of state sovereignty as a symbol of national independence and international stature. The resentment is further manifest in those post-colonial discourses fuelled by a perception that 'Europe' has maintained a posture of superiority long after the end of formal colonialism. This includes a posture of moral superiority in relation to issues such as human rights. A speech by Ambassador Tommy Koh of Singapore, founding director of ASEF, on 'Differences in Asian and European Values' illustrates some of these points very clearly:

> [The] West has not yet come to accept Asia as an equal. The West has dominated Asia for the major part of the past two hundred years. Most people in the West, including its intellectuals, still regard Asia and Asians as inferior ... I suspect that the West cannot accept the concept of Asian values because the latter could pose a challenge to Western intellectual hegemony. The truth is that we still live in a world which is economically, culturally, intellectually and morally dominated by the West ... [But] East Asia has the potential to challenge ... Western domination in the economic, cultural, intellectual and moral spheres, in the 21st Century.[42]

Cultural regionalism in Europe has also drawn on images of European culture and/or civilisation. Among the early founders, we find that one of Jean Monnet's motives in promoting European integration was a fear that Europe's role in the very civilisation that it had created was declining. Some of Monnet's successors, such as Jacques Delors, have been committed to nurturing a certain regional cultural homogeneity as a means of maintaining unity.[43] Those who focus on postures of superiority among Europeans at large, however, miss some of the interesting points of friction within the EU.

Significant sections of the British population, for example, are notorious for their Europhobia. Indeed, some British attitudes have, at least in the perceptions of their neighbours, verged on the insufferable: 'Through a long period of imperialism and hegemony, British people had developed a sense of their uniqueness that bordered on condescension ... [which] was particularly pronounced in the attitudes to France and Germany ... '.[44] It is further suggested that such attitudes made Britain ill-suited for participation in the early experiments in European integration, and still form 'a cultural barrier' between Britain and the rest of Europe. These attitudes are also related to a concern with defending national sovereignty, which is comparable to attitudes found in the Asian region.[45]

The defence of national sovereignty has underpinned virtually all aspects of regional governance norms and principles in what is perhaps the most influential grouping within ASEM to date – the ASEAN countries. Certainly, the identity of 'Asia' in the ASEM process has been heavily influenced by its general approach to regional identity, which has been articulated very largely in terms of the 'ASEAN Way'. This emerged in a post-war historical context shaped by a rejection of both communism and liberal democratic institutions in favour of a form of patrimonial authoritarianism which nonetheless attempted to describe itself as 'democratic'. Acharya observes that, in Indonesia, Suharto denounced Western political and social values and substituted 'guided democracy' for liberal democracy, urging a return to traditional principles such as *gotong-rotong* and *musjawara* – translated more or less as 'community mutual assistance and discussion leading to consensus'. The turn to indigenous conceptions of political authority also came to shape foreign policy and regional cooperation and, eventually, to underpin the 'ASEAN Way'.[46]

Acharya has summarised this amalgam of ideas and practices as supporting 'a narrow elite-centred and sovereignty-bounded framework of regionalism' that provided little scope for collectively addressing emergent transnational issues such as the environment, migration and refugees as well as for involving broader social forces in the regionalism project. These features of the 'ASEAN Way' that include an emphasis on regional culture and identity, avoidance of legalistic norms and institutions, dependence on top-level leadership, state-centredness and a tendency to downplay or ignore conflicts so as not to introduce what were seen as Western-style adversarial negotiating and bargaining postures, effectively combined to produce Southeast Asia's 'patrimonial regionalism'.[47] Another commentator notes that, if Europe, along with North America, has provided a benchmark for 'high legalisation', the Asian region has offered 'an important example of low legalisation and possibly an explicit aversion to legalisation',[48] with a suggestion that ASEAN members tended to cast this antipathy to legalisation in terms of a cultural predisposition.[49]

However, changes within ASEAN and some of its member states – due in part to a changing international environment over the past fifteen years which has seen communism recede as any sort of threat, along with financial and environmental crises enveloping the region at various times, and a strengthening of democratisation processes among some members – has impacted on aspects of cultural regionalism and the norms of both domestic and regional governance. Following these developments, as well as continuing concerns with Myanmar, where domestic political problems have also had significant spillover effects in the immediate region, a reformist agenda was proposed by Surin Pitsuwan, the Thai foreign minister appointed in 1997 (and currently ASEAN Secretary-General), who urged ASEAN to moderate its 'cherished principle of non-intervention ... to allow it to play a constructive role in preventing or resolving domestic issues with regional implications'.[50] Pitsuwan's ideas gave rise to the notion of 'flexible engagement' which, for a time, became embodied in Thailand's official foreign policy. Nonetheless, other ASEAN members remained cautious, opting for a more restrained posture styled as 'constructive engagement' and, later, an even weaker notion of 'enhanced interaction'.[51]

Acharya suggests that the Pitsuwan formulation failed to secure support because it was not grounded in any prior regional tradition. More specifically, he has argued that:

> ASEAN was founded as a grouping of illiberal regimes with no record of collectively promoting human rights and democratic governance ... The campaign by human rights activists against Burma failed because advocacy of human rights and democratic government had no place in ASEAN, which did not specify a democratic political system as a criterion of membership.[52]

While there is some merit in this argument, it tends to endorse a deterministic standpoint which holds that norm change only occurs when supported by previous traditions. However, that norm change can and does occur in the absence of a pre-existing tradition whenever it is perceived to serve the interests of those in a position to effect change.[53] Clearly, ASEAN members had not yet felt that it was in their interests to make more significant moves towards weakening the principle of non-intervention, despite signs of increasing dysfunctionality in the 'ASEAN Way'. This was evident in the lead-up to ASEM V in Hanoi in October 2004, when membership issues came to a head.

The dynamics of regional expansion and generational change

Since the EU had expected its new members to participate fully in the ASEM process, it was only to be expected that ASEAN would adopt the same approach. However, while the admission of Cambodia, Laos and Vietnam proved relatively unproblematic, the push to admit Myanmar as a full member of the ASEM process inevitably created problems for the EU, given its desire to retain an identity as an international actor that does not officially do business with such regimes. This led to a rather tense diplomatic stand-off in the lead-up to the Hanoi Summit, which was resolved only when the EU accepted Myanmar as a participant, but not at head-of-state level. This was accompanied by a renewed commitment by the EU to maintaining pressure on the regime, including sanctions, and to pursuing the matter in other fora.[54]

The resolution of the immediate problem amounted to a partial concession by both sides, but was never likely to prove more than a temporary and problematic solution. The 2005 ASEM economic ministers' meeting in Rotterdam was boycotted by the ASEAN members when the Dutch government refused to grant a visa to Myanmar's delegate. In 2006, a visa was issued to Myanmar's finance minister to attend an ASEM ministerial meeting in Vienna only after it was agreed that the country's political development would be discussed. It has been suggested that the latter course of action has come to typify a modus vivendi for Myanmar's participation in all ASEM gatherings: 'the critical evaluation of the junta's self-proclaimed commitment to democracy, Myanmar's human rights situation and the country's involvement in money laundering and human trafficking are considered default items in return for the regime's high level representation'.[55]

There are signs, however, that things may be moving in new directions. In 2004 an ASEAN Inter-Parliamentary Caucus for Democracy in Myanmar (AIPMC) was established, consisting of a group of parliamentarians and law makers drawn from among ASEAN members. One of their first significant moves was to force Myanmar to relinquish the chairing of ASEAN, which it was due to take up in 2006.[56] A meeting held in Kuala Lumpur, organised by the Pro-Democracy Myanmar Caucus of the Malaysian Parliament, was attended by parliamentarians from Malaysia, Indonesia, the Philippines, Thailand, Singapore and Cambodia as well as parliamentarians-in-exile from Myanmar who were elected in 1990 but never able to participate in a government. The three-day meeting resolved to establish a committee of ASEAN Inter-Parliamentary Caucuses on Democracy in Myanmar 'to promote the establishment and coordinate the activities of parliamentary pro-democracy Myanmar Caucuses in individual ASEAN countries' as well as to proactively oppose Myanmar's chairing of ASEAN until such times as there are 'meaningful and tangible results in political reforms in Myanmar on democratisation and national reconciliation'.[57] Since then, it has continued lobbying both in the region and further afield to effect meaningful, long-term reforms in the region's most politically troublesome country.[58]

The ASEAN Inter-Parliamentary Caucus joins other forces for democratisation in the region, which include the Forum of Democratic Leaders of the Asia-Pacific (FDL-AP), established in 1994 'with the mission to promote democracy, including all its necessary pre-requisite conditions and institutions, within the Asia-Pacific region and beyond', and headed by an array of pro-democracy regional figures such as its founder, Kim Dae-Jung, along with Corazon Aquino and Sonia Gandhi and others from more distant locations, such as Costa Rica's President Sánchez.[59] The emergence of a new generation of parliamentarians in Southeast Asia, in particular, may see these pressures increase, although whether they succeed in effecting significant change remains to be seen. At least one analysis sees little changing in the foreseeable future, with the regimes of Southeast Asia, in particular, remaining committed much more to norms of non-interference and illiberalism than to democratic values.[60]

Beyond these regional networks there are also signs that ASEAN is becoming less tolerant of Myanmar's internal politics and the implications these have for regional norms of governance. The drafting of the ASEAN Charter (discussed in Chapters 1 and 2) saw a renewed focus on the issues of human rights and the ability of ASEAN to expel members who were not behaving in a manner appropriate to the organisation. While there are other countries to whom these recommendations may have posed a threat, the public and policy discussion at the time focused on their implications for Myanmar. Although the expulsion clause was ultimately dropped from the Charter and it is not yet clear how the regional human rights mechanism will develop, it is noteworthy that ASEAN expressed 'revulsion' at the Myanmar regime's crackdown on protests in September 2007.[61] Moreover, in the lead-up to the May 2008 political referendum in Myanmar, the ASEAN Chair – Singaporean Foreign Minister George Yeo – was heavily critical of Myanmar's decision to ban Aung Sang Suu Kyi from participating in the process.[62]

With respect to ASEM itself, it also remains to be seen whether it can move beyond the formula of cultural regionalism. It was initially constituted as an explicitly interregional dialogue that not only posited an 'Asia' grouping alongside a 'European' one, but also engaged in a form of exchange that in its formative period was constantly portrayed as a 'dialogue of difference', not least with respect to issues such as human rights.[63] A further testing of identity politics in both regions will inevitably occur as membership issues advance to another stage. As suggested earlier, Turkey's possible accession to the EU is certainly going to provoke vigorous debates on 'European identity' over the next decade. It may not affect ASEM issues directly, but if there is a perception of heightening anti-Islam prejudice within the EU – highly likely in the event that Turkey is not admitted at the conclusion of the present accession process – it could well provoke strong reactions in Malaysia and Indonesia.

The possible expansion of the 'Asian' side of ASEM, to include the countries of South Asia which more or less 'fit' in a culturalist sense into the existing Asian bloc – at least to the extent that they are not 'Western' – is not likely to be a major issue for identity politics, although it may be for other, more pragmatic reasons. The possible inclusion of Australia and New Zealand, however, is another question altogether, although with the departure of Mahathir, who was always deeply antipathetic to the idea that Australia and

New Zealand could possibly join the club on the Asian side, the climate is likely to be more receptive in the future. Japan has been fairly consistent in its support for Australasian incorporation and the more democratic of ASEAN's members may also warm to the idea. What is certain is that if Turkey were to join the EU, and therefore the ASEM process on the European side, and Australian and New Zealand on the Asian side, the culturalist aspects of interregional relations would almost certainly diminish. Both sides would be able to reinvent themselves as being regional, yet cosmopolitan and pluralistic at the same time, giving far less scope to the play of cultural politics in regional and interregional governance.

Conclusion

The ASEM process to date has thrown up some interesting governance issues, especially in relation to cultural regionalism as manifest in both regional and interregional relations. The review of developments in the ASEM process presented above shows that participants from both 'sides' have invested in constructions and representations of region which have generated certain problems and tensions between them. The EU presents the principles underpinning liberal conceptions of human rights and democracy as integral not only to its own governance but to the conduct of its foreign and security policies. These principles, however, clearly do not underpin the identity of the 'Asia' of the ASEM process to date, nor other governance norms in the region. This version of Asia consists of a cluster of states of which the ASEAN group constitutes the most coherent entity. Further, as Camilleri has noted, ASEAN has been the principal engine of East Asian multilateralism and has played a critical role in the emergence and consolidation of East Asian regionalism.[64] It is not surprising, then, that ASEAN norms of governance have tended to dominate the region and its related fora. In summary, governance in both regions has been founded on what seem to be quite different sets of norms – norms that have come into conflict over the Myanmar issue and which present continuing problems.

Nonetheless, norms and values are not static and neither is 'the culture' to which they are attached. Rather than seeing 'culture' as a bedrock akin to reinforced concrete on which the institutions of governance are built, an approach to the culture concept that recognises its inherent dynamism and the fact that it is through culture that change actually takes place, is far more appropriate. This is why approaches based on a narrow cultural and historical contextualism are problematic, for they tend to overemphasise the deterministic elements of both history and culture. In turn, these feed into assumptions about relatively inflexible norms and values among those actors involved in governance processes. 'Europe' and 'Asia', as represented (at least partially) by the ASEM process, have indeed been formed through different historical/cultural dynamics and contingencies. But then, so has been each of

the national entities within each grouping, not to mention subnational entities, local dynasties, modern elites and so on. Furthermore, the respective
histories of 'Asia' and 'Europe', and many cultural elements as well, are
deeply intertwined, sometimes in an antagonistic manner, at other times in
alliance, but always in a state of flux.

The final point is that culturalist interpretations of politics often mistake
'values' and 'beliefs' for 'interests', and perhaps even 'prejudices'. It was
suggested earlier that norm change may occur in the absence of a pre-existing
tradition whenever it is perceived to serve the interests of those in a position
to effect change. This suggests that the 'context' that matters most is the
present. Again, although not always explicit in constructivist thought, this
accords with Acharya's argument that norms change over time and are
context and issue dependent: 'Norms that were initially conceived as moral
and functional could become immoral and dysfunctional with the passage of
time and with the advent of new challenges.'[65] Instrumental interests may
not be the only driving force in politics, but one does not need to be a realist
to recognise that they are sufficiently powerful to assist in effecting significant 'cultural change' as and when circumstances require. Arguably, this
has occurred in certain parts of 'the West' over the last five years or so as
liberal values of governance have declined, while far more conservative and
decidedly illiberal ones have been making an impact in the sphere of social
and legal norms as part of the 'war on terror'. Thus, forms of governance,
whether in Europe, Asia or anywhere else, do not emerge simply as clusters
of institutions, practices, values, beliefs and interests determined in advance
by any given historical and/or cultural legacy. For while these are undoubtedly important, they are only ever part of a complex and never-ending story
of both continuity and change in political, social and economic relations that
defy reduction to any one explanation or set of factors.

Notes

1 For more on the precursors to ASEAN see: Curley, Melissa and Nicholas
  Thomas. 'Advancing East Asian Regionalism: An Introduction', in Melissa
  Curley and Nicholas Thomas (eds). *Advancing East Asian Regionalism.*
  (London: Routledge Curzon, 2007), pp. 1–25.
2 Beeson, Mark. 'ASEAN Plus Three and the Rise of Reactionary Regionalism'
  Contemporary Southeast Asia. (Vol. 25, No. 2, 2003), p. 252.
3 Gilson, Julie. *Asia Meets Europe.* (Cheltenham: Edward Elgar, 2002), p. 3.
4 Lawson, Stephanie. 'Regionalizing the Pacific Rim: Economic, Political and
  Cultural Approaches', in Stephanie Lawson and Wayne Peak (eds). *Globalization and Regionalization: Views from the Pacific Rim.* (Sydney and Guadalajara: University of Technology Sydney and University of Guadalajara, 2007),
  pp. 21–38.
5 See Marchand, Marianne H. 'North American Regionalisms and Regionalization in the 1990s', in Michael Schulz, Fredrik Söderbaum and Joakim Öjendal
  (eds). *Regionalization in a Globalizing World: A Comparative Perspective on
  Forms, Actors and Processes.* (London: Zed Books, 2001), p. 199.

6 Severino, Rodolfo C. 'Regionalism, Culture and Information', *Remarks at the opening of the 34th meeting of the ASEAN Committee on Culture and Information.* 10 May 1999. http://www.asean.org/3334.htm. Accessed 7 September 2007.

7 Some regionalist projects, such as APEC, have been relatively open-ended, relying on broad physical geographic factors to establish initial coherence, with subsequent norm building depending on the perception of economic interests.

8 Quoted in Teitelbaum, Michael S. and Philip L. Martin. 'Is Turkey Ready for Europe?', *Foreign Affairs.* (Vol. 82, No. 3, May/June 2003), p. 98.

9 The concept of a collective regional identity in terms of ASEAN's diplomatic mode is said to be based on shared structures of meaning, mutual identifications and norm compliance within the organisation. See Nischalke, Tobias. 'Does ASEAN Measure Up? Post-Cold War Diplomacy and the Idea of Regional Community', *The Pacific Review.* (Vol. 15, No. 1, 2002), pp. 89–117. For one defence of the 'ASEAN Way' see: Katsumata, Hiro. 'Reconstruction of Diplomatic Norms in Southeast Asia: The Case for Strict Adherence to the "ASEAN Way"', *Contemporary Southeast Asia.* (Vol. 25, No. 1, 2003), pp. 104–121. A more circumspect assessment is provided by Haacke, Jürgen. 'ASEAN's Diplomatic and Security Culture: A Constructivist Assessment', *International Relations of the Asia-Pacific.* (Vol. 3, No. 1, 2003), pp. 57–87.

10 Jayasuriya, Kanishka. 'Introduction: Governing the Asia-Pacific – Beyond the "New Regionalism"', in Kanishka Jayasuriya (ed.). *Governing the Asia-Pacific – Beyond the 'New Regionalism'.* (London: Palgrave Macmillan, 2004), pp. 1–2.

11 There are many different versions of constructivism, and there is not the space to enter into great detail here. Suffice to say that as far as my reading has taken me to date, virtually none of the constructivist literature in IR really delves into the various meanings and conceptualisations of 'culture', or shows an awareness of the history of ideas from which the concept emerged in the human sciences.

12 See Lawson, Stephanie. *Culture and Context in World Politics.* (Basingstoke: Palgrave, 2006), pp. 3–6.

13 For an interesting comparison, note Gamble and Payne's point that the 'political culture and political identity of Latin America and the Caribbean has for much of the twentieth century been framed in opposition to the United States.' Gamble, Andrew and Anthony Payne, 'Conclusion: The New Regionalism' in Andrew Gamble and Anthony Payne (eds). *Regionalism and World Order.* (London: Macmillan, 1996), p. 251.

14 Interestingly, if one compares historical culturalist rhetorics from Africa through to the Pacific, one finds remarkable similarities among them. See Lawson, Stephanie. *Tradition Versus Democracy in the South Pacific: Fiji, Tonga and Western Samoa.* (Cambridge: Cambridge University Press, 1996), esp. pp. 1–9.

15 Bell, Daniel A. and Kanishka Jayasuriya. 'Understanding Illiberal Democracy: A Framework', in Daniel A. Bell, David Brown, Kanishka Jayasuriya and David Martin Jones. *Towards Illiberal Democracy in Pacific Asia.* (London: Macmillan, 1995), p. 1.

16 Ibid. p. 9.

17 Lawson. *Culture and Context in World Politics,* p. 51.

18 The meeting included the ten ASEAN countries – Brunei, Cambodia, Indonesia, Laos, Malaysia, Myanmar, the Philippines, Singapore, Thailand and Vietnam – as well as China, India, Japan, South Korea, Australia and New Zealand.

19 Heisburg, François. 'Envoi', in Hans Maull, Gerald Segal and Jusuf Wanandi. *Europe and the Asia-Pacific.* (London: Routledge, 1998), p. 231.

20 Goh Chok Tong. 'Europe-Asia Partnership for Growth, in Singapore Ministry for Information and the Arts'. *Speeches.* (Vol. 19, No. 1, 1995), pp. 18–19.

21 European Union. *Towards a New Asia Strategy.* http://ec.europa.eu/external_relations/asem/asem_process/com94.htm. Accessed 20 October 2007.

22 Which at the time did not include Myanmar, Cambodia, Laos and Vietnam.

23 'The Asia-Europe Cooperation Framework (AECF) 2000: III Key Principles and Objectives', EU External Relations website, http://europa.eu.int/comm/external_relations/asem/asem_process/aecf_2000.htm. Accessed 16 June 2002, p. 2 of 6.

24 EU External Relations. *Chairman's Statement of the Third Asia-Europe Meeting, Seoul, 20–21 October 2000.* http://europa.eu.int/comm/external_relations/asem/aecf_2000.htm. Accessed 16 June 2002.

25 See: 'Asia-Europe People's Forum (AEPF) between 3 and 6 September 2006'. http://www.asem6.fi/events/other_events/en_GB/aepf/. Accessed 17 September 2007.

26 See Gilson, Julie. 'Making Uncommon Cause: Forging Identities on the Margins of ASEM', in Stephanie Lawson (ed.). *Europe and the Asia-Pacific: Culture, Identity and Representations of Region.* (London: RoutledgeCurzon, 2003), p. 63.

27 See: ASEF. 'History'. http://www.asef.org/index.php?option = com_content&task = view&id = 17&Itemid = 62. Accessed 7 September 2007.

28 Ibid.

29 European Parliament. P6_TA-PROV(2005)0186, 'Human Rights in Burma/Myanmar', *Texts Adopted at Sitting of 12 May 2005.* http://www.unpo.org/news_detail.php?arg = 02&par = 2486. Accessed 9 March 2006. This reiterates existing EU policy and urges stronger pressure on the junta from other bodies, including ASEAN.

30 Wesley, Michael. 'The Politics of Exclusion: Australia, Turkey and Definitions of Regionalism', *The Pacific Review.* (Vol. 10, No. 4, 1997), p. 526.

31 See, for example, O'Connell, James. 'The Making of Europe: Strengths, Constraints and Resolutions', in Preston King and Andrea Bosco (eds). *A Constitution for Europe: A Comparative Study of Federal Constitutions and Plans for the United States of Europe.* (London: Lothian Foundation Press, 1991), p. 25.

32 'Political culture' is another highly problematic term. There is insufficient space to discuss this in detail, but for a very thorough critique see Formisano, Ronald. 'The Concept of Political Culture', *Journal of Interdisciplinary History.* (Vol. 32, No. 3, 2001), pp. 393–426.

33 EU External Relations. *The EU's Human Rights & Democratisation Policy.* http://europa.eu.int/comm/external_relations/human_rights/intro/index/htm, pp. 1–2. Accessed 28 June 2005. All emphases in the original. Note that the document went on to outline other declarations, including a Declaration on Human Rights adopted at the Luxembourg European Council in June 1991 and another resolution on Human Rights, Democracy and Development in November 1991 and a further Declaration on the Occasion of the 50th Anniversary of the Universal Declaration of Human Rights outlining practical steps to be taken in strengthening the EU's human rights policy. It also outlines measures on human clauses in agreements with third countries and the funding of activities to promote human rights, including EuropeAid and provision for funding NGO activities. The most recent developments may be found at ec.europa.eu/external_relations/human_rights/intro/index.htm#1. Accessed 17 September 2007.

34 European Commission. 'The European Union's Role in Promoting Human Rights and Democratisation in Third Countries', COM (2001) 252 final. (Brussels: 8 May 2001), p. 3. http://ec.europa.eu/external_relations/human_rights/doc/com01_252_en.pdf. Accessed 20 September 2007.

35 Ibid. p. 16.

36 The record of the US in the international sphere has become increasingly tarnished since the invasion of Iraq, the denial of due process to its captives in Guantanamo Bay, and the possibility that some of those suspected of involvement in terrorist activities have been 'rendered' to countries such as Jordan and Egypt where they can be tortured to extract information. It is also interesting to note significant differences in the norms underpinning US and EU approaches to regionalism,

and which points up the mistake of oversimplifying 'the West'. On the difference between EU and US approaches, see Grugel, Jean. 'New Regionalism and Modes of Governance – Comparing US and EU Strategies in Latin America', *European Journal of International Relation*. (Vol. 10, No. 4, 2004), pp. 603–626.

37 Portes, Richard and David Vines. 'European Integration: Retrospect and Prospect', in Peter Drysdale and David Vines (eds). *Europe, East Asia and APEC: A Shared Global Agenda?* (Cambridge: Cambridge University Press, 1998), p. 79.

38 Lee Hsien Loong. *Speech at Lloyd's City Dinner*. (London: 7 September 2006). http://www.13thaseansummit.org.sg/asean/index/php/web/layout/set/pr. Accessed 7 September 2007.

39 More recently, a massive 16-year project on Confucianism, due to run until 2020 and sponsored by the Chinese Ministry of Education, aims to produce the first-ever comprehensive literature on Confucianism, employing some 300 scholars from twenty-five universities and research institutes. See 'Modern Confucian Scholars Stir Revival of Ancient Philosophy', *China Daily,* 12 July 2005.

40 There was also an experience of Japanese colonialism and occupation which introduces another dimension to historical experiences in the region, but which cannot be pursued here. Suffice it to say that Japan, for this and other reasons – including an obsession among some Japanese with their absolute 'uniqueness', as well as significant ambivalences about its own regional belonging and its inclusion as a member of 'the West' in some cases – has problems in its historical relationship with other ASEM members.

41 See Lawson, Stephanie. 'Perspectives on the Study of Culture and International Politics: From *Nihonjinron* to the New Asianism', *Asia-Pacific Review*. (Vol. 6, No. 2, 1999), pp. 24–41.

42 Tommy Koh. 'Differences in Asian and European Values', *Speech to the 2nd Informal ASEM Seminar on Human Rights*. (Beijing: 27 June 1998). http://www.asef.org/documents/speech_june27_tommykoh_99.html. Accessed 19 June 2002. Note that despite the reference to 'Europe' in the title of the speech, he talks almost exclusively about 'the West'.

43 Ibid. pp. 538–539.

44 George, Stephen and Ian Bache. *Politics in the European Union*. (Oxford: Oxford University Press, 2001), p. 182.

45 Ibid. p. 182. The authors note that France has also made sovereignty an issue at times.

46 Acharya, Amitav. 'Democratization and the Prospects for Participatory Regionalism in Southeast Asia', in Kanishka Jayasuriya (ed.). *Asian Regional Governance*. (London: RoutledgeCurzon, 2004), p. 131.

47 Ibid. pp. 131–132.

48 Kahler, Miles. 'Legalization as Strategy: The Asia-Pacific Case', *International Organization*. (Vol. 54, No. 3, 2000), p. 549.

49 Ibid. p. 567.

50 Quoted in Acharya, Amitav. 'How Ideas Spread: Whose Norms Matter? Norm Localization and Institutional Change in Asian Regionalism', *International Organization*. (Vol. 58, No. 2, 2004), p. 260.

51 See Haacke, Jürgen. 'The Concept of Flexible Engagement and the Practice of Enhanced Interaction: Intramural Challenges to the "ASEAN Way"', *The Pacific Review*. (Vol. 12, No. 2, 1999), pp. 581–611. For a critical assessment of expectations that ASEAN's diplomatic and security culture may see a significant diminishing of the 'ASEAN Way' as a 'normative shield' against external interference in the foreseeable future, despite some shifts in attitudes by some individual countries, see Haacke. 'ASEAN's Diplomatic and Security Culture'.

52 Acharya. 'How Ideas Spread', pp. 262–263.

53 A point which much of the evidence produced in Acharya's article actually seems to support. See also Thomas, Nick. 'Towards and East Asian Community:

Implications of the EAVG Report', in Kanishka Jayasuriya (ed.). *Asian Regional Governance: Crisis and Change*. (London: RoutledgeCurzon, 2004), pp. 189–211, on the dynamics fuelling norm change after the financial crisis, especially the norm of strict non-intervention.

54 See: 'ASEM 5: The Fifth Asia-Europe Summit Meeting', Hanoi: 7–9 October 2004. http://europa.eu.int/comm./external_relations/asem/asem_summits/asem5/ index.htm. Accessed 25 August 2005. The following sanctions remain in place: arms embargo; ban on exports of equipment for internal repression; ban on certain services; freezing of funds and economic resources, with certain exemptions, restrictions on admission; suspension of certain aid and development programmes; suspension of high-level bilateral governmental visits; reduction of diplomatic relations. See: EU External Relations. http://europa.eu.int/comm/ external_relations/cfsp/sanctions/measures.htm. Accessed 9 March 2006. The EU continues to issue press releases condemning the junta's actions.

55 Dorsch, Jörn. 'The Impact of EU-Enlargement on Relations Between Europe and Asia', *Asia-Europe Journal*. (Vol. 5, No. 1, 2007), p. 36.

56 These developments are described at http://www.aseanmp.org and http://www. siiaonline.org. Accessed 1 November 2005.

57 Lim Kit Siang. 'Speech at the DAP Save Bukit China 20th Anniversary Dinner', http://dapmalaysia.org/all-archive/English/ 2004/nov04/lks/lks3242.htm. Accessed 9 March 2006.

58 See, generally, http://www.aseanmp.org. Accessed 17 September 2007.

59 See: *The Forum of Democratic Leaders in the Asia-Pacific*. http://www.nancho. net/fdlap/. Accessed 17 September 2007.

60 Martinez Kuhonta, Erik. 'Walking a Tightrope: Democracy Versus Sovereignty in ASEAN's Illiberal Peace', *The Pacific Review*. (Vol. 19, No. 3, 2006), pp. 337–358. See also: Narine, Shaun. 'The English School and ASEAN', *The Pacific Review*. (Vol. 19, No. 2, 2006), pp. 199–218.

61 'Burma High on Agenda as Southeast Asian Leaders Gather for Summit', *Voice of America News*. 16 November 2007.

62 'ASEAN Expresses Concern Over Burma's Election Ban Against Aung San Suu Kyi', *Voice of America News*. 20 February 2008.

63 Gilson. 'Making Uncommon Cause', pp. 58–59.

64 Camilleri, Joseph. 'East Asia's Emerging Regionalism: Tensions and Potential in Design and Architecture', *Global Change, Peace and Security*. (Vol. 17, No. 3, 2005), p. 255.

65 Acharya, Amitav. 'Do Norms and Identity Matter? Community and Power in Southeast Asia's Regional Order', *The Pacific Review*. (Vol. 18, No. 1, 2005), p. 102.

13 New modes of regionalising governance in Asia

Kanishka Jayasuriya

Introduction

Regional governance, the principal theme of this volume, refers to the management of the conflicts created through growing interdependencies within a specific – albeit ideologically constructed – geographical region through the creation of institutional forums, policy instruments and networks of private and public actors. As such, regional governance encompasses those institutions, instruments and mechanisms that allocate political power, influence material stakes and shape the ideological representation of the region itself. In other words, as Thomas (Chapter 1) observes, governance is principally concerned with policies and politics; or rather, various techniques of governance represent a particular form of political rule over the region. The advantage of approaching governance as a technique of political rule is that it enables us to ask these basic questions: Who rules? What is the domain of rule? How is political rule organised?

Regional governance, viewed through this prism, is a distinctively political exercise and to the extent that particular forms of regional governance become dominant, it is only as a component of a particular governance project underpinned by a favourable conjunction of national coalitions and international, political, economic and strategic conditions. Regional governance, as the activation of political projects, is a notion well exemplified in Caballero-Anthony's chapter (Chapter 2), which explores the potential of the ASEAN+3 (ASEAN states along with China, Korea and Japan) process to become the basis of a governance project within the Asian region. This is a similar approach to analyses of the domestic foundation of open regionalism and its underlying political economy of embedded mercantilism which have been undertaken elsewhere.[1] However, as several chapters in this volume suggest, this political economy of embedded mercantilism and its associated theory and practice of regional governance is now in transition. But the question is: transition to what?

This is not a question that is easily answered. The governance processes identified in this volume not only reflect a transition to a new phase in the ongoing process of creating and making regional order, but more

significantly they involve the creation of a new form of regionalised governance in which the 'regional' becomes a particular spatial scale on which
economic, political and social governance takes place. It is this regionalisation
of governance that leads to the emergence of a new mode of regulatory regionalism that is as much located within the national state as it is within regional
institutions. As Cammack has noted, this involves a meta-governmental role
that is geared 'towards promoting states to compete with each other in ways
that promote rather than run counter to competitiveness on a global scale'.[2]
This regulatory regionalism is complex, more diffused, uses a variety of both
public and private actors, works within functionally defined policy sectors,
and often involves policy instruments that are negotiated and implemented
at multiple levels governance.

In effect, the transition being witnessed here is from inter-governmental
institutional forms to policy-specific regional governance arrangements that
operate at multiple scales of governance; in short, the regionalisation of governance.[3] But alongside this regulatory regionalism there exists a more state-
centric, geopolitically driven, ideologically constructed form of East Asian
governance. From this geopolitical perspective, the crucial transition is from
a Pacific-based, US-centred order to a more Sino-centric organisation.[4] In fact,
many of the chapters in the volume straddle these competing notions of regional
governance. While the regulatory mode of regional governance is increasingly dominant over the state-centric mode, in the foreseeable future regional
politics will continue to be shaped by the contradictions and tensions between
these two modes of regional governance. The struggles within, and between,
these systems of governance are at root a question of politics and power.

In some ways these two competing systems of governance could be analogous to the shift from government to governance within systems of
national politics and policy-making institutions. Government is usually
viewed as a mode of policy making focused on its traditional instruments of
public administration, which are centralised, hierarchal and dependent on
modes of governing that require 'rowing rather than steering'. On the other
hand, governance is focused on the use of a variety of actors both public and
private, fragmented forms of governance, the creation of meta-governance
systems to regulate the governance of governance, and dependent on flexible
modes of governance.[5] It is exactly these new modes of governance that
feature prominently in the transition to regulatory regionalism. Here, I propose to identify the central themes of this volume by examining key aspects
of this transformation of regional governance. This transformation is analysed in terms of its causes and consequences, new issues and actors, and
policy instruments.

Causes and consequences of regionalised governance

Regional governance has changed considerably since the mid 1990s. Some of
the essays in this volume examine these in relation to the structural changes

in the patterns of geopolitics and economics. Without doubt the most significant transformation identified across many of the essays relates to the rise of China and the challenges this poses for the theory and practice of regional governance. To be sure, none of the contributors suggest that there is a coherent Sino-based regional order to compete with the US-based Pacific regional order, but all detect an underlying change in regional governance structures stemming from deep-seated changes in wealth and power produced by the rise of China. In fact, as Thomas makes starkly clear in Chapter 1, one of the most striking changes is the emergence, albeit weakly, of East Asian institutional structures as reflected in the ASEAN+3 (APT) process, as well as a decidedly more normative construction of regional identity in terms of 'East Asia' rather than the 'Asia-Pacific'.

Together these developments suggest a considerable weakening of the American-led 'hub and spokes' strategic system on the one hand and the Japanese 'flying geese'[6] driven production and investment regimes on the other. In fact, to the extent that there are attempts afoot to reinvigorate the US strategic relationship within the region, these have been driven by a perceived need to contain or balance China. Clearly, then, at the geopolitical level the emergence of China as a powerful regional player is reflected in the initial stage of a transition towards a putative East Asian regional order.

Nevertheless, a far more substantial reordering of the economic order is the fundamental shift in the nature of production in East Asia. As Moore (Chapter 8) notes, one of the significant features of the emergence of China is not to be found in the dominance of the Chinese economy per se, but in the fact that the various subregions of China are key locations in the international production networks that now cross national boundaries. In this respect this analysis exemplifies Breslin's argument that:

> by considering the nature of post-Fordist production and globalisation, different conceptions of the location of power emerge that are not necessarily territorially bound. Instead they draw attention to the role of supra or transnational 'commodity driven production networks' that have done much to generate Chinese economic growth in recent years.[7]

These production networks have become especially important in the information technology sector, where manufacturing production is relocated in China and other parts of Asia, but control of production standards and research – structural economic power – still remains with foreign companies. The proposition here is that the rise of China, rather than leading to an emerging Sino-centric regional order, represents a new form of production that is not necessarily bound to national territorial space. Therefore, the regional transformation catalysed by China's economic and social transformation is more appropriately conceptualised as a symptom of a new system of regionalised economic governance that transcends national territorial boundaries.

The broader point here is that globalisation as an economic process needs to be conceptualised not so much as an externally driven process through the increasing flows of trade and capital but more as an internal process that fundamentally transforms the internal and external aspects of sovereignty. In this respect, regional governance is as much about developing new forms of regulatory regimes within the state as it is of developing governance between national states. This is a crucial dimension of the argument because it implies that adopting a governance framework allows us to locate the development of regionalised governance within broader political contexts of market making and state transformation of individual countries. On this understanding, the process of state transformation is the key to the analysis of regulatory regionalism.

The process of global economic integration rescales the nature of local activity so that, at one level, it is much more localised (for example, the part played by Southern China and its connection to international production networks), but at the same time these localised developments sit within a set of globalised international and finance and production structures which now cross national boundaries. It is these activities that now take on distinctive regional shape and form. The globalisation of production and finance makes problematic the very idea of 'national economic space' and in this context regionalism denotes restructuring of both 'national' and regional space.

In this sense, regionalisation reflects a structural process of the rescaling of economic activity at the regional and local level. Yet, it is not only transnationalised production that operates regionally. Domestic capital also increasingly operates on a regional rather than a national scale – consider here the vast regional connection of Singapore state capitalist companies – and, as it does, it seeks to influence or promote regional levels of political governance. Hence, the ASEAN Free Trade Agreement (AFTA) or the web of bilateral agreements between regional states can be considered as part of this ongoing regionalisation of activities and functions of domestic capital – be they private or state controlled.

Consequently, regional space becomes an important scale of governance through which these new economic processes are regulated and governed at the regional level by means of mechanisms of regulatory regionalism.[8] Katzenstein describes a similar process as 'porous regionalism', which comes about through:

> global and international processes and also by a variety vertical relations linking them to other political units. A world of regions is therefore not simply a territorially bounded system of geo economic blocs that extends national mercantilism onto a supra national plain.[9]

From this perspective, regional strategies need to be analysed and understood as strategies of economic and political governance, which are causally associated with a fundamental restructuring of the scales of economic governance.

Implications of regionalised governance

In this sense, regional governance is not an agglomeration of 'national eco-nomic units' at a higher regional level; it is a more fundamental regionali-sation of economic governance. Phillips aptly observes that regionalisation of governance does not 'imply the wholesale elimination of more "national" forms of economic governance, and progressively the trend is towards con-vergence upon a regionally coordinated policy norms and objectives and the location of market governance at the sub regional level'.[10] As implied in this argument, regionalisation or regional governance runs through the tracks of the national state apparatus such that new modes of regional governance are located within national or domestic governance institutions.

Regionalisation of governance has two important implications for the regional political economy. First, instead of the obsession, in much of the mainstream international-relations literature on the Asia-Pacific, with pat-terns of state power within the region, the new 'network' forms of produc-tion demand a more systematic examination of the nature and location of power within these private networks rather than in terms of shifts from a Japanese to a Sino-centric form of economic organisation. In short, to answer the question of 'who rules' we need to be much more cognisant of how regional integration, particularly in the Asia-Pacific, leads to the reor-ganisation of production across national boundaries in a way that makes simple calculations of national economic power much more complex.

Moore, in his contribution on the US relationship to East Asia, takes up the issue of structural power within these private networks and the under-lying question is: 'who rules?' He notes that, despite the growing economic clout of China, US companies still dominate these production networks. Consequently, cross-border economic global commodity chains promote the conditions for the influence of non-state economic actors in regional gov-ernance. It is the control of these production networks, rather than the location of production itself, that matters and we need to be cautious of arguments about a new Sino-centric form of regional governance.

Second, these new production networks facilitate the development of dif-ferent and various forms of privatised governance, such as private legal arbitration, new standard-setting organisations such as international accountancy boards, and even the monitoring of labour standards through private non-governmental organizations (NGOs). For example, various forms of corporate conduct have evolved, and in the aftermath of 'several well-publicized scandals involving child labour, hazardous working condi-tions, excessive working hours, and poor wages in factories supplying the major global brands, multinational corporations have developed their own "codes of conduct"'.[11] Corporate codes of conduct, the role of standard-setting organisations, or indeed the role of transnational actors such as Transparency International (TI) suggest that private governance systems seek to incorporate principles and practices of public governance within transnational production chains or networks. Within these networks private or non-state actors have played a growing role in public or regulatory functions in the region, shaping an evolving structure of regulatory governance that operates outside of traditional inter-governmental arrangements.

Regional governance: new issues and actors

One of the striking conclusions of this volume is the fact regional governance now includes a far broader range of governance issues than the usual trade-related issues that dominated in the 1990s. Cotton (Chapter 6) illustrates the importance of the bilateral and regional governance of new policy issues such as, for example, terrorism and people smuggling in shaping Australian foreign policy towards the region. He identifies the growing role of networks of specialist policy makers such as police and security officers – quite different from the usual governmental and 'official' non-governmental streams of Asia-Pacific policy networks[12] – in spearheading Australia's response to new regional problems. In a related vein, Arner, Lejot and Wang (Chapter 10) stress the importance of the East Asian network of central bankers – or to give its proper name the Executives' Meeting of East Asian-Pacific Central Banks (EMEAP) – in the oversight and management of the Asian Bond Fund initiative. Similarly, the SARS crisis presented new challenges in governance for the countries of the Asia-Pacific region. These new issues not only extend the regional governance agenda away from the traditional issues of trade integration, but more significantly require harmonisation of national policy and the cooperation of national regulators and policy makers.

But nowhere is this shift in the domain of governance more pronounced than in new forms of regional financial coordination. In their chapter on financial integration and governance, Arner, Lejot and Wang are critical of the inflated rhetoric that accompanies proposals for financial integration when the policy outcomes are much more limited. On these grounds they remain rightly sceptical of the potential in the Asia-Pacific for the development of a European-style, highly formalised and rules-based financial and monetary system along the lines of the European Monetary Union. Despite these reservations they argue that recent regional initiatives such as the Asian Bond Fund indicate the potential for regional financial governance based on the principles of mutual recognition and harmonisation to common minimum standards.

In this context there has been a range of significant regional initiatives to coordinate financial governance within the region. The Chiang Mai Initiative (CMI) provided for emergency funds for currency stabilisation in the event of another financial crisis such as that of 1997–98. The initiative is limited in scope as well as in terms of the volume of funds available for emergency funding. However, the very fact that currency stabilisation schemes such as the CMI are on the policy agenda is itself a major step away from the Asia-Pacific region's traditional emphasis on trade liberalisation. Similarly, the networks of East Asian central banks manage the Asian Bond Fund, which invests in a basket of US dollar-denominated bonds issued by Asian sovereign and quasi-sovereign issuers in East Asian economies. That these initiatives have a substantial degree of policy support within the region is a significant facet of the new governance in Asia.

In this respect, Dieter offers a provocative and highly stimulating argument, namely that regional integration projects driven by trade liberalisation have only a limited viability for the newly industrialising countries of East Asia and Latin America. Instead, he proposes a shift towards what he terms 'monetary regionalism' that will offer a degree of protection to increasingly vulnerable national economies. Dieter has argued that countries

> participating in a conventional integration project do not enjoy additional protection against financial crises. Neither with regard to the stabilization of the exchange rate of their currencies nor with regard to the stabilization of capital flows do conventional integration schemes strengthen the economies of their member countries.[13]

In the proposals and initiatives on financial governance since the turn of the century we can plausibly see the development of a putative East Asian monetary governance that contrasts with the trade-oriented regionalism of the 1990s.

Equally significant in these forms of regionalised governance is the emergence of new private actors who take on pubic regulatory roles. The regulatory roles are reinforced through the development of international production networks. These systems of private governance often intersect with national state institutions and organisations so that distinctive arrangements of regional governance are created at the intersection of these private and public bodies. For example, the Cambodia–US bilateral textile trade agreement, which included labour standards, is especially revealing on this score[14] in that it required substantial compliance with core international labour standards. As a result of this agreement the Cambodian government, together with the International Labour Organisation (ILO)[15] and the Ministry of Commerce requires registration with the inspection regime of the ILO's Better Factories Programme in order to export.

These private–public partnerships can be found in other policy sectors. Yoshimatsu (Chapter 3) in his chapter documents how the Japanese government has sought to foster collaboration with non-state actors in the management and monitoring of environmental issues. Similarly, Guilloux too (Chapter 11) observes that a concerted regional response to humanitarian crises in Asia has been limited. In this context, NGOs together with national agencies have played a crucial public policy role in the management of and response to humanitarian crises. It is to be expected that the importance of bilateral arrangements to the Asian region will accelerate these private–public forms of regional governance. Consequently, the focus of much of the mainstream international relations literature on geopolitics misses the more important dimension of the regional governance which is to be found in the migration of political authority from both the national and the regional level to novel forms of privatised governance. The important feature identified in these contributions is the development of innovative methods of regionalised governance that incorporate private and public–private arrangements.

The instruments of regional governance

One of the characteristics of the new regional governance in areas as diverse as terrorism and finance, is a recognition that region-wide regulatory frameworks such as monetary coordination and macro-economic policies can be implemented and policed at a local level. From this perspective, the regulatory state is not a state form confined to the territorial boundaries of the national state. Rather, it should be seen as a system of multilevel governance which embeds international organisations such as the International Monetary Fund (IMF) with regional entities such as the Asian Development Bank (ADB) and various national agencies, and even subnational or local entities, so that regionalisation runs on the tracks of the national policy process.[16]

Caballero-Anthony's chapter in this volume sketches the evolving regional governance project of ASEAN, and pointed attention is drawn to the central role of ASEAN in the emerging project of regional governance. ASEAN, it is argued is at the hub of an emergent form of multilevel governance that has shaped not only the dialogue and cooperation between the APT countries, but also between these East Asian countries and others outside the region. Certainly, this multilevel governance is different from that of the more formalised system within the European Union, but nevertheless Caballero-Anthony's analysis indicates the fuzzy outlines of a new form of multilevel governance. Furthermore, this analysis also depicts another important feature of multilevel governance: a mechanism through which regional norms can be localised and articulated. Reinforcing this observation, Choo's (Chapter 4), points to the importance of Korean participation in the APT forum as a way of localising regional normative practices. This point is also supplemented by Saint-Mézard's suggestion (Chapter 7) that India's participation in various forms of multilevel governance and bilateral arrangements may lead it to adopt certain kinds of regional norms.

Further supporting this multilevel governance is the system of transnational policy networks analysed by Cotton, which includes the EMEAP that has contributed to the development of the Asian Bond Fund (as noted by Arner et al.). Indeed, policy networks such as EMEAP are also embryonic systems of multilevel governance. Nesudurai has pointed out that the Asian Bond Market Initiative (ABMI):

has already stimulated domestic reforms in tax and regulatory regimes in some countries, therefore provides a mechanism for regional capacity-building in these areas. Incidentally, none of these cooperative projects has been designed to oppose market-based financial systems nor to sever East Asia's ties with global markets.[17]

In effect, the ABMI is also a system of multilevel governance. These policy networks complement the multilevel governance identified by Caballero-Anthony (Chapter 2). Breslin, in an analysis of China and the new global political economy, notes the emergence of a group of globalised bureaucrats pointing out that:

> This group, epitomised by the policies of Zhu Rongji, is engaged in a process of making the investment regime within China more and more liberalised and 'attractive' to international capital, and reforming the domestic economic structure to reduce domestic protectionism, and institute a more neo-liberal economic paradigm.[18]

In short, the articulation of regional norms by regional governance in the way suggested by many of the contributors to this volume needs to be materialised in the nuts and bolts of policy networks. Not only do these policy networks reflect the emergence of regulatory regional institutions within the state, but they also embody ideological and political preferences and interests often ignored in some of the cruder constructivist approaches to regional governance.

Noteworthy in this respect is the contribution made by key regional states such as Japan in linking regional policy networks with transregional policy networks and agencies. Yoshimatsu argues in Chapter 3 that development of regional financial governance has been facilitated by the epistemic communities linked to, and sponsored by, the Japanese Ministry of Finance. It is clear that middle power regional states such as Korea or Australia may perform similar functions within the emergent systems of regional multilevel governance. Core regional states, or rather specific societal and state actors within these states, provide a pathway through which regional governance is linked to a global order dominated by the United States. Hence, the 'fusion of globalisation and internationalisation and the vertical links between regions, the American imperium, core regional states, and other actors resembles a swirly marble cake rather than a neat layer cake'.[19]

These inter-governmental arrangements within the regional order are not the only forms that multilevel governance may take. For example, the Mekong Project of the Asian Development Bank envisages the creation of a new, functionally specific jurisdiction that links local-level organisations with transnational agencies and authorities.[20] Hirsch has noted that the Mekong is managed by a complex system of governance that includes ministerial councils of the relevant countries, a secretariat to manage its affairs and a parallel system of national-level committees that serve as a conduit between transboundary water management and internal national management structures. In some countries, such as Thailand, these governance arrangements also incorporate local non-state actors into the system of water management. Hence it may well be that the Asian region is likely to be distinguished by different and overlapping systems of multilevel governance.[21]

The other important new mode of governance within the region is the emergence of systems of peer review and monitoring. A nascent example of this system of regional multilevel regulation is the ASEAN Regional Surveillance Process (ARSP), which was endorsed by ASEAN finance ministers in December 1998.[22] The peer review process serves to link both national and international regulatory governance through the internationalisation of various state agencies and actors. The latter became part of a regional system of surveillance and regulation, which transmits the disciplines of a globalised economy. Again, the role of specialised policy networks – both public and private – is likely to prove crucial in these forms of peer review.

However, one mode of Asian integration that challenges the notion of the region as a coherent system is the existence of transregional and pan-regional policy and political networks which require participating Asian states to engage with or adopt different norms. This issue is clearly raised by Davidson in Chapter 9, with his discussion of APEC, and is echoed by Lawson in Chapter 12, with her analysis of the tensions within ASEM. In both cases, it is clear that these other processes require the participating states to be open in their identification of the region, contributing to the development of norms and institutions beyond their APT-centric governance structures. As both Davidson and Lawson show, this more open consideration of regional associations brings benefits and challenges for the policy elites, subnational and private sector actors as well as civil society representatives.

In any case, regulatory regionalism – be it through multilevel governance or peer review – requires the increasing harmonisation of standards and codes such as corporate governance, transparency standards, and broad macro- and micro-economic policies. Hence, regulatory regionalism requires collaboration with global and other levels of governance to establish standards and mechanisms of policy coordination as well as norms of conduct. New modes of regionalised governance serve to incorporate standards and mechanisms of policy coordination across all levels of governance. Of course, as the authors in this volume point out, the regional governance of this kind is at best rudimentary, but it is clear that, at least in an embryonic form, a new type of regulatory governance is taking shape within the region.

Conclusion

This volume is a first cut at a new and innovative agenda on regional governance. The various chapters in the volume have convincingly pointed out the strengths of the governance approach to regionalism in contrast to the realist and constructivist approaches that have been influential in the international relations literature. The various contributions have demonstrated the value of an approach that seeks to examine more closely the nature and form of the issues, actors and instruments of regional governance. By analysing the nature of policy networks, the forms of multilevel governance and the patterns of monetary and financial governance they have confirmed the emergence, albeit in fuzzy outline, of new modes of regulatory governance. Perhaps the key distinguishing feature of these new modes of regional governance is the fact that they operate at the boundary between national and regional governance. In other words, regional governance works in, through and beyond the regulatory state. Equally, the regionalisation of governance also takes place within cross-border production networks and, in the long term, these privatised forms of governance may well provide the backbone of regional governance.

To conclude, three major questions can be are posed for future researchers. First, what is the role of private actors in structures of regional governance? More detailed analysis is needed of the nature of private governance within the production network, and especially the of way in which private governance and networks link in with public actors at levels of government.

Second, what is the role of multilevel governance within the region? In particular, we need to do more work on the prospects and possibilities of specialised systems of multilevel governance as seen, for example, in the governance of the Mekong. Equally, it would be useful to explore the extent to which the role of key regional states such as Korea, Japan and Australia have become a conduit through which multilevel governance is established with extraregional actors and organisations.

Third, it is clear that policy networks such as the EMEAP are the glue which holds together many of the new modes of regional governance. However, further analysis is needed of the nature of the actors within the networks, the rules and norms that govern these networks and their relationship to other national and regional actors and international organisations.

It is to be hoped that this volume will open the way to a rich and fertile research agenda on regionalisation of governance.

Notes

1 Jayasuriya, Kanishka. 'Embedded Mercantilism and Open Regionalism: the Crisis of a Regional Political Project', *Third World Quarterly*. (Vol. 24, No. 6, 2003), pp 339–355.
2 Cammack, Paul. 'Competitiveness and Convergence: the Open Method of Coordination in Latin America', *Papers in the Politics of Global Competitiveness*. (No. 5, March 2007), p. 17. http://e-space.mmu.ac.uk/e-space/bitstream/2173/11064/1/omc.pdf. Accessed 15 January 2008.
3 For an analysis of the transformation of regional space by the processes of global economic integration see Agnew, John and Stuart Corbridge. *Mastering Space: Hegemony, Territory and International Political Economy*. (London: Routledge, 1995).

4 Macintyre, Andrew and Barry Naughton. 'The Decline of a Japan-Led Model of the East Asian Economy', in T.J. Pempel (ed.). *Remapping Asia*. (Ithaca, NY: Cornell University Press, 2005), pp. 77–100.

5 For an excellent analysis on these lines see Sudo, Sueo. 'Regional Governance and East and Southeast Asia: Towards the Regulatory State?', *Japanese Journal of Political Science*. (Vol. 4, No. 2, 2003), pp. 331–347. This study examines the emergence of new actors and issues within regional governance.

6 On the flying geese model see Beeson, Mark. *Regionalization and Globalization in East Asia: Politics, Security and Economic Development*. (London: Palgrave Macmillan, 2006). This provides a comprehensive analysis of Asia-Pacific regionalism over the last two decades.

7 Breslin, Shaun. 'Power and Production: Rethinking China's Global Economic Role', *Review of International Studies*. (Vol. 31, No. 4, 2005) pp. 735–753.

8 This has been accelerated by the rapid growth of tangled webs of bilateral trade and economic agreements. For an excellent analysis see Dent, Christopher. 'The New Economic Bilateralism and Southeast Asia Region: Region Convergent or Region-Divergent', *IPEG Papers in Global Political Economy*. (No. 7, April 2004). http://www.bisa.ac.uk/groups/ipeg/papers/7%20Christopher%20Dent.pdf. Accessed 24 January 2008.

9 Katzenstein, Peter. *A World of Regions: Asia and Europe in the American Imperium*. (Ithaca, NY: Cornell University Press, 2005).

10 Phillips, Nicola. 'Regionalist Governance in the New Political Economy of Development: "Relaunching" the Mercosur', *Third World Quarterly*. (Vol. 22, No. 4, 2001), pp. 565–583.

11 Locke, Richard, Fin Qin and Alberto Brause. 'Does Monitoring Improve Labour Standards? Lesson from Nike', *Sloan School Working Papers*. (No: 4612–06, 2006).

12 See Thomas (Chapter 1) in this volume for a description of Track 1 and Track 2 policy processes.

13 Dieter, Heribert. 'Monetary Regionalism: Regional Integration Without Financial Crises', *CSGR Working Paper*. (No 52/00, 2000, University of Warwick), p. 2. http://www2.warwick.ac.uk/fac/soc/csgr/research/workingpapers/2000/wp5200.pdf. Accessed 28 January 2008.

14 Polaski, Sandra. 'Cambodia Blazes a New Path to Economic Growth and Job Creation'. *Carnegie Papers*. (No. 51, 2004). Washington, DC: Carnegie Endowment for International Peace. Given the increasing pressure on developed states to include labour standards in trade agreements, the US–Cambodian agreement may well become a template for such agreements.

15 The programme is built around a series of random inspections and uses both ILO standards and Cambodian labour law to provide a checklist of more than 500 items. For an overview of the Better Factories programme, see http://www.betterfactories.org/LO/efault.aspx?z = 1&c = 1. Accessed 26 May 2007. An astute analysis of this is in Hughes, Caroline. 'Transnational Networks, International Organization and Political Participation in Cambodia: Human Eights, Labour Rights and Common Rights', *Democratization*. (Vol. 14, No. 5, 2007). pp. 835–853.

16 See: Sudo, Sueo. 'Regional Governance and East and Southeast Asia: Towards the Regulatory State?', see note 5 above.

17 Nesudurai, Helen. 'APEC and East Asia: the Challenge of Remaining Relevant'. http://rspas.anu.edu.au/ir/pubs/keynotes/documents/Keynotes-7.pdf, p. 25. Accessed 28 January 2008.

18 Breslin, Shaun. 'IR, Area Studies and IPE: Rethinking the Study of China's International Relations', *CSGR Working Paper*. (No. 94/02), p. 25. http://www.warwick.ac.uk/fac/soc/CSGR/publications.html. Accessed 28 January 2008.

19 Katzenstein. *A World of Regions*, p. 41.

20 Hirsch, Phillip. 'Water Governance Reform and Catchment Management in the Mekong Region', *Journal of Environment and Development*. (Vol. 15, No. 2, 2006), pp 184–201.
21 Ibid.
22 Manupipatpong, Worapot. 'The ASEAN Surveillance Process and the East Asian Monetary Fund', *ASEAN Economic Bulletin*. (Vol. 19, No. 1, 2002). pp. 111–122.

Index

Page numbers in **bold** refer to figures. Page numbers in *italics* refer to boxes or tables.

For Product Safety Concerns and Information please contact our EU
representative GPSR@taylorandfrancis.com
Taylor & Francis Verlag GmbH, Kaufingerstraße 24, 80331 München, Germany